The Dream Weaver
One Boy's Journey Through the Landscape of Reality

Anniversary Edition

Jack Bowen

New York   San Francisco   Boston
London   Toronto   Sydney   Tokyo   Singapore   Madrid
Mexico City   Munich   Paris   Capetown   Hong Kong   Montreal

College ISBN-13: 978-0-205-52886-8
    ISBN-10: 0-205-52886-4

Sourcebooks ISBN-13: 978-0-205-60540-8
    ISBN-10: 0-205-60540-0

1 2 3 4 5 6 7 8 9 10—DOH—10 09 08 07

Praise for *The Dream Weaver*

An intriguing tale that will instill readers with an abiding sense of philosophical wonder. If you're smitten with *Sophie's World*, you're sure to be entranced by *The Dream Weaver*.

—*Christopher Phillips, author of* Socrates Café

Jack Bowen's novel is like traveling with Alice to a Wonderland inhabited by the greatest philosophers and scientists who ever lived. This is must-reading for anyone who wants to understand how the teachings of the great philosophers apply to today's world. A triumph!

—*Wenda O'Reilly, Ph.D., Author,*
The Art Game; *President, Birdcage Press*

The Dream Weaver is a terrifically written, plot-driven, clever, smart, and sassy introduction to philosophy. Bowen's verbal facility, narrative grace, and structural inventiveness are very impressive indeed. . . . Bowen has enough narrative talent and philosophical background to pull off the very difficult combination.

—*Dr. Rob Reich, Assistant Professor,*
Stanford University; Founder of the Stanford
Summer Philosophy Discovery Institute

There's value in the application of knowledge. That's an underlying girder in [the book], and also a kind of faith in the possibility of human choice.

—*Michael Krasny, KQED*

Like Merlin and Arthur, Bowen's Old Man and Ian examine important issues—identity, God, good and evil, love, ethics and morality, free will—through a series of highly inventive adventures. . . . *The Dream Weaver* is a philosophical odyssey that tackles the mysteries of life, of science, and of the meaning of reality.

—*Susanne Pari, Author,* The Fortune Catcher

As Ian plumbs the depths of the human mind and the history of philosophical thought, [readers] will inevitably begin to ask [the] big questions themselves. Now, that's something worth thinking about.

—*Edutopia*

The Dream Weaver serves to introduce the relevance of traditional philosophic questions to people in a new and engaging manner.

—*Reginald Raymer, University of North Carolina-Charlotte*

A lively, rigorous introduction to philosophy that most browsers in bookstores should gobble up . . . I see the main emphasis as a call for fierce but fair debate of the philosophical issues. I love it. . . . Bowen's presentation of the philosophical positions is right on target.

—*Dr. Jean-Paul Vessel, Assistant Professor*
of Philosophy, New Mexico State University

To Mom and Dad.
For your gifts of the mind and heart.
But mostly for your love.

You embrace both heart and mind / In seeking what you find
"Beautiful Colors"

Contents

Foreword

For a certain percentage of the population, philosophy is one of the great joys of life. Thinking about basic problems of human existence—or basic problems about the existence of numbers, for that matter—reading what the philosophers of the past have written, talking about philosophical issues with friends: for some of us these intellectual pleasures rank very high. The habits of mind encouraged by philosophy are valuable, and a certain number of people who get involved in philosophy have ideas and write things that make a difference. Philosophy is a gift.

It is incumbent on each generation of philosophers to make this gift available to those in the next generation who have the habits of mind to enjoy it, engage in it, and perhaps make important contributions to it. This is not something we do very well. By my reckoning, at least half a dozen students in each sixth grade class are potential lovers of philosophy. They are the ones who spontaneously begin to wonder if their classmates could all be automatons, have worries about living in a Matrix even before seeing the movie, ponder the difference between the past and the future, and speculate whether the things taken for granted by their teachers could be as wrong-headed, intellectually and morally, as the assumptions of past generations. If we reached all of these potential philosophers, our classes would be bursting, and there would be as many philosophy majors as there are English majors. In my forty years of teaching philosophy, countless seniors, having discovered philosophy late in their college careers, have complained that it was kept hidden—they had no idea that there were classes on campus where the deep questions that bother them were approached carefully and imaginatively.

That is why I was twice delighted to discover Jack Bowen's wonderful book, *The Dream Weaver*. First, I was thrilled to read in the preface that a book I edited, the blue book of readings about personal identity that he stumbled across while wandering around a bookstore, had played an important role in his discovery of philosophy. Second, I found the book itself a wonderful contribution to the cause of making the gift of philosophy available and accessible to the uninitiated. Readers of *The Dream Weaver* will find that a whole new world awaits them, just as Jack Bowen did when he stumbled across my book. Do you wonder whether the world exists, just as we perceive it? Whether you really continue to exist through all the changes you undergo? Whether there is really any difference between what we call "right" and "wrong," or whether morality is just a bunch of practices our culture foists upon us? If so, this is the book for you.

Dialogue has often been found to be a good genre for introducing, and pursuing, philosophy. Dialogues by Plato, Berkeley, and Hume have long been a staple of introductory classes. Bowen creates dialogues within the larger setting of a readable and engaging novel, so the plot and character can keep the reader going from idea to idea, problem to problem. He deftly handles a wide range of philosophical problems, from skepticism and personal identity, to faith and knowledge, to ethics and morality, in a way that manages to be both sophisticated and engaging. The text is supplemented by diagrams, asides, quotes, and reading suggestions in a way that comes close to integrating the flexibility of a website with the experience of reading a book. Ian—Bowen's protagonist—and his family and friends are characters with whom the potential philosophers of the world will readily identify. I identify with the Old Man.

The Dream Weaver is a wonderful addition to the tools that philosophers can use to share the gift of philosophy with the next generation. May this Anniversary Edition be, as the original release was, that rarest of books, a philosophical best seller.

JOHN PERRY
Cohost of Philosophy Talk
Henry Waldgrave Stuart Professor of Philosophy
Stanford University

Preface

> If I have seen further, it is by standing on the shoulders of giants.
>
> —*Isaac Newton*

> The mind is not a vessel to be filled but a fire to be kindled.
>
> —*Plutarch*

One afternoon while in the university bookstore perusing books for my senior year spring term, I found myself in the philosophy section. I think I literally *stumbled* into it. It was nestled near the physics and psychology sections, both of which had become my mainstays as a Human Biology major. I certainly didn't venture there intentionally. At the time, I had no idea what philosophy "stood for" or what philosophers did. As I regained my footing there in the philosophy section, a light blue book caught my eye. The binding had the words "Personal Identity" in white, providing a nice contrast to the sky blue. I peered over my shoulder, concerned that someone might see me reaching for a book in the philosophy section and think whatever people think about those sorts of things. I opened it to find a collection of essays on *The Self*: on what it means to be human and to be a person, on how we are the same person over time; it discussed the concepts of the mind and the soul; it drew on scientific notions of consciousness and the brain, the psychology of memory, and it explored the *essence* of being human.

I sat on the itchy industrial carpet perched up against the bookshelf and read. I frantically flipped through the pages, devouring them, half rapidly skimming to see what would be next, and half stuck on each article, contemplating the issues. I read until that ultimate moment when I had just enough time to get to my next event—that moment when, if I know exactly where I'm going and if there is very little bike traffic, I would get there right on time. I left the bookstore that day racing with an intellectual curiosity that I had never experienced. It was as if I had been led behind the curtain of facts and information previously taught to me. I actually felt, in some sense, like I was walking out into a new world.

I returned to the bookstore every afternoon that week. I sat on the floor and read that book, as if I had discovered a secret treasure. It was all I could do to focus on this one book, ignoring the others whose titles alone piqued my intellectual curiosity: *The God Question*, *The View from Nowhere*, *The Metaphysics of Morals*, *Free Will and Its Consequences*, *The Philosophy of Love*, *The Meaning of Life*. But I sat and focused on the light blue, bound treasure.

Eventually, I gave in and bought the book along with a handful of others in that same section and found more comfortable places to read it. From there, my story takes its own twists and turns, which I will not belabor at this point. Needless to say, it culminates with my writing this preface to the story of another boy's journey in a world that I was fortunate enough to have the chance to experience quite intimately.

I remember my first day with that little blue book so fondly—like that first enriching experience with anything, when it hits you with an aesthetic feeling of intensity unique to that first time. I am eager to share that with the readers of this book, and to provide them an opportunity to go on their own journey.

Acknowledgments

If I could thank passion I would, though I wouldn't know where to direct it. I would thank it for creeping through so much of the worldly cynicism, sneaking into myself and those around me, and making every thought, interaction, and experience that much more radiant. To those mentioned here, I mean it not so much as a "thank you" but, aptly, an opportunity to *acknowledge* your fingerprints on this book and, more importantly, on this fruitful journey.

To start from the start, I want to recognize the teachers and professors who have kindled the intellectual fires. Ariela Lazar, for making time for that gawky senior-year athlete at Stanford who expressed a curiosity in your area of expertise: a one-unit directed reading . . . who'd have known? To the entire philosophy department at CSU Long Beach—yes, the entire department—what a fortunate series of accidents (or not, depending on your outlook) that I landed there. I want to acknowledge not just your teaching, but your nurturing. For instilling in your students much more than just *what* to think, but *how* to think— a considerably more difficult mission, yet immeasurably more enriching. I am especially grateful to Sara Goering, Paul Tang, and Al Spangler for both trusting me and challenging me, and mostly for the true passion you devote to your students. I hope you see your reflection in the characters here.

A number of people have gone above and beyond in their involvement with this book: Howard Wolf at the Stanford Alumni Association (and his daughter Rachel—a true cohort of Ian's), Norris Pope and Louise Herndon at Stanford Press. All of the readers at Longman who offered feedback, including Marina Banchetti, David Beck, Mary L. Bringle, Jaymes Buick, John Clark, Houston Craighead, L. Garrett Manning III, Paul Hodapp, John Holmes, Steve Horst, Nicholaos Jones, Andrew Kelley, Hye-kyung Kim, Hans-Herbert Koegler, James Mahoney, Maria Paleologou, Michael F. Patton Jr., Reginald Raymer, Daniel Skubik, Joshua Thompson, and Larry J. Waggle, and especially Rob Reich of Stanford University, Jean-Paul Vessel of New Mexico State University, and Louis Yock of West Shore Community College.

To friends who read that early draft of a first-time novelist: Brian, Dean, Dave, Bryan, Dr. Charles, Matt and Summer. To Dr. Michael Shermer at *Skeptic* magazine for your comments. To everyone from our Menlo Water Polo Family—players and parents—who have supported this in so many ways, to my students for being so open, thoughtful, and engaged, and to Mamm for an amazingly creative and relevant web design that Ian would be proud of.

Thank you Susanne Pari, for your ability to empower me and make me feel like a writer even before I thought I was. And Wenda O'Reilly for your incessant encouragement and willingness to challenge me to push myself creatively. I have been touched by the energy you both devoted to mentoring me while in the midst of your own creative endeavors.

Angela, you somehow found a way to tease my true inner voice out of me. Thank goodness you didn't let me get away with some of my lazy moments and instead urged me to challenge myself in new ways. I don't know if I learned more from Ian or you in this process.

Lastly, I have read about the downsides of publishing and heard the stories of authors' hopes gone awry. I feel fortunate to be able to say that I have experienced nothing like that. For this I feel indebted to my publisher and, more specifically, my editor, Priscilla McGeehon—for your vision, your trust in Ian's wily ways, and for putting up with my skittish excitement about it all.

I suppose it's strange for anyone—especially the supposedly cerebral philosopher type—to thank passion, but in the five years of writing and working on this, my sense of awe has only grown. As Matt Bowen so passionately sings in the book's theme song, "Beautiful Colors"*: If you look with eyes wide open/You realize the world wonders.

Indeed.

JACK BOWEN
Menlo Park, California, October 2005

An additional thank you to my sponsor, BTC Elements, not only for the support but for living your philosophy (thus, Gandhi's "Be The Change") and to Alisa Poppen for sharing your expertise on the beginning of life. And lastly to all of the great independent bookstores who opened your doors to Ian and I, and for allowing reading to remain a part of the life well lived.

Note to Reader

Throughout Ian's adventure that follows, you will find annotations lining the margins. I became so intrigued with the story that I wanted to find out more about it. In doing so, I realized that everything Ian experiences stems from a very rich history of thought: science, psychology, history, sociology, religion, and primarily philosophy. What began as a project to satisfy my own curiosity grew into almost a reader's guide—a chance for the reader to see just how connected Ian's journey is with the work of history's greatest thinkers and those of today. It became almost like two books—one being the trials and tribulations surrounding one boy's adventure, and the other, an overview of philosophy and its relevance to our own struggles and enlightenment.

*To download "Beautiful Colors," go to www.dreamweaverphilosophy.com.

Chronological List of Philosophers Encountered by Ian

BC

570–510	Lao Tzu	c. 400	Eubulides of Miletus
570–495	Pythagoras	399–295	Chuang Tzu
555–479	Confucius	384–322	Aristotle
535–470	Heraclitus	365–300	Euclid
510–445	Parmenides	365–270	Pyrrho of Ellis
490–430	Zeno of Elea	341–270	Epicurus
469–399	Socrates	287–212	Archimedes
427–347	Plato	c.3BC–65AD	Seneca

AD

46–119	Plutarch	1632–1677	Benedict Spinoza
55–135	Epictetus	1632–1704	John Locke
121–180	Marcus Aurelius	1642–1727	Isaac Newton
c. 200	Sextus Empiricus	1646–1716	Gottfried Leibniz
354–430	St. Augustine	1685–1753	George Berkeley
480–524	Boethius	1686–1769	Hakuin Ekaku
540–604	Pope Gregory I	1694–1778	Voltaire (François Marie Arouet)
670–762	Shen Hui		
1033–1109	St. Anselm of Canterbury	1709–1784	Samuel Johnson
		1711–1776	David Hume
1225–1274	St. Thomas Aquinas	1712–1778	Jean Jacques Rousseau
1285–1349	William of Ockham	1723–1789	Paul-Henri d'Holbach
1295–1361	Jean Buridan	1723-1790	Adam Smith
1400–1464	Bishop Nicholas of Cusa	1724–1804	Immanuel Kant
		1739-1795	Lawrence Kohlberg
1452–1519	Leonardo da Vinci	1743–1805	William Paley
1473–1543	Nicolaus Copernicus	1806–1873	John Stuart Mill
1561–1626	Francis Bacon	1809–1882	Charles Darwin
1588–1679	Thomas Hobbes	1813–1855	Søren Kierkegaard
1596–1650	René Descartes	1818–1883	Karl Marx
1616–1703	John Wallis	1820–1903	Herbert Spencer
1623–1677	Blaise Pascal	1825–1895	Thomas Huxley

1832–1898	Lewis Carroll	1898–1963	C. S. Lewis
1839–1914	C. S. Peirce	1900–1976	Gilbert Ryle
1842–1910	William James	1901–1976	Werner Heisenberg
1844–1900	Friedrich Nietzsche	1902–1994	Karl Popper
1845–1879	W. K. Clifford	1904–1990	B. F. Skinner
1854–1912	Henri Poincaré	1904–2005	Ernst Mayr
1856–1939	Sigmund Freud	1905–1980	Jean-Paul Sartre
1857–1939	Pope Pius XI,	1905–1982	Ayn Rand
	Ambrogio Ratti	1905–1997	Carl Hempel
1858–1947	Max Planck	1906–1998	Nelson Goodman
1861–1916	Pierre Duhem	1908–2000	W. V. Quine
1861–1947	Alfred North	1911–1990	Norman Malcolm
	Whitehead	1912–1954	Alan Turing
1863–1952	George Santayana	1913–1960	Albert Camus
1869–1948	Mohandas Gandhi	1914–2003	I. B. Cohen
1870–1966	D. T. Suzuki	1916–2004	Francis Crick
1872–1970	Bertrand Russell	1917–1981	J. L. Mackie
1873–1958	G. E. Moore	1919–2003	Richard Taylor
1874–1939	Gilbert Keith	1920–1997	Julian Jaynes
	Chesterton	1921–2002	John Rawls
1875–1916	Carl Jung	1922–1974	Imre Lakatos
1877–1962	Herman Hesse	1922–1996	Thomas Kuhn
1878–1965	Martin Buber	1924–1994	Paul Feyerabend
1879–1950	Alfred Korzybski	1927–1987	Lawrence Kohlberg
1879–1955	Albert Einstein	1929–2003	Bernard Williams
1881–1956	H. L. Mencken	1931–2007	Richard Rorty
1886–1967	W. T. Stace	1933–2004	Susan Sontag
1887–1948	Ruth Benedict	1938–2002	Robert Nozick
1889–1951	Ludwig Wittgenstein	1941–2002	Steven J. Gould
1892–1949	Homer Adkins	1941–2003	James Rachels
1897–1941	Benjamin Whorf		

Currently Living

Annette Baier	Martin Gardner
Fritjof Capra	Edmund Gettier
Peter Cave	Carol Gilligan
Noam Chomsky	Trudy Govier
Patricia Churchland	Dalai Lama, Tenzin Gyatso
Carl Cohen	John Hick
Eve Cole	John Hospers
Susan Coultrap-McQuin	Alison Jaggar
Richard Dawkins	Robert Kane
Daniel Dennett	Jean Kilbourne

Jaegwon Kim
David Lewis
Alisdair MacIntyre
Colin McGinn
David Myers
Thomas Nagel
Taleb Nassim
William Newcomb
Justine Oakley
John Perry
Steven Pinker
Hilary Putnam

James Randi
Richard Rorty
R. M. Sainsbury
John Searle
Michael Shermer
Peter Singer
J. J. Smart
George H. Smith
David Solomon
Roy Sorenson
Stephen Stich
Mary Anne Warren

This Is the Title of the Prologue

Wonder is the feeling of a philosopher, and philosophy begins with wonder.

–Plato

There was no telling what people might find out once they felt free to ask whatever questions they wanted to.

–Joseph Heller, Catch 22

Ian walked down his neighborhood street—a street lined with billowing, bushy trees, allowing the sun to shine only down the middle. He had his latest *slice of the sky* tucked under his arm. "A slice of the sky," he called it. The sky was especially blue and the whiteness of the clouds provided a sharp contrast like some surrealist painting, though strangely more real. Ian's interest in the sky dated back as far as he could remember. He had a great appreciation for the sky, just as others have for flowers or music. It had something to do with the feelings he associated with it—that it is always different though somehow the same; that the sky is all around him yet he can only perceive it as far away; that different people see different things in the clouds; that it goes on forever; and that his vision captures only a small part of the sky's essence, though that was somehow magical for Ian.

His paintings seemed to portray feelings more than anything purely aesthetic. He had blue, white, and black paint, and nothing more. The slices didn't seem to have any particular artistic quality since Ian cared more about sentimental value than anything else, although maybe that added to the artistic quality all the more.

On the wall in his room he had framed his favorite two pieces: his first slice which he made at age four—basically a smattering of blue and white paint, more like abstract art than anything else—and the other, the slice that he and Alexis made on the day they first met two years ago in the sixth grade. One could only wonder what sentimental value today's slice had.

1

He held it tightly, shielding it just as one would any meaningful object. Ian's body language often gave away his happy-go-lucky disposition; that is, unless you already noticed the smile he typically had—a perfect smile with perfect teeth, almost imperfectly so. He had a resiliency in his step, with his big brown eyes always perked up. Any noise or object even slightly out of the ordinary got his immediate attention, as though his head were a motion-sensitive surveillance camera inside a bank vault.

His coffee-colored hair usually appeared as if it had just been freshly tousled by one's aggressively affectionate grandmother. Ian, though, had never had a grandmother. And there was something peculiar about Ian's parents, although Ian couldn't have seen that for himself. After all, as he himself realized, *if yours is the only world you know, how could it be strange?*

"Ian!" A shout came from someone behind him. He couldn't hear it as he had his usual gray sweatshirt on, hood up.

"Ian," the boy said again, reaching out, grabbing Ian's shoulder in the way that someone grabs another's shoulder to wake them up. Ian turned to see his best friend Jeff brimming with excitement. "I need to talk to you," Jeff said, obviously flustered as he panted heavily, not his usual calm self.

"Ian, I think I've figured out what's going on with the Old Man—that guy you've been meeting with, or think you've been meeting with, or whatever it seems like."

"You've figured *it* out?" Ian said, as if surprised that Jeff assumed he would know what *it* was. Ian was so happy with his latest slice of the sky that he held it out for Jeff to see.

"Nice one," Jeff said to appease him, obviously more interested in other things.

"Yeah," Ian said, seeming to ignore Jeff's fervent demeanor. "You know, *this* blue, *this* is the color of the Old Man's eyes."

Jeff's disposition changed from disinterested to interested, though he was still swaying back and forth a bit to help alleviate his excitement. "I thought you said his eyes were *piercing*," he said to Ian, knowingly. "Remember?"

"Yeah," Ian answered, a bit despondently. "I was scared of him at first though. Scared of him as much as I was scared of what he was getting me to believe, what he was teaching me, all the things he was showing me. But sky-blue is much closer to his eyes. You know, I kind of like him now. It's changed the whole way I see him."

Jeff nodded and continued as the two walked together. "So his bushy eyebrows don't scare you anymore either? From what I remember, they made his whole face seem dark or something. And his beard? And that little scar?"

"I know," Ian responded, pausing to look up at a bird whistling in a tree. "But like I said, my view of him has changed. The facts are still the same, I just see them differently. His eyebrows, for example. I *did* feel like they hid his eyes, made his face dark. But now I sometimes put us in a weird situation on purpose just to watch him crinkle them up and raise them at me. Remember the re-creation of the universe? His eyebrows were crinkling up in ways I'd never seen that day.

"And his beard—it was like he used to hide behind it. Now, when we're talking, he sits and strokes it like it somehow makes him wiser, giving him some sort of brain power. And of course his scar at first made him seem like some kind of villain—I could see it whenever a gust of wind blew his whitish-gray hair aside. He always says it's the result of too much thinking—'the philosophical battleground,' he calls it. I think it gives him a lot of character." Ian nodded, almost proudly.

They had been walking together as Ian explained his gradual change of heart regarding the Old Man. Jeff continued his anxious fidgeting, though he was now a bit more interested, assessing Ian's view of the Old Man to see how he might react to the theory he had to share. They arrived at Ian's house as Ian continued with his exposé. "His big hands, good for comforting. His pursed lips that scream out *brilliant point* better than any words could." Jeff was nodding encouragingly.

As they got to Ian's front door—a larger-than-life oak door that took two hands (and often a shoulder) to open—Ian invited Jeff in.

"You know I can't come in your house," Jeff said, getting excited again. "That's one of the things I've figured out."

"But my parents are waiting for me. I wasn't even supposed to be out getting any sky today. I had to, though, to celebrate my last meeting with the Old Man. Or more like, to help me deal with it. But I'm already late." Ian seemed to be covering something up, almost as though *he* was the one who knew what *it* was. Or maybe he just didn't want to hear what Jeff had to say. He couldn't possibly have figured it out.

"Ian," Jeff was now more hesitant, with a cautious kind of excitement. "Your parents. . ."he paused, "I've figured that out too. They've never been outside with you, except when all those strange things happen. And where do you think we've gotten all the ideas for everything we've been doing lately—those binoculars, that crazy place with those 'people,'" he said, making the bunny-ear motion with his fingers when he said "people." "The town that we visited, the porcupines, mice, and squirrels—all of it? You could stay out all night and the only way you'd get in trouble with 'your parents'—as you say—is if you *think* you will."

Now Ian really didn't seem to want to hear it. "I have to go inside now. I'll meet you here tomorrow, same as usual."

"But Ian, there's good news too." Ian turned back to face Jeff. "About Alexis."

Ian smiled. "Of course there is. I'll see you tomorrow." And he leaned on the big oak door and went inside.

A time will come, in the not too distant future, when Ian will emerge from that very doorway and finally understand what everything that happened with the Old Man had meant. And everything with Jeff, Alexis, his parents. And he will discover himself, his purpose—his future as a Dream Weaver.

A Note from the Old Man

> The unexamined life is not worth living.
>
> *–Socrates*

> The great virtue of philosophy is that it teaches not what to think, but how to think.
>
> *–The Times of London*

I am the "Old Man"—at least that's what Ian calls me. In a way, that makes me a person just like you. Though, in a very important way, I am not like you. Regardless, you can know Ian and the fruits of this endeavor that I have been working on for years. This project was originally intended to stay in my world—a world only slightly different than yours. A world that, instead of explaining, I will let you experience for yourself.

Part of the initial reasoning behind keeping all of these discoveries and adventures in my world was pragmatic: I didn't know how to get it to you. This issue has been solved, obviously—you're reading it. Part of the problem was that I was thinking only of myself and failed to realize how pertinent this would be for all of you. I now see that it is equally important, if not more so, for you to have access to all of this knowledge as we do.

As you will realize by the end of this journey, the insights gained from our travels directly relate to your world. And the job for which Ian has been trained will also have a direct effect on your life to come. Much of what he and I experienced involved examining the world around him and how he and others fit into it. I suppose you could say that we were exploring *reality*, for lack of a better word. How we accomplished this, though, will become apparent only after you travel with us.

While this is an adventure in reality, it is as much an adventure into the unknown. This is where I must introduce this word, "philosophy." The word comes from the Greek words *philo*, meaning "love," and *sophia*, "wisdom." This is Ian—a true lover of wisdom. At fourteen, Ian is the perfect age, still young enough to really learn. It's often been said that young people are the best philosophers—never afraid to ask "Why?" and always wide-eyed, seeing many things for the first time. He has not yet been indoctrinated into civilization—"educated" I think it's referred to, or maybe "domesticated" is more accurate. After all, it took a child to notice that the Emperor's new clothes weren't actually clothes.

Our question-asking can lead to the most enlightening of answers or to the depths of the unknown. Admittedly, it can be a somewhat dangerous venture. As they say, "Ignorance is bliss"—sometimes what we discover may not be so well received, but it will be knowledge, which many believe is better than the alternative.

I think of philosophy like a crime scene investigation. The investigators examine the scene, asking "Why?" and taking nothing for granted. Why is this hair here? Why is this chair like this? Why is this door open? Why is this glass broken? All of these questions may not produce answers, but that doesn't stop them. And when they *do* get an answer, it leaves the "investigation" department and is taken to another department—maybe forensics, maybe judiciary—where it becomes part of the *evidence*. Your world is our crime scene.

Your journey with us will often leave you without immediate answers. This is a virtue of our journey, though, not a vice. Philosophy is on the cutting edge of the unknown.

For this reason, we—Ian, me, you the reader—can ask whatever questions we want. Anything. This questioning leads us to learn how to think "outside the box," so to speak. (Of course if everyone is thinking outside the box then occasionally we need to think *inside* again—Ian actually does this a number of times.) And philosophy deals with more than just "why." Just as importantly, it explores the "what" and "how," helping to frame the questions we ask. It does so through a method of reasoning and logic that can illuminate previously perplexing issues and provide answers unique to the philosophical arena.

You too can gain access to our adventure, which tells the story of a boy, and a story of philosophy. It has been carefully orchestrated so that you can experience them both.

A brief note on this orchestration—the chapters that follow are divided into three parts:

The first part consists of Ian's nightly adventures with me. You are given access to this through Ian's journal entries of these events; it is a personal account and, thus, more fruitful as it remains in his words.

The second part consists of Ian's discussions with his parents the morning after. Here, I was able to observe these parent-son "debrief-ings" from afar and catalog them.

The third part, also taken from Ian's journal, includes Ian's excursions that are either solo missions or jaunts with his friend, Jeff. It is here that Ian starts to apply the knowledge gained from his encounters with me to his own journey.

Now you are on board with us. You know all that Ian knew—if not more—as he began his journey. He's going to his room now . . . time for me to get to work . . .

Chapter 1

Knowledge

I am, therefore I think.

–Skeptic *magazine credo*

Appearances are often deceiving.

–Sixth-century BC *fable by Aesop,*
"The Wolf in Sheep's Clothing"

It was like I was dreaming. I supposed that I was, or else how would some man have gotten inside my room? He just stood there with his back to me, as if he were examining that poster of the moon on my wall, though there's nothing really interesting about it. I'd always just liked the moon because it gave me that small-yet-big feeling, like nothing mattered, yet *everything* mattered. He just stroked his grayish beard as if he were genuinely interested in it.

How *did* he get inside my room? I felt strangely comfortable about it. It was as though I'd realized I was dreaming and so was able to enjoy his being there, instead of being scared and probably waking up. Then again, how could I know if I were really dreaming? Instead I felt like I was awake and for some reason he had the right to be in my room.

He moved on to my poster of the flat Earth—when people actually believed the Earth was flat. He was nodding in the way someone would if they agreed with what they were reading. Then he moved his noticeably big hands over to the picture of 1,001 words. It was called "Inflation." I loved the concept. It seemed like he was going to count all the words. I already had: 1,001. It had exceeded its worth—

> "Have you ever had a dream . . . that you were so sure was real? What if you were unable to wake from that dream? How would you know the difference between the dream world and the real world?"
>
> –The Matrix

now worth more than just the usual thousand words. Then he moved onto the framed picture of a baseball, deformed at the exact moment of impact. Did he even realize that I was in the room, peering out over my comforter?

"So how do we know what's really there, Ian?" he asked in a gentle tone, as if he really were supposed to be there.

"Really there?" I said.

"Yes. *Reality*, if that's what you want to call it."

"Well, I suppose I just look and see."

"Of course." He turned to me. His white beard and grayish hair framed a face that featured two bushy, angled eyebrows pushing down a pair of glasses onto his large nose. It was all accented by a comforting though inquisitive smile, which seemed to be saying, "Great answer: look and see." He pulled out an apple from his pocket. "Look at this ripe Rome apple. What do you see?"

I sat up in bed. I grabbed my gray sweatshirt off the floor and pulled it over the T-shirt I had on. Now a little more intimidated, though not enough to start genuinely worrying, I responded, "A red, smooth, somewhat spherical object."

"I agree. Describe red. What is red?"

"*You* know what it is. It's red. Look at it." I pointed at the apple, trying to somehow point only at the redness of the apple alone. Admittedly, my response wasn't very satisfying. "Well, I guess it represents anger, and sometimes love. Ironically. It's supposed to make you hungry—that's why all the fast-food chains put it in their logos. That's what my mom says." He just stood there, apparently dissatisfied with my attempt at an answer. "It's just red. It's reddish. Look at it."

"I am."

"Okay. *That's* red."

"Let me show you something." He reached into his pants pocket and pulled out some sort of device. It looked like a wire with a little transmitter on it. He worked one end deep into his ear. The other end he held in his hand. The end-piece looked small in his rather large hand. I sat, almost paralyzed, as he approached me and fitted the piece into my

---

Navigating "Reality"

Thinkers in various disciplines throughout history have explored the difficulty in deciphering reality:

"Reality is merely an illusion, albeit a very persistent one."
    –Albert Einstein

"Exterior perception is truthful hallucination."
    –Nineteenth-century psychologist Hippolyte-Adolphe Taine

"We don't see things as they are, we see them as we are."
    –Anaïs Nin, French novelist (1903–1977)

ear. I felt a strange mix of curious and very scared. Then we just sat there for a moment, looking at the apple. Staring at it. I saw him shut his eyes for a moment very deliberately, and at that instant my vision became blurry. When it cleared up a second later, I was startled.

"What happened? What did you do? That apple's purple. It looks rotten. What is this?"

He sat, calmly. "It's purple . . . to you. You try it. You blink while we're still attached and let me see what you see."

I tried doing just what he'd done. I stared at the apple, then blinked really tightly. I opened my eyes and the apple was back to red. Then he spoke, again calmly, "Yes, of course, this apple now looks purple *to me*."

"But your purple is my red," I said.

He nodded. "And this could be the same for *every* person. We have no possible way—aside from this one-of-a-kind device— for knowing what someone else's *red* is really like. What someone else's perception of *anything* is really like.

"So I'll ask you again: How do you know what's really there?"

"I think I see what you're getting at."

The Old Man continued, "Ian, I think it's important that we make a distinction between the way things seem and the way things are. The first—how things seem—we'll call the 'phenomenal.' The latter—the way things are, independent of any perceiver—we'll call 'noumenal.' Okay?"

This seemed a little silly, giving an already complicated concept even more complicated titles; though I felt like there was something important there. "Okay. But where else could there be things like this besides with the color thing? Everywhere else it's pretty easy to figure out the," I really wanted to impress him here, "the difference between phenomenal and noumenal."

He seemed unimpressed. "Well, there are many. Let's take a simple example. When you put a straight stick in the water, how does it seem?"

"Well, aren't straight sticks just straight, by definition?"

"Yes. But how do they *seem* in the water?" he asked.

The Importance of Reason

German philosopher Immanuel Kant wrote that the noumena— *"thing in itself"—is essentially unknowable. It lies behind the* phenomena—*the observable world experienced through the senses.*

He claimed that we can know the world through "concepts of understanding"—our mind's innate tools used to categorize reality:

"Although all knowledge begins with experience, it does not necessarily all spring from experience."

"Bent. They seem bent."

"Good. How about the moon? How big does the moon seem when you look at it?"

"About as big as a dime."

"But we know it's much bigger. *Empirically*, we measure it and know it's not as big as a dime. And doesn't the moon seem bigger on the horizon than in the sky?"

"Yes. I think it's closer when it's on the horizon though. It sure seems that way."

"Yes, it does. But it isn't. That's just something that your visual system does incorrectly. Because there are more immediate objects between you and the moon on the horizon, your visual cortex sees the moon as being closer when, empirically, it's the same distance as when it's high in the sky."

"My visual cortex *tricks* me?"

"Sure." He took out a piece of paper from my desk and drew two lines. "Which of these lines seems longer?"

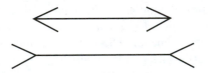

This illusion was discovered by nineteenth-century psychologist F. C. Müller-Lyer.

The brain makes this mistake because it wrongly adds depth to each line: the brain sees the bottom line as closer, like the outside corner of a building, with the roof and ground sloping away from us.

"The bottom one is a bit longer."

He measured them and we realized that, empirically, they were both the exact same length. "Again, another trick by your visual system. The brain's unconscious constantly fills in blanks left over by our limited sensory perception. How it does this is rather complex. But *that* it does—this is what we're concerned with."

"Okay, so my vision's not perfect. But my other senses are right on. I know that this apple and this table feel smooth. I can tell how things *are* by how they *feel*—that can't be in the object."

"Sure, the table feels smooth. But look." He grabbed one of a number of microscopes from the shelf. It was as if he knew I was going to bring that up. "Look at the table through this."

I did. I now saw small ridges in the table's surface. "There are little ridges. Okay, so it's not smooth. But there aren't a lot of ridges."

"Okay," he said as he grabbed another microscope. "Look at it under *this* microscope."

There were many more ridges now. It looked like there were ridges *within* the other ridges from before. "Even more ridges. But how could I ever see this with just my eyes?"

"That's just the point. If we looked at it under an even stronger microscope we would see that the table is just a conglomeration of molecules that are primarily *space*. The apparent solidity that you see as this table is really just energy and space. The table *appears* smooth. But is it? Can we know? Which of these many views shows us the *actual* table?

"Ian, there are so many examples of this around you. Look in church next Sunday: people fanning themselves with the pamphlets. This makes it seem as though it cools them off, but the energy required to do this actually raises their temperature, making them warmer. Likewise, when people drink coffee: it *seems* like it should warm them up but it actually dilates their blood vessels, letting *out* heat, cooling them down.

"You know, part of the problem lies in our language. We're somewhat confined by it and somewhat bewitched by it."

He must have noticed my confusion.

"Let's go back to our experience of color. We say that the apple is red—as if there's somehow redness *in* the apple. But you and I have already seen one problem with that. Regardless, we know that objects can't *have* color."

Is the Heat and Cold "in" the Water?

Our skin does not have "hot" receptors but only "cold" and "warm." These cold-receptors are responsible for detecting all extreme temperatures.

If one places his left hand in a bucket of very hot water and his right hand in a bucket of ice water and then immediately places both hands in a bucket of room temperature water, that water will feel simultaneously warm and cool.

Can We Be Certain of a Table?

"Is there any knowledge in the world which is so certain that no reasonable man could doubt it?"

This is one of the most difficult questions that can be asked, according to philosopher Bertrand Russell, winner of the Nobel Prize for Literature in 1950.

He concludes, "The real table, if there is one, is not immediately known to us at all."

Mass Is Energy

Albert Einstein demonstrated the relation of mass (m) to energy (E) in his famous equation, $E = mc^2$ (c = the speed of light). From this we see that mass is proportional to energy: $m = E/c^2$.

"It followed from the special theory of relativity that mass and energy are both but different manifestations of the same thing—a somewhat unfamiliar conception for the average mind."

English physicist Sir Arthur Eddington writes that a table, "is mostly emptiness. Sparsely scattered in that emptiness are numerous electric charges rushing about with great speed; but their combined bulk amounts to less than a billionth of the bulk of the table itself."

Again, more confusion.

"Think about the case of an object comprised of colorless atoms. Likewise, collections of these atoms are colorless. Yet objects are just collections of atoms. The color is more in us than in anything. Same with hearing. Do things *have* sound? Do atoms? Objects cause sound waves to be compressed and then our inner ear translates these compressions into sound. The sound is in *us*. It's the same with smells, tastes, tactile sensations. You name it."

This was frustrating. It went against anything I'd ever been told, against my own experiences even. "But we can all *see* things," I responded, "how they really are. You and I both see the apple, the desk."

"Ian, I want you to put these glasses on. You won't be able to use them for very long or you'll become overwhelmed. But I think this will be very illuminating, pardon the pun."

On my head, he put a sleek-looking helmet with glasses attached that came down over my eyes. As the glasses settled on my nose, he locked them down. What I saw next was so beyond anything I'd ever

A Blank Slate

British philosopher John Locke argued that qualities such as sound and color (which he called "secondary qualities") are in the observer and not the object. He gave the example of fire that can be both warm/comforting and hot/painful, suggesting that these conflicting sensations cannot be in the fire, but must be in us. Thus, he writes, if we did not see, hear, taste, nor smell then, "all colours, tastes, odours, and sounds . . . vanish and cease."

He wrote, "The mind is at birth a clean sheet, a tabula rasa [blank slate]; and sense-experience writes upon it in a thousand ways, until sensation begets memory and memory begets ideas."

seen, so beyond anything I could think to describe. I felt as though I were seeing colors I'd never known, that I was almost *feeling* with my eyes. I didn't see the objects in the room as objects, but almost more as collections of energy. Within what felt like seconds, he unlatched the glasses from the helmet. I stood in amazement.

"What was that?" I asked softly.

"That," he replied, equally softly, "was much closer to reality. That was *all* the wavelengths of the electromagnetic spectrum."

"You mean not just visible light, but all of it?"

"Exactly. You know, humans can see only an extremely small part of the spectrum of waves." He got out a piece of paper. On it he drew a line and then continued talking. As he spoke, he drew more. "Humans see only from 400 to 700 nanometers—what we call 'visible light.' But the entire spectrum runs from 10^{-12} to 10^4 centimeters, with visible light coming in at around 10^{-7} centimeters. It includes gamma rays, X rays, ultraviolet rays; *then* comes the visible spectrum, then infrared rays, microwaves, and the biggest, radio waves. Much more out there than you can see."

"To be [exist] is to be perceived."

Irish philosopher and bishop George Berkeley espoused the view known as "immaterialism." He agreed with Locke that our ideas come only from our senses. Berkeley went further to argue that nothing material exists. We simply experience our various perceptions and learn to attribute them to an outer world. Thus we cannot directly experience a three-dimensional world.

By the end, he had written the following on the paper:

WAVE:	radio	micro-	infrared	Visual	UV	X rays	gamma rays

Wavelength: LONG...VERY SHORT

A View from Nowhere

Thomas Nagel discusses the impossibility of obtaining a purely objective view—the observer always involves his or her own view. He writes, "An objective standpoint is created by leaving a more subjective, individual, or even just human perspective behind." This is not necessarily a problem—the subjective nature of our consciousness is itself a feature of reality, "without which we couldn't do physics or anything else—and it must occupy as fundamental a place in any credible world view as matter, energy, space, time, and numbers."

"Many of the truths we cling to depend greatly on our own point of view."
–Obi-Wan Kenobi, *Return of the Jedi*

Sight . . . and Smell . . . and Reality . . .

Do human senses grasp reality?

Pit vipers can see infrared light.
Honey bees can see UV light.
X-rays are so short that they go through the human body—except the bones.
Humans can detect 10,000 different odors. Dogs, on the other hand, have 25
times more olfactory (smell) receptors than humans and can detect odors at a
concentration of nearly 100 million times less than humans.

"It was amazing. I felt like I could hardly make anything out."

"Yes, it's ironic in a way. If people could see more," he continued, emphatically, "they'd be blinded by it all. Having our vision somewhat limited actually allows us to see. If our vision accounted for more of what is really there, then we'd be overwhelmed with all the information. Either that or we'd get used to it and adapt." He shrugged his shoulders.

"Okay. So without having any more experiments done on me, what's the point of all this?"

"The point is, things very often seem to be what, in actuality, they are not. And very often, our lowly senses are not the proper devices to use in determining reality. Though it sure *seems* like they are."

"Yeah."

"And *so* we don't want to rely on them for such an ever-so-revered thing as *knowledge*. When we claim to know something, we want it to mean something more than being *somewhat certain*, or *might be*. We want *is*. We want *knowledge*. But it turns out that this *knowledge* is impossible. We don't get it through our senses. They've lied to you in the past, and you wouldn't go to a friend who'd repeatedly lied to you and ask him about something very important to you. Would you?"

"No. No, I wouldn't." There I was, believing that I couldn't trust my senses to help me know things. It was very strange, sort of a dull

Looking into the Past

When we look at a star, we're actually seeing it the way it was in the past. It takes light from the nearest star about 3½ years to get to us. The star Arcturus had been shining for 200 years before we could see it. Thus, we might imagine that a number of stars we see today are really not there and what we see is their "leftover" light. When we see the sun set, it has "actually" set 8 minutes earlier. This effect is even greater with sound as it travels much more slowly than light.

"It is sometimes proved to me that [my] senses are deceptive, and it is wiser not to trust entirely to anything by which we have once been deceived."

—René Descartes

feeling. Scary, even. I thought of all the things I thought I knew. It seemed like I knew them all through my senses. Though I also recalled all the times that my senses had failed me. But I still was certain of some things. There were still things I could know for sure. I thought of all the things in school that people claim to learn. Things I could learn even if I were deaf and blind, with no sensation at all. I could still know that one plus one equals two. I certainly know *that*.

"Did you know that one plus one equals two?" I asked him, somewhat rhetorically. No response. "See. There's something I know. I relied on *reason* there for knowledge. It's through reason that one can attain the *knowledge* of which you said there was none."

He shook his head slowly, seriously.

"How? How could I be wrong that one plus one equals two?"

"What are numbers?" he asked.

I couldn't really answer.

"What are they, really? Here's what I want you to do. Go destroy the *number five*."

I must have looked dumbfounded. How in the world could someone destroy a number? I couldn't imagine how that would even be possible.

"I'll save you the effort, Ian. You can't. Couldn't it be possible that numbers aren't real, that they're just another figment of your imagination? That one plus one could just as well equal five? We just decided ourselves, at some point in the past, to say that it equals two. How many clouds would you get if I added one cloud plus one cloud?" He was rattling all

> **A Life of Skepticism**
>
> *A form of skepticism was developed by the Greek physician Sextus Empiricus, ca. 200 AD. It was not based on doubt but on the Greek word* epoche—*suspension of judgment. Once one could consistently suspend judgment, he would achieve* ataraxia—*peace of mind.*
>
> *A more current practice is based on the Greek* skepticos—*thoughtful*—*and the Latin* scepticus—*inquiring, or reflective. Editor of* Skeptic *magazine, Michael Shermer writes, "Skeptics are the watchmen of reasoning errors, aiming to expose bad ideas."*

---

2 + 2 = 5

In George Orwell's novel 1984, *the protagonist considers the government's declaration that two plus two equals five. He wonders if everyone believes it, would that make it true? This not only questions the truth of math, but also the power of the government.*

"I agree that two and two make four is an excellent thing; but to give everything its due, two and two make five is also a very fine thing."

—Fyodor Dostoevsky

Math and Reality

"As far as the laws of mathematics refer to reality, they are not certain; and as far as they are certain, they do not refer to reality"
—Albert Einstein

"Mathematics may be defined as the subject in which we never know what we are talking about, nor whether what we are saying is true."
—Bertrand Russell

of this off rather quickly. It was kind of agitating. *"Reason* can't provide you with absolute knowledge. Otherwise, how could I know what red was like? I could reason what it would be like, you could tell me about all the wavelengths of light and how they make you feel angry, or hungry, or how a rose is red, but reason *alone* wouldn't yield absolute knowledge. We'd have to go back to our not-so-trustworthy foe, the senses."

I guess his shotgun approach worked for now. Kind of overwhelming. Destroy the number five? But I had moved on to something even more certain. I held my hand up between the two of us. I stood there, looking at him, for what seemed like five minutes—phenomenal—but was probably more like five seconds. After feeling as though I'd set the tone I said, matter-of-factly, "This is my hand." It felt kind of silly, saying something so obvious. But *that* I knew.

"Ian," he began, "I want you to tell me if it's possible that the devil, let's say, has deceived you. He's deceived you that one plus one equals two, maybe. Or that you were seeing something that was red, that your hand was in front of your face; he could even deceive you as to your own existence. Isn't this at least a possibility?"

I supposed it was. "Yes. It's a possibility. But not a good one."

"I agree. But a possibility, nonetheless. We're just looking at the potential ways in which we may not be certain of anything. And if there is a way to doubt something then we lack certainty. And without certainty, what good is this so-called knowledge? I have something else I want to show you."

He motioned to me to walk with him to the back corner of my room. I got out of bed, wearing my shorts and sweatshirt, sliding my feet into my sandals. He lifted the poster of the moon to reveal a big hole in my wall. There was a ladder that came up to the hole, leading down to somewhere I'd never seen

"I can prove now that two human hands exist. How? By holding up my two hands, and saying . . . 'Here is one hand,' and adding . . . 'and here is another.'"

G. E. Moore was a leading twentieth-century thinker classified as an "analytical philosopher." He attempted to show that everything that we seem to see—such as visual afterimages—will not necessarily be "met with in space."

before. It had a tube around it that made it all seem a little claustrophobic.

He crouched down and climbed onto the ladder. It seemed safe as he slowly walked down it. I could see the light at the end of the tunnel, so to speak. So I got on. Walked down. Slowly. Wondering why I trusted this man.

At the end I stepped out into a corridor that certainly wasn't there before. We walked down it, the Old Man nodding in an attempt to be encouraging. Amidst my worry about what would happen next, I was able to produce a little confusion as to where this corridor came from. It looked vaguely like something I'd imagined from a book I read once.

At the end of this corridor was a large steel door. The Old Man opened it and we entered what seemed to be a science lab. It looked a lot like the science lab that was in my biology textbook—in the "Scientists at Work" section, meant to show the students that scientists are people too. The white walls, silver tables and steel door gave it sort of a cold feeling, though I wasn't cold, though I felt like I should be.

By itself on a table sat a glass container with a human brain in some liquid. It had wires running in and out of it. A placard on the table in front of the container read, "The Brain of Ian Pinkle." I felt my stomach drop. The Old Man sensed my discomfort.

"This process is completely safe," he explained. "While you were sleeping, a doctor removed your brain from your skull, kept it alive in this solution, and was just stimulating it to make it seem as though you were experiencing certain things." He paused to let his explanation sink in. It didn't really sink in. "How could you differentiate your *own* experience yesterday from today's experience as a brain floating in this jar?"

I didn't know how to answer. If my sensations really did relate to a certain brain state, it seems like there would be no way to tell. I could manipulate the brain in the jar, but that would do no good because this brain could just be an illusion, created by the *actual* brain—my brain—in a jar somewhere else.

The Old Man jiggled one of the wires in the brain and I immediately saw a red apple appear on the adjacent table. He probed again

Doubt Yields Knowledge?

Descartes proposed a "Method of Doubt" very similar to the text here. Ironically, he did this not to show that we can't know anything, but after a closer analysis, that knowledge is possible.

Of the notion of an evil deceiver he writes, "I shall then suppose . . . some evil genius not less powerful than deceitful, has employed his whole energies in deceiving me; I shall consider that . . . all . . . external things are but illusions."

Phantom Limbs

In approximately 80 percent of cases in which people have a limb amputated, subjects report feeling sensation where that limb origi- nally was. These sensa- tions range from warmth and itching to slight pain and discomfort. Some people who have lost their arms even report feeling that their arms swing while they walk.

What Is Real?

The 1999 film The Matrix *poses the follow- ing question:*

"What is real? How do you define real? If you're talking about what you can feel, what you can smell, what you can taste and see, then real is simply electrical signals interpreted by your brain."

The Old Man's quote paraphrases Chinese philosopher Chuang Tzu (369–286 BC).

and I smelled a freshly baked apple pie. And then again, and I felt a pain, like a pinprick, on my arm. But there was no pin near my arm. Just the sensation. Pain without any- thing there to cause it. He did it again. Pain. But *nothing* there on my arm. Could it be that pain is an illusion? That it's just phenomenal? I had really begun to doubt that there was anything I could know. I mean, *really know*.

"I've got a third alternative for you, to go along with the Deceptive Devil and the Brain in a Jar."

I paused, intrigued by what could possibly follow those examples. He looked at me in an assuring way, as if to quiet my fear that my brain just might be floating in a jar of liquid.

"How can you be sure that you're not dreaming right now?"

"Up until now, completely sure," I responded. "Dreams aren't really anything like reality. Dreams are, well, they're more *dreamy*. You can just tell. Things happen in dreams that don't happen in reality. Usually, anyway."

A strange look came over his face. He could sense that I maybe wasn't so sure about the dif- ference anymore. He slouched down and began speaking in a slow, deliberate Eastern accent:

"I was Old Man who dreamed I was butterfly. Or was I butterfly who dreamed I was Old Man?"

He raised his eyebrows at me. Smiled.

I nodded. He seemed to enjoy saying things without really saying them. "Now that I think about it, I have had times when I can't really remember if something actually hap- pened or if it happened in a dream. Alexis actually got mad at me last week because I told her that I had returned her phone call and when she told me that she was home all day and didn't get a call from me, I recalled that it actually might have happened in a dream. It was just so real. And I've woken up so . . ."

"Alexis?" he asked, as if giving me a hard time. He seemed interested that I'd confided in a stranger about a girl I had been calling. "Yes, Alexis," I thought to myself. Her name even sounded good to me. And I *did* bring her up because I felt like talking about her. I like her. But he doesn't need to know that.

"She's a friend of mine." I had been thinking about her a lot lately. She's definitely cute. Plain and simple . . . and cute. Her hair just falls to her shoulders—she doesn't seem to care much about it, except when she braids it into pigtails. And none of that make-up ever. Her clothes are always just regular, I guess. She does always have cute shoes, though. I can hardly describe myself so I wouldn't know how to describe her. Not that I'd need to. She's just really fun to be with.

Someone outside caught my attention. Alexis was peering in. Alexis? She smiled her perfect smile. She flipped her pigtails back and forth and had her usual journal tucked under her arm. Her writing had always been interesting to me. She waved for me to come outside. As I smiled back at her and stood up to go see her I stumbled a bit. I had been asleep. I shook my head and looked at the Old Man. He was smiling at me. "It sure looked like you were ready to go greet someone outside." He walked up to the window and, seeing no one, turned to me continuing to smile.

He squinted his eyes. Nodded. "So you were saying . . . about your waking up?"

"Yeah. I've woken up lots of times from situations that seemed so real at the time. It would be hard to imagine that this whole conversation was just a dream. And my feeling the pain of my brain in a jar being prodded and, all the while, it happening in a dream. It seems unlikely. But I do get your point."

"And what is that?" he asked, tilting his head slightly.

Solipsism—the theory that one's self is the only reality. While not a popular view amongst philosophers, it derives from the skeptical view that no public sort of knowledge is possible due to the subjectivity of individual experience.

Justifying Why We Can Doubt Anything

1. *The senses constantly deceive.*
2. *Reason can't explain everything.*
3. *A devil could be deceiving us.*
4. *The brain can be misleading or, worse, could just be floating in a jar.*
5. *We could be dreaming.*

"If you would be a real seeker after truth, it is necessary that at least once in your life you doubt, as far as possible, all things."
    –Descartes

"Doubt is the beginning, not the end, of wisdom."
    –George Iles

"I know only one thing—that I do not know."

–Socrates

"The wise man is he who knows that he knows nothing."

–Plato

Socrates taught Plato until Socrates was sentenced to death in 399 BC for "corrupting the youth."

The Socratic Method

Socrates' approach to teaching focused on asking versus telling. This allowed the students to work towards answers for themselves, thus providing more "ownership" of the ideas. Though often this method of questioning reveals what one does not know. By interrogating the brightest orators of his time, Socrates repeatedly revealed the lacking of their knowledge simply in asking the right questions. Ironically, admitting one's ignorance in a discussion can often provide greater clarity or can better expose another's erroneous belief.

"My attempts at knowing something—at knowing *anything*—all fall short. I can't trust my senses; reason doesn't consistently lead us to truths; there are possibilities, however small, that I may be deceived by another being or that I am no more than a brain in a jar, and I obviously have trouble deciphering reality from dream. So it seems that I can doubt everything to some extent. So there is nothing I could know for certain. Not even my own existence. Not even my own existence? So what can I know? Anything? Don't I know anything?"

As he walked away, or more like faded away shaking his head, he turned to me and said, "All you can know is that you know nothing." He turned to me, still grinning, "Enjoy those binoculars of Jeff's—should be fun."

Binoculars? If he's something in *my* dream, how could he know about something in reality that I don't even know? Jeff doesn't have any *fun* binoculars.

And I can only know that I know nothing? I began to feel restless.

As much as I loved meeting with Ian, one thing I liked even more was to watch him sort through everything, trying to make sense of it. I was really looking forward to Ian's someday having to make sense of *me* and, more importantly, of *himself*. For now though, reality seemed to be challenging enough.

So I sat, perched outside the kitchen window, peering in. I couldn't help noticing the simplicity of his home. This little breakfast nook, for example. Secluded from the rest of the house, it seems like its own entity in a way. It has an almost sterile feel, except for the warmth brought to it by the conversations. All of the family's conversations happen around the square dining table, draped in an off-white tablecloth and surrounded by four chairs, only three of which are ever occupied. It's connected to the home by a hallway that leads to the stairs descending from the upstairs where Ian's room is. The only other way out of the kitchen nook is up the small flight of three stairs that lead to the entryway (or exit, depending on which way you're going) and out the big oak front door to the porch.

It was another Friday morning in the Pinkle home. Ian's mother and father were eating breakfast, talking casually about the latest news in the papers. As usual, Ian was making his way downstairs after an early morning of reading—though not the typical books his eighth grade peers read. Because of his parents' backgrounds as scientists, Ian had always wanted to find out *the answers* for himself. It was more of a personal conviction—a challenge that he took on himself to see if *he* could figure it all out without having to ask mom and dad. Last weekend, instead of asking his parents why sticks bend in water, he read about it. His parents were not surprised as he proudly arrived at the table the next morning exclaiming, matter-of-factly, "Thank goodness for Snell and his law. Without him, we'd probably think that sticks actually bend when dipped in water. Light travels slower in water than it does in air. That makes the stick look bent."

This morning, it was rainbows. He had some trouble, though, and admitted to not

> *"To be a philosopher is not merely to have subtle thoughts, nor even to found a school, but so to love wisdom as to live, according to its dictates, a life of simplicity, independence, magnanimity, and trust."*
>
> –Henry David Thoreau
> Nineteenth-century
> author

Not-So-Straight Sticks

Sticks appear to bend in water because, as Willebrord Snell discovered in 1621, light moves more slowly in water than in air. When we view a stick in the water, the light from the submerged stick takes longer to get to us than from the part above the water.

Snell's discovery of the law of refraction was published by Descartes in 1637 as "The Law of Sines."

Biologist Richard Dawkins provides an evolutionary explanation of our senses: "You might think that our sense organs would be shaped to give us a 'true' picture of the world as it 'really' is. It is safer to assume that they have been shaped to give us a useful *picture of the world, to help us survive."*

He references very small particles—neutrinos—which can pass through solid objects. Yet if we saw these seemingly solid objects as mostly space, we would not be able to navigate around these objects without repeatedly running into them.

fully grasping why we can see only a certain, very small portion of light rays. His father, an evolutionary biologist, explained that this was actually an *ability* and not a limitation: "If people saw it all," he explained, "then they'd be overwhelmed with all the information. Imagine making sense of it all simultaneously: gamma rays, X-rays, ultraviolet rays, infrared light, microwaves, on top of our present color spectrum. Impossible. Ironically, if we could see more we'd be blinded by it all."

Ian obviously felt an overwhelming sense of *déjà vu*. He shook his head slowly, trying to figure this out. Then his mother, a practicing psychologist, explained that we actually create what we see—that we are much more active in our observations than we consciously realize. Our brain fills in blanks, reconstructs the input gathered by the senses, and makes it understandable for us. Our consciousness—or subconsciousness—is much more active than we realize.

They continued their explanation until Ian seemed satisfied with it. But he remained silent. He didn't eat, moving his toast around on his plate. "Are you feeling okay?" his father asked. "Did you sleep well?"

"Well, I guess I did," Ian responded. "But I feel as though I was asleep for, like, a day—so much seemed to happen last night that it couldn't have happened in just a few hours."

"What makes you say that?" his mother asked.

Rules of Seeing

"You construct every figure you see. So, in this sense, every figure you see is subjective."

Psychologist Donald Hoffman explains numerous "rules" that our visual system follows. In following these rules, we have a much more active role in perception than we consciously realize. He writes, "Your rules allow you to construct what you see, but they also restrict what you can construct." For example, Rule 31:

"Construct motion to be as uniform over space as possible." This helps explain why our vision makes it seem that a wagon wheel on a moving stagecoach spins the wrong way.

"Nothing," he said, hesitantly. "Nothing."

His parents seemed confused but let him think through what he wanted to say. They sat quietly, ready to listen.

Ian scooted his chair away from the table a bit, as if his time here was not about eating breakfast, but instead about something bigger. He looked up at them, already with ink on his face from something he must have been writing before coming downstairs.

"I really mean that nothing—the actual *nothing*—made it happen. I think I actually dreamed nothing last night. And after dreaming nothing, I dreamed a very big *something*.

"I had a very strange person visit me in my dream. He confronted me with all these strange thoughts." He shook his head nervously. "Thoughts that convince me of things that I was totally sure weren't the case. I remember now, why I felt *nothing* at one point. This man—an older man, with a nice smile, but nice in a crafty way—told me that not only do I know nothing, but that I could never know anything. He even went so far as to say that I couldn't know that I exist. I told him he was obviously wrong. That I knew he was standing right in front of me. That I knew he had a small scar on his forehead. I could touch him. How could he say that I didn't know anything?

"He asked me if I'd ever had a friend who lied a lot—who had told lies in the past and who, when I really needed to know something, I would avoid for fear of being given false information. I thought about that guy Jerry who you always made me play with in the summers at the cottage. I could never trust him. Whatever he said I didn't totally believe because he'd deceived me so many times before. He's like the exact opposite of Alexis—whenever I really need advice, I go to her because she's never lied about anything."

The Shock of the Torpedo Fish

Plato refers to Socrates as often acting like a "torpedo fish" (an electric ray with a shock powerful enough to knock over a grown man). In doing so, Plato describes Socrates' ability to "shock" people into realizing their own ignorance through his questioning. This shock provides an ideal moment for learning.

Socrates uses this term just after he has forced a boy into doubt, which leads to the boy's realizing mathematical truths:

Socrates: *If we have made him doubt, and given him the "torpedo's shock," have we done him any harm?*

Meno: *I think not.*

Socrates: *We have certainly . . . assisted him in some degree to the discovery of the truth; and now he will wish to remedy his ignorance.*

Ian sat still, amused that he was recalling a dream, but with a sense of frustrated confusion as well, as though the dream had really bothered him.

"And then . . ." he went on zealously, retelling the experience of seeing purple apples, of the Color Spectrum Helmet, of seeing his own brain, of all the phenomenal-versus-noumenal examples. He sat and retold the entire dream experience so fast, at times, that it all seemed "stream of consciousness," like he had actually lived it.

"That's it. I woke up and tried to make sense of it. Even though this man was just in a dream, he seemed to have stumped me. We do know things, don't we? Or is *knowing something* just not as strong a statement as I thought it once was?"

His parents looked at each other. They were more impressed than anything. Their son, who thrived on *knowing*, had obviously been disturbed by this dream. And this wasn't the kind of dream where one simply hugs one's child and says, "It was just a bad dream." This one had some actual consequences to deal with. There were some questions that needed answering.

His mother raised her eyebrows as if to speak. His father nodded subtly, as if to thank her for taking the responsibility. Very cautiously, she asked Ian, "Do you really believe what the man in the dream told you in the end—that the only thing you know is that you know nothing?"

A Life of Doubt

"Doubt is not a pleasant condition, but certainty is absurd."
–Voltaire
Eighteenth-century philosopher and author, best-known for *Candide*

"Doubt is useful for a while. . . . To choose doubt as a philosophy of life is akin to choosing immobility as a means of transportation."
–*Life of Pi*, Yann Martel

"I wouldn't have," he replied, "but I don't see any way out of it. All the ways I could possibly know anything, the man in my dream showed were flawed. It seems like it's true—I now know that I don't know anything."

"But, son, you must know *something*. One couldn't get very far in life without knowing anything. How would you ever do anything?"

Ian didn't seem happy with this. He obviously *was* concerned that he might not know anything.

His mom spoke again, this time more thoughtfully. "Isn't there a problem inherent in that statement that you and your dream character have made?"

"I thought there was during my dream, but now I feel like he might be right."

"Don't look at all the instances that he explained to you. Look at the last statement." She paused for a moment. Ian raised his eyebrows and looked as per his mother's instructions. No response. She continued, "It's a paradox. Completely impossible, logically. If you do know that you know nothing, then you know *that*." Ian nodded hesitatingly, though with a subtle smile as if his mom might be on to something. "And, either you do know nothing *or* you don't. If you *do* know nothing, and you know it, then you know something. If you *don't* know nothing, then, by simple logic, you know something: *that you know nothing*, which is inherently paradoxical. So, either way you're better off than you seemed to be a moment ago. You should be somewhat relieved that you know *something*."

"On top of that," his father added, "it seems that you can know one specific thing for sure."

"How, dad? What could you use to know something if not your senses or your reason? I think this man and I successfully doubted every possibility."

"That's just the point, son. You *doubted*. Or maybe I should reemphasize that: *You* doubted. In your dream, you repeatedly proclaimed, 'I doubt *x*.' I doubt that the apple is red. I doubt that I hear someone calling my name. I doubt that one plus one equals two. I doubt

Paradox

para—*beyond or against*
doxa—*belief*

Typically, a paradox is a statement that either forces us into a logical contradiction, or drastically overturns our present viewpoint or belief system.

"How wonderful that we have met with a paradox. Now we have some hope of making progress."

–Niels Bohr

"The problem is, if there's no objective truth, then no statement is objectively true, including the statement, 'There's no such thing as objective truth.' The statement refutes itself."

–T. Schick, Jr. and
L. Vaughn
How to Think About Weird Things

"I think, therefore I am."

Translated from the Latin, "Cogito ergo sum," *Descartes' statement served as his foundation for all knowledge. Descartes' quest was to,* "find just one thing, however slight, that is certain and unshakable."

He referred to the term, "Archimedian Point." *Second-century BC Greek thinker Archimedes believed that by finding a single fixed, immovable point, he could move the Earth. To find truth, then, one must first find an enduring, immovable truth.*

that I exist. The man in your dream even did this exercise with you. What he failed to recognize, though, was that when something doubts, or when something does anything, that thing must exist to do it. So if *I doubt*, then *I* must exist. And that's something about which you can be certain."

Ian looked somewhat satisfied that his parents had come to his rescue, showing him flaws in the reasoning of this frightful man in his dreams. Still, he seemed a bit perturbed. "So according to you guys, I can know two things: that I don't know nothing and that I exist. That's not very much. What's the point of going to school if that's all I can know?"

"Well, Ian, I'll suggest some quick criteria for that before we have to be going," his mother answered. "I argue that knowledge is achieved if the following three criteria are met. You can see if everything that you think you know fits this."

Ian nodded. "Finally, some answers."

"First, you must be *justified* in believing something. Right? If you ask what year Abe Lincoln died, imagine that I answer, 'The number on my soccer jersey was eighteen and my favorite numbers are six and five, so he died in 1865.' I'm hardly justified in *knowing* what year he died, despite the fact that I was right. I have no good reason for holding that belief.

"Secondly, what you claim to know must be *true*. This should seem obvious. You can't *know* something if it's not true. How we determine something to be true is another story, but we all agree that to know it, it must be true.

"And thirdly, you must *believe* what you know. You can't *know* it's Jeff's birthday tomorrow if you believe that it's next week.

"So that should help for now. In order for you to know something, you must have a 'justified true belief.'"

Ian's dad was nodding in a complimentary way following his wife's suggestion. Ian furrowed his brow as if using her criteria to test things that he knew.

Things We Know

Kant distinguished between two types of knowledge:

a priori—*prior to or independent of experience, determined by reason.*
Includes statements like:
"All bachelors are unmarried men," and "All triangles have three sides."

a posteriori—*through experience. For example, "Lemons are yellow," and "Water expands when frozen."*

Justified True Belief

In Plato's dialogue, Theaetetus, *he proposed the three criteria for knowledge:* justified true belief. *He added the "justified" criterion because people were often tricked into believing things by crafty orators, yet these things couldn't be "known" as they were not properly justified.*

"Does that help, honey?" she asked.

Ian shook his head, upset that he might disappoint his mother following her thoughtful suggestion. "You're saying that *every* time we have a justified true belief that we have knowledge. So if I can show you one time that you have a justified true belief yet do not have knowledge, then your criteria will not be sufficient. Right?"

She smiled an approving smile.

Ian took out what looked like a silver dollar and he put it on the table. He looked at both of his parents and smiled somewhat mischievously, leaning forwards with his hands on the table, left hand palm-down, right hand on top.

"Do you *know* that there is a silver dollar on the table?"

His parents looked at each other and nodded hesitantly.

"Yes, son, I do," his mother responded.

"Does that knowledge pass the criteria you just gave?"

"I certainly *believe* there's a silver dollar on the table. That much is for sure. And I'd say I'm *justified* in believing it—I'm sitting here looking at it in plain lighting. Honey," she motioned to Ian's dad, "do you see the silver dollar on the table?"

His dad nodded.

"So all that's left," she continued, "is the 'truth' criterion. Is it true that there's a silver dollar on the table? If so, then it's *knowledge*."

Is "Justified True Belief" Knowledge?

In his 1963 paper of the above title, Edmund Gettier provides numerous examples that he suggests show the JTB criteria—justified true belief—do not suffice for attainment of knowledge. His examples are cases in which the JTB conditions are satisfied yet the agent still does not really know the proposition in question.

Ian nodded, happily. "Yes, it's true." He leaned forward and turned the coin over. The back showed it to be not an authentic silver dollar, but instead a video game token with the face of a silver dollar on one side and the video store emblem on the other.

"So it's not true," Ian's dad noted. "That's *not* a silver dollar."

Ian nodded confidently and lifted up his left hand. Under it was an authentic silver dollar, which they all could see as Ian turned it over on both sides and handed it to them.

"What's the point, son?" his mother asked, curiously.

"You claimed to *know* that there was a silver dollar on the table, and you did so by applying your three criteria. But do you think you really *knew* there was a silver dollar on the table? It would seem strange if you do—it's almost like you were accidentally right. It was only true because there was a real one under my hand. In this case, the statement passed the criteria, though I don't really think you *knew* it. Seems like maybe there's a flaw somewhere in your criteria. Though, I admit, they're pretty good criteria. The point is, they don't work all the time."

She looked at Ian's dad. They shook their heads. "We've got to get going, dear." She smiled. She seemed proud of Ian's thoughtfulness. "And you have science homework to get to—a class full of learning about things you can know."

Ian responded, proudly, "I'm not so sure about that. You know, years ago, people said they *knew* that the Earth was the center of the universe. They didn't say 'We think it might be the center,' they said, 'It *is* the center. We know because our best scientists with the best tools say so.' I guess they didn't *know*—because it wasn't *true*. It would be strange to say that it was true then but not now, especially because the

---

Pragmatism: Truth in Use

Pragmatism was introduced in the early 1900s by William James and C. S. Peirce. It holds that an idea is true if it has practical consequences and provides results. Pragma *is Latin for "action."*

James wrote, "Ideas become true just so far as they help us to get into satisfactory relations with other parts of our experiences." And also, "We have to live today by what truth we can get today, and be ready tomorrow to call it falsehood."

More recently, Richard Rorty expanded on this notion, claiming that truth is socially and historically constructed, arguing that truth results from agreement upon common conclusions.

"The map is not the territory."

Noted by semantics expert Alfred Korzybski, he refers to the notion that a description of something is not the thing itself. Likewise, when we perceive reality, it is not the same as reality itself. Due to the active way in which we perceive—because we see things from our own point of view—*no two people see things exactly the same way. Though as Korzybski continues, if the* map we *use is correct, "it has a similar structure to the territory, which accounts for its usefulness."*

Surrealist painter Rene Magritte illustrates this in his painting, "The Betrayal of Images"—a pipe with the text, "This is not a pipe."

In Lewis Carroll's novel Sylvie and Bruno, *he portrays a map that has a one to one scale: every mile represents a mile. One character notes, "We now use the country itself, as its own map, and I assure you it does nearly as well."*

Earth's position hasn't changed." He paused for a moment to think through this. "But how do we know our current scientific knowledge is any more reliable today?"

"Look at it as a nice story, for now. A good way to explain the world around you. You need to pay close attention in that class anyway. Your teachers say that's the class where you struggle the most."

As Ian was stepping out the front door, he remembered getting his last exam back earlier in the week. He poked his head back in the door. "Hey mom, dad," he said excitedly, "did I tell you I got an 'A' on my last test? Or was that in a dream? It really is hard to decipher the two sometimes."

"No, son, you didn't."

"Oh, well, I did. I got an 'A' on my last chapter test."

They smiled at him. "Well done, son," his father said, sincerely. Then, his parents stood up, walked to the door, opened their wings and flew off the porch like giant eagles. He watched them soar over the treetops and then he looked back to where they were just standing.

"I am dreaming now?" he said softly to himself. "Tomorrow, I will tell my parents about my initial dream and then about this strange dream. I can't wait to hear what they will say. But what they just said in my dream seemed so real. When I retell this tomorrow, how will I know if I'm really telling them or if it's another dream? If they pinch me it won't help. I could dream that I'm being pinched.

"I wonder if I should let myself do homework now," he was mumbling to himself. "I spend enough time doing homework already, it would be silly to do it in my dream. Though what if I'm not dreaming and I just had a hallucination of my parents flying away? What can I really know and how can I know that I know it?"

> *"The last creature in the world to discover water would be the fish, precisely because he is always immersed in it."*
> –Ralph Linton
> American
> anthropologist

What Really *Really* Happened

After this discussion, I needed some fresh air. My head hurt a little, though I was also somewhat refreshed. Kind of a strange feeling. I went up the stairs to the front door and out to meet Jeff. Jeff and I had planned to go to the big high school baseball play-offs. We didn't know any of the players who were playing, but there was something exciting about a championship game of guys who were barely older than we were. The thrill of competition, I suppose. Jeff and I got to the game pretty early—early enough to get very good seats, close to home plate, and near all the parents and teachers of each school. As we watched the players finish their warm-up, we listened to each group of parents talk about how well *their* team or *their* son had done all year. Listening to them talk, it sounded as if both teams had won the last time they played each other. Funny thing.

Just as the game was getting ready to start, Jeff pulled out his binoculars. They looked pretty high-tech. "These are no ordinary binoculars," he said.

Of course they weren't—Jeff loved gizmos and gadgets. More importantly, the Old Man had told me that Jeff would have "fun" binoculars. How could he—or was it *I*—have known that?

"Here," he said, "let's turn this dial to 'sporting event.'" There were about ten different options on the dial. I wondered how it could be that binoculars would do different things depending on the event. He continued, "Now all we have to do is wait. I'll watch the game through them and then we can adjust the other dial. *That's* when it gets really interesting."

I was already interested.

The game began. Both pitchers were obviously strong and it seemed that earning runs was going to be tough. I actually preferred a pitching duel, so that was fine with me.

Then in the third inning, with a runner on second, the batter hit one that landed in right field. As the runner came around third, the outfielder threw the ball toward home. The catcher caught the ball and as the player was sliding into home base, the catcher tagged him with his glove. It was really too close to tell from my angle if he was out or safe. I was anxious to see what the call was. The crowd was screaming a mix of "Out!" and "Safe!" The umpire checked to see that the catcher still had the ball and then proclaimed, "Out!" and the crowd went wild. Everyone was now screaming even louder. The runner looked up and yelled something at the umpire and his coach ran out to the field to confront him. Then Jeff turned to me. He flipped the second switch on the binoculars. "With this we can see how everyone else saw what happened."

I gave Jeff the "you can't be serious" raised eyebrow.

"I'm serious," he said. "Look. You can flip this switch to see how anyone in the area saw what happened. With this ear piece you'll hear their thoughts and you'll get to see what they saw. Basically, you'll see things through their eyes." He paused, as if awaiting my amazement. I assume he translated my silence as amazement. "Here. Try it."

I put the ear piece in and looked through the binoculars. There was nothing different. Jeff pointed to the switch. The first notch on the switch read "Parent of Runner." I looked at the person screaming "No way, ump! What are you looking at?" This was the runner's parent. So I flipped the switch and the binoculars went blurry for a second and then it went back to the hit to right field, just like a video camera would. I saw the hit just like it happened originally, except it looked like the ball went a little farther than I remember. In the ear piece I heard the voice of the same parent who was yelling. As the runner was coming around third base I heard, "My son works so hard. He was so cute as a kid. He's struggling with acne and scoring a run in a big game like this would really boost his self-esteem. Plus, he obviously touched home plate before getting tagged." As I watched the replay through the binoculars, the runner slid into home plate, clearly before the tag. Definitely safe.

"Wow, Jeff, the umpire was wrong. I just watched the replay. That runner was safe by a long way. The umpire must have had a bad angle or something."

Jeff seemed unimpressed. He nodded toward another parent who was cheering enthusiastically. Then he directed his attention back toward the dial.

The next notch read "Parent of Catcher." I flipped the switch and looked through the binoculars. Again, the hit to right field. This time it was at about the distance I remembered, maybe a little closer. Then I heard, "My son works so hard. He was so cute as a kid. He's struggling with algebra and preventing a run in a big game like this would really boost his self-esteem. Plus, he obviously tagged the runner before he got to home plate." As the runner slid into home plate, the catcher grace-fully tagged him almost a yard before he got to the plate. Clearly out. Wait, clearly *out*? In the first replay he was clearly safe. I looked at Jeff and as he anticipated my next comment he just nodded his head as if to say, "Yeah, I know. Kind of a problem."

Now I wanted to get to the bottom of this. I moved the switch to the "Coach of Runner" notch. Hit to right field. Audio: "These guys train so hard. My career hinges on how we do today. I should have worked more with them on sliding. If we lose because of this I'll look so bad. Run! Run! Winning is everything to me." Video: Player slides, has great tech-nique, and, in a close play, from that angle, he appears safe.

I quickly clicked to the next notch, "Teacher." Audio: "Come on, Bulldogs. Bulldogs are never out. Only safe. He's a Bulldog so he must be safe. Go Bulldogs." Video: As the runner rounds third, the view shifts to a woman on the other side of the stands. Audio: "Oh, she *did* come.

I've got to go say 'hi' to her." And then back to the play, but it's already over. With the "Teacher" view I didn't even get to see the play. Then the Audio: "Clearly safe!" I looked at the teacher—he was yelling, "Clearly Safe!"

The last notch was the "Umpire" setting. This should be interesting. This was the one that mattered. I looked through the binoculars. I didn't even see where the ball landed because the view focused on the runner's feet and whether he touched the bases. He did. Then I hear, "I hope that my mortgage comes through this week. What am I doing here, judging balls and strikes and people sliding into bases? I don't feel so well today. Oh, geez, there's a lot going on here. This guy's fast. Here comes the ball. This is going to be close. I wonder where I should stand so that I can see this best. I don't want either of them to get in the way of my seeing the tag. Okay, there's the ball. Looks like he touched the runner's leg. Looks like the runner touched the plate too but maybe not in time. Let's see, tie goes to the runner. I wish I'd been able to see the tag *and* his foot hit the plate so I could know what happened first. What does he mean, 'What am I looking at?' I'm looking at the catcher. Now at the runner. I don't think this guy made it in time. I need more time to assess what just happened here. I know this coach is a screamer but I can't let that influence me. More time. What did that person mean, saying I need glasses? Maybe I do need to start wearing those glasses. I just feel so old in them. But I do see better. I wonder if he knows that. Looks like the catcher still has the ball. He's holding it up to show me so he must have tagged him on time. I think he got him."

Wow. That seemed like a lot to deal with. I wondered if he was really out or not. Jeff seemed to anticipate this as he saw me sitting there, obviously dumbfounded. "Did you see the last notch?" he remarked. "It's on the bottom of the dial."

I looked at the dial. There was one left: "What Really Happened." I looked at him, surprised. I clicked it to "What Really Happened" and started watching. The ear piece was silent this time. I began to watch as the runner approached home plate. I thought of how impressed I was that these guys could throw a small ball like that so hard, from so far away, and have it end up in the catcher's mitt. The catcher had thrown his mask off and he looked like a nice guy—the kind of guy you'd want to be friends with. He was obviously a great athlete, but had a sort of carefree attitude too. Wow, this game really was a defensive battle. I love a zero-zero tie. As the catcher caught the ball, the runner began his slide. The catcher effortlessly swept his glove across the runner's calf, clearly before he reached the plate. Good for the catcher.

"Looks like the umpire made the right call," I said to Jeff. "Definitely out."

"Yeah," he smiled, "is that what happened on the 'What Really Happened' section? Good to know. Let me see."

"Why do *you* need to see if I just told you?"

He smiled. Nodded his head. "Just curious. That's all."

Understandable. I handed him the binoculars and sat as he watched the play for himself, as it *really* happened—to see the truth. This device could really come in handy. It could certainly settle many disputes in the future. Once you have the truth, there's really not much left to argue about.

Jeff turned to me. I said to him, "See. The umpire was right. He was obviously out."

His face showed signs of doubt. "That's not what I saw."

Chapter 2

Self, Mind, Soul

This body holding me, Reminding me that I
am not alone in/
    This body makes me feel eternal, All this
pain is an illusion.

–Tool, Musical group

 A few million Earth-years whirled into the
past; then suddenly the physicist found
himself standing in the presence of God.
He was overcome with confusion. "I
cannot understand! How by all the laws of
science could I exist again?"
    "How by all the laws of science," God
replied, "could there be laws of science?"

–Martin Gardner

I was asleep—or so it seemed—and the Old Man was right there with
me. "Good to see you, Ian. I was expecting you to come back."

Did I really have a choice? Though it was my dream, so if anyone
were expecting someone, it would be me. And I hadn't decided yet if it
was good to see him. "Hi," I greeted him.

He waved to me to follow him once again
down the tube-like contraption connected to
my room. I walked toward him, accepting his
invitation, though somewhat hesitantly.

"It's the only other way out of your room
except for the stairs," he said. He obviously
never had the need to sneak out of my window

> *"Dreams are . . . illustrations from the book your soul is writing about you."*
>
> –Marsha Norman
> 1993 Pulitzer Prize
> Winner

and along the tree limbs. And he didn't need to know about that potential exit. "And we can't use the stairs," he said, shaking his head slowly. "We just can't. Not at night. Follow me."

As we crawled out of the tube, I followed him toward the door of a big auditorium. Before things got weird again, I told him of my solution to the whole "knowledge" problem from the night before. I had a feeling that once I could dissuade him with my intellect, or I suppose the intellect of my parents, he would go away—a mild sort of exorcism.

He stood there, shaking his head, as if he were reading my thoughts. When I mentioned the knowledge problem he acted as though he'd never heard of such a thing. I explained to him how I know things and he said that everyone knows things, and that I had gone mad. I told him to look at the table and feel its smoothness. To look at my sweatshirt and see its grayish color. That I exist. He repeated again that I'd gone crazy. I grabbed his hand and demanded that he feel mine. He looked at me, nodded, and said, "You've got a bigger problem on your *hands.*" He chuckled as he admired his attempt at a pun. I didn't find it so amusing.

"And what's that?" I asked cautiously.

"It turns out that you've been named 'Student of the Decade' by *World Scholastic Magazine.* Not only is this a prestigious award, but it carries a hefty monetary sum as well. You have been selected based on your scholastic performance tracked from kindergarten through this, your eighth grade year."

"So what's the problem with that?"

"No time for that now," he said. As we entered the back door of the auditorium, I heard the master of ceremonies announce, "And now, our Student of the Decade, Ian Pinkle."

As the audience applauded, there was nothing for me to do but go onstage and accept the award. I supposed I would find out what was so problematic about it afterwards. As I stood onstage in front of a huge audience, a man stood up and pointed at me. He was scruffy looking, wearing old jeans and a tattered flannel shirt. This caught everyone's attention and it quickly became very quiet. He just stood there, pointing, like he was really aiming his finger right at me, like something was going to shoot out of it. After what seemed like a minute he shouted, "This kid is an impostor! This is not the same person now who was in kindergarten."

To me, this seemed like a phrase that people just use rhetorically— that I had changed since I was five. But the changes this man referred to were extreme. He got out of his seat and walked deliberately toward the stage. "Nothing about you is now the same. You may, as you argue, *exist*, but as *what* I'm unsure. Certainly not as Ian Pinkle, the same Ian Pinkle that was in Ms. Londay's kindergarten class."

"This is ridiculous," I protested nervously. *Was* I an impostor? What would that even mean?

"Before we get into this," he said cautiously, "I need to make things clear. I don't want to know how things *seem* or how they *appear*. While interesting, psychologically, I want to know more—how things *are*. Take the example of viewing a movie. It seems like there really is continuity, like the motion on screen is really part of the movie. But when you look at the actual movie reel, you see only static frames. It is only when we view these frames in succession very rapidly that it gives the impression of motion. It *seems* like there's consistent motion—sameness—but it's actually one frame after another."

"I'm not like that," I responded. "I seem the same, but that's because I *am* the same."

"Then I will let you prove this thing of which you are so sure. I will overlook your temporary insanity. Though if you cannot, then know that the committee would take drastic action against an impostor attempting to receive this coveted award."

"Nothing could be easier," I thought. "I am Ian Pinkle. I was born as Ian Pinkle and have remained Ian Pinkle for the past fourteen years. I've had the same hands, my brain is the same, I have always liked chocolate better than vanilla." Apparently I was thinking out loud.

He asked, "If I find one person who liked chocolate ten years ago and then find another person who likes chocolate today, does that make these two people the same person?"

"Not necessarily, of course. But, with *all* these other factors, it makes me the same person over time. Just *look* at me," I began to plead, "I've had the same body."

"The same body? You have the same body now that you had as a one-month-old baby? I hardly think so—you should check your photo

One Cell's Lifetime

The lifetime of one skin cell is about three weeks. This comprises its journey from the bottom layer of the skin to leaving the body. Every minute, you lose about 30,000 dead skin cells.

Whose Ship?

Plutarch (45–125 AD) told of a ship completely reconstructed over time. He wrote:

"Insomuch that this ship became a standing example among the philosophers for the logical question of things that grow; one side holding that the ship remained the same, and the other contending that it was not the same."

The Type/Token Distinction

"Your car is the same *as mine."*

Two ways to use the word same*:*

1. Type—*two people have the same year, make, color, and model of car.*
2. Token—*two people have the exact same car (i.e. they share it).*

albums to make sure. And did you know that your cells regenerate themselves over time? Your skin cells get sloughed off just as a snake sheds its skin. In fact, from the time you were in kindergarten ten years ago to now, *none* of these cells are the same. Physically, you are completely different."

"That doesn't matter. People have called me Ian Pinkle my whole life."

Then this scruffy-looking man sauntered onstage. From backstage, he dragged a raft made of three pieces of wood lashed together. "Take this raft here, made of three pieces of plywood. I call it 'Voyager I'" He laid the boat down on the stage and pulled one of the pieces of wood out and replaced it with a new piece. He looked up at me and grinned, asking, "Is this the same boat as the one I brought up here initially?" He shook his head as he went back to work on the boat. I stood silently, unsure of what this had to do with me, though very curious.

He pulled the next plank out and replaced it, looking up and asking, "Still Voyager I?" Shaking his head. Finally he took the third plank out and removed the rope. He threw the old plank and old rope in a pile with the others and tied the three new pieces together with new rope.

He stood up with his foot on top of the raft and asked, "So, is this Voyager I? Actually, regardless of what you call this, the real question is: *Is this the same raft?*"

I stood there, shaking my head, like he'd just worked some bit of magic on me or something. Nothing about it was the same.

"And if you do think this is still Voyager I," he continued before I could answer, "then tell me what that is," he said, pointing to the wood and rope that had been reassembled off to the side of the stage. "There may be two

Voyager I's" he said, "but they're the same in name only. They're certainly not the same actual entities. If a museum wants to put Voyager I on display, what are they to do? Which do they display? They can't *both* be the *same* boat. Identity isn't in the physical. Your physical body cannot be your actual *self*."

This new boat seemed like it was a completely different object. Just calling it the same thing wouldn't matter. The physical composition of the boat was really important in determining its identity or sameness. So if a thing changes physically over time, it can't be the same thing over time. I started to feel almost a twinge of anger.

"That doesn't matter," I exclaimed. "I'm not a boat. I'm a person. I'm more complex. I have thoughts. Consciousness. Memories. Those make me who I am, not my hair, or skin, or cells."

Then it got really weird. He began speaking more cautiously. "Ian, while you were sleeping, I had an exact replica made of your memories and thoughts. I used a computer program to transfer all your mental stuff into a computer, configure it digitally, and then reinsert it into the brain in another body." Out walked another younger boy. He didn't look like me, and he walked in a rather awkward way. But once I began to talk to him I realized that he talked, thought, and even bit his nails just like I do. He knew everything about me that I did. It was very strange. I didn't much like it.

Where My Consciousness Goes, My Self Goes

Seventeenth-century philosopher John Locke wrote, "For it being the same consciousness that makes a man be himself to himself, personal identity depends on that only."

How Important Is Memory . . . ?

Nineteenth-century French physiologist Pierre Flourens discovered a major problem with medical anesthesia. When it contained chloroform, he believed that this actually allowed patients to feel the pain of the surgery, while still immobilizing them. Yet, it would also cause the memory to fail when they woke up, so they would not remember experiencing pain. This has caused many to question the relevance of memory to consciousness and to ask what happens to the "self" under anesthesia.

"I'm still amazed, even after thirty years of doing [anesthesiology], that consciousness goes away. It makes me wonder where [the patients] go but more importantly why we're conscious in the first place."

–Stuart Hameroff, anesthesiologist and co-founder of
the Center for Consciousness Studies

Could Memory Comprise My "Self"?

In the 2000 film, Memento, *the main character, who has lost the ability to create new memories, states, "Memory can change the shape of a room, it can change the color of a car. And memories can be distorted. They're just an interpretation, they're not a record."*

In George Orwell's novel 1984, he writes about changing one's memory to intentionally distort historical facts: "If it is necessary to rearrange one's memories . . . then it is necessary to forget that one has done so. The trick of doing this can be learned like any other mental technique."

"So," the man asked, "are there now two of Ian Pinkle? If there are two of you then can I keep you—the Ian I am talking to—in the dream and let your mental replica go to school? Would people think it was you? More importantly, would it be you? And what if I killed the thing that I'm talking to and let this other live? He's got all your mental stuff, so wouldn't you, Ian, still be alive?" He smirked as if playing the role of an evil villain.

I just shook my head. It sure didn't seem like it.

"And I'm sure you've heard of amnesia—losing one's memory? Would that mean one is no longer one's *self*? What about when you go to sleep? You don't remember much and you're not even conscious—does your self disappear? Tell me, can you even remember what you had for lunch last Monday, much less a year ago? Is memory really necessary or even sufficient for selfhood? Is consciousness?"

I was a little scared. I was claiming that all that mental stuff was what made *me* me. I responded, "But this guy doesn't have my brain—he just has all the stuff that was *in* my brain. And my brain cells don't regenerate over time like all my others. I may lose them and not have them replaced, but new ones aren't created." That had to be the difference, I thought. I was running out of options.

"Well, Ian," he continued, in an even more somber tone, "I have two options for you. You can think through the following 'brain transfer' scenario, or I could perform it on you."

I wanted no more taking my brain out of my head. "I'll think through it. What is it?"

Whose Brain?
Whose Body?

Harvard Professor of Psychology Steven Pinker explores the identity ascribed to people's bodies and brains. He writes, "Journalists sometimes speculate about 'brain transplants' when they really should be calling them 'body transplants,' because, as the philosopher Dan Dennett has noted, this is the one transplant operation in which it is better to be the donor than the recipient."

A core Buddhist tenet is the doctrine of "no self," which holds that no constant element designates the self over time. A Buddhist dialogue between someone named Nagasena and a king illustrates this:

". . . although parents give us names such as 'Nagasena' . . . it is, however, only a generally understood term, a designation in common use. For there is no permanent self."

The King then suggests many qualities of the self and realizes, "I fail to discover any 'Nagasena.' Truly, now, 'Nagasena' is a mere empty sound . . . there is no 'Nagasena.'"

Nagasena concludes, "'Nagasena is only a way of counting, a term, a label, a convenient designation, or a mere name . . . In the absolute sense there is no self here to be found."

"A wise choice. It's simple, really. Imagine that I took your brain out of your head and put it in someone else's head— we'll call him "Joe." Then, imagine that I did another memory transfer and transferred all of your memories out of your brain and into another brain that we then put in your head. Got that? So your body has your consciousness and memories, yet Joe's brain. Would you really be Joe?" he asked, shaking his head. "It seems unlikely. Your identity can't just be in that piece of gray matter you call a brain."

I nodded. "Yes, I understand. Thanks for leaving my brain in my head."

"So, this whole personal identity thing seems a little implausible after all. It's not your body, nor your brain, nor, as you say, your 'mental stuff' that makes you the same person over time." He paused, nodding as though the discussion were over and now it was time for the moral of the story.

"The moral of the story is," and he raised his eyebrows, as though he anticipated my anticipation of this, "that you may not have this *self*, this consistent identity. Your creation of a *self* may just be a defense mechanism that you've developed—a tool for survival or maybe psychological comfort. This isn't to say that it's a bad thing, just that it's not really *reality*."

"I think I understand that, but I have one last solution," I paused, somewhat overwhelmed

Dualism—*Humans have a body and a nonphysical attribute like a mind or soul.*

Materialism—*Humans are just physical creatures.*

Idealism—*Humans are just non-physical minds and contain nothing material. "Matter" is just a collection of immaterial ideas. Physical entities exist only in the sense that they are perceived.*

The Afterlife

In ancient Egypt, the dead were buried with food and clothing their soul would need in the afterlife.

Hinduism holds that the "atman" (unchanging essence) has karma—*this self carries the previous bodily experiences through each subsequent lifetime.*

Christian doctrine holds that, upon death, the soul separates from the body and goes on to be judged so that it spends eternity in either heaven or hell.

by the last hour's activities. "It's not the body that's important, you've already shown that. And, after this experiment, I've seen that it isn't the brain or even the thoughts and memories that are completely necessary in maintaining identity over time."

The Old Man chimed in from the side of the stage, asking, "What could it possibly be if not those things?"

"My *mind*," I responded.

"Your mind?" the Old Man asked.

"My *soul*."

"Your soul? Which is it?"

"Both," I responded, shaking my head, waving my hands frantically. "Either."

I felt as if it could be both. As if both were the same. I'd heard people use them interchangeably. After all, if there wasn't something nonphysical about me that lived on, how could I go to heaven, or be reincarnated, or have any sort of afterlife? That was it. That was the answer. "There is something about me, *Ian*, that is nonphysical, which makes me who I am. My mind interacts with my body, which then gives a physical representation of who I am." I finally felt relieved.

The Old Man began laughing. A deep laugh. He shook his head at me as though I had forgotten something obvious. "Do you really believe that whole statement of yours?" After I nodded my head somewhat assertively he asked, "How in the world can something nonphysical—a mind, a soul, whatever—affect your physical body?"

Descartes defended a view known as "causal interactionism" which held that the soul could interact with the body. He wrote that the soul affects the pineal gland which in turn, "thrusts the spirits which surround it towards the pores of the brain, which conduct them by the nerves into the muscles, by which means it causes them to move the limbs."

It seemed easy. I couldn't see why he was so amused. "Well, my mind tells my arm to lift, and my arm lifts. My mind tells me to think about my favorite color, and I think about it."

The Old Man walked over to me. He put his arm around me and we left the auditorium stage, walking through one of the side-door exits and into an adjacent room. He asked me, calmly, "Tell me, Ian, what do you know about ghosts?"

More Than a Kleenex Box . . .

In a dialogue written by philosopher John Perry, a character defends the position that the mind or soul is immaterial. He compares the body to a Kleenex box, arguing that the body is much more than that:

"If you were merely a live human body—as the Kleenex box is merely cardboard and glue in a certain arrangement—then the death of your body would be the end of you. But surely you are more than that, fundamentally more than that. What is fundamentally you is not your body, but your soul or self or mind . . . I mean the nonphysical and nonmaterial aspects of you, your consciousness . . . . Your mind or soul is immaterial, lodged in your body while you are on earth. The two are intimately related but not identical."

Unsure of what his question had to do with the issue, I responded, "A lot, actually." I explained to him the book that I'd read last summer about the ghosts that haunt graveyards.

He interrupted, "Do these ghosts pass through doors or do they have to open them just like people do?"

"Of course they can float through doors. Doors, walls, anything. Ghosts aren't material things. They're spirits, so material objects like doors aren't obstacles as they are for people."

"Okay. So is it possible for a ghost to do something like knock over a candlestick?"

"Sure. We've all seen that in tons of movies. That's one way that ghosts scare people."

He was nodding his head. "You think so?"

My stomach dropped. I pointed. "Behind you. Behind you!" It definitely looked like a ghost. It was hard to see its definition, but I could tell it was a ghost. It floated right through the door.

"Yes, this is Nightshade the Ghost. I thought you'd like to meet her. Nightshade, this is Ian."

She nodded, kind of. I nodded back, nervously. She was kind of wispy-looking. She didn't have any real definition unlike the ghosts in the movies. She had a smile that

Out of Body . . .
Near Death

Research shows that nearly 50 percent of subjects who had near-death experiences felt like they left their body and floated above it looking down on it, while others recall being drawn towards a light. Some argue that these "out of body" experiences prove the existence of a soul which exits the body upon death.

Other hypotheses have been put forth to explain this phenomenon, such as: chemicals that cause hallucinations are released by the brain during a near-death experience; the brain relives unconscious birth memories; the visions result from the brain trying to place order within an unknown, disordered event.

was half-comforting, half-scary. Her bluish hue gave off a pleasing light. The movies hadn't really gotten the ghost thing right—she looked nothing like the movie-ghosts.

The Old Man turned to her, "Nightshade, we saw you just float through that door. Could you also knock over this candlestick here?"

She shook her head. She reached out her hand, or arm, or whatever, and swiped at the candlestick. It went right through it.

"Ghosts are unable to affect the physical world," the Old Man said, smiling at this ghost named Nightshade. For some reason I thought it was more strange that this ghost had a name than that there was an actual ghost floating in front of me. "It's a slight limitation, but this is what allows them to float through physical objects. If they could affect physical objects, then they couldn't float through doors. Non-physical things like ghosts can't affect anything physical."

The Old Man paused, allowing Nightshade an affirmative nod. He continued, "Ghosts can't have their cake and eat it too. I know there was a cartoon in which the ghost could do both. But that's just not logical: something can't both be immaterial *and* affect the material world."

He seemed to have a point. I smiled at her.

"Thank you, Nightshade. It was nice to see you again," the Old Man said. I waved at her timidly, still not sure of ghost protocol.

She smiled and floated back through the wall. He looked at me knowingly.

"Okay. I get it," I said. "Something immaterial—like a *mind*—can't affect something material, like a *body*."

"Good, Ian. So you must admit that either your mind is immaterial or it isn't. If it is immaterial, then it should have no effect on your physical self, just like an immaterial ghost can't knock over a candlestick because its hand would go right through it. And if your mind isn't immaterial—that is, if it's a material thing—then we're back to the original problem of your being a merely physical entity."

I started to feel sick again. Even though I felt like it was a dream, I noticed that I couldn't even prove that I maintained a *self*—that I was Ian Pinkle. Maybe the interaction between my mind and body wasn't like usual things like pool balls bouncing off each other. "Listen," I began, a little ahead of myself, hoping my thought would come out making sense. "The

Smoke and Shadows

The theory that the mind resembles a shadow was recently reexamined by contemporary philosopher Jaegwon Kim and dates back to Thomas Huxley and William James in the late nineteenth century. It was later named epiphenomenalism *by historians of philosophy.*

mind isn't like a pool cue acting on the rest of the balls. Maybe physical brain activity causes non-physical mental states, yet these mental states just don't cause things to happen in the physical body. But the mental is still there."

I obviously hadn't been as clear as I'd hoped, so I continued. "Think of the mind as a shadow cast by the brain. Just as a tree's shadow depends on the tree and doesn't have any effect or any control over itself, it's still *there*. Shadows still exist. Or, better yet, it could be like the smoke from a fire. That's what the mind could be like—it's the result of the physical brain, but it doesn't affect the physical brain." That seemed pretty clear.

"Ian, I must say, you're a thinker. And this is a cute one."

A cute one?

"But I'm not sure it accomplishes what you want." He paused. He waited for me to look a bit let down, and then with a slight chuckle he continued, "What's the point of a mind that has nothing to do with who you are, what you do, or how you act? Are you saying that you have a mind, and yet this mind doesn't serve a purpose or do anything at all? It's just somehow *there*? This theory of yours results in a pointless conclusion. And if you want to over-

Gremlins in Our Watches

Jeffrey Olen imagines someone who has never seen a watch and then finds one. This person believes that an invisible gremlin causes the watch to tick. When the watch stops, he assumes it is because the gremlin died. But when he winds the watch it starts again. Others tell him that something physical—i.e. the gears inside—make the watch tick. However, the finder still believes that the gremlin is inside and just has nothing to do with running the watch.

Olen writes, "A nonphysical mind is just as suspect as the gremlin." He asks, "If we do not need the gremlin to explain how the watch works, why continue to believe that it exists?"

Keep It Simple

Medieval philosopher William of Ockham developed the principle "Ockham's Razor." It holds that:

When choosing between two competing theories, both equally plausible, we should choose the simplest explanation of a phenomenon. In doing so, we minimize the number of steps needed for the explanation. The simpler the theory, the less chance it has of being mistaken. Thus, in explaining human existence, Ockham's Razor would "cut" the mind away, as it only adds unneeded complexity.

"Nature is pleased with simplicity."   –Isaac Newton

What Is It Like to Be a Bat?

Because one can only answer this question by imagining what it's like for oneself to be a bat, we miss out on the complete answer to this question. It is for this reason, argues Thomas Nagel, that our own experience is subjective and thus more than just physical.

ride it, then you're back to explaining how something nonphysical can affect the physical."

He stood there, shaking his head slowly. "You're making things more complicated than they need to be, Ian."

I was becoming more dejected. It just seemed so much like I was the same person. That I was me. And maybe that was enough to make a *self*—that feeling of sameness. That there was something nonphysical that formed what it was like to be me. He couldn't possibly know what it's like to be me. There was something about me that *couldn't* be only physical.

"Okay, listen," I started in. "Remember yesterday, when you told me that the color red was just a certain matrix of light waves that resonated at a certain frequency and caused a certain sensation in my brain? Well, it seems like actually *experiencing* red gives someone an impression that they just can't get from knowing absolutely everything about it physically. If a blind man got a Ph.D. in the physics of color, he would know a lot about what it means for a person to experience the color red: how light reflects and absorbs, what the rods and cones in one's eyes do when this light hits them, etcetera. But, if he then had surgery allowing him to finally see, it seems obvious that he would learn something new about experiencing red. 'Red-experiences' couldn't *only* be physical. The same is true of a lot of things: what it's like to be an animal, to taste something, to use language, to do math." I paused. "To *be me*. They all require something more than just physical processes. There's something subjective about them. They require something nonphysical. A mind. I have a mind."

"I didn't do that, you did."

Neurosurgeon Wilder Penfield stimulated the motor cortex of his patients' brains, causing not only limb movement, but also head turning, swallowing, and even talking. Numerous patients inevitably responded, "I didn't do that, you did."

He sat there, nodding his head slowly, pursing his lips. His eyebrows crinkled up in kind of a scary way—like he could contort them as easily as I could bend my fingers. "Thoughtful." He paused. "Are you saying that if something can *do* language or math then that thing must have a mind, something more than merely physical parts?"

"Yes, that's part of what I'm saying."

"Okay. First, before I take out my calculator, I want to try something with you. I promise this won't harm you in any way, but it certainly will enlighten you."

I nodded apprehensively, "Okay." Somehow, in our short time together, I'd come to trust the Old Man, though I really had no good reason to.

He took out a very thin needle, thinner than I'd ever imagined any needle could be. He put it against my scalp. "Can you feel that?" he asked.

"Not really. It feels like a leaf landed on my head or something."

"Okay, good. I want you to relax and not move at all, okay?" So I sat still, not moving, focusing on my stillness. Just then, my right arm raised.

"What was that?" I asked, alarmed.

"Watch this. Now I'll have you raise your left arm."

I thought to myself, no way, not this time, not now that I know it's coming. Despite my thinking, my left arm raised up above my head and then landed back in my lap. It was like my body was moving behind my back.

"Ian. I think that this alone is enough to show you that your movements and all your actions are a result of your physical brain. All I'm doing is prodding your brain in just the right spots. This is what happens when you move on your own, though instead of this needle nudging your brain, you have physical chemicals do it for you. Chloride. Sodium. They flow down physical neurons and, after a chain reaction, they result in your body movement. It's purely a physical process.

"And now that we've shown that all of your *actions* result from a physical process, let's look at your feelings."

"How I *feel* can't be physical. *That* is where my mind comes into play," I said.

He nodded, as if he expected me to say that. "Okay. I want you to take each of these

From Physical to Non-Physical?

Colin McGinn asks how something physical could give rise to consciousness:

"The problem is how any *collection of cells . . . could generate a conscious being . . . . How can mere matter generate consciousness? . . . If the brain is spatial, being a hunk of matter in space, how on Earth could the mind arise from the brain?"*

Part of the issue, he admits, is, "The mind-body problem is the same kind of problem as the problems of physics and the other sciences; we just lack the conceptual equipment with which to solve it."

The Physiology of the Mental

The drug Prozac blocks the re-uptake of serotonin so that it remains in the system. This is one example of how a drug can physically alter one's brain chemistry and thus change one's mental state.

Twentieth-century Spanish-American philosopher George Santayana explains the material roots of all mental processes:

"If I want water, it is because my throat is parched; if I dream of love it is because sex is ripening within me.... Conscious will is a symptom, not a cause; its roots ... are ... material."

Reduction—to simplify or break down human actions and emotions into their basic components: physical chemicals and brain activity.

little pills that I give you. Then, I want you to tell me how you feel afterwards." He pulled out a very small white pill. In my trusting way, I opened my mouth and he placed it on my tongue and I swallowed it. I sat, waiting. I had no idea what to expect. I smiled at him. He really was a nice old man. Very trusting. Very nice. This whole thing wasn't so bad. Kind of nice, actually.

"How do you feel?"

His question kind of surprised me. "How do I feel?" I looked inside, so to speak. "Well I guess I feel happy. Yeah, content. And I'm not hungry like I thought I was. Just happy I guess."

"Exactly. That was serotonin. That's the chemical that makes you feel happy and curbs your appetite. Your brain makes it naturally. Try this one now. Open up."

On my tongue it went. I waited. I was getting a little curious about just what this was all doing to me. I was starting to feel a little sorry for myself, realizing that I was just a physical thing and that I could be controlled like a puppet. And who does he think he is? I took back my Mr. Nice Guy thoughts about the Old Man. He was just toying with me. I wanted to give him a punch right in the nose.

"You mad at me yet?" he asked. "That last pill neutralized all the serotonin I put in earlier and even depleted some that you already had. This decrease in serotonin results in depression and aggressiveness. So, for my safety, I'll give you this neutralizer pill."

And I was back to normal—whatever that was.

"I want you to try one last one. Open up." And I felt nothing. Nothing toward the Old Man anyway. I was tired of thinking about him.

Feeling Pain and Seeing Demons

Richard Rorty imagines how a scientist of the future might reply to someone who reports feeling pain, "You were reporting the occurrence of a certain brain-process, and it would make life simpler for us if you would in the future, say 'My C-fibers are firing' instead of saying 'I'm in pain.'" He compares this to when shamans see demons after taking "sacred mushrooms." Both the demon-seeing and pain-sensing, Rorty writes, are just fabrications of the brain.

Instead I thought of Alexis. Her smile. Her hair. Her love of baseball cards. She was definitely the first girl that I'd ever thought was cute. She is cute. Really cute.

He spoke up, "Recently, biological psychologists have argued that these two chemicals—dopamine and norepinephrine—are the chemicals of love. Even being in love can be broken down—*reduced*—into physical chemical components. I won't ask you to explain how you're feeling now—I'll just imagine for myself. Here's the last neutralizer." I put it under my tongue and, when he turned to make his next point, I spit it out into my hand. No harm in thinking nice things about Alexis.

"Chemicals. Everything you do and everything you feel can be broken down to something physical. There's no need for a mind here. There's no place for it."

He spilled right into his next question. "Do you know about the phenomenon of phantom pains?" He continued immediately. "When people lose a limb, nearly all report feeling sensations, often pains, where their limb used to be. Yet, obviously, if you lose your hand in an accident, you can't then hurt that same hand."

"That's weird."

"Yes, it seems odd, but it's highly verified. It turns out that pain is another physical process that occurs in one's brain. Remember this from our last meeting? If I numbed the proper section of your brain, and then stuck a pin through your hand, you wouldn't feel a thing." He noted my obvious fear of this happening and he assured me this wouldn't be an experiment we would do today. "Pain is just another physical process."

I feared continuing this pain-related conversation, but I had to ask, "Pain? Physical? Whatever it is, it sure seems *real*."

He shook his head. "Sure, in a sense it is. But when you feel a pain in your hand it's not really in your hand, it's just chemicals firing in your brain. Try something simple for me. Stare at this light for ten seconds." I did. "Now look away and blink your eyes. What do you see?"

"Well, I see the light."

"Exactly. And that is real. You *really do* see the light. But in a more important way,

Philosopher J. J. Smart explains what we mean when we say we "see" an afterimage:

"When a person says 'I see a yellowish-orange afterimage,' he is saying something like this: 'There is something going on which is like what is going on when I have my eyes open, am awake, and there is an orange illuminated in good light in front of me.'"

Can Computers Think?

Alan Turing developed a test (the "Turing Test") that he hoped would answer this question. In his test, a human judge engages in a text-only (i.e. typed) conversation with two entities: another human and a computer. If the judge cannot distinguish between the two, then the computer passes the test and is said to have achieved thought.

Since 1991, the Cambridge Center for Behavioral Studies has held an annual contest: $2,000 for the most human-like computer-generated conversation and $25,000 for any computer undistinguishable from a human (awarded only once).

it's not real. You don't really think that this light is all the places you're seeing, do you? Of course not. Again, more of your physical brain."

I changed the subject as quickly as possible to avoid the potential "brain numbing" that might follow. "Got it. So what were you going to do with your calculator?"

If It Behaves Like It Is Conscious, Then It Must Be Conscious.

"If it looks like a duck, quacks like a duck, and walks like a duck, then it is probably a duck."
—Old saying

Behaviorism identifies mental features (such as thoughts) as represented through behavior. Thus, thoughts are not activities that occur somewhere in the "mental" realm, but instead are reduced to actions of the agent. This view alleviates the mind/body problem, as there is nothing mental to separate from the physical to begin with.

He gave me a pencil and paper. "What is 200,100 divided by 15?" As I started writing the numbers down, I heard someone exclaim, "It's 13,340." I turned to the voice. It looked like it came from something like a toaster with a few wires running out of it.

"That's an easy one," it said in a robot-like voice. "Division is a cake walk for me. Give me something more difficult."

"This basic computer can do math," the Old Man commented, happily. "Better than you actually. So, I guess by your logic, this thing has a mind." He paused again so that his point could sink in before he explained it. "Or, more likely, doing math can be reduced or broken down into physical parts. Just like the little computer in your skull.

"And regarding your language claim, can you spell 'euphemism'?" he asked us.

As I thought about both the point of his question and how to spell the word, I heard that voice again. "E U P H E M I S M. Euphemism. Let's see. 'Asphyxia': A S P H Y X I A. Spelling is easy."

The Old Man smiled, "Yes, it seems so for you," he said to the toaster. He turned to me, "And my computer at home knows the English language better than I do. It always corrects my spelling and even corrects my grammar. Yet you stated that doing language and doing math was above and beyond something purely physical—that it required a mind. So, by that argument, your choices now are either: a) this computer has a mind or, b) doing math and language is merely a physical process. Is there a computer heaven in that religion of yours?"

"I'm still not sure how you overcome my argument," I said, not being totally truthful as I did see some relevance.

He continued, "You said that in order to use language, one needs a mind—that language can't be a *purely* physical phenomenon. But computers do language; they're learning how to do it better and better, to the point where many actually have trouble distinguishing a conversation with a person from one with a computer. So this being the case, it seems that computers have a soul or a mind, according to you. Or, more likely, since we build computers and see that they are made up of wires, plastic, and metal, we see that they are just *physical* things. So there really is no truth in your claim that we must have a mind in order to use language."

"I suppose you're right," I said. I just wasn't ready to give up on having a mind or a soul. There must be a difference between the physical body and the mind or soul. And if there were, then the mind would have to exist to be different.

I remembered what my father had said yesterday about doubting the "I." I finally felt that I'd come upon the answer. "The mind has qualities that the body doesn't." This time *I* paused to drive home the point. "The quality of *indivisibility*, for one."

Determining Uniqueness

Seventeenth century German philosopher Gottfried Leibniz proposed the "Law of Identity": for any two things to be identical (i.e. the same actual thing), they must have identical properties.

This law has been used to argue that the mind exists separately from the body—namely, that the mind exists. Descartes writes, "The fact that I can clearly and distinctly understand one thing apart from another is enough to make me certain that the two things are distinct."

Descartes explains, "There is a great difference between mind and body, inasmuch as body is by nature always divisible, and the mind is entirely indivisible. . . . When I consider the mind . . . I cannot distinguish in myself any parts . . . yet if a foot, or an arm, or some other part, is separated from the body, I am aware that nothing has been taken from my mind."

"And the other?"

"*Knowability*, I'll call it."

"I demand an explanation," he proclaimed, as if we had momentarily switched roles.

"First of all, I can divide my body. I could cut off my hand, for example. Or, more simply, my skin cells could fall off, remember? I hope you don't need me to show you this." Being in the driver's seat was nice. "But I *can't* divide the mind; unlike the body, the mind is indivisible.

"And as for 'knowability,'" I paused for a moment. "I perceive my body through my senses—by looking at my hand, for example. But I know my mind simply by closing my eyes—I know it directly. Because the body exists in three-dimensional space and is divisible and the mind is *not*, and because I can know my mind with greater certainty than any physical part of my body, then the brain and the mind are not the same things as you seem to be arguing. If they have different qualities then they must be different things."

The Old Man nodded as if he was half proud, half expecting this. "I have someone I want you to meet, Ian. He's from ancient Greece."

In walked a man looking just as I would expect a man from ancient Greece to look. He even had dust and dirt all over him, like he'd been walking through those big buildings with dirt floors.

Just then, we saw lightning strike outside. The Old Man asked the man from Greece if he knew what it was. The man responded, "Zeus is angry. He's throwing lightning bolts."

The Old Man turned to me, "Actually, it's the separation of electrical changes produced by the clouds. It may not *seem* this way, but it is."

Then he asked the man from Greece, "What is now falling from the sky?"

"Water."

The Old Man responded tritely, "H-two-O. H-two-O is falling from the sky."

He smiled at me, obviously ready to make his point. "This thing you call the mind *is* the

The Ghost in the Machine

Modern philosopher Gilbert Ryle referred to dualism as "the dogma of the ghost in the machine."

While standing in the courtyard of Oxford University, viewing the bookstore, classrooms, and dormitories, Ryle wittingly asked, "Where's the university?" He hoped to show that the university isn't some nonphysical "thing" above and beyond those buildings. To ask that would be to make a "category mistake." All of those things together are the university. Likewise, it would be wrong to say there is a body, brain, and a mind. Just like it's wrong to say, "There's a left-handed glove, a right-handed glove, and a pair of gloves."

The Intensional Fallacy—*when one acts as if his or her beliefs about a thing are actual qualities of that thing. For example:*

1. *Oedipus wants to marry Jocasta.*
2. *Oedipus does not want to marry his mom.*
3. *THUS, Jocasta is not the mom of Oedipus.*

While (1) and (2) are true, (3) is not. (In Greek mythology, Oedipus unknowingly marries his mom, Jocasta.) The beliefs that Oedipus has about her are not qualities of her. This fallacy is often applied to the proof of the soul's existence using Leibniz' Law: it's not enough to say that the mind and brain are different just because you believe that you know one better than the other.

brain. Like water is H-two-O. They're not separate; 'mind' is just another term for 'brain.' Look at the clouds. It would be wrong to say that clouds have water in them, separate from them. Clouds *are* water—condensed water. There's no water separate from clouds, or clouds separate from water. We'd be wrong to say, 'I have a mind and a brain' just like we'd be wrong to say, 'Look at the cloud *and* the water,' or, 'Look at the water *and* the H-two-O.'

"Your 'mind-is-indivisible' argument assumes that the mind exists to begin with. If the mind doesn't exist, then it can't be indivisible. Just like little invisible Martians under your bed can't be red if they don't exist.

"Just because someone perceives two things differently, doesn't mean they are uniquely different things; that has more to do with the perceiver than the thing being perceived. How I perceive something is hardly a quality of *that thing*."

I was in a real quandary. Not only had he argued that I wasn't the same self over time, but he had me starting to believe that I had no soul, no mind, that I was just as physical as a rock, a monkey, or a computer.

He started peppering me with questions about my "soul theory." "Tell me, Ian, where would this mind of yours come from anyway? In our evolution from apes to humans, did minds or souls just pop into existence,

Michael Shermer writes in Scientific American, *"The reason dualism is intuitive is that the brain does not perceive itself and so ascribes mental activity to a separate source."*

He writes, " . . . Either the soul survives death or it does not, and there is no scientific evidence that it does." He then addresses the question as to whether this view diminishes the meaning of life: "I think not. If this is all there is, then every moment, every relationship and every person counts—and counts more if there is no tomorrow than if there is."

"All Souls"

The view known as "panpsychism" (from the Greek "all" and "souls") holds that all things maintain consciousness or even have souls. Versions of this view have been held by a few philosophers, such as Leibniz and Spinoza.

out of nowhere? If so, how could something come from nothing—or do you think primates, dogs, one-celled organisms have souls too? And where in one's body does this nonphysical thing reside? How can you contain something that's nonphysical? Your view is much more complicated than you need it to be."

Not only had he disproved all my claims, but he seemed to have more and more arguments against them. In the span of a dream, I'd been convinced by my*self*—or I suppose I should say *by my brain*—that I am just that: a physical thing.

Then he put his hand on my shoulder and I could feel how big it was, though also somewhat comforting. "Ian, you really are ideal for this," he said, changing his tone from before. "Once we get all of this to Jack, it will greatly influence the lives of others and how they view their world around them."

I stared at him, like I was looking through him. "Jack? What are you talking about? Who's Jack? And I'm ideal for what? What am I ideal for?"

I got restless. I literally got restless. I woke up. I sat up and looked at myself in the mirror for five minutes. I looked at myself as a thing. Just like the computer on my desk in the background. It was depressing. I told myself that my having a soul or a mind of my own made me more special. I would just believe in that because it made me feel better. I certainly felt that I must be unique from all other organisms, all other objects. But this rationale wasn't very satisfying.

Then came my daily call from downstairs.

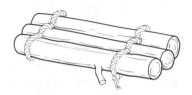

Ian walked into the kitchen, rubbing his eyes.

"Ian," his mom said cautiously. "Ian, what's wrong? Did you not sleep well again? Are you feeling okay?"

He shook his head, obviously not feeling okay. He wasn't feeling like himself—literally. He slumped down into his chair at the breakfast table where his father greeted him. "Would you like to share your dream with us, son?" Ian nodded. He went through everything. He retold the entire dream, every strange occurrence, every frustrating discussion. He shared his conclusion that he had no soul, no mind, nothing to identify him as the same person over time. While he talked his father buttered some toast and slid the plate of toast towards him, along with a glass of juice. Ian began eating the moment he stopped talking, as though he really had been out all night on some sort of adventure.

Realizing he was taking a break from talking given his ravenous eating, his mom attempted to comfort him. "Well, son, this man in your dreams is really forcing some tough questions on you. I always knew, from the day you were born, by the way you looked curiously around the room, hardly crying, that you had a special interest in the world around you, a unique perspective." Ian started to get that uncomfortable, awkward look. "You know, dreams are often vehicles by which people can delve into their inner selves and get a more honest look at what's bothering them, at what they're really concerned about. I have a couple comments for you about your recent dream, if you want to hear them."

"I do, mom. I feel like this man confuses me about things I'm really certain about. *I am Ian Pinkle.* That seems simple. *I have been Ian Pinkle. I will be Ian Pinkle tomorrow,* hopefully. He makes me sound like I really have gone crazy."

"You haven't. You are grappling with some important psychological and philosophical issues. While this might make you feel insane, my guess is that once you realize what's going on, you'll actually have a much better perspective about who you really are. You've taken care of the first big step: asking the right questions.

"So, first of all, I'm curious about this 'Voyager' boat that you mentioned."

"That *he* mentioned! That *man*."

> *"The philosophy of one century is the common sense of the next."*
> –Henry Ward Beecher (1813–1887)
> Orator who strongly opposed slavery in the U.S. while it was legal, and also supported women's right to vote before they had it.

Knowledge Through Dreams

Two well-known psychiatrists, Sigmund Freud and Carl Jung (pronounced "yoong"), believed people can acquire great knowledge of themselves from dreams.

> *"The dream is a little hidden door in the innermost and most secret recesses of the soul."*
> –Jung

> *"The interpretation of dreams is the royal road to a knowledge of the unconscious activities of the mind."*
> –Freud

The Same Band . . . ?

The Latin teen musical group "Menudo" maintains an "essence" despite rotating different people into and out of the band—once a member turns 16, he is forced to leave. The group has had over 30 musicians come and go since its inception.

"Yes, that one. After all the parts have been changed over time, do you really need to change the name of it? At what point would you change it? What if you'd replaced ninety-nine percent of something, would that remaining one percent be the thing that allows it to still be the *same* thing? So, would that one percent just *be* that thing—its core? That's unlikely. So what is it that's important in maintaining identity?"

Ian raised his eyebrows on his already tilted head.

His mom continued, "A lot of people believe that consistency allows something to maintain an identity over time. For example, over long periods of time, nothing about a river is the same—the water is different, its path is different as it's eroded new parts of the land, it may have dried up and then been replenished with new water years later. Yet it's still the same river. Likewise, you too have consistently been Ian Pinkle, from that very day when I first saw you. You weren't somehow destroyed when you were five, only to return years later."

"Yes son, and if I may interject, one of my favorite bands when I was a kid went through a lot of changes. From their first album to their last, all the members changed—one per record, over time. There was something that remained, though. An *essence*, I suppose.

"And take this frozen cube of water. If we let it sit here on the table for another hour, every property of the ice that you *perceive* changes: it will look different, feel different, taste different, sound different, even smell different. We don't think that it becomes different water. Its essence remains."

His mom cut back in. "And I'm still stuck on this boat thing. Instead of a boat, I want you to imagine a church. You're really not much like a boat."

Ian nodded happily.

"Imagine that our little church, the Holy Palace, burned down and they rebuilt it. Okay? The original church was made of wood and is rebuilt out of brick. It would still be the same church, right? Good ol' Holy Palace." Ian bobbed his head agreeably.

She continued, "Imagine that they then had a big truck come and move the church to a different part of town. They just picked up this newly-built church and moved it, in its entirety, a few blocks down from where it was." She paused so that they could imagine this. "Still the same church.

"Finally, imagine the Holy Palace in a hundred years, after every current parishioner had passed away and the entire congregation was made of new people, with new priests and all. Is that still the same church? Do we really need to change its name?"

Ian jumped in, excitedly. "Yeah, it *is* still the same church. It can change over time, and still be the same."

"I agree, dear, as I think most people would. Even though *nothing* about it is the same. It just maintained consistency. An essence. Something nonphysical, metaphysical. "

The "Same" Wax

In Descartes' "Wax Example," he explains that he perceives the wax not with his senses but with his intellect. When the wax melts, it retains none of the sensible qualities it had when solid. The true nature of the wax, then, is known by reason, not the senses.

This defends the position that things may have a nonphysical essence known only through reason. To perceive the wax in its true form, Descartes writes, "at least my perception now requires a human mind."

His father picked up from there. "You know, part of this is a problem, or fact, of our language. By that man's skewed definition of 'same,' *nothing* is ever the same. But that would be ridiculous. Using that definition, our home wouldn't be ours, I wouldn't drive the same car to work. It's a pretty silly way to use the word. It would be meaningless."

Ian nodded.

"And on top of that, we live in a day and age where science is king. What science says, goes. But science doesn't have a language for the spiritual, for the immaterial, certainly not for minds and souls. Science

The Science of Souls and Minds?

Thomas Nagel writes, "I believe that physics is only one form of understanding." He suggests that relying on the physical sciences to explain a nonphysical mind is, "both intellectually backward and scientifically suicidal."

Physicist Freeman Dyson of the Institute for Advanced Study believes that nonphysical, mental phenomena could exist and if they did they would be, "too fluid and evanescent to be grasped with the cumbersome tools of science."

The Ise Shrine in Japan is one of the most important Shinto shrines. Every 20 years it is dismantled and a new shrine is built. The present shrine was constructed in 1993 and serves as the 61st, with the 62nd scheduled for 2013.

Metaphysics

meta—*beyond*

physics—*the physical*

Derived from the Greek, meta ta physika, 'after the things of nature,' "metaphysics" was the name given to Aristotle's work which came immediately after his book on physics.

Metaphysical issues include time, numbers, mind, soul, spirit, God, free will.

won't allow for us to talk about it. This may be something we want to talk about later."

This all seemed to make Ian feel somewhat better. "But what about how my mind affects my body? How could something nonphysical do that? Remember the whole 'ghost' thing?"

His mother replied, "That does seem somewhat tricky. I had problems with that when I watched scary ghost movies. It went so far as to prevent me from ever being scared. That is, until I read about some cutting edge experiments and thought about some real-life examples." Ian's eyes perked up. "Some authors in my field have suggested that seeing is actually a two-way process. They posit this to suggest a possible explanation for the oft-noted feeling of being stared at. That's one example of nonphysical— someone staring—affecting the physical."

She smiled and continued, "And I've seen a hypnotist put a room-temperature penny on someone's arm and, merely through the suggestion that it was hot, it resulted in a physical blister. It just may be the case that nonphysical phenomena can and *do* affect the physical realm. We may not even know all there is to know about this." When she was done, she'd devised a chart:

Nonphysical	⟶	Physical
Seeing	⟶	feeling of being stared at
Hypnosis	⟶	burn marks
Mind	⟶	Brain Activity!

The Study of Souls

The term "psychology" is derived from the Greek words psyche *meaning "soul," and* logos *meaning "the study of." In its present use, it has come to mean the study of the mind.*

"The point that I find most interesting, son," his dad chimed back in, "is this notion of yours—or this man's—that computers can really do math and language. It seems that these activities require the knowledge that you're doing them, not just the action. For example, although a computer can divide numbers, it seems unlikely that it could develop unique mathematical proofs. In fact, it's yet to happen. Only humans are capable of this type of thought. And

I'm curious too, if you think a conversation with a computer could really be placed on the same level as a conversation with me."

"It seems like it is," Ian replied. "What would be the important difference?"

"Imagine that a man, who knows no Chinese, stands inside a room. This room is filled with books that indicate how to properly give answers in Chinese to questions in Chinese. So people can go to this room, give the man a question in Chinese, and receive an answer in Chinese. The man basically receives a sheet of paper with symbols whose meanings are unknown to him, and he then finds these symbols in a book and jots down the corresponding symbols—again, meaningless to him—on another sheet of paper and hands it back. After many years of doing this, the man becomes very proficient in this process: the symbols come in, he finds their corresponding symbols in one of the books, and he gives those out. Chinese-speakers from all over go to this man to have their questions answered. But it would seem odd to say that the man, or the room, actually knew Chinese, wouldn't it? It seems that the man has a good grasp on the syntax—how to put symbols together correctly—but not the semantics—what those symbols actually mean. Yet, isn't it just the meaning that we're concerned with when we use language?"

"I agree, dad. But I'm not sure if I see the connection with my dream."

"Well, in your dream, the Old Man said that since computers can do language and computers are purely physical things, then it seems that the act of linguistics is merely a physical process. But this example shows that computers don't do language in the way that is important to us. They certainly don't *know* language."

Ian nodded affirmatively.

Minds That Reach Out

First-century BC scientist Leucretius questioned whether the process of seeing involves something coming from an object into our eye, or if our eyes somehow intertwine with the object.

In a review of experiments done on the phenomenon of being stared at, Rupert Sheldrake writes, "Our minds reach out to touch everything we see."

Can Computers Really Think?

"Artificial Intelligence"(AI) posits the theory that machines can think.

Philosopher John Searle uses the "Chinese Room Argument" to argue against AI. He explains that computers don't know that a "6" stands for the number six, or that a plus sign stands for the act of addition. The calculator doesn't know anything, but we have them because they calculate quickly and more accurately than we can, "without having to go through any mental effort to do it."

When Computers Come Up Short

In 1630, French mathematician Pierre de Fermat posited a math puzzle that remained unsolved for 350 years. Known as "Fermat's Last Theorem," the trouble was finding "n" in the equation:
$$x^n + y^n = z^n \text{ (for } n > 2\text{)}.$$
While computers were able to plug in numbers for n (they reached n = 4,000,000) the complete proof of the theorem wasn't given until 1993, in a 150-page proof by human mathematician Andrew Wiles.

"Computers are useless. They can only give answers."

—Picasso

The Third Eye

Scholars of ancient Egypt and Greece as well as Descartes believed that the "seat of the soul" was in the pineal gland, which rests near the exact center of the brain. This organ controls the body's biorhythms and is connected to photoreceptors. It is this gland that many believe drives the power of meditation and causes the "seeing" that occurs in a deep meditative state.

His dad finished, saying, "So just like knowing language is something subjective and requires a mind, so is seeing color, or even just *being* something—being conscious. You know, if a blind woman has a Ph.D. in color vision, she's still missing out on maybe the most important aspect of seeing red." His dad was bobbing his head back and forth, almost a bit nervously. "She's missing out on what it is like to see red."

Ian stared intently at his father, almost like he was staring right through him. "Did you make up that 'Ph.D. in red' example, dad? Where did you get that?"

His dad nodded sheepishly, "Yeah, made it up I guess. It just seems to help drive home the point."

Ian nodded, as though tentatively accepting that. "So I was right," Ian responded, "at least about that. Language can't be broken down into something physical.

"I just wonder though, if I had a mind where could it be? The Old Man asked this along with a bunch of questions at the end. How could my body contain a mind? Where would it be?"

"Why does it have to *be* somewhere? Let's look at something similar. You know that every object has a *center of gravity*—a point in the object that represents its concentration of weight. For humans it's somewhere around our abdomen, just below and behind the navel. That's why your soccer coach puts so much emphasis on your doing sit-ups. But you can't *find* your center of gravity somewhere. You can't somehow take it out.

"And look at this chair. Its center of gravity isn't even located within its physical parts. It's here," he was pointing to the space under the seat between the legs, "in this space here. It would be silly to argue that the chair had no center of gravity just because you couldn't *find* it somewhere and take it out. And even when you did calculate it, it wouldn't *be* there, in the way that your stomach is somewhere. It wouldn't even *be* the one atom that resides nearest to where the center of gravity is calculated to be—it only exists because humans invented it and found a use for it.

"That's just what your 'self' or your 'mind' could be like—a very useful way of describing our experience. A human construct that's quite useful," Ian said.

"A mind or soul that is only real in theory isn't very rewarding, though."

His father shrugged and nodded, as though he were sorry the way his example had worked out. "It's still real though, in some sense," he concluded.

"Yeah, that's better than nothing," Ian responded. "So if the mind is real, how would it exist? I mean, what would make it what it is? It really does seem like there is something above and beyond just our physical selves."

His mom smiled. "You could almost say that your mind 'emerges' from the physical. You know, just like no *one* player on your soccer team *is* the team. Only when you're together is there a *team*.

"In the same way, no one molecule of water is 'wet.' And, you know those CDs you listen to—all they contain on their surface is ones and zeros. But, together, they produce the music you listen to. No single one or zero *is* music. Also, no one cell of yours *is* consciousness or *is* your mind. It is from water molecules that water emerges, from ones and zeros comes music, and from your individual cells emerges your soul."

> ### What Center of Gravity?
>
> "A centre of gravity is not an atom or a sub-atomic particle or any other physical item in the world. It has no mass; it has no colour; it has no physical properties at all. . . . It is not one of the real things in the universe in addition to the atoms. But it is a fiction that has a nicely defined, well-delineated and well-behaved role within physics."
>
> –Daniel Dennett
> Contemporary
> philosopher

The Weight of the Soul?

In his quest for a proof of the soul's existence, physician Duncan Macdougall examined six patients by placing each on an ultrasensitive scale. He looked for any change in weight at the moment of their death (and after their final exhalation). Each patient showed an exact change of three-quarters of an ounce. He concluded in his 1907 "American Medicine" article that this is the weight of the human soul. He did a follow-up study with dogs and, finding no change after their death, concluded that dogs have no soul. His conclusions, though, were not highly accepted.

The Soul's "Emergence" from a Body

The concept of "emergence" was initially posited by John Stuart Mill in 1843. It relates to the notion of "holism," that the whole is greater than the sum of its parts.

Reducing Beethoven's Ninth

John Searle explains that many phenomena—including consciousness—are best explained not by their molecular behavior, but by their surface features. He writes of a music critic who, upon hearing Beethoven's Ninth Symphony, *writes, "All I could hear were wave motions." This critic, writes Searle, "has missed the point of the performance." Likewise, by defining humans merely as a collection of cells and chemicals, we have "missed the point" in describing what it is to be human.*

Ian was smiling a big smile now, nodding affirmatively.

"I wish I had you guys in my dream to talk to this man. He just seems so smart when he talks, like he's using magic or something. I just sit there and accept his claims: *You can't know anything; You can't maintain an identity; You're just another physical thing.* I hope he doesn't visit me tonight. I can't imagine what else he'll have to show me."

His parents looked at each other, heads tilted, eyebrows raised, as if to say: *You have no idea, son. Your journey has just begun. If you look with open eyes, you'll often find more questions than answers. As long as you let the questions spark your curiosity and not thwart it, you'll find this to be purely enriching. And you'll find that answers only lead to more questions.* They could say a lot with one glance.

His mother hugged him. "Ian, you really are ideal for this. Once we get all of this to Jack, it will greatly influence the lives of others and how they view their world around them."

Ian looked quizzically at them, actually almost like he was looking through them. "Jack? Wait, how do you know about him? And who is he? What is he? What's going on?"

She looked to his father as though she had definitely said something she wasn't supposed to—and rightly so. "Nothing, honey. Aren't you meeting Jeff? You should really run along. Your father and I have some work to get to. Forget that I mentioned Jack. I just got distracted."

What's in a Name?

(The names have been omitted to protect the "identity" of those involved.)

After all that discussion, I decided I'd had enough for one day. My head even hurt a little bit—in a good way though, kind of like my body feels after playing a hard soccer game. I walked up the small staircase to the front door. I always thought it strange that we had to walk upstairs to go outside. It was like all of the outside was upstairs.

I also thought of how strange it is that Jeff never comes inside my house. He had never been in my house. Neither had Alexis. We'd always meet somewhere. Or they would just wait outside for me.

Jeff came bounding up the sidewalk. "Hey Ian. You want to go invent another game?" he asked, knowing I'd almost always say yes. We currently have 17 games of our own.

"Nah, I actually want to go see that place that we've always wondered about. You know, down on the edge of town."

"You mean, 'We The People'?"

"Yeah. You haven't been there yet, have you?" I asked, hopeful that he hadn't.

"No. I don't even know what it is. You really want to go there?"

"Yeah. I think it would be interesting, especially because of some of the things I've been thinking about lately."

Jeff nodded trustingly. It was like we had a pact that when the other guy suggested something new, we always had to agree.

We got to the building that we'd walked by so many times. It looked kind of like a regular house on the outside. Above the door hung a big sign, like it was made out of gold. It said "We The 'People'". I'd never noticed the quotes around "People" before. The little sign on the door said "Come In." We did. A nicely-dressed man sat behind a counter that looked like the one in my doctor's office when I was a kid—well, when I was a younger kid.

"Hello," he greeted us, in a friendly tone. "Can I help you? Would you like a tour?"

Jeff looked to me. "A tour. Yes. We'd like a tour," I said.

"Very well, come with me. I'm Doctor A."

"Ian," I mumbled.

"Jeff," Jeff said.

The doctor nodded at us and proceeded through a door that led to a long hallway of more doors. He seemed happy to see that we had names.

We stopped at the first door on the left. The doctor turned to us, "Our mission here at We The 'People' is two-fold. First, to determine what constitutes a person— which beings are people and which are not? 'Person' here is a moral term, unlike 'human being' which is normative, descriptive. 'Human being' is easy—a being with human DNA. 'Personhood' can be much more difficult. Establishing personhood is very important in establishing who should have rights.

"Secondly, we attempt to ascertain just how it is that beings maintain an identity over time—what it means to be the same person you *were* and how you could possibly forgo that sameness."

Jeff and I looked at each other. Jeff looked half curious, half How-Hard-Can-That-Be.

"Meet our first study-case, B." We walked into the room. It looked like a normal kid's bedroom. It had a bed, a desk with pens and paper on it, a basketball hoop stuck on the wall. A chimpanzee sat on the desk with its back to us. "You think *that's* a person?" Jeff asked. "Or even *could be* a person?"

The chimpanzee turned to us. "Oh, hello Dr. A. How's it going?" It was in perfect English. No accent or anything—except for whatever accent we speak with.

"Hi B. It's going well. You?"

"Not bad." The chimpanzee turned and sat down in the chair at the desk. It crossed its legs. "More of the same, I suppose. You showing these guys around?"

"Yeah. Ian and Jeff, right?" the doctor confirmed.

We nodded. I nervously grinned at the chimpanzee.

"Hey guys. Enjoy the tour. Nice to see you," the chimpanzee said, grinning a big grin.

The doctor patted us on the back and walked us out of the room. As we were leaving I heard the chimpanzee whisper to the doctor, "Definitely people, right?" The doctor nodded.

"In most instances, it's very easy to distinguish a person from a nonperson," the doctor announced as we left the room. "I am a person, and it seems as though you are both people, though this will require a bit more observation. Years ago, we pioneered 'in vitro fertilization'—we created a person by combining a man's sperm with a woman's egg in the laboratory. This is now a widely accepted practice—the only way that some couples are able to have their own children. At the time, critics claimed that we were 'playing God' or that the creatures we created were not natural people. As if doing anything that wouldn't happen naturally is 'playing God' and is therefore wrong."

He chuckled to himself. "Playing God," he grinned. "It seems silly, really. Didn't this God give humans our amazing intellect?" We nodded. That seemed sensible.

He continued, "These critics say, 'Don't interfere with nature,' and then they go off and enjoy food grown in greenhouses with pesticides, they take aspirin and get shots at the doctors, heart surgery, you name it. They say humans should not give and take life, yet they benefit from so much that literally keeps them alive considerably longer than they would 'naturally' live, whatever that means. They use contraception—birth control—for God's sake, pardon the pun." He grinned. "They brush their teeth with fluoride-enhanced toothpaste they got from their dentist and then *they* say *we're* playing God because we do something that wouldn't happen otherwise. 'Nice teeth,' I always say to them." He shook his head. "They never get it."

As we approached the next room in the hallway, I wasn't surprised that no one ever got the "Nice teeth" comment, though he had a point.

Before we opened the next door I mentioned some of the ideas from my last visit with the Old Man. "You know what I wish I'd suggested as a criteria for personal identity? The *thumbprint* that's unique to every person. *That's* one way to tell if somebody is the same person over time—no two peoples' thumbprints are the same."

"You'll really like this room then," our tour-guide responded. He opened the door to a room that looked exactly like the last, except there were three beds. On each bed, reading a book, were three younger girls who all looked the same. I assumed they were triplets.

The doctor turned to us, "Clones."

Jeff and I looked at each other blankly. "You mean triplets?" Jeff said.

"No, these are clones. Made out of the same DNA. They all have the same DNA—and the same thumbprints." He grinned. "Hello C, D, and E."

"Hello," they responded in unison. I noticed what they were reading. One a music magazine, one a textbook of some sort, and the other a book of poetry.

"Why are they reading different stuff?" I asked.

"Because they have different tastes," the doctor responded. "Some believe that a being who is cloned isn't really a person. They think that a clone will be just like the person whose DNA we used. But they forget about how the environment acts on people, how it lets them develop their own personality. I'll admit, the first 200 attempts at cloning a human turned out pretty drastically; they had a lot of physical and mental complications. And people are worried that we're creating clones for the wrong reasons.

"But we feel it's what you *do* with the knowledge that's important," he continued, as if he were reading from a script, "not the knowledge itself. If you create clones to be slaves or solely for research purposes, then it's bad. Otherwise, they're people just like me—and you, I suppose."

Jeff suggested, "It's like that bumper sticker, 'Guns don't kill people—*people* do.' Guns aren't bad, but it's sometimes bad what people do with them." The doctor nodded and Jeff added, "Though I always say, 'Guns don't kill people—*bullets* do." The doctor seemed unimpressed. I thought it was kind of funny.

We looked at the girls and smiled. I definitely looked at them differently knowing they were clones. They smiled back. Two waved, one nodded her head at us. We all said goodbye.

The doctor was nodding his head as he motioned us to the next room. We entered it and saw what certainly looked like a person. An older man was typing on a typewriter. "Hi F," the doctor said. "Hello Dr. A."

"Why wouldn't this be a person?" Jeff asked the doctor.

"F is a recovering brain-dead person. A year ago he drowned and due to lack of oxygen, his brain literally died. The doctors were able to keep his heart beating and get everything else back to normal. Some of our engineers acquired him and for six months they worked on his brain, inserting wires and conductors in all the right places. A majority of brain activity is due to electricity anyway—different ions and electron gradients firing at all the right times. So they just wired his brain so everything would mimic that. It's all done electrically. When he goes to bed he has to plug his head in."

"Everything okay?" Dr. A asked.

"Yeah, all is well, thanks," F responded. "You good?"

"Yup. All is well."

As we left, Jeff asked, "Why wouldn't that be a person?"

"Some argue that a being whose movements and brain function is run by manmade electricity is not a person," the doctor responded.

"That seems silly," Jeff suggested.

The doctor shrugged his shoulders. He opened the next door.

"Hi G, how's it going?"

This man was cleaning something off of his fingers. He looked up and responded, "Oh, not bad. You?"

"Pretty good. More of the same, ya know?"

"Yeah, I hear ya. What have you been up to lately?"

"Not much. You?"

"Yeah, nothing new. Just hanging out."

"Good to hear."

"Yeah. Thanks for stopping by."

"Definitely. It was good to see you."

"Yeah, you too. Talk to you later."

We quickly left the room.

"What was that?" I asked.

"That," the doctor responded, "was our robot. Our most advanced robot. He's actually got tear ducts in his eyes. And we trained him to converse with people. I think he did a good job with the 'conversation,' don't you?" He made the little bunny ear quote signs with his fingers in the air when he said "conversation." We nodded.

"You know what I mean, though," he continued, "that conversation that you have 20 times a day when you see someone that you have nothing real to say to. It's a longwinded way of saying 'hello.'" We smiled uncomfortably. "Or really just a long goodbye.

"A lot of people discount robots as people. But as you saw, G is certainly self-aware. And you couldn't tell the difference between him and any other person. We basically created him as a computer, but we made him mobile and let him receive input through a camera. Then we programmed him to learn from his mistakes and to self-correct. Just like humans. It took humans millions of years to evolve and so it's taking him some time too. Of course, we had to put skin on him—people are very human-centric. They're very tied to their own species. So if he looks like a person, and acts like a person, then he must be a person. Of course, he has to have a name." He nodded again, that confident nod.

He interrupted his nodding to open the next door. We walked into a room with someone asleep on the bed. His face looked odd because there were a number of small scars on it. He had the same marks on his hands. He looked somehow peaceful though, just lying there.

The doctor sensed our interest in this man and whispered, "This is H. He's actually the result of combining a lot of people. His body is constructed out of 311 different bodies. At the time of the person's death, we extract one body part and keep it alive. Then we put them all together to form a new body. He is the result. He's got the heart of I, the lungs of J, the fingers of K, the left hemisphere of his brain is from L, the right from M, the brainstem of N. He's quite a cornucopia of people. The question is, is this new thing a person and, if so, *who* is he? We don't show this one to many people, but you two seem trustworthy enough. Let's move on shall we."

We were both wide-eyed. And silent. I was sort of glad that guy was asleep.

"Here's our last room. It's slightly different, as we need an apparatus unique to this being."

This room looked the same except for two tall metal cylindrical chambers, connected by wires and tubes. A man was standing in one of them. When he saw us, he said "hello" and nodded at the doctor, smiling. The glass on the cylinders closed and the doctor lifted the cover on a switch and then flipped the switch. A loud humming noise startled us a bit and then the man disappeared. Jeff and I stared in amazement.

"Vaporized," the doctor yelled over the humming noise. "I'm sure you're at least somewhat familiar with Einstein's 'E-equals-M-C-squared.' With energy proportional to mass, we just reduce this man's mass to energy. Many claim that it's physical consistency that's important to their maintaining some sort of identity—that even though people change over time, it's not like they stop existing and then reappear. Well, we've challenged that."

We looked at the opposing chamber. The man reappeared there, looking like he had seconds ago in the other chamber. "Hello," he said again in the same voice. The doctor smiled at him giving him the "thumb's-up" sign of approval. "The question is: Is he the *same* person now that he was moments ago?" We left the room and walked out of the hallway into a sort of waiting room.

The doctor turned to us, "I hope you enjoyed the tour. As you can see, determining personhood and identity can be tricky, especially with the nuances of technology. And it's become an increasingly important field. Everyone thinks that 'persons' should have certain rights, like the right to life. So this is important when we look at issues like cloning, artificial intelligence, animal rights, human rights—for both the beginning-of-life fetus and the end-of-life who are dying—and even potential extraterrestrials.

"If I were from another galaxy, what kind of rights would you give me?" he asked, pausing with an almost eerie smile on his face. "If the only real difference between me and other human beings was my lack of human DNA, would that somehow change my moral status?

"Or what if I were a mix of a mouse and a human—a chimera? How would you treat me then? We're currently working on this technology, you know, even as we speak," he said, as he motioned with his head towards a closed door.

We nodded thoughtfully and I thought about the questions. He stood there, as if he were really asking them. I shrugged my shoulders and shook my head longer than I would have normally. Jeff did the same.

He smiled and shook our hands and we left the building with a different sort of excitement than when we entered. I felt so overwhelmed that something like one's *identity* and *personhood* could be so complex, yet so important. I looked to Jeff. He nodded his head like he was in complete agreement with me on this. I could tell we had hours of discussion ahead of us.

Chapter 3

Science

There is no such thing as philosophy-free science; there is only science whose philosophical baggage is taken on board without examination.

–*Daniel Dennett*,
Darwin's Dangerous Idea

Student: Professor, this is the same question as last year's final.
Einstein: True, but this year the answer's different.

"Hello, Ian . . .

"Good evening, Ian."

I just lay there, pretending that I was asleep. But I *was* asleep, wasn't I? I guess I pretended in my sleep that I was asleep. As soon as I became conscious of this thought process the Old Man said to me, "Don't pretend that you're asleep and that you don't see me."

How would he know I was pretending?

"Because you're *thinking* that," he responded.

But I didn't say anything. How could he know what I was thinking?

"I see that you've been talking to your parents about our conversations."

He was bluffing. He wasn't real. He couldn't possibly know that.

Controlling Your Dreams

In a "lucid dream," the dreamer is aware that he or she is dreaming. It is usually triggered by something in the dream that wouldn't normally occur or is impossible in a waking state. Some psychologists argue that, with practice, individuals can learn to control what happens in their dreams.

"Man is a genius when he is dreaming."

–Akira Kurosawa,
filmmaker

The Quality of a Student's Work

"Quality . . . you know what it is, yet you don't . . . If no one knows what it is, then for all practical purposes it doesn't exist at all. But for all practical purposes it really does exist. What else are the grades based on?"
–Robert Persig, *Zen and the Art of Motorcycle Maintenance*

"A man in a room regurgitating Chinese symbols—pretty crafty. Was that little story enough for you to believe that you really have an immaterial soul, mind, whatever you call it?"

He *was* real. He'd have to be to know about that. "What do you want? Haven't we solved it all? Or haven't you confused me enough? I'm fine not thinking about any of this. It does me no good in school and certainly won't help me get a job. What's the point of all this?"

"Are those really the only reasons that you think about things, your only purpose for wanting to know things? So that you can have someone judge you by giving you an 'A' or so that an employer can judge you by this list of silly, subjective judgments? You subscribe to 'Ignorance is Bliss'? That's a pretty dangerous ideal. To not want to know about one's self, about what it means to know. About

"Ignorance is not bliss— it's oblivion."
–Phillip Wylie

how much of what they teach you in your science class is based on *non*-objective reasoning. Okay. Sleep tight. Enjoy your time amongst the *shadows of your reality.*"

"Wait. What about my science class? Science is the one thing that's clear. Science and math. Those are things we're really confident about. No subjectivity there. All my science tests are multiple choice—it's either right or wrong."

Shadows of Reality

In Plato's "Allegory of the Cave," he portrays cave dwellers, chained down, who know only the shadows on the wall that are created by the light from outside. To know reality, the dwellers must arise and overcome the blinding light outside, thus becoming educated. In doing so, they will come to know reality— what Plato calls the "Ideal Forms." Yet many choose to stay in the cave, enjoying the cool, shaded comforts of the false reality.

"Education" means "to lead out."

*I tell them that I'm doing fine,
Watching shadows on the wall.*

–John Lennon

"I know. I've seen your tests. I've seen your textbooks. I've seen the language in them. They all seem to have finally figured out how everything *actually is*. From the smallest particles to the grandest galaxies. That is, until a new edition of the book comes out, and changes are made for the new 'things that are true.' Very crafty, those textbooks."

"How can you say that?"

The Old Man laughed to himself and nodded as if to say, "I expected this." He reached down, under my desk, and pulled out a stack of big textbooks. Some of them looked new, but most were worn and very out-of-date, almost like antiques. He looked at me with his big hands resting on the top book in the stack.

"What are those?" I asked, as if performing a sort of conversational ritual.

"These are science textbooks I've collected. They each have exams in them that were given to the students at the time. I thought you'd find them interesting."

"Why? I've got my own textbook."

"Well, look at this exam. This eighth grader got an 'A + ' on it. Pretty good. A perfect score."

I looked over the test to see how hard it was. "This teacher missed something. This kid put the Earth at the center of the universe."

"Well, look what his textbook says." I did, and I saw just what the student drew on his exam.

"But that's wrong," I pointed out.

"Look at these." He opened the oldest one and in it was a photo of the finest scientist of the time. His name was Aristotle. The text explained how Aristotle had shown that things fall at speeds proportional to their weight. Then we looked at a separate text that showed how Galileo proved Aristotle to be wrong, and that bodies fall at a constant acceleration.

A chemistry text explained some supernatural thing called "phlogiston" that was responsible for certain kinds of reactions, and then another, years later, which explained Lavoisier's discovery of oxygen. (How, I

When Philosophy Becomes Science

Until very recently, philosophy was part of a much broader scope of academia. Aristotle was also a scientist, and Newton and Darwin were both natural philosophers. Along with the traditional philosophical issues, philosophers also examined physics, psychology, biology, mathematics, astronomy, and many other areas. When philosophers discover answers in these areas, the ideas are escorted out of the philosophical arena.

Bertrand Russell writes, "As soon as definite knowledge concerning any subject becomes possible, this subject ceases to be called philosophy, and becomes a separate science."

> *"We cannot identify science with truth, for we think that both Newton's and Einstein's theories belong to science, but they cannot both be true, and they may well both be false."*
> —Karl Popper, twentieth-century philosopher of science

thought, can someone *discover* oxygen?) This overturned the phlogiston theory.

Next was a biology book that looked at how all living things came to be, and yet another that showed Darwin's theory of natural selection, which overturned the earlier theory.

And again, another schoolbook showing the great Isaac Newton and his theories of physics. But the Old Man shook his head, gave me an even more recent text, and showed me that Einstein's theory of relativity replaced even that.

"And there's a test for each book . . . " the Old Man said as if he was happy he'd so rapidly shaken my faith in science, "testing students' memorization of each theory."

It was a bit troubling and frustrating. I was tempted to say, *Well, at least we have it all figured out now—how could Einstein be wrong?* but that was obviously his point. No one who read those textbooks at the time or took those exams figured the information was probably wrong, that it was *not* how things *really are*. And so, here we are today. With our new textbooks and our new scientists, and their new equipment—

How Many Planets in the Solar System?

500 years ago:
Seven—Earth wasn't considered a planet; sun and moon were.

1846: Eight—Neptune discovered.

1930: Nine—Pluto discovered.

2007: Eight—Pluto no longer considered a planet.

Future: Unknown. Some astronomers speculate there may be another.

and our new teachers making us memorize all their theories. "But now we really do have *universal laws*," I said.

"Universal?" His response was somewhat trite. "Have you ever been bothered by the phrase, 'never say never'?"

I shook my head. I hadn't. But I saw how *he* probably had. So I suggested, "Because, when you say it, you're saying 'never,' but the phrase is telling you never to do that."

"Exactly." He nodded. "Universal laws." He was shaking his head. "'Always.' That's a strong word. It's just like saying, 'always never say never.'

"Make sure you see the difference between 'universal' and 'true,'" he instructed. "Just because a law is true doesn't mean it's universal. If a law holds in certain situations, that doesn't mean it will hold in *all* situations. Einstein overturned Newton not because

Newton's laws weren't universal but because they were only *approximately* true."

Then he continued, in a lighter tone, "So what do you know about shadows?"

"Just the basics, I suppose."

"Okay. Well, let's make two of these laws about shadows, shall we? Tell me if you agree with these:

1. A shadow cannot go through a non-transparent object."

He paused.

"Well of course that's true," I responded. "Shadows don't go through walls or anything solid."

"Okay. Here's the other:

2. An object must have light shone on it in order to cast a shadow."

"That's how shadows are made. That's certainly true."

He then set up what looked like an "Ian-trap." It involved a flashlight, a statue, and a rubber ball. He turned off all the lights. The room was pitch-black. Then he turned on the flashlight, which shone directly on the statue. It looked like this:

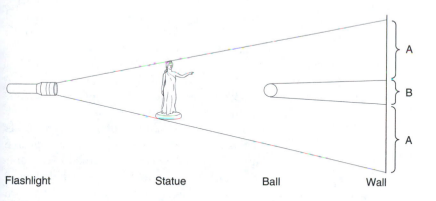

Flashlight   Statue   Ball   Wall

He walked to the wall and asked, "What casts the shadow represented by 'A'?"

Could this simple question be the trap? "The statue. We even know that by applying Law Two."

"Okay, good. Now, tell me, what casts the part of the shadow represented by 'B'?"

The shadow problem has been attributed to Bas van Fraassen as an illustration showing that science involves more than just speculation.

Solar Eclipses

(S) We see things when
light is shown on them.

*During a total solar
eclipse, the moon com-
pletely blocks the sun's
rays and we see this as
a dark round disk. Yet,
there is only light on the
back side of the moon,
facing the sun. The side
nearest us has no light.
So, in an eclipse, do we
see the lit far side (as
"S" suggests) or the dark
near side? Neither seems
plausible.*

The Scientific Method

*Sir Francis Bacon is
credited by many with
the modern view of sci-
ence. Before his* Novum
Organum *(1620), scien-
tific practices relied heavily on theory, reason, and
logic. Bacon emphasized
an empirical ('with the
senses') approach based
on observation and data
collection. This paved the
way for the modern
method of induction by
which hypotheses are
confirmed or disproved
based on repeated obser-
vations.*

*He urged us to,
"command nature . . . by
obeying her," thus leav-
ing no room for supersti-
tion or supernatural
forces in a quest for truth.*

"The statue," I blurted out. "I mean the
ball." Neither worked with our laws. The Old
Man sat patiently. I thought out loud, "With
Law Two, I figured it was the statue. It can't
be the ball because it's completely in the dark.
No light is on it. But by Law One, it can't be
the statue. If it were the statue, then the
statue's shadow would have to go through the
ball. But we know that *can't* happen. So
what's wrong here?"

He was nodding. "Not only are our laws
not universal, but it doesn't appear that they
are true either."

"Is that what went wrong with all those
scientists in the textbooks? All the ones you
just mentioned?"

"That's a small part of it. Part of the
problem is that we relied only on theory to
make our two laws—we totally ignored any
sort of empirical approach—you know, running an experiment like we just did, making
observations."

"So what's the big part? What caused all
the problems with their science?"

"Induction," he said forcefully.

"That's it? That's your answer?"

"Well, yes, that's one important reason.
Certainly not the only reason."

He pulled a handful of coins out of his
pocket and opened his hand, exposing five
dimes. They looked especially small because of
how big his hands were. "There is a sixth coin in
my pocket. What do you think it will be?"

"Well, obviously I *think* it will be a dime.
But I don't know that."

"Exactly. You just used the inductive
method."

I stood there, happy to have used the
inductive method.

"You assumed that the future would
resemble the past. Because each coin I pulled

out of my pocket was a dime, you assumed that the next coin would be a dime. That's induction. It's a weak example because you made your inference based on only five examples—five 'instances.'" He pulled out the last coin in his pocket. It was a video game token. He shrugged his shoulders. "Obviously, there's no need that the future be just like the past." He smiled. "Here's an example of a much stronger inductive claim: *The sun will rise tomorrow*. It's true on the basis of induction. We only make that claim with great certainty because it's happened so many times in the past. We think: *Every day the sun has risen, and so the next day the sun will rise*. That's inductive reasoning."

"But what's wrong with that? It works. We use it all the time."

"That's just the point, Ian. *Induction* has worked in the past, so it will work in the future. You see the circle? Basically, you have to say, 'inductively speaking, induction works.' That's a shaky foundation on which to build a system of attaining *truths*.

"We couldn't be sure that the last coin would be a dime, though we believed that it would. We can't be sure the sun will rise, though we have a very strong belief that it will. And, now, we can't be sure that induction will work, though we have a belief that it will. Not only does induction itself have a logical flaw, but you need induction to prove induction."

"So, what's the point of all this?" I asked, genuinely concerned.

"Well, this is how science gathers information, makes predictions, develops theories—through induction. Simply put:

The *generalization*, 'All Xs are Ys' is supported by the *confirming instance*, 'This X is Y.'"

He paused for a moment.

Deduction—*if all the premises (P) are true, the conclusion (C) must be true. For example:*

P1. Socrates is a man.
P2. All men are mortal.
C. Thus, Socrates is mortal.

Induction—*inferring that a general statement is probably true, based on observations; the conclusion could be false even if the premises are true. For example:*

P1. The first 100 swans I saw were white.
C. Thus, all swans are white.

David Hume's "Problem of Induction"

There is no logical, non-circular way to support the notion that the future will be just like the past.

Hume writes, "It is impossible that any arguments from experience can prove the resemblance of the past to the future, since all these arguments are founded on the supposition of that resemblance."

In other words, to prove that induction works, we must use induction.

Russell's Chicken and Horse

Bertrand Russell tells the story of a chicken who reasons inductively: Every day it has been fed at a specific time. Thus, this will continue every day. He writes, "The man who has fed the chicken every day throughout its life at last wrings its neck instead, showing that more refined views as to the uniformity of nature would have been useful to the chicken."

"The 'law of universal causation' . . . [is an] attempt to bolster up our belief that what has happened before will happen again, which is no better founded than the horse's belief that you will take the turning you usually take."

Or the *generalization*, 'When X happens, Y will happen,' is supported by the *confirming instance*, 'X happened, then Y happened.'

"For example, the generalization 'All swans are white' is supported by repeatedly noting, 'This swan is white.' Once we confirm that enough times, we come to believe that the statement '*All* swans are white' is true.

"Do you see that? Do you see the inductive principles science is based on?"

I guess I did. It didn't seem like anything Earth-shattering, but it was somewhat interesting to realize how it is that scientists know things. "Yes, I suppose I do. Is that how Einstein's theories work too?"

"Exactly. He made predictions—generalizations—and then went out and tested them to see if they held up. His theory of gravity held that heavy bodies, like planets, would attract things. So, we look at objects. They move toward the Earth. Even light. During an eclipse, we can see that light from distant stars *bends* toward the Earth. His theory has been confirmed by countless instances."

That was pretty cool. "That makes sense."

"There are a couple scientists doing work right now who could illuminate a few of the issues with induction. Come with me."

I got out of bed, slid into my slippers, and went through the ladder-and-tube routine that had already become so, well, so routine. We ended up in a laboratory that seemed to be right in the middle of my backyard.

The Old Man pointed out a group of scientists digging outside of the lab.

"What are they looking for?" I asked.

"Grue emeralds."

"You mean *green* emeralds?"

"No, grue ones."

"Grue?" I asked, causing one of the scientists to glance our way. We had obviously distracted her. As she walked towards us removing her glasses on the way over, the Old Man nudged me in the same way Jeff would have and said, "Ask her."

"How do you do?" the woman greeted us, politely.

The Old Man nudged me again so she could see. I then felt obliged to ask. "Hello ma'am. What exactly are *grue* emeralds?"

She swung her glasses by one of its arms and responded, "'Grue' means:

Green until the year 2100 and blue afterwards.

We're looking for grue emeralds."

"Do you mean emeralds that will change overnight from green to blue?" I asked.

"No, the sense data—the actual color that is viewed—won't change. Basically, if an emerald is viewed before the year 2100 and is green then it is grue. And if it is viewed on or after January 1, 2100 and is blue then it is grue."

"But how will you know if you find them?" I asked.

"Well, I will first ask *you* what you know of emeralds," she said, motioning with her hand out toward me.

"Not much. Just that they're green," I shrugged.

"And how do you know that?"

"Well, I suppose at some point, scientists went out looking for emeralds. When they found one, they saw that it was what we call 'green', and through many instances of this, they determined that emeralds are green." I looked to the Old Man and smiled. I felt like I was kind of showing off for him.

"So, you're saying that even though we haven't seen all emeralds, we've seen enough to confirm the generalization, 'All emeralds are green.' There have been enough *confirming instances* of green emeralds to confirm this hypothesis?"

"Yes," I said proudly. "That's how science works."

"Well good, then you will likely approve of the work we do here. First of all, we don't

"What we observe is not nature itself but nature exposed to our method of questioning."
     –Werner Heisenberg

In the movie, The Man Who Wasn't There, *a lawyer applies Heisenberg's relevance to a case:*

"He's got this theory: you wanna test something, you know, scientifically . . . you gotta look at it. But sometimes you look at it, your looking changes it. Ya can't know the reality of what happened, or what would've happened if you hadn't-a stuck your own [nose in]. So there's no, 'what happened?'. . . . Because . . . our minds get in the way. Looking at something changes it. They call it the 'Uncertainty Principle'. . . . Even Einstein says the guy's on to something."

Testing a Single Hypothesis?

Quine and Duhem noted that any group of observations actually supports numerous hypotheses. Thus it is impossible to test one hypothesis alone. For example, a green emerald confirms that emeralds are green and that they are grue. In another example, the curved shadow of the Earth on the moon during an eclipse supports the notion of the Earth as spherical and as disc-shaped.

Similarly, disconfirming evidence refutes numerous hypotheses: the unexpected motion of Uranus disconfirmed Newton's Laws and it refuted the hypothesis, "There are only seven planets." This led to the discovery of Neptune. Later data consistent with Newton's theory showed evidence for a planet ("Vulcan") between Mercury and the sun. Instead, Einstein's relativity replaced Newton's theory and Vulcan was dismissed.

use 'green' as a way to classify the world like you do. You made up *green* to explain your world. Right? The word *green* didn't just come in a package with the universe like a hamburger comes with pickles. People made it up. Right? And now it's embedded in your language."

I shrugged my shoulders in agreement.

She continued, "Keeping that in mind, we are testing the hypothesis, 'All emeralds are grue.' We do it by digging for emeralds and, when we find one, we determine if it's green. If it is, then it confirms our hypothesis. So far we have had great success. We've found thousands of emeralds, and each has satisfied the hypothesis. We're going to publish our findings at the end of the month."

"But that can't be right," I said now more boldly, though partly to cover up my concern that she might be on to something. "We already know that all emeralds are green."

"Yes, but you know it in the *same way* that we know that all emeralds are grue. We both used the same process: develop a hypothesis, go find instances that confirm the hypothesis, and then make a generalization.

"The trick will be what to do when both our group and your group hear of emeralds located at some undiscovered place after January 1, 2100. You will say the emeralds are green and we will say they're grue. When your group asks what 'grue' means they'll find that it signifies the emeralds to be blue. Both blue *and* green emeralds," she said, laughing at the absurdity.

"But *grue* is just a made-up word anyway. We can't just use anything we want as words," I said, as if these people were breaking the rules of some game just to make it work in their favor.

She nodded, "First of all, we *both* use made-up words. But in the case of *your* scientists, just because they use *their* words doesn't mean they're getting it right. It just works for them. *Green* has come to be accepted by them. Likewise, *grue* has come to be accepted by us."

I nodded, waiting for her to say, *And secondly*.

"And secondly, scientists make up new words all the time to explain things: *electron*, *quark*, *muon*. We wouldn't want to claim that we can't test an electron's force on an atom because the word 'electron' is *made up*."

I shook my head. I shook it not out of confusion but out of amazement. Amazed that I'd never consciously realized that we *do* make up words. And we use these words to try to explain how the world *really is*.

She smiled looking up at the sky. The Old Man looked up with her, saying, "Great day. Beautiful *bleen* sky."

"Bleen?" I asked, though I could anticipate the response.

The woman smiled at the Old Man and answered for him, "Blue before 2100, green afterward. Beautiful bleen sky." She shook the Old Man's hand, waved to me, and went back to her work.

"Words are our servants, not our masters."
–Richard Dawkins

Many "particles" in scientific theory are seen only as a blip on a screen.

Contemporary scientist Rupert Sheldrake writes, "It is sometimes suggested, in a joking way, that nuclear physicists do not so much discover new subatomic particles as invent them. . . . If enough professionals believe they are likely to be found, costly accelerators and colliders are built to look for them. Then, sure enough, the expected particles are detected, as traces in bubble chambers or on photographic films."

I thought about their bleen-sky comments. With my own powers of induction I suggested to the Old Man, "I happen to think the sky will be grue in the year 2100. Don't you think?"

"Blue after the year 2100," the Old Man responded, affirmatively. "Yes, I suppose so," he said, smiling to himself.

He diverted his attention, pointing in another direction and said, "I have another group I want you to see. They're in the laboratory next door." As we entered the next room, a group of people were walking around yelling out, "Non-raven . . . Not-black. Confirming instance!"

"What in the world is going on here?" I asked.

"Well, this group is testing to confirm the generalization, 'All ravens are black.'"

"But don't we already know that?"

"My first question for you is, how *could* we know that? We haven't seen all ravens. Or, do you just want to claim that anything raven-like,

Ad hoc Hypotheses

If a hypothesis is disproved, often we can simply add a clause to "save" it. For example, given the hypothesis, "All swans are white," when a black swan was found in Australia, one could formulate the ad hoc *hypothesis, "All swans are white except those in Australia." At some point, a subjective decision must be made as to when to reject* ad hoc *hypotheses.*

"Scientists also come up with elaborations to explain away the short comings of a dud theory, just as sorcerers conjure up excuses for the shortcomings of a dud spell."
—Roger Highfield,
The Science of Harry Potter

which isn't black isn't a raven? You know, humans did that with each other at one time, except they just reversed the colors. Pretty silly, don't you think?" He paused to let this apparent life lesson sink in. It gave me time to wonder just why being black was essential to "ravenhood." And then, I wondered what *was* essential to "personhood." Certainly not our color.

He continued, "And for a long time, Europeans posited that the statement, 'All swans are white,' was true. Then, when they visited Australia they found swans that were black. Everything about these creatures was exactly the same except the color of their feathers. They had to come out with new editions of all their books on swans.

"This is the first, general problem with induction: we'll never be able to test *everything*. Instead, we have to make a generalization and then confirm it with *a lot* of instances, or confirmations. Then, at some point in our confirming something, we declare it a law. We almost take a leap of faith in a sense. *When is enough testing enough?*" he exclaimed, his eyes bigger, as if he really did struggle with this.

I asked, "So, how does that guy—over there, the one holding up the green apple—think he's confirming the hypothesis, 'All ravens are black'?" I was waving my finger somewhat frantically.

"Well, let's look at two principles that almost all people believe are true. First:

> The Principle of Confirmation (which we've already mentioned): If one finds enough confirming instances of a generalization, then that generalization holds true.

"For example, every instance of a white swan gave more credit to the hypothesis, 'All swans are white.' The second principle is:

> The Principle of Logical Equivalence: For example, the statement 'All politicians are literate,' is logically equivalent with, 'No politicians are not literate.'

"This principle is really not controversial at all—just a simple, though necessary, principle of logic."

"Yes, I understand all of that."

"Okay, so I'll just explain in plain English what these scientists are doing. Take the generalization,

A. All ravens are black.

"This statement is *logically equivalent* with the statement,

B. There are no ravens that are not black.

"This may not seem very interesting, but it must be true if the first statement is true as well. Do you agree?"

"I do, but I don't see the relevance." *Another "Ian-trap"?* I thought.

"Okay, given that statement then it must also be true, *logically*, that:

C. All non-black objects are non-ravens.

"Do you see why that must be logically equivalent?"

"Yes. Since no ravens are non-black then all non-black things must, at the least, not be ravens."

"Good. Well, since statements A, B, and C are all logically equivalent, *and* given the Principle of Confirmation, then these scientists are just confirming the hypothesis, 'All ravens are black.' They're doing it by finding instances that confirm the *logically equivalent* hypothesis, 'All non-black objects are non-ravens.'"

I looked over in the corner of the room where a scientist shouted, "A thousand confirming instances over here, all in a little pile. One thousand pieces of white computer paper. And next to these, a yellow banana. One thousand and one!"

When Is Enough Enough?

Abduction—*the logical term for the "creative leap" required of scientists. Because scientists can never confirm any hypothesis* absolutely, *they must determine, at some point, that they have done enough testing and that it can be considered a law.*

Francis Bacon posited that there should not be any such subjective speculation in science. He wrote, "Facts should be assimilated without bias to reach a conclusion."

Philosophers of science typically see Bacon's view as unrealistic and incorrect. Science historian William McComas calls bias-free science "absolutely impossible." Charles Darwin believed it to be, "ridiculous to even try to reach a conclusion without bias because it's that bias that allows you to reach that conclusion."

Carl Hempel developed the "Paradox of the Ravens" in 1940. He is also well known for developing one of the leading models of scientific explanation.

"Do you find this silly?" the Old Man asked.

"Yes, it is silly," I suggested.

"You agree, as do I, that Statement C is *equivalent* to Statement A. These scientists are just confirming Statement A by confirming the *equivalent* statement, C. By finding a yellow banana, they confirm Statement C, which confirms Statement A. You yourself accepted the two principles. Which one do you want to get rid of? They are both deeply entrenched in your language and the current paradigm of science."

"Paradigm?"

"Yes. A paradigm—the way that a community or culture views things. It can apply specifically, as in how different sports leagues have different rules, or it can apply in a broad way, as was the case years ago when all of humanity was viewed as the center of the universe."

"But why does this matter for scientists?"

"Well, because the paradigm determines how one does science, how one observes things. It literally determines the way we see the world around us. One's paradigm can cause two people to see the exact same thing totally differently."

I raised my eyebrows.

He went to the hallway and called in two people: one, a modern-day scientist, and another, from what looked like medieval times. As we looked out the window, dawn was occurring. The Old Man asked the contemporary scientist what he saw and he responded, matter-of-factly, "It's a result of the Earth spinning on its axis, so the sun appears to rise up over the horizon." The Old Man turned to the other scientist, queried him, and he responded, "Well, because the Earth we are standing on is stationary, obviously the sun is, as we say, 'rising' and will continue its path around us."

"Thank you, gentlemen." And he escorted them out of the room.

"Ian, can you see why one's paradigm is important, especially when doing science? It completely changes the way scientists do tests

Historian of science Thomas Kuhn explores the notion of scientific paradigms in his 1962 book, The Structure of Scientific Revolutions. *The* Arts and Humanities Index *lists this book as number one of the "most cited works of the twentieth century."*

Kuhn writes: "Paradigm changes do cause scientists to see the world of their research engagement differently . . . [W]e may want to say that after a revolution scientists are responding to a different world."

He explains that instead of science somehow evolving, it is actually a "series of peaceful interludes punctuated by intellectually violent revolutions." In these revolutions, "one conceptual world view is replaced by another."

in their lab, make hypotheses, explain phenomena. What we call a 'conceptual framework' practically forbids someone from seeing what is *really* there."

"This really happens? This is a problem?"

"It's a problem because most people would like to believe that science is purely objective—that scientists just go out and objectively view the world and the things in it. But their paradigm completely taints what they see. Even the hypotheses they test are a product of their current paradigm. Likewise, how they test them—they already know what they're looking for. And they also make subjective judgments regarding the number of instances they need to test. Remember from above, how five coins in my pocket didn't quite seem to be enough? Well, scientists make the determination when enough testing is enough—yet *another* subjective determination made by supposedly pure 'objectivists.'"

In Aldous Huxley's, A Brave New World, *one of the main characters, Mustapha Mond, proclaims,*

"I was a pretty good physicist in my time. Too good—good enough to realize that all our science is just a cookery book, with an orthodox theory of cooking that nobody's allowed to question, and a list of recipes that musn't be added to except by special permission from the head cook."

I sat, somewhat overwhelmed, dumbfounded. I think he could sense this.

"Let's try something," he said as he pulled out a deck of playing cards. "I'm going to hold up a card for a brief moment and then put it back, facedown. Then, I want you to tell me what card it was. It's simple."

He held up a Queen of Diamonds for about a half-second.

"Queen of Diamonds," I responded.

He held up a Two of Spades.

"Two of Spades."

Six of Clubs.

How We Observe

Karl Popper writes, "the belief that we can start with pure observations alone . . . is absurd." He recalls a time that he instructed a group of physics students: "Take pencil and paper; carefully observe, and write down what you have observed!" He explains, "They asked, of course, what I wanted them to observe. . . . Observation is always selective. It needs a chosen object . . . a point of view." He continues, quoting another author (Kaltz), "A hungry animal . . . divides the environment into edible and inedible things. . . . Generally speaking, objects change . . . according to the needs of the animal."

"The way our brain is wired up, we only see what we believe is possible. We match patterns that already exist within ourselves through conditioning."
    –From the movie *What the Bleep Do We Know!?*

Read the title of a book by Robert Martin:

*There Are
Two Errors In The
The Title of This Book*

Most people fail to see the repeated word in the title because they are not looking for it or, more likely, have been conditioned to see it in a particular way. (I leave it to the reader to deal with the second "error.")

"Six of Clubs."

He held up a Three of . . . something. It was black, I think.

"A Three of Spades," I said hesitantly.

"Interesting. Let me show you again what card I just held up." He held up what was, in fact, a Three of Hearts and the heart was actually black.

"So? How was I supposed to know that? I've never seen a black Three of Hearts. How could you expect me to get that?"

"I didn't expect you to get that one right. You're a human. You have a 'conceptual framework' which *prevents* you from seeing things. But in another sense I *did* expect you to get it. You know the number three, you know hearts, you can distinguish black from red, you got the other three examples correct. Because your *paradigm* allows you to see only red diamonds and hearts, and black spades and clubs, that's what you see."

"But hasn't science progressed? Isn't *this* paradigm better?"

"One would think so. But, as you saw earlier, I'm sure that everyone in the Aristotelian paradigm, Newtonian, Ptolemaic, etcetera, thought that *his* paradigm was *the one*. You know, the term *mass* in Einstein's paradigm differs from that in Newton's—each of their conceptual frameworks uses the term differently. They'd have trouble even talking to each other about *mass*—it means something different to each of them. This makes comparing paradigms with each other somewhat difficult. How could we say that one is necessarily better than the other? It's almost like comparing apples to oranges—one might be better at the time, given our tastes, or what we want at the time. So we see that choosing between paradigms is somewhat subjective."

"I think I understand. And that's what leads to all the other issues with science?"

"Yes. Right. You know, people are very uncomfortable with *not knowing*. That's the whole purpose of a myth. If you can't explain why there are loud noises in the dark skies and visible electricity shooting

Comparing Apples to Oranges?

Newton's theory holds that mass is conserved. Yet, Einstein's holds that mass can convert to energy. Some argue that Einstein improved upon Newton, and thus that his theory was better. As historian of science George Sarton writes, "progress has no definite and unquestionable meaning in other fields than the field of science."

Though Kuhn explains that because the concept of "mass" is different in the two theories, the two cannot be compared with each other. This is known as the "incommensurability thesis"—that theories of different paradigms cannot be compared and thus can't be said to improve.

---

everywhere, then exclaim that the chief god in the clouds is angry with everyone and is punishing them by throwing lightning bolts."

I nodded.

"People are designed to want to know. They'll even hold on to certain beliefs despite discrediting information. Many people associate their sense of self-worth with knowing things or with just plain being right all the time."

"Yeah, I guess so. Plus, there's that whole problem, that people play such an active role in what they see. Remember, from before?"

"Exactly, Ian," he paused and crinkled his bushy eyebrows at me like he realized I was not only listening but actively thinking. It made me feel like I was an equal of his, just for that moment.

He continued, "We don't always—or, as we discussed a few nights ago—we *rarely* see what is *actually* there."

This almost caused *me* to experience a paradigm shift.

"Good. So this discussion will provide a very good background when you meet this next person," he suggested.

I was curious. Certainly curious. And excited to see who it was.

In walked a medieval-looking man. He wore a plain gray robe made of fancy material tied at his waist with a green cloth. His old leather shoes looked perfectly tattered and he carried a small black bag. There was a piece of cloth tied around his head too as sort of a bandanna to keep in his hair, which was long and shaggy.

Immunity to Change

Social scientist Jay Snelson explains what he calls the ideological immune system. *He writes, "Educated, intelligent, and successful adults rarely change their most fundamental presuppositions."*

Similarly, Kuhn writes, "In science, novelty emerges only with difficulty."

"Idols" That Distort the Truth

Bacon wrote that before pursuing scientific truths, we must first become aware of the "idols" (prejudices) that distort the facts and thus prevent an accurate view of nature: These are the Idols of the . . .

1. Tribe—*flaws inherent to human nature such as our imprecise senses, wishful thinking, and subjectivity.*
2. Den—*prejudices of the culture, such as racism and sexism as well as bias towards one's religion and cultural norms.*
3. Marketplace—*shortcomings and lacking of language.*
4. Theater—*ideas handed down by authority (i.e. politics, religion, education) which may be blindly accepted as true.*

"Ian, this is Copernicus, the great scientist of the revolution. I invited him to tell you about his major discovery and how it all happened."

"Hello, Ian. It's very nice to meet you. Great that the Old Man here could enlighten you as to how scientists work. Most kids your age think that scientists just plug in formulas to the world and get their answers."

I nodded and smiled. What could I possibly say to Copernicus? He spoke in a very friendly tone, though I don't know why he shouldn't.

"Ian, as I don't have much time, I want to explain some of the major factors in what happened with this major scientific paradigm shift. So first, I must tell you that I realized the heliocentric truths—that the Earth is *not* the center of it all—twenty years before I published the book that explained it. I even wrote a few papers on it. I was just too shy—too intimidated to go out and battle the big minds at the time. That was a big issue for me. So that's one major reason for the delay.

"The Planck Problem":

"An important scientific innovation rarely makes its way by gradually winning over and converting its opponents. What does happen is that its opponents gradually die out and the growing generation is familiarized with the idea from the beginning."

"Secondly, and more importantly, was the social and religious situation at the time. The Catholic Church was battling the Protestants. Many cardinals in the Catholic Church accepted the supposed *fact* that the Earth was the center of it all. So the Church was not terribly supportive. It was almost as though they had a lock on the *truth* and they didn't want to lose it. Likewise, the government at the time—a monarchy—depended on the notion of a geocentric universe. This way, everything was closed and finite. Just as God could easily rule over this system, the king could run the country. They somehow thought that overturning Ptolemy was akin to overturning the king.

"And, lastly, the scientific paradigm of the time couldn't handle the change. With the Earth no longer the center of the universe, the laws of physics no longer held. We had to do more than just change the pictures of the Earth in the textbooks, we had to change it all. It was pretty major.

"So all of this combines to show why things took so long. And scientists have to deal with this all the time. It wasn't just *my* revolution. It was much bigger than that—Kepler, Bruno, Galileo, Newton—they all played a major role. Instead of its being one big event, it more accurately happened over a long period of time.

"I hope that helped. Old Man, thank you for having me here. I think it is so valuable for young students to learn how science works and the beauty behind its methods. I wish you two the best. I must go."

Copernicus left the room. The Old Man looked at me, proudly. I nodded and agreed with his look, "That was pretty amazing. I had no idea. I really did think that scientists just dealt with facts. There's so much more."

He nodded, "Well, I assume you now grasp the concept—and *importance*—of scientific paradigms. Pretty key idea. Now I want to get back to where we were before this talk of paradigms. Let's see."

"The effect of scientists on the world?" I suggested, partly to help him, and partly to show that I'd been paying attention.

"Yes. Good. So, when scientists study their environment, they affect it. Scientists go into experiments expecting to see certain things. They actually limit what they can see. Doing experiments is sort of a self-fulfilling prophecy in a way: expect to see something and you will."

"So when you say that we affect our environment, do you mean by assigning color to objects that may really be colorless? Like those things?"

"The resistance of a scientist to a new theory almost invariably is based on ideological reasons rather than on logical reasons or objections to the evidence on which the theory is based."

–Ernst Mayr

"All great truths begin as blasphemies."

–George Bernard Shaw

"Theories and paradigms are social in nature and the marketing of an idea is at least as important as its creation."

–Michael Shermer,
The Borderlands of Science

"People only see what they are prepared to see."

–Ralph Waldo Emerson

"The Experimenter Effect"

Rupert Sheldrake explains how expectations can affect a scientific experiment:

1. *They affect the kinds of questions asked and, thus, the answers found.*
2. *They affect what the observer sees (and what he ignores).*
3. *They affect what actually happens, as the observer's subconscious is involved.*

When asked what his reaction would be if an experiment yielded a result that didn't match with the theory, Albert Einstein commented, "So much the worse for the experiment. The theory is right!"

"Well, not just that. For example, a scientist cannot simultaneously measure *both* the speed *and* the position of a quantum particle; in order to measure one, we affect the other. And on a grander scale, it provides insight to all of our observations. In order to observe *anything* we must interact with the thing and its environment at least slightly. So we can only know what we're testing when we're testing it."

"Wow. This is all amazing. And it all seems so important to how we know things scientifically. I guess I just never realized that scientists are subjective people just like you and me, making subjective, value-laden decisions."

Heisenberg Uncertainty Principle

"The more precisely the position [of a particle] is determined, the less precisely the momentum [of that same particle] is known in this instant, and vice versa."

"Science cannot solve the ultimate mystery of nature. And that is because, in the last analysis, we ourselves are part of nature, and, therefore, part of the mystery that we are trying to solve."

–Max Planck

"Enlightening, isn't it?" he said, like he had just finished a marathon and could finally rest. "And they're real issues. After a complete indoctrination by your school system instructing you that scientists have somehow achieved pure objectivity—that they follow some rigid scientific method procedure—some find it offensive that these claims would be made. And just think, this same indoctrination is going on now, throughout the world. The next generation of scientists, being told how to think, what to know, how to know it. Almost like being taught how to dance. Though in this case we're not sure who's leading whom."

I exhaled, dejected.

"Yes, Ian, it does seem to debase science from its all-knowing pedestal. Grue emeralds. Ravens as black because bananas are yellow. Induction. Theory-laden human scientists. Scientists affecting their environment. Made-up constants. Black Threes of Hearts," he sighed. "Ahh." It was as if he'd just seen a therapist and passed on all of his problems for them to deal with. I was that therapist.

He raised his bushy eyebrows for one last suggestion. "On the flipside though, we do realize that science is amazingly useful and successful. The 'inference of the best explanation,' they often comment. Your dad will know what I mean. And look at the creativity of *real* science. Pretty enlightening, I'd say.

"Good luck with your science class, Ian."

Ian awoke. As he walked downstairs, his face seemed to show almost a twinge of anger as opposed to the anxiety he'd felt earlier. Maybe he'd gotten used to these dreamy visits. "Mom and dad will really like this one," he mumbled as he stormed into the kitchen shaking his head. "That they're frauds just like the astrologers they'd made fun of and called 'pseudo-scientists.'"

"Dad, I have something to share with you, and I don't think you'll like it very much," he said confidently, sitting down at the table. He recounted the dream in a very serious tone. It was available to him in quite clear detail. The smells of the laboratories, the lines on the scientists' faces as they crinkled with inclination, the now-familiarity of his guide through these troubling puzzles.

"Dad," he then queried, "are my science teachers aware of this and just not telling me so that they'll have something to grade me on? Do they not know about these issues? I've never thought about them because science is presented to all my classmates as the *absolute truth*.

Even Einstein Makes Constants . . . and Mistakes

Einstein's equations of general relativity resulted in the concept that the universe has a beginning (versus being infinite). Initially he didn't like this result. So he added a "cosmological constant" to change this result. He later removed it as he realized there was an origin of the universe. He referred to this as the "biggest mistake" of his career.

Defending Society

Philosopher of science Paul Feyerabend gave a talk in 1974 entitled "How to Defend Society Against Science." In it he stated,

"My criticism of modern science is that it inhibits freedom of thought. If the reason is that it has found the truth and now follows it, then I would say that there are better things than first finding, and then following such a monster."

But they're not. Not really. So what's up with all of this?"

"Well, son, I don't think it's as bad as your dream—or should I say your nightmare—makes it appear. Actually, you've had a chance now to think about science in a way that I only just began to do a few years ago. You're thinking about not just *what* we know, but *how* we know it. It's very tricky. And what you'll come to see is a more realistic view of science in doing this. You'll come to realize *how* scientists work and this will provide you with a more accurate view of what scientists do. They gather information. They make hypotheses. They all have interests, friends, desires, likes, dislikes. This doesn't make scientists bad people in any way; as a matter of fact it makes them *people*, just like you and me. Kind of refreshing."

Ian nodded in an affirmative way as if thinking of his dad as someone who also had interests, friends, desires. His dad seemed to be excited about exploring the humanity of his profession. He continued, "You know, scientists are actually very creative in their approach to doing good science. Most people don't realize how much creativity is involved. Now you're starting to see this. It makes it a very enriching experience.

"And scientists have to put food on the table too. I don't know if you've ever heard of the phrase 'publish or perish,' but it certainly rings true. I hear colleagues of mine talk about it all the time. The main way that scientists earn their living is by doing science and then telling everyone about it. And they tell people about it in scientific journals. So you can imagine the pressure on scientists to come up with some *truths* here and there. And these days, there are over a hundred thousand science journals. It gives us more chance to publish, I suppose. And less chance to perish. But that's also a lot of new *truths* coming out every month."

Ian nodded his head slowly. His father's pace had picked up a bit as he was obviously speaking on something that hit home a little more than usual.

"But dad, what about all these problems with the scientific method I mentioned? What about the two groups of scientists whose labs I visited? Grue emeralds? Non-black objects?"

"These can actually be very illuminating—not necessarily problems, but insights as to how this method works. Take grue, for example. What that woman's group did was to assign a seemingly unimportant regularity to emeralds."

"What does that mean?" I asked.

"The concept *grue* is not important to us. You probably think it's rather silly. But things do often change their appearance. Your folder that you left out all summer in the backyard faded from blue to white. We just refer to color as the reflection of light rays of certain wavelengths. But couldn't we just as well use color-language to refer to color as relative to time? We could have chosen anything. We're humans. We're liberated by language but, at the same time, it constricts us."

Ian blurted out, "Yeah. So that folder that I had was actually *blight*." He sat, proud of his grue-like joke.

His father smiled.

Once Ian realized the potential implications he asked, "So scientists choose which regularity they want to test and then they test it?"

"Yes. They could have chosen any number of them. We could find a regularity or generality in anything. Anything at all. So what are scientists to consider as acceptable regularities? For example, it's been suggested that the Egyptian pyramids were actually built by creatures from space. We could 'prove' this," he said, both hands making bunny ears around *prove*, "by dividing the base of the Great Pyramid by twice its height. This equals *pi*—three-point-one-four, which is a very important number in mathematics. And the height of the pyramid times ten to the ninth power—nine, being the number of

"Regularities are where you find them, and you can find them anywhere."
–Nelson Goodman, who developed "The Paradox of Grue" in 1955

Regularity—*a pattern that allows us to predict events.*

The Washington Monument and Regularity of "Fiveness"

Height: 555 feet and 5 inches
Base: 55 square feet
Window height from base: 500 feet
The base times 60 (a number that is 5 times the months in a year) equals 3,300—the weight of the top stone in pounds
"Washington" has 10 letters—2 times 5
It takes the average mathematician 55 minutes to figure this all out.

This parody was "discovered" by mathematician Martin Gardner.

Making Order from Chaos

Psychologist David Myers writes, " . . . human nature abhors chaos. Show us randomness and we will find order, pattern, clusters, and streaks." He quotes the author of How We Know What Isn't So, *Thomas Gilovich: "The tendency to impute order to ambiguous stimuli is simply built into the cognitive machinery we use to apprehend the world."*

planets—equals the distance to the sun in miles. But, the problem here is *something* had to result in that distance—if not this, then something else. Either that, or this number must add up to *something*—maybe the distance to Venus, maybe the distance to Virginia. *That's* a regularity."

Ian nodded and grinned, as if envisioning the latest findings that the pyramids were actually built by Virginians.

"Likewise here—the *grue scientists* have a regularity of their own. So there's a problem that we can now be aware of: either we can't know what a regularity is—but this seems silly as it is what the whole inductive practice of science is built upon—*or* we have to include things like *grue* into our account of regularity. It seems problematic, but it's a good heads-up for scientists who assign regularities to things."

He spilled right into his next point without pausing, "This is part of what I meant when I said that scientists *choose* to assign regularities. Most scientists choose *green* as a regularity of emeralds. It's a subjective choice, just as *grue* was chosen by the scientists in your dream. Though, in a deeper sense, it is imbedded in our language like that woman mentioned. Think about it, she probably thinks that when you say something is green, you mean it is grue before the year 2100 and bleen afterwards. Why is it any better to refer to color as a result of randomly chosen wavelengths, versus as a result of time?"

Are Names and Categories Arbitary?

In Robert Martin's review of The Grue Paradox, *he suggests that this paradox illustrates "category relativism"—"the view that how you categorize things is just an arbitrary matter, an accident of culture or language."*

"So the point is?"

"The point is that we—*humans*—choose how to classify facts in the world. The world doesn't somehow whisper it to us in some secret members-of-science-club manner. Science describes the world in *our* terms, yet we typically think of us as describing the world as it is, in its own language. Though, actually, any quality or predicate used in science is totally relative to the scientists involved." His dad smiled for a moment.

"Okay, that actually is somewhat insightful," Ian said. "But what about the Raven

Problem that I encountered with those other scientists?"

"Well, it seems that this presents a similar problem with induction. It forces you to either:

1. Change the principle of confirmation (on which science is based), OR
2. Change the principle of logical equivalence (on which our language is based), OR
3. Accept that a yellow banana *confirms* 'All ravens are black.'"

Ian raised his hands helplessly, "But the first two seem totally necessary and the last seems silly. What do we do?"

"Well, I agree that it does seem somewhat silly to accept these particular scientists' findings. But there's a lesson to be learned here. When we talk about *confirming* something, instead of saying that we've *proved* it, we could just say that we've found *very strong support* for it."

Ian butted in, "Yeah, that's like the idea that we don't have to find all the non-black non-ravens everywhere in order to prove our hypothesis. Instead, we just have to find a number of them that scientists think is enough."

"Yes," again, proud of his son's genuine interest and ability to introspect on his own profession. "You know it's funny but people sometimes try to debase a scientific theory *just because* it is a theory—as if that's somehow a weakness. Theories can be highly confirmed and accepted and considered true. This is something that we will probably revisit," he said, smiling. "Maybe you can explore this in another dream," he interjected, as though Ian had control over that. "*Science Revisited.*"

"And secondly . . . " his dad continued immediately, not wanting to tip Ian off. Ian looked around suspiciously, almost as if he suspected a hidden camera somewhere. "Regarding this 'Raven Problem,' you can see here that this view of confirmation is *relative*—it's relative to what we already

Language and Reality

"If we spoke a different language, we would perceive a somewhat different world."

"The limits of my language are the limits of my world. All I know is what I have words for."
–Ludwig Wittgenstein, student of Bertrand Russell at Cambridge in the early 1900s. *Russell described meeting Wittgenstein as "One of the most exciting intellectual adventures [of my life]. He soon knew all I had to teach."*

"Language shapes the way we think, and determines what we can think about."
–Benjamin Whorf

"No amount of experimentation can ever prove me right; a single experiment can prove me wrong."
–Einstein

"Theory"

The National Academy of Sciences defines a scientific theory as: "a well-substantiated explanation of some aspect of the natural world that can incorporate facts, laws, inferences, and tested hypotheses." A theory is often the result of a hypothesis that has been highly confirmed. Theories often include very well-received notions, such as "cell theory"— that humans are comprised of cells, and Einstein's theory of general relativity.

Creativity and Subjectivity in Science

Scientists . . .

1. *Choose what language to use to describe the world.*
2. *Choose which regularities are significant.*
3. *Choose how many confirming instances are enough.*
4. *Choose which hypotheses to test.*
5. *Affect what they test.*
6. *Have biases which affect how they view the world.*

know. We already have to know about ravens, color, non-ravens, and on and on. And how do we find out about those things? We use knowledge that we already have. This obviously becomes circular, then, but at least allows a more realistic view of confirmation."

Ian nodded, and suggested, "It also seems like a yellow banana confirms the hypothesis 'All ravens are *blue*' too. Maybe it's the principle of logical equivalence that we can get rid of, or at least modify."

"Exactly. Imagine that I hope to prove my hypothesis, 'All boys who play baseball live outside Nebraska.' If I find baseball-playing boys everywhere, other than Nebraska, according to this principle that would confirm my hypothesis. But it seems that, actually, this would also lead us to think that there *are* some baseball-playing boys in Nebraska: if they're everywhere else, why wouldn't they also be in Nebraska? It doesn't account for *positive*, or actual, information."

"Geez, dad. There's really a lot going on in science that I've never thought of. It's really got a lot of issues: logically, sociologically, psychologically. I wish our science books taught us *this* stuff. Maybe I'll stop bothering with this subject in school and just study it with you."

His dad grinned, "Well, son, I'm not sure that's really the lesson here. With this background, you can really look to science not for just what we know, but *how* we know it.

"Science is our most successful method of attaining truths. The 'inference of the best explanation,' they often comment."

Ian interrupted him, "Yeah, the Old Man said that same thing right before I woke up."

His dad nodded, almost as though he knew that.

Science and Reality

Scientific Realism—*science provides a literal translation of how the world really is. Theories are true because they relate to real entities in the world. For example, a chemistry law is true because there really are molecules that behave in a certain way.*

Scientific Anti-Realism—*a useful scientific theory isn't necessarily true. Theories are tools that help us classify the world. For example, a chemistry law works because the world behaves as* if *there are molecules that behave in a certain way.*

W.T. Stace suggests that scientific notions such as gravity and atoms are metaphors that help us make predictions. He writes, "Gravitation is not a 'thing,' but a mathematical formula, which exists only in the minds of mathematicians." And also, "In reality the atoms no more cause sensations than gravitation causes apples to fall." Instead, atoms and gravitation are just concepts to help predict occurrences in the world.

"What does that mean, anyway?" Ian asked, visibly perturbed by his dad's mention of something from his dream that he had not shared.

His dad clarified, "When we make observations and then try to explain them, we must assume that we've come up with the best explanation— that it's *true*. To take a simple example, when your mom and I saw mouse droppings and nibbled cheese in the kitchen, we explained it by inferring, 'A mouse was here.' We didn't think this was just some hypothetical story useful in explaining why cheese disappeared. We never actually saw a mouse, but we inferred it was there. We thought it was *true*. It's the same with science."

"But dad, does a scientific theory really have to be true to be successful? I mean, even if something like quantum particles don't exist, theories about them could be good if they allow us to predict and explain the universe."

"You know, son, that's very insightful. Some scientists today support what they call 'Superstring Theory.' It basically holds that somewhere within 10 to 26 dimensions there are ultra-thin strings and the vibrations from these strings provide the energy needed to sustain the universe. I have to think that this is just a metaphor—a concept that helps us explain. These proposed strings are way too small to ever be observed anyway."

Ian shook his head astoundingly, "Yeah, I can't even think of what ten dimensions would

> "In science a successful theory is not necessarily a correct theory."
> –Michael Behe, biochemist

The Limits of Science

In The End of Science, *John Horgan argues that we may have reached a time in which there are few, if any, major scientific discoveries to be made. And if we did continue these discoveries, we may not be able to understand them given our limited cognitive ability. He quotes mathematician Ronald Graham: "We're not very well adapted for thinking about the space-time continuum or the Riemann hypothesis. We're designed for picking berries or avoiding being eaten."*

Horgan discusses Gödel's "Incompleteness Theorem." It holds that any system of axioms (such as mathematics) results in questions that cannot be answered with those axioms alone; new axioms must be added. In doing this, new unanswerable questions arise and this continues infinitely. Gödel initially posited this theorem in regards to math, yet the idea has been expanded to other systems such as science.

---

mean. And how would scientists even test this if there's," he paused, dragging his 's' like the air being let out of a tire, shrugging his shoulders, "nothing to test?"

"You don't really *see* gravity, do you?" his dad quickly responded, rhetorically.

Ian shrugged again, then asked, "So how can we tell the difference between science and science fiction?"

"We're actually going to talk about that another time, maybe after a dream of yours deals with that."

"How do you know if I'll have a dream that deals with that?"

"Just seems like a logical progression, I suppose," his dad responded hesitantly, and continued in a more lively manner, "Just wait until we distinguish between science and pseudo-science—people making claims based on what they pretend to be science or, more realistically, what they *believe* is science.

"Maybe you could become a little more open-minded, as could I, to areas of knowledge-gathering other than science. Science provides answers to the great multitude of questions that are testable. It might not be able to answer questions on ethics, on spirituality, on metaphysics. But it *can* answer a lot

> *"Science is a particular way of knowing about the world. In science, explanations are limited to those based on observations and experiments that can be substantiated by other scientists. Explanations that cannot be based on empirical evidence are not a part of science . . . Science is not the only way of acquiring knowledge about ourselves and the world around us. Humans gain understanding in many other ways, such as through literature, the arts, philosophical reflection, and religious experience."*
> –The National Academy of Sciences

of other questions and has done so throughout history. With the background you have now, I think you'll embrace science even more—and you'll know what you're embracing."

> "All our science, measured against reality, is primitive and childlike—and yet it is the most precious thing we have."
> –Albert Einstein

Seeing that he had successfully satisfied Ian's intellectual turmoil yet again, his dad got up to leave the kitchen. On his way out he remarked, "That was quite a little dream—*grue* emeralds, yellow bananas, and *that black Three of Hearts*. Pretty crafty. Pretty insightful."

As his dad left the room, Ian almost seemed to interrupt his own contentedness. "Dad, I told you about the black Three of Hearts?" Ian was shaking his head. "Dad. Dad." No answer.

"Dad, how did you know about the black Three of Hearts?" No answer. "I didn't even tell you about that."

Ian sat thoughtfully for a moment. He grabbed an apple from the table and went up the short staircase and out the door.

We Are *It*

I know I didn't tell my dad about the Three of Hearts. I didn't mention the Blind Color Ph.D. the other day either. I couldn't wait to talk to Jeff about it. I wondered if there was such thing as *déjà vu*? This wouldn't even be *déjà vu* though. *I don't know what* this would be.

As I walked down the sidewalk, I saw Jeff on the corner, looking through binoculars at the sky. When I got to him he acted like he didn't notice me. "The binoculars again?" I asked Jeff, actually surprised that we didn't use these more often.

"Yeah," he responded half-heartedly, gazing at a bird flying above. He acted like he was too busy or maybe just too interested in it to talk to me.

"So are you trying to figure out what *really really* happened with this bird, or something?" I asked, somewhat sarcastically.

He turned his head slowly towards me, leaving the binoculars aimed at the birds. "Somewhat. Yes."

I furrowed my eyebrows at him.

He responded to the eyebrow furrowing, "You already know that with these ear plugs you can hear what someone else is thinking. Animals think too, you know."

"Let me see."

He begrudgingly took the binoculars down from his self-made perch. The bird soared above, circling us like a preying vulture would a carcass, like it was trying to figure us out in the way we were studying it.

I focused the binoculars on the bird. As I fastened the earpiece in my ear, a voice came through—a female voice, in very clear English. " . . . Wouldn't that be nice," she thought to herself, as though I'd caught her mid-sentence. It was the inner voice of the bird. I held the binoculars in their perch and looked at Jeff excitedly.

"I know," Jeff said, smiling. "Pretty cool, huh."

I rushed my eyes back to the binoculars: "Poor, poor human. Still unevolved, walking around on two feet. I don't know how they can stand it—ha, *stand* it—all day long. If I walk for ten minutes, I want to go sit in my nest and relax. I guess that's the fate of being stuck in the middle of the evolutionary hierarchy. I'm just glad I made it where I did—as a bird. Those humans plan months ahead to fly, and then they have to wait around for two hours to cram into one of those big metal bird-machines, trying their best to be just like us. I've read all the works by the smartest birds throughout history using the finest scientific tools and they all confirm that we are the pinnacle—we evolved wings and then evolution came to a halt. I'm sure there will be subtle changes throughout the rest of time—bigger wings, more flaps per minute, prettier colors or maybe colors that better camouflage—but, basically, we are *it*.

"And carrying their young around in their stomach for nine months—how archaic. I can't imagine having to carry my eggs around with me for nine months before their birth.

"Though I'm still up in the air about something—up in the air, hah, I should remember that one. Since God is a bird and created us to be like Him, I wonder what happens to humans when they die. With no souls, they must just stop existing. Then again, if they had souls like birds do, that would allow them to be light enough to fly just like us. But they don't have wings, so of course it would be silly to say they have souls.

"Is that a worm over there? It would be unlikely that I get the worm at this point in the day—I'm hardly the *early bird*. Though I wonder if maybe the worms have also figured out that the early worm gets eaten. I should really stop hovering here and get further north. The weatherbird predicted a nice warm stream of air up there."

I laughed in amazement. "This works for all animals?" I said to Jeff.

"All animals," he responded, matter-of-factly. "All organisms. You should hear what sharks think."

"You've pointed these at a shark before? What did it say?" I asked.

"I remember one thing very clearly. He thought that we humans have no grasp of ethics. We trespass when we go into their waters—they have a very strong system of property rights; we act unethically when we kill their neighbors; they don't even think ethics apply to us—that ethics are a shark-made concept. This shark thought it made as much sense to say that a human acts unethically as it does to say that a jellyfish does."

"Ethics are a *shark*-made concept?" I repeated.

Jeff nodded and continued, "The shark thought through how he had read books by the most well-traveled sharks and that they had swum the length of the universe and came to realize that they were certainly the most evolved, with all other creatures either less fast, less strong, or stuck floating on boats like humans. This shark recalled seeing a human swim and he practically choked laughing about it.

"He kept saying to himself, 'We've covered the entire universe, and we are *it*.' It was pretty interesting, actually."

"This is amazing, to get their perspective. What if I point these at this puddle here below us?" I asked, pointing to a small, murky puddle of water.

"Try it," he said, nodding encouragingly, though somewhat unsure if I'd be able to hear anything.

I focused them on the dark edge of the puddle and adjusted the knob. Eventually, a tiny bacterium came into focus and I heard a voice. "Nice and clean, this water. Nice and clean. Not like those clear days when you can see for inches—yuck. I don't know how bacterium can stand that. Everyone's different, though, I suppose.

"I'm just glad I am alive. More than that, I'm glad I've evolved and am here, at the apex of evolution. I mean, we as a species have traveled to the edges of the universe and interviewed the most intelligent bacterium—and thus the most intelligent organisms—known. I'm always amazed when I think of how we were able to cover this entire aquatic universe. All the way to the edges, and all the way down to the bottom and the top, we've seen it all. But now that we have, we realize there is nothing more. There may be other lifeforms out there, but we may never know it. And how *could* anything conceivably evolve more than us, with our flagellum for maximized transportation, and our simplified digestion system, and the capability to reproduce all by myself, a thousand times over. I couldn't imagine depending on another member of the species for reproduction, and then being able to reproduce just one offspring per year. How unsophisticated that would be! But now, we are here. And we are *it*."

The little organism was shimmying a little, almost like it was dancing. "Here's some nice sludge over here," it thought to itself, "'Tis a beautiful world we live in. A beautiful world."

I looked at Jeff, "'Tis a beautiful world we live in, Jeffrey." I said grinning, now with a slightly new sense of being.

He looked at me as though something were wrong. "*Jeffrey?*" he asked, his eyebrows raised. "Since when did you call me that?"

"We made it, Jeffrey. Things have been evolving for billions of years and producing the finest specimen. I'd have to say that, at this point, we are *it*—the finest six billion beings in history."

He shrugged, nodded, and smiled puffing out his chest in a joking way, "*I* am it. I was born a few weeks after you." We laughed.

"So, Jeff," he looked at me as if he knew I was ready to change the topic. "Is it possible that someone could know about something in your dream without you telling them?"

He scrunched his face up like he didn't really understand the question—like he didn't understand why the answer would be anything but a resounding 'no.' He mumbled, "Well, telepathy maybe?" shrugging his shoulders, almost embarrassed that he'd mentioned it. "Or just like how some people think that dolphins can transmit images to each other through their sonar, maybe you accidentally did something like that," he suggested, gritting his teeth together and scrunching up his nose.

I continued, "Hardly, Jeff. It's just that I am positive that I didn't mention part of my dream to my dad this morning. And then *he* mentioned it. How would that be possible? Could he have the same dreams that I'm having? Could there be some dream world or something where dreams are created and then shared with people?"

"And *you* think *my* telepathy and dolphin sonar suggestions were weird?" he suggested, more to defend himself.

"I just can't figure out how my dad would know this. In the same way, that man in a dream of mine knew what you and I were going to do the other day with the binoculars. Do you think dreams are more powerful than just something your brain does when it's bored sleeping?"

Jeff had a blank stare on his face, like he was actually considering my question.

He mustered up an, "I'm sure it's nothing" response, to show that he at least heard the questions. "Maybe you did mention the cards and you just don't remember. Or maybe the prediction about the binoculars was like one of those self-fulfilling prophecies. Like your dreaming it and thinking about it aided in your actually doing it."

"But *you* brought the binoculars. How could I have anything to do with that? And I *didn't* mention the cards to my dad. There's always a way to be skeptical about everything—to explain it all away. But what if something *is* going on with my dreams, something more than just a bored brain?"

Jeff nodded. I would have expected him to be even more blank-faced, but instead he looked thoughtful, like he was really considering my last questions.

"'Tis a beautiful world, huh Ian?" he said reluctantly as a way to break the tension of the unknown.

I smiled at him, "'Tis. I'll see you tomorrow."

Chapter 4

The Liar, Motion, and a "Surprise"

It might turn out that people either are not intelligent enough to understand the world or that the world is unintelligible.

–Daniel Kolak and David Goloff

If this sentence didn't exist, somebody would have invented it.

–Douglas Hofstadter

I figured I'd actually try the ladder-and-tube experience on my own without the Old Man leading the way. I wanted to go to school and see what happens there.

As I emerged from our little portal, everything seemed pretty much the same. I did have that excited feeling though, like the first day my parents let me walk to school by myself.

On my way to school, though, I saw the Old Man from a distance. He was with someone. From behind it actually looked like Alexis. I always think that any girl with pigtails is Alexis. I wondered why they would be together. I tried to sneak up closer to them and I caught up to a group of people a half-block away and walked close enough to them to disguise myself as part of their group. The people looked at me, probably wondering why I was walking so close to them. I immediately started counting on my hand, like I was trying to figure something out and was

> *"If the dream is a translation of waking life, waking life is also a translation of a dream."*
> *–Rene Magritte*
> Surrealist painter
> (1898 –1967)

oblivious to everything going on around me. I do this a lot when I feel like people are looking at me. It's like if you're counting then you must be busy, must be figuring out something really important, and certainly must not be eavesdropping on people. I kept my eye on the Old Man, watching him stroke his beard, talking to this girl who I was becoming more certain was Alexis. She had that little bounce to her walk.

A few of the people looked at me again. I counted. One of the women stared into the sky and exclaimed, "What is that?"

"What? What is what?" another group member asked.

"I honestly think it's a UFO," the woman responded immediately. "Actually, I'm sure it is. We should call this in to someone."

"Well, *now* we can't. It's not a UFO."

"I swear it is. I know what I'm seeing. It is definitely a UFO."

"Well, it's not. You've just identified it. As soon as you identify an object you can't then say it's also *un*identified. At the very least it's an FO."

"FO?"

"Flying Object."

She nodded, as if she understood but wasn't happy about it.

"And now it looks like it's landed. So now it's an O. Nothing terribly exciting about that. What are you going to say when you call this in: *Hello, I'd like to report an object?*"

This was all very strange. And it caused me to lose track of the Old Man and Alexis (or was it an Alexis look-and-act-alike?). It was like I had forgotten what I was doing. Kind of like when you're riding your bike and then all of a sudden you realize that you haven't been aware of the fact that you've been pedaling and steering —you're kind of amazed that you're even alive. I'd probably make a bad private investigator. I'd get distracted by everything going on around me. I wonder if psychologists have a name for that. I've heard that lots of famous artists and thinkers were like that though. Good thing no one *cured* them.

This all brought me to school. The Old Man was nowhere to be found. More importantly, Alexis was nowhere to be found.

I walked into my classroom and saw a bunch of students that looked vaguely familiar. There was no one that I could recognize, though no one there that I'd never seen before either. I sat down and the seat was especially cold, the desk exceptionally scrunched, the teacher in this now-I-remember-it's-a-dream was a little overdone.

On the board it said, "Please don't erase." This usually wouldn't be odd—our teacher would sometimes write this so that whatever was on the board would remain so she didn't have to rewrite it. But today that's all that was on the board. Why would someone write "Please don't erase" if that's all they were writing? Did they want "Please don't erase" to not be erased?

As I adjusted myself in my seat I spied the Old Man sitting in the back. Curious. I felt both anxiety and comfort from his presence.

The teacher announced that she was giving a quick true/false exam. She assured us that the questions were on things that we knew well, so there was really no need to have studied for it.

Before she handed out the exams, she notified us of a surprise exam that she would be giving next week. She stood and smiled for a moment, like she was genuinely happy to have created an entire week's worth of anxiety for us.

As she placed the test on my desk, my eyes quickly landed on the first statement: "The test sheet is white."

That seemed obviously true: as far as whiteness goes, the paper was white. So I marked "T" for "true." The next few seemed similar, and equally (strangely) as simple:

2. The janitor has six arms.
   False.
3. This sentence is part of a test.
   True.
4. This sentence is black.
   True.
5. This sentence is false.
   True. I think.

There were some extra credit questions that I ignored for a moment —question five bothered me. It seemed like it would be true. This particular sentence should *know* best, I supposed. But I thought of the consequences of my answer.

If I answered "True," then what the sentence says would be true, just like the other statements. For example, if I marked "True" for number *two*, then it would be true that the janitor has six arms. So, for number *five*, answering "True" meant that it was true that the particular sentence was false. That being the case, the sentence was *false.* Aha! I knew who was behind this part of the test. It was a trick. While the answer may *appear* to be *true*, it was actually *false.* So, I scratched out my previous answer and changed it.

The Liar

"What I am now saying is false."

[The sentence printed in the brackets on this page is false.]

The "Paradox of the Liar" dates back to the Greek philosopher Eubulides of Miletus in the fourth century BC.

A Cretan once said, "All Cretans are liars."

In the New Testament of the Bible, St. Paul says, "One of themselves, even a prophet of their own, said the Cretans are always liars."

If a prophet says that all Cretans lie, and this prophet is a Cretan then he may be lying. Though, if he lies and he is a Cretan, then he is telling the truth. But . . . if he is telling the truth, then he's a liar, because what he is saying is that he is a liar.

I looked back at my not-so-guardian angel with pride. He shook his head slightly, as if we were somehow conspiring on the exam and he didn't want to get caught.

Was I wrong? I thought through it. If this statement was false then that would mean that what the sentence said was not the case. If the answer was "False" then it would turn out that the statement, "This sentence is false," was not the case, and would actually be *true*! Aha! "The answer," I thought to myself excitedly, "is," and then remembered my recent train of thought, "True?" But that can't be.

If it's "True," then it's false.
If it's "False," then it's true.
What was I to do?
What if it were you?
I haven't a clue.

I was going delirious in my own dream. I was proclaiming that true statements are false and false ones true. Impossible. The statement must be true or false, and it certainly can't be both. *Neither* works!

I jumped ahead to the extra credit. I had always found that concept funny—if it's given on an exam, how is it extra? Isn't the whole exam extra?

I read through the questions, now somewhat cautiously:

a. Don't read this statement.
b. Spell the word "penultimate."
c. With one line make VI a seven.
d. With one line make IX a six.
e. Carry out the next instruction.
f. Carry out the previous instruction.
g. Do you know how many meetings you have left?
h. Is it time to go see Alexis?

Alexis?

I immediately looked back at the Old Man. He was getting up to walk out the door and subtly motioned for me to follow him. I turned in my exam (not remembering how I decided to answer number five) and went with him. We walked silently together until we stopped on the front steps of the school. As I gazed out onto the lawn, I noticed a lot of kids, all just standing around talking. I did see Alexis—sitting under a tree reading a book. She looked up, as if she felt my stare and motioned to me. "Come over here," she mouthed as she stood up, her arms waving at me.

Could this be for real? I looked at the Old Man who stood there (like everyone else) watching all of this. He nodded his head as if to say, "Alexis is awfully cute."

"I have to go see her," I said, thinking of how the word *cute* somehow fell short. *Perfect* was more like it.

"I have bad news, Ian," he said.

Of course. Too good to be true.

"You will never make it to Alexis' arms," he stated.

"Please," I begged him. "I really like her. She's the only girl I've ever liked, and she wants me to go over there. Can't I at least go see what she's reading?"

He shook his head. "It is not that *I* will prevent you. It is something much greater than merely me."

"God?" I thought. What else could be greater than the Old Man?

"Listen," he continued, "do you agree that in order to get there, you will have to go halfway?"

"Of course:

Every journey has a halfway point."

This couldn't be so bad. What is the big deal with having to go halfway before you can go all the way? Probably another life lesson he was trying to teach me.

He continued, "Well, given that, then once you get to the halfway point between you and her—let's call it 'H'—you will then embark on another journey: from H to Alexis. But because this is another journey, you must agree—as you have already stated—that you will once again have to go halfway."

"I *do* agree that every journey has a halfway point."

"That's the problem," he said, matter of factly. "Your journey from here to Alexis involves an *endless* number of halfway points. And seeing as how you only have a finite

Zeno of Elea (born 490 BC) is best known for his creation of paradoxes relating to space and motion. At the time, his mentor Parmenides asserted that, "All is one." He claimed that all of existence was just a single unchanging whole: if it were not, then the separate things would have to be separated by nothing, which seemed to him incorrect. In his paradoxes, Zeno supported this by showing that motion and change were false notions.

lifespan, you can never reach her. Nothing personal—it's just a logical fact. You don't want to start ignoring simple logic all of a sudden, do you?"

I looked at the Old Man, hopeful, with my best puppy-dog face. There must be a way out of this. "That's not true, is it? It *is* possible for me to go give Alexis a hug, isn't it?"

"I'm afraid not. Let me show you." He got out a pad of paper.

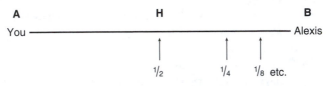

> *"Space isn't made up of individual things (parts) . . . [I]t gives to reality an infinite opportunity for division."*
>
> –Wittgenstein

> *"It is a paradoxical but profoundly true and important principle of life that the most likely way to reach a goal is to be aiming not at the goal itself but at some more ambitious goal beyond it."*
>
> Arnold J. Toynbee
> British Historian,
> 1889 –1975

> *"Math—the most logical of sciences—shows us that the truth can be highly counterintuitive and that science is hardly common."*
>
> –K.C. Cole

"You yourself admitted that *every journey has a halfway point*. So, every time you make it to a halfway point, you can be said to have started another journey. We certainly agree that once you get halfway from A to B, at H you'll have to go halfway from H to B. This continues, as philosophers say, *ad infinitum* –forever."

The logic seemed correct. Even though I knew I could get to Alexis, I wanted to prove it to him first. I do have to go halfway before getting anywhere. That's a fact. But this gave me a good idea.

I turned to him and said, "You see that tree over there, way behind Alexis? It's about twice as far from us as she is. So, I've changed my mind—I *now* want to go stand under that tree."

"Changed your mind?" the Old Man asked, smiling, realizing what I was trying to do.

"Yes. I'm going to that tree, okay? And in doing so, I'll have to go halfway. And," I bobbed my head back and forth a little, now even more excited to see Alexis, "while at that halfway point, I just might stay awhile before continuing my journey."

The Old Man took a deep breath, "It gets worse, Ian. Not only can you not reach your destination, but *all* motion is impossible. Look." And he drew again:

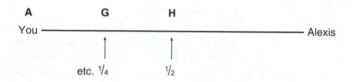

"In order to get to Alexis, we both agree that you must go halfway, or to H. *But*, in order to get to H, you must get halfway to that—the journey from A to H is just another journey. We'll call that point 'G'. As you can see, this works its way back to where you are now standing. You can never move. Change and motion really do seem totally paradoxical. Actually, they're impossible."

This seemed ridiculous. I could disprove this just by walking over to Alexis and giving her a hug. As I began, nothing happened. I didn't know what to do. It was as if someone had told me to make a rock move only by using my mind—it wasn't like I struggled against something, I just didn't move. I looked to the Old Man.

"Listen, Ian. I fear this theory might be right. I've got two pieces of evidence that seem to support it."

I looked towards Alexis and she looked back, perplexed.

The Old Man showed me his pad of paper. "First, as you know, we can repeatedly make these halfway divisions on the paper only until my pencil becomes thicker than the space left to divide. But that doesn't mean that the divisions stop there. If we get down to where there's only a centimeter left between the division and the destination, we can just take a photograph or make a photocopy of that segment and enlarge it. In doing so, we can go right back to the same procedure, dividing up halfway points until the distance became one centimeter thick and then enlarging again. This can go on forever."

I agreed, nodding slowly.

"So then, in order for you to ever get to Alexis, you'd have to somehow magically jump one of these distances. You'd have to *travel without traveling*. I'm sorry. I'll tell Alexis that this was out of your control. I'm

Motionless Arrows

Zeno's "Paradox of the Arrow":

1. *At any instant an arrow is motionless (imagine a photo).*
2. *A span of time is just a composition of instants.*
3. *THUS: During any span of time an arrow is motionless.*

Aristotle summarized Zeno's argument: "What is moving moves either in the place in which it is or in the place which it is not. And it moves neither in the place in which it is, nor in that which it is not. Therefore nothing moves."

So often times it happens that we live our lives in chains,
And we never even know we have the key.
—The Eagles, Musical group

sure she'd come over here, but, obviously, she's run into a similar problem." I looked up. Alexis was standing in the same spot, sadly, tilting her head. I looked around at all the others, expecting them to think this preposterous. Everyone was just standing there. No one was moving.

Maybe I would like a little time in that *cave* of false reality the Old Man mentioned earlier. Being here, not able to move, my only solace that 'at least I'm in *reality*' hardly seemed worth it.

Just then, I saw a dog walk right up to Alexis and lick her hand.

Wait a minute! How did *he* move?

Ian woke up to the sound of, "You want to come downstairs, son?" His mom yelled, "Breakfast is ready."

Ian deliberately stood up as if to work on perfecting his posture. He had a startled look as he walked into the kitchen, as if he hadn't slept at all, yet felt strangely refreshed. He walked over to his mom and hugged her. He smiled.

"Many people would sooner die than think. In fact, they do."
—Bertrand Russell

"Are you okay? Were last night's events traumatic?" she asked.

"No, not particularly. But troublesome. I think our whole 'logic' thing really may be flawed. Otherwise, there's no way I should have been able to do what I just did to you."

"We'd love to hear about it."

As he recounted the experience to his parents, his father shook his head slowly grumbling, "self-referential . . . self-referential," while his mother mumbled, "time and space . . . time and space." She smiled though, learning the significance of the morning's embrace.

"Is there a solution to these two problems —the test question and my motionless standing? Or are they unsolvable—just a fluke in our logic?"

"A fluke?"

"Well, yeah. Like with the test question. I mean, sentences about things must either be true or false. And sentences can't be true *and* false. The sentence on the test seems to avoid these two logical laws."

"Well, son, there are two problems with this sentence, and they reveal illuminating issues about language and logic.

The Principle of Biva- lence —any proposition is either true or false.
The Law of Noncontra- diction —any proposition cannot be both true and not true. Aristotle wrote, "One cannot say of something that it is and that it is not in the same respect and at the same time."

"First, let's look at Question One on your exam. This particular statement—which you're testing to determine its truth-value—refers to something other than itself: it refers to the sheet of paper. The second sentence on your exam refers to something other than itself: it refers to the janitor at your school. The third, to the test. The fourth, to the color of the sentence—and while this is *part* of the sentence, its color is something outside the sentence. But the fifth statement refers to itself. There is nothing outside itself which we can use to test. Thus, it is 'self-refer- ential.' It *is neither* true nor false."

"Self-referential?" Ian was obviously bothered by this. "Why is that so important?"

"Well, let's change the sentence a bit; we'll keep the structure the same and just change what it says slightly. This new formulation will take away the trick- iness of the true/false, false/true dilemma which you encountered."

"Okay. What is it?" Ian asked.

"This sentence is true."

"How do we know?" Ian quickly responded. "If it is true, then it is the case that the sentence is true and so the sentence would be true. If it's false, then it's not the case that the sentence is true and so it's false."

"Yes, but that's just the problem. The sen- tence refers to itself, not to something outside itself. There's no way to justify the truth or fal- sity of a self-referring statement. Statements

Wittgenstein explains the problem of "self-refer- ence":

"It is correct to say 'I know what you are thinking,' and wrong to say 'I know what I am thinking.'"

To "know" what one is thinking is self- referential. To "know" what another is thinking refers to something out- side oneself.

need to refer to something *outside* themselves in order to be judged as true or false. Look." He wrote: "The janitor has six arms."

"See how different this one is compared to, 'This sentence is true'? The second claim isn't grounded in anything outside itself. No outward criteria. Like, 'This sentence is meaningful,' or 'This sentence is meaningless.'

"There's nothing we can do with sentences that refer to themselves."

"Okay, I think I see that," Ian responded. "But it's funny, in a way. The sentence, 'This sentence is meaningful' refers to itself, so it should be meaningless, but it actually helps me understand this problem and, by doing that, it *does* have meaning."

His father nodded, proudly, smiling.

"So, dad, you said there were two reasons this statement was flawed."

"Yes, the second concerns something that you mentioned, albeit briefly, in your discussion of the true/false dilemma you encountered above. You said that a statement that isn't false is true."

"Isn't that right?" Ian responded. "Look at all the other questions. Even if you've never met the janitor at our school, Ron, you would know that he either *does* or *does not* have six arms. Likewise, the sheet of paper was either white or not. Every statement seems to be either true or false, even if you can't determine that right now."

"Yes, it does at first glance *seem* that way. Let me ask you, is it true that you've stopped kicking 'Opus the Dog' in the head?"

"Huh?" Ian got quickly defensive, and a bit confused by his dad's implications.

"Is the following statement true or false: 'Ian Pinkle has stopped kicking Opus in the head'?"

"But you know I would never do that."

"What *I* know is not the question. Tell me, is that true or false?"

"I don't think I want to answer that. Have you had dreams with a crazy old man in them who's planted questions for you to ask?"

"No, thankfully I've avoided him."

"But it seems that this statement here isn't true. I believe, and you say, that you've never kicked Opus in the head even once and, thus, you can't now *stop* something you never started."

"Exactly."

"But that would suggest that the statement is false. But if it's false that you've stopped, then that implies that you are *still* kicking her in the head, which isn't the case. Try these statements:

It is 3:00 on the moon.
Anchovy pizza is good.

"Are these statements either true or false?"

"I'm starting to get it. Though I wouldn't have thought that a sentence could be *neither* true *nor* false." He smiled for a moment, thinking through his new knowledge about language. He suggested, "I'm not so sure that really solves the problem, though. Because the statement was, 'This sentence is false.' So if it's neither true nor false, that means it's not false, so what it says is false?" He sat, smiling.

His father added, "Well, try to forget about all of this for now. Your school tends to like true-false exams. Assume—at least while taking these tests—that statements *are* either true or false."

Ian continued smiling.

His dad asked, "So why the question about me meeting with an Old Man, anyway?" He was half-joking, though somewhat concerned.

Ian looked up at him, obviously sensing the concern, yet also showing signs of becoming distraught as to why his dad should be concerned with a simple joke. "What do you mean, dad? I guess I was just joking with you because you asked me that weird question about Opus."

"Oh, ok," his dad responded, now somewhat relieved. "Good. Because I don't have anything to do with the Old Man, you know. After all, how could I?"

Ian smiled, seemingly more relaxed. This lasted only momentarily, as he then brought up the surprise exam that his teacher promised.

"No such thing," his dad quickly retorted.

Ian sneered at him, almost like a caricature of some cartoon character.

"Tell me," his dad started in immediately, "Can that exam be on Friday?"

Ian seemed unsure.

"Not if it's a *surprise* exam," his father quickly responded, answering his own question. "If you didn't have an exam Monday through

Logical Positivism

Founded in the 1920's by a group of academics in Austria known as the "Vienna Circle."

Logical Positivism posits the "verificationist principle"—in order for a statement to have meaning it must be testable and able to be verified. More strongly, for a statement to have meaning, its subject matter must be able to be verified by observation. Thus, for example, because we cannot test or verify moral statements, value judgments and, some argue, statements relating to God, they are neither true nor false.

The "Paradox of the Surface Exam" was first presented by philosopher W.V. Quine.

Designated ... and Unknown

Roy Sorenson explains a similar paradox involving the concept of a "Designated Student" (DS). Two features distinguish the DS from other students:

1. *They have a gold star pinned to their back, while the others have silver stars.*
2. *They do not know they are the DS.*

Five people stand in a line, with person five facing the back of four, four facing the back of three, etc. Obviously, person five would know if she were the DS as he could see the backs of persons four through one. Because of this, person four knows the DS can't be five, and thus, that it can't be her as she can also see the backs of persons three through one. This problem occurs for each person.

Thursday, then you'd *know* the exam was Friday. It certainly wouldn't be a surprise. So it can't be Friday."

Ian smiled, "Yeah, I agree. But that's only one of the days."

"True, but once you realize that it can't be Friday, then that only leaves four days, right?"

Ian nodded.

"We can apply the same logic to the remaining days. Given that the surprise exam can only be Monday through Thursday, if you haven't had the exam by Wednesday, then you'd know it would be Thursday. Again, you can't know about a surprise. That logic applies all the way to Monday. No surprise exam," he said tritely. "Good news, indeed."

Ian nodded, though somewhat subtly, as if not totally satisfied. "Okay, well, you're two for two," he paused. "But what about the third problem—what about our logic not even allowing for motion?"

"Well, son," his dad began, "this is just a problem of mathematics." As he was about to continue, his mom chimed in, "And, dear, it may have its real solution in one's view of space." His dad raised his eyebrows, curiously. "You begin, though, dear," she continued, "I'm curious to hear your solution first."

"Okay." He handed Ian a pen and paper. "Have you learned the Roman number system at all, son?" He nodded. He knew the basics.

"Let's see the Roman depiction for 'ten.'"
Ian wrote, "X"

"Good. How about 'twenty'?"
"XX"

"Yes. And 'one-hundred-and-three'?"
"CIII"

Ian was anxious, like he wanted his dad to ask the tricky ones, where you put the smaller numbers first and then they are actually *subtracted* from the big number instead of just added. But he never did.

Last he asked, "Let's see the Roman depiction for 'zero.'"

Ian sat blankly, thinking. He seemed disappointed in himself, as he thought he would pass this test with flying colors. Dejected, he looked up at his dad.

"Exactly, Ian. You passed with flying colors," he said, drawing a zero on his paper. "The Greeks, like the Romans, didn't have a zero in their system of mathematics. The zero didn't come around until years later, in 300 BC, when the Babylonians used it to differentiate between their numeric symbols. Although they only used the concept as a placeholder, it was a zero nonetheless: a lack of something. The Greeks didn't have this, so issues like the one you raise here were legitimate."

"Weird, dad. But what does this mean for us now?"

"Zero and infinity play on each other. They're very much related. But most importantly, the zero is needed to calculate what we call a 'limit.' And, when you get to high school, you'll see the importance of zero in what we call 'calculus.' We can use these things to solve this problem of motion you experienced."

Apparently this hadn't helped yet.

"Basically, calculus allows us to treat infinite sets of points as a whole. That's just what you're dealing with here, an infinite set of divisions within a finite distance. Within this infinite series of additions are finite distances, and they all approach a specific goal, or, limit.

"Kind of interesting, really. Without a proper set of mathematical axioms, we can't even allow for simple motion," he said, raising his eyebrows enthusiastically. "The Greeks didn't have this so it created problems –changed their view of reality in a way."

The History of Zero

300 BC: Babylonians use it as a placeholder.
300 BC: Euclid writes major math book, Elements, *though it deals only with geometry and not a number line.*
630: It appears as a number in Indian math, represented by a dot.
665: The Mayans use it as a placeholder.
1247: The Chinese begin to use the symbol "0" as a zero.
1876: Dewey Decimal System developed by Melvil Dewey. It included numbers from 000 –999 and is used to classify library book collections — subdivisions are designated by numbers after a decimal point.
Jan. 1, 2000: People celebrate the new millennium, though this was a celebration of only 1999 years since there was no "year zero."

The Lazy Eight: ∞

English mathematician John Wallis is credited with first using the "lazy 8" to represent infinity. He introduced it in his 1655 treatise, Arithmetica Infinitorum.

Numbers and Reality

Greek mathematician Pythagoras (c. 500 BC) is commonly known for the "Pythagorean theorem" (which relates the sides of a right triangle to each other). He noted:

"All is number."

"Numbers rule the universe."

"Number is the substance of all things."

"Numbers are the highest degree of knowledge. They are knowledge itself."

—Plato

"Dear," Ian's mom chimed in after listening patiently, "I realize that this use of zero, limits, and infinity is important in solving the problem, but it may help to think of it in terms of space. Even theoretically."

Ian and his father looked at each other, tilted their heads, shrugged their shoulders, and got ready for the theory to begin. Ian could tell that his dad really liked listening to his mom talk about these sorts of weird things in a smart way.

She began, "Nowadays, scientists and mathematicians use a term called a 'Planck Length' to represent what they believe to be an indivisible space: a space that can no longer be divided. It runs counter to what the scientists in ancient Greece thought, which was that space is infinitely divisible. We can think through the ramifications of this ancient way of thinking for ourselves. Okay?"

They nodded. They were ready.

"Okay. So, for the Old Man's sake, let's assume the following: space *is* infinitely divisible—it can be divided forever and ever, just like he suggested. This would need to be the case for his view to hold. Given this, a line must then be made up of an *infinite* number of segments. The problem is, what is the size of each segment? The only answers are," and she held up her right thumb,

A. Each segment has *no* size."

They nodded. She held out her left thumb. "Or . . .

B. Each segment has *some* size."

Very Small . . . and Very Quick

The Greek word "atom" derives from: a ("not") and tomos *("cut"). Some ancient Greeks held that the atom was "undividable."*

Today the Planck Length assumes the role of the indivisible. It is roughly equal to 1.6×10^{-35} m, which is about 10^{-20} times the size of a proton.

There is also a Planck Length of time, which is the shortest measurement of time. It equals the time it would take a photon of light traveling at light speed to cross the distance of a Planck Length. This time is equal to 10^{-43} seconds.

They nodded again.

She continued, "If it is 'A,' then the line would not exist: if you have segments of no size—*zero* length—then no matter how many you have, the length of the line would be zero. Anything multiplied by zero is zero. This seems absurd."

They nodded. Absurd.

"And if it is 'B,' then the line would be infinitely long. If you have an infinite amount of segments of any length then that would be infinity: anything multiplied by infinity is infinity. Equally absurd."

"Yes. An equal amount of absurdity," Ian remarked, playfully.

"The conclusion, then, is that space is not as the Old Man suggested. It is *not* infinitely divisible. We must get to a smallest particle—a Planck Length—which we can then cross over and give hugs to each other."

"But this distance—even if it's very small—must be *something*. So we just magically cross this?" Ian asked.

"Yes. A Planck Length."

Ian nodded his head affirmatively, though with a hint of lingering doubt. His dad got up, took four deliberate steps over to Ian's mom and hugged her. As they stood there, arm in arm, his mom finished, saying, "You know, Ian, I'm surprised your friend didn't take you inside a black hole up in space. In these things, where stars have collapsed, there is no time at all, and no space. Nothing ever reaches its destination there. Light can't even escape from it. There you would have a real problem getting a hug from Alexis." They smiled.

"I didn't even know what black holes were. Can a black hole be in my dream if I don't know what it is?" He paused.

"We talked about them last year on our night hike together, remember son?" his dad asked, hopeful. "Probably buried somewhere in that subconscious of yours with everything else you learn."

His mother changed her tone, "And now we've got to get going. I have a surprise for you when you get home Ian. And, now that you expect to get something when you get home, maybe I'll give you nothing, and *that* will be your surprise."

Black Holes

Black holes are formed when a star uses up all of its fuel. Then, the force of gravity on the outside of the star forces it to collapse upon itself. The effect is so powerful that it forms an infinitely dense area of matter, with a gravitational force so strong that not even light can escape from it.

Although the concept dates back to English geologist and astronomer John Michell (1724–1793), the term was coined by physicist John Wheeler in the 1960s.

"When I came home I expected a surprise and there was no surprise for me, so, of course, I was surprised."

–Wittgenstein

"Is this one of those not-so-instant-gratifi-cation-esque motherly ploys? Do you really have a surprise for me?"

"Yes, actually I do. I'll have a *surprise snack* ready for you when you get home."

Silent Lonesome Tree

As I walked out the door, I thought back to earlier visits with the Old Man. Some things I'd thought about a lot since then. Who would have thought that what we perceive is subjective? I'd been thinking about this for the past few days. How strange it is that we actually are part of what we perceive—that we play such an active role in what is out there. So I guess I got my answer to the big question:

If a tree falls in the forest and there's no one there to hear it, does it make a sound?

It doesn't. Hard to imagine, really. But, what we perceive is subjective. Sound is listener-dependent. Amazing. How's *that* for a *true* statement!

As I was walking and thinking, the road split into three—a three-pronged fork, I suppose. It made me think of my dislike for three-pronged forks. Four prongs are so much better: they hold more and can hold small things like rice. They can basically do everything a three-pronged fork can do and much more. They give you a twenty-five percent chance more that you'll stab what you're trying to stab.

As I looked up, I noticed that each of these roads ended at a sort of greenhouse—a big transparent dome with what looked like a dense forest inside. In front of each greenhouse stood a very official-looking man wearing a coat and tie.

So I walked to the dome at the end of the left prong of the fork. I said hello to the man. He nodded. Inside the dome were lions roaring, monkeys swinging through the air, leaves rustling. But we couldn't hear a thing outside. It was sealed and soundproof. Strange. I looked at the man with my eyebrows raised as if to say, "This is obviously a very strange exhibit you have here, and you know that I must be very curious as to why it's here, can't you just tell me?" Then he spoke: "Strange exhibit, isn't it?" I nodded. "You must be very curious as to why it's here." I nodded. He motioned with his head toward the forest. Just then, a large tree came crashing to the ground. I nodded. He went to the door of the exhibit and opened it. All the forest sounds came alive. He picked up a tape recorder and we walked out, closing the door behind us.

He pushed *play*. I heard a lion roar and then heard the squeaking of wood, the sound of brush crackling, and the loud thud of a tree hitting the forest floor. He turned to me, "No one was in there at the time of that falling tree. How do you account for this sound?" He walked away.

I walked quickly to the man at the middle prong. He must have the answer to this. When I got to him, he was with another official-looking man. The first man waved to me and signed to me in Sign Language with his hands. The second man translated, speaking plainly, "Hello. Welcome to Prong Two. Enjoy." Just then, an airplane flew nearby, behind the supposedly deaf person. He turned toward the sound and I raised my eyebrows—you didn't need to be much of an investigator to figure out that this person was just *posing* as a deaf person. I actually used to do this trick with Jeff's old dog. When you told it to sit, lie down, "bad," "no"—anything it didn't want to do—it ignored you as if it were deaf. Even when you'd sit behind it and say its name, it wouldn't turn around. But when you whispered the word "food" behind it, it would immediately turn around. Selective deafness is no deafness at all. Then the apparently deaf person began to sign again. The translator spoke, "I knew I heard something."

"How could you?" I asked the translator. It felt strange to say "you" to someone who I wasn't speaking to, but I assumed that's how you do it.

He responded, "For me, sound *is* the displacement of air molecules. That's all. That's all it really is anyway. For people with functioning inner ears, the molecules from that plane just vibrate a part of the inner ear and then the brain relates it to an airplane. I am just very sensitive to disturbances in the air. I *feel* them. *That's* sound—the displacement of air particles. It's all in your definition, really."

He turned and walked into the forest. Just then, a massive tree came crashing to the ground. Being outside, I didn't hear a thing. He came out, signing, "Wow. That was a loud *sound*."

"Sound?" I said. "It made a sound? But there was no one there to hear it."

He signed to me, "I was there. And air particles were definitely displaced. I felt them. It was quite a sound indeed."

And the two of them walked off. I yelled to them, but they pretended to be deaf.

Logically, then, I made my way to the third prong. I had become glad that this particular fork was only three-pronged. As I arrived, the official-looking man greeted me.

"Hello, young man," he began. "Please, could you explain to me the concept of a bicycle?"

Could he be serious?

"I'm serious."

Okay. That answered that.

"I have heard the term many times, though don't know what it is. I've often heard it described using such words as 'wheels,' 'handlebars,' 'pedals,' 'frame,' 'chain,' 'transportation.' But this never helps. Please describe the concept of bicycle without using those terms."

This is impossible. All those things together *are* the bicycle. What was I supposed to do here? This guy was really in trouble. Without having those things, bicycles would be impossible. "I'm sorry, sir." I really did want to help him. "But you need those things to describe a bicycle. Without those things, a bicycle would be incomprehensible. But we obviously do have bicycles—we've seen them everywhere. So I think you have asked me to do the impossible. Bicycles have to have those things."

"Thank you for your honesty," he replied. He was smiling. It was as though he was mocking me. So I figured I'd play along with him a little.

"Sir. Could you describe the concept of a falling tree for me please?" As he was starting to nod I continued, "But could you do it without including the concept of sound?"

That stopped his nodding in its tracks. "But, young man. Without sound, falling trees would be incomprehensible, impossible—we just plain wouldn't have falling trees. But *trees fall* all the time." Just then, he motioned into the soundproof forest chamber, just in time to see a tree come crashing to the ground. He nodded. "So, I think you have asked me to do the impossible. Falling trees *have to* have sound." And he walked away.

I turned to walk back down the handle of the fork. This fork seemed to overturn my original hypothesis, that lonely falling trees didn't make a peep. As I looked up at the handle, I saw one last official-looking man in front of a last forest-in-a-bubble. I was obviously intrigued by this one, because he wasn't there earlier. I approached him and he greeted me officially. He was holding a camera. He opened the door to the forest and we walked in. At least this time I'd be there for the inevitable falling tree. The forest, though, was amazingly quiet. No lions roaring. No monkeys screeching. Nothing.

Then he whispered, "Did you hear that?"

I shook my head. "No. Nothing happened."

"No? Look at my micro-camera." It showed leaves up close. They were rustling.

Well, I guess I just didn't hear the rustling leaves. Then he whispered again, "Did you hear *that*?"

I shook my head.

The video camera showed ants walking along the path. By definition, their little feet must be making noise, but a noise that my ears couldn't detect.

"What about *that*?"

More head shaking on my part. I couldn't imagine what he was going to show me this time. We looked in the camera. He bumped it up to *super magnification*. And there were two molecules colliding with each other. Couldn't quite hear them. I imagined that we were done with the exercise at this point.

He began, "So, is silence possible?"

"Of course. Why have the word if it's not possible? It was silent here in the forest, just now."

"Then you'd agree that you need someone to hear something in order for it to make a sound." He paused. "Correct?" He continued. "Because there were obviously things making sounds though you just didn't hear them. You need someone to hear something for it to make a sound."

"Yes, that seems to be right."

We walked out of the forest and he closed the soundproof door behind us. "So, if a tree falls in the forest and no one is there to hear it, does it make a sound?" I stood still. We turned. A tree fell. No sound. "Obviously not."

"If a ripe *lemon* is in the forest and there's no one there to see it, is it yellow? If a rose is in the forest and there's no one there to smell it, is it sweet?" I looked to the forest for a lemon and a rose. I turned back. He'd walked away.

Chapter 5

God

I'll have to believe it to see it.

–The New Yorker comic

DOROTHY: We want to see the wizard!

EMERALD CITY DOORMAN: The wizard? But nobody can see the great Oz, nobody's ever seen the great Oz. Even I've never seen him!

DOROTHY: Well then, how do you know there is one?

–The 1939 movie, The Wizard of Oz

I figured the Old Man and I were off to the classroom.

"So, I saw you with Alexis the other day you know," I said to the Old Man as we walked right past the school. I blurted it out without even thinking—probably somewhere subconsciously I knew that if I thought about confronting him I might not go through with it. I looked at him, trying to be strong.

"Oh yeah, I forgot to tell you that I ran in to her," he suggested, as if he really had forgotten that she was one of my best friends and that I kind of liked her. What was he trying to hide? And how could he just *run in* to her in *my* dream?

> *"All that we see or seem/ Is but a dream within a dream."*
>
> –Edgar Allan Poe

"Oh, nice," I said, so that he wouldn't suspect anything. "So what did you guys talk about?"

"The Final Excursion." He responded, nonchalantly, almost as if he forgot he *was* trying to hide something.

"The final excursion?" I asked. "What do you mean?"

"Oh, just some chatter. You know, what her last outings have been like. Just stuff. You know."

I didn't know, and it looked like he had his guard back up. He changed the subject, "Quite a surprise snack yesterday, eh?"

"Hardly." How could he think I was surprised by apples and cheese? "I have apples and cheese *every* day when I get home."

"So didn't it surprise you then? You were expecting the unexpected. And because of that, you got what you *least expected*. Sounds like quite a surprise to me!" He laughed as though he had put my mom up to it. I suppose I *was* surprised in a way.

Apparently we had arrived at our destination. We walked up to the front door of what looked like a regular house. I assumed it was the Old Man's. Inside there was a living room. In it a TV, two seats, carpet. It was very plain. And now it was time for lesson number *who-knows* about *who-knows-what*. The Old Man went to the TV and turned it on. It was the top of the hour—I could tell because the minute hand of the clock on the wall was on the "twelve," though there was no hour hand. The voice-over announced the upcoming program.

"Whew. Just in time," the Old Man sighed, halfheartedly.

Of course we were just in time. After all, he was in charge. If he wanted us to miss the program, we'd miss it. If he wanted me to almost win "Student of the Decade," then I'd almost win. If he wanted us to turn on the program *just in time* then, well, here we are.

"I think you're really going to like this, Ian. I've been waiting a long time to see this interview."

Of course I'll like it.

The program began. The music was very dramatic, and the broadcaster sat there, seeming nervous, though proud, awaiting his cue. After the music died down, the camera zoomed in and the broadcaster welcomed us. "Today we will be a part of broadcasting history. Something never before attained at any level, by any medium.

"In a recent poll, when people were asked to whom they would most like to speak, living or dead, real or imaginary, 72 percent responded, 'God.' Today we will come closer to that than ever imagined. I will sit with God's agent, his right- and left-hand man, the man behind the scenes. People have pursued him for ages—eternity really—and we are fortunate enough to have him with us here today." The Old Man looked at me, eyebrows raised, smiling, nodding.

"I admit, this is pretty cool," I said.

Then the music came up, the camera panned out and he continued, "It gives me great pleasure to have God's Agent here today." Out walked a man dressed all in white: white shoes, slacks, button-down shirt, white belt, necklace. He looked like an average person. Nothing special. Though he did have sort of an aura about him. I was excited to hear what he had to say.

BROADCASTER: Welcome. It is such a great honor to have you entrust God's word with me and my listeners today. I know you are extremely busy creating universes, working on heaven admissions, building souls. Let's get right to it, shall we?

GOD'S AGENT: Yes, thank you. Thank you for having me. God and I decided that the people need some answers to all the questions they've had throughout the years. People are naturally curious—I should know, I see them constructed and see how their brains are built. You know, we actually built the brain such that it naturally seeks to investigate the world around it—we really created all humans to be philosophers. I think the name some of you have given to this is the "cognitive imperative." You guys come up with some great names for things. This is just the brain's way of making sense of the world. Ironically, it was with the advent of *this* thing—*the television*—that people started ignoring their cognitive imperative; they started to ignore their innate desire to learn, and they let the television do their learning for them. It's much easier for them. You know, one of our creations—you all called him "Plato"— referred to this as staying in a

Try not to think.
The Cognitive Imperative (CI):
An automatic, involuntary process in the brain. If there is too much going on, the CI will immediately categorize it. If there is not enough going on, the CI will create complexity. Try not to think, and the CI will think for you.

"All human beings, by nature, desire to know."
    –Aristotle

A Cave with No Books. . .
In Ray Bradbury's novel, Fahrenheit 451, *he portrays a society that burns all books. The leaders reason that people thinking on their own makes them unhappy. So they eliminate porches, gardens, and rocking chairs and replace them with big TV's on their walls, filling them with countless irrelevant facts.*

"You ask why *to a lot of things and you wind up very unhappy indeed," one character says. "If you don't want a man unhappy politically, don't give him two sides to a question to worry him; give him one. Better yet, give him none."*

cave, chained down, watching only the shadows of reality. He was on to this idea way before the television came around. Because it is easier on the eyes to stay in the cave, people would do so and avoid learning about reality. Quite literally, they were blinded by the light. [Chuckles] It's much easier to sit and watch TV, to sit in a cave. This, God and I find interesting, seeing as how you were all designed to see the light, and to like it. That's why we're so excited by the institution of philosophy: humans doing what they were made to do. Anyway, sorry about that. I spend so much time with God that when I finally get away I really become quite a chatter box.

B: Of course. This is all very interesting. You're uniquely insightful. I want to start with a quick question, one about which I know many of our viewers are curious. Why did God send you, his only agent?

GA: Well, He and I talked about this. It was really a difficult decision and we had to be careful about how we handled it. You see, we realize there are many religions—and this topic is really a Pandora's Box for me, as you could well imagine. There are just so many questions and we want to help people out with this. We don't want to give them *everything*, but just a few insights to help them out. Instead of providing them with the *knowledge* that God exists, we give them the gift of *faith*.

B: Got it. But couldn't science eventually prove God's existence—give people that *knowledge* you speak of?

GA: One might think so. A number have tried, though a definitive proof seems very unlikely. And as I'm sure you know, science has its own little set of rules and may not be the exclusive means for knowing about the true universe. It excludes the metaphysical by definition. But don't you all think that the existence of an intelligent designer is obvious? I mean, the odds that all of this would just *happen*—by *chance*—are astronomically low.

Think about it: the Earth and the humans that inhabit it are exquisitely constructed for life. There are millions—actually billions—of things that have to be *just so* for humans to exist. The exactness of hydrogen for example, or your planet located within the spiral of a galaxy just the

---

Intelligent Design

Eighteenth-century archbishop William Paley presented the "Argument from Design." He used the analogy of a watch: if you found a watch on the beach, it would seem unlikely that all of its parts just came together by chance, especially given that it exhibits such order and design. Instead, like the ordered universe, we think it had a creator.

What Are the Odds?

Some scientists estimate the odds of our universe happening by chance as somewhere between 1 in 10^{53} and 1 in 10^{112}. (10^{62} is the number of atoms in a trillion planets the size of Earth.) This supports the "Anthropic Principle"— that the conditions in the universe needed for our existence have to be exactly as they are. A slight difference in the weight of any specific atom or in the force of gravity and life as we know it would not exist. Thus, the universe seems to be designed specifically for humans.

Theoretical physicist Paul Davies writes, "The impression of Design is overwhelming."

---

right distance from a perfectly hot star, and the millions of chemical pathways in your body that need to function exactly the way they do— and I mean *exactly*, down to the nth degree.

B: [Nods. Wide-eyed.]

GA: You didn't really think this perfection came into existence through a bunch of random mutations do you? Off the record, what do you really think?

B: Well we're really not off the record right now [he gestures towards the camera]. And anyway, I don't really know at this point.

GA: Okay. Well I'm also curious as to how you all think that some of these complex organs of yours could just evolve out of nowhere. For evolution to occur, one individual must have some sort of advantage over another, right? So he is selected—chosen by nature, we could

---

A Critique of Evolutionary Science

In Jonathan Sarfati's book, Refuting Evolution, *he cites two critiques of the theory of evolution:*

1. Science is like a game with rules that prohibit creationists from "playing." He quotes evolutionary scientist Richard Dickerson: "Science is fundamentally a game . . . with one overriding and defining rule: . . . Let us see how far and to what extent we can explain the behavior of the physical and material universe in terms of purely physical and material causes, without invoking the supernatural."

2. Science too requires faith. Loren Eiseley writes: "The philosophy of experimental science . . . began its discoveries and made use of its methods in the faith, not the knowledge, that it was dealing with a rational universe controlled by a creator who did not act upon whim nor interfere with the forces He had set in operation . . . . It is surely one of the curious paradoxes of history that science, which professionally has little to do with faith, owes its origins to an act of faith that the universe can be rationally interpreted, and that science today is sustained by that assumption."

say—for having a better chance to survive. By surviving, he passes on his genes and thus his advantageous physical traits.

B: Sure [nodding in agreement].

GA: But how would this happen with a complex organ that needs to be fully intact to function? First I want you to look at these two mouse-traps here [he pulls out two piles of pieces and puts them on the table]. This one on the left has the *spring* and the *hammer* and the *catch*, but no *holding bar* and no *platform* for holding it all. This one on the right has all of that but, in addition, it has a *platform*.

B: [Nods, staring at the piles of metal curiously.]

GA: Which will catch more mice?

B: Neither, I suppose. You need all five pieces for it to work. They are both pretty much useless.

GA: Exactly. If these were like organs of an animal, the animal on the right would have no advantage over the animal on the left, at least in regards to that particular organ. Yet, there *are* organs like this.

Take the eye, for example. I won't bore you with the details, though I happen to find them amazing. But in order for an eye to properly function, it requires that a great many pieces be in place. For simplicity, let's say that the eye needs 100 components or ingredients to allow for vision—the iris, cornea, retina, ion channels, optic nerve, specific proteins, molecules, and so much more. So, an individual with an eye containing 44 of these ingredients would have no advantage over one with an eye containing 43 of them. That being said, the individual with 44 wouldn't see *more* than the one with 43—he wouldn't catch more prey, or have a greater chance to avoiding being eaten, etc. Basically, he wouldn't have any sort of advantage

---

Too Complex for Darwin?

Biochemist Michael Behe explains irreducible complexity—*"an apparatus that requires several distinct components for the whole to work." He gives the example of a simple mousetrap with five parts, all of which need to exist and function for the trap to work—a trap with four parts is as successful (i.e. totally unsuccessful) as a trap with three. Because there are so many examples of this in nature (e.g. the eye, cilium, etc.) he writes, "Natural selection is powerless when there is no function to select. We can go further and say that, if the cilium can not be produced by natural selection, then the cilium was designed."*

He quotes Darwin in hopes to show that even he would agree with this: "If it could be demonstrated that any complex organ existed which could not possibly have been formed by numerous, successive, slight modifications, my theory would absolutely break down."

over the other. So there's no good reason to think he would have a better chance to pass his genes along. And there are numerous examples like this throughout the organic universe, examples in which *all* the components are needed for the organ or entity to function, including considerably more simple things than the eye—like basic proteins or even the cilia that serve to transport fluid on cells.

Since it is so unlikely that these things *evolved*, I think it's considerably more likely that these organs and features were designed. By a designer, of course. And intelligent, at that.

God's a smart guy. Infinitely smart, really.

B: I imagine so. Thank you for sharing. And that really touches on the heart of our time here today. You see, human beings have a difficult time comprehending qualities like "all-knowing," "all-powerful," "all-good." Today, I'd like to focus on these three attributes of God and see if you could help shed some light on these concepts.

GA: Of course.

B: So, is it true that God is, in fact, omnipotent?

GA: Omnipotent. Love it. You guys really come up with some good ones. *All-powerful.* Yes. God can do anything.

B: Well, I'd ask if he can just create a universe, but it seems that he's already done that.

GA: Yes. We're very proud of it. It is good.

B: Could God make this interview interesting? [Pause] Well, he's done that too. [Laughter] How about, could God give man a tool that might help him to better cope with the world?

GA: He's actually done that numerous times. Let's see. We have this video entitled, "The Wheel." [Camera pans to a caveman sitting next to a pile of boulders. The screen reads "3500 BC." He seems dejected. Just then, we see God nod his head deliberately. The caveman says "Aha!" and puts the boulders on a fallen tree and rolls it. Another comes along and adds an axle and a third adds wooden pegs that allow the wheels to move and transport the boulder.]

Spinoza writes of humans' view that everything was made perfectly to suit their existence: "eyes for seeing, teeth for chewing, plants and animals for food, the sun for light, the sea for supporting fish . . . Hence they consider all natural things as means to their advantage. So, looking at the universe as the means to my end (my own advantage) I come to hold that the universe must have been made for that purpose. And if it was made for that purpose, it did not make itself but rather was made by a ruler of Nature, endowed with human freedom, who had taken care of all things for men, and makes all things for their use."

B: Wow. He works in mysterious ways. Looks like you have a whole library of those films.

GA: Actually, yes. Here's the "Safety Pin" videotape. Microwave. Typewriter. Did you know that the placement of the keys was initially done to *slow down* the typing so that the first typewriters wouldn't jam. Let's see here, what else. Hmm, lasers. Penicillin. You all think that was a fluke. God all but shouted this one out, putting moldy penicillin on Fleming's work bench killing all the surrounding bacteria. Then there's sliced bread, of course, everyone's standard for inventions. Let's see here. Ahh, the frisbee. And . . .

B: [Nodding emphatically, hoping to stop the barrage of examples.] He really works in mysterious ways. He really does.

GA: Quite true. You know, because God is omnipotent, he really can do anything. So, for any question that begins, "Can God . . . "—and then you fill in the blank—the answer will be "Yes, God can do that." He is, as you say, omnipotent.

B: Well, then, here's a question sent in by one viewer. This one is from someone who calls himself, "The Man in Your Dreams." I guess he wants to remain anonymous. I suppose only God knows who this is [he chuckles]. It reads, "Can God create a rock so heavy that He can't lift it?"

GA: Well, of course He can do that. God can do anything.

B: [Now somewhat anxious.] Yes. But I fear there are some pretty serious complications that arise from answering this question positively. [A pause, as though he'd hoped the Agent would realize this for himself. Silence.] You see, if God can do that, then it appears he's created something that he can't do, namely, lift the rock. Yet, if there is something that God cannot do, that renders him as *not* omnipotent.

GA: True, I suppose. Well, we can't have that. So the answer must be an emphatic, *no*.

B: [Looks from side to side as if in need of assistance.] But isn't that problematic too? If God is really all-powerful, then he should be able to do anything, not just *most* things. After all, this question *was* phrased in the form, "Can God . . . "

GA: Right again. I suppose we're stuck on this one. Maybe we should move on to the next attribute of God, if you don't mind.

B: Yes, of course. [He appears somewhat dejected.] Okay, well I'm very interested to hear about this one: omniscience. What is it like working with someone who knows everything?

GA: It's a very humbling experience. Though amazingly enriching. Did you know that the Earth weighs 5.97 times 10^{24} kilograms?

B: Now that's an interesting bit of knowledge. Did he know if Oedipus would actually marry his own mother?

GA: Of course. God knows everything. He knows that Oedipus will marry his own mom. [Camera pans to Oedipus who proclaims, "I will never marry my mother."] Now watch this. [Later, we see Oedipus on one knee, in front of his mother, asking, "Jocasta, will you marry me?"]

B: He really knows all. Does God know about everyone? Everything? How about this: does God know what flavor ice cream Ian Pinkle will order today?

GA: Let's see. Ian Pinkle. Ah yes, curious little fellow. He's being trained right now for, let's see ... what was is that he was being trained for ... ?

B: Oh, never mind telling us about Ian. [He looks to the camera and dejectedly mouths the word, "sorry."] Could you just tell us if God knows what flavor ice cream he is going to get today?

GA: Certainly. Chocolate. I'll even get God to sign his name to that. [He goes behind the curtain and there is a strange noise. He comes back with a slip of paper and hands it to the broadcaster.]

King Oedipus by **Sophocles, 425 BC**

Oedipus is told by the future-telling Oracle of Apollo that he will kill his father and marry his mother. He strongly disapproves and does all he can to avoid this fate. Yet, in the end, he unknowingly fulfills this prophecy: he kills his father as a passerby on the road and then, after solving the Riddle of the Sphinx, he is dubbed king and given the hand of the recently widowed Jocasta, his mother.

Thus the term, "The Oedipus Complex," in which Freud posited that sons subconsciously desire their mothers and view their fathers as competition.

[Ian stands up. "Wait a minute. I wasn't even going to get ice cream today. But this trip will be worth it. I have a chance to prove God as not all-knowing." He runs out of the house.]

[Camera follows Ian to the ice cream store. He rushes in and asks for a strawberry ice cream cone. "A double," he says emphatically, looking up, smiling. He walks back to the home and finishes his cone. He looks at the Old Man, nods his head proudly, and sits down. Then the camera goes back to the interview.]

B: [Slightly uncomfortable.] Well, everyone makes mistakes.

GA: Read the signature I handed you.

B: [He unfolds the sheet of paper, and reads.] "Not only will Ian get ice cream today, but he'll go against his natural inclination to order chocolate and will instead order strawberry." It's signed, "God." Truly amazing. It seems that God *does* know everything.

GA: [Nods.]He's pretty amazing.

B: Now, the obvious question must then follow. If God knows—I mean *really knows*—what I will do, or what flavor Ian will order, then in what sense do we act freely? There is a lot of hype about our apparent free will. Free will seems to be a major tenet of almost all religions and moral systems. It's obviously important in the story of Adam and Eve, and determining who gets into heaven. But, to what extent does man have free will if it seems that he couldn't do otherwise?

GA: Is that really a problem for you?

B: Sure. Since God can't be wrong, then Ian couldn't have ordered anything *but* strawberry ice cream. So to what extent did he *choose* it?

GA: Maybe Ian could have changed his mind at the last second and ordered chocolate.

B: That's just my point. If Ian had done that, then God would have been wrong—he wouldn't know everything. *That* obviously can't be the case. So, in *all* instances where humans make decisions, it seems that they couldn't choose any differently than God knows they'll choose. If God *knows* Ian will order strawberry ice cream today, it doesn't seem as though Ian could *choose* to do any other thing. That doesn't seem like free will at all.

GA: [Nodding slightly.] I'm afraid that's all I have time for. Many works to be accomplished . . . only eternity to do them. I know we still have

All-Knowing God *and* Free Will?

"Man, like a feather in the wind, cannot have will, ability or choice. All events and human acts are created by God. It is not true to say man has his own acts; rather he has them metaphorically. For instance, when we say the tree bears fruit, the water flows, or the sky rains, truly it is God who performs the acts of tree, water and sky."

–Jahm ibn Safwan (d. 746)
Islamic theologian

"If God foresees all things and cannot in anything be mistaken, that, which His Providence sees will happen, must result . . . just as, when I know a present fact, that fact must be so; so also when I know of something that will happen, that must come to pass. Thus it follows that the fulfillment of a foreknown event must be inevitable."

–Boethius
(AD 480–524)

one attribute left, but God is obviously all-good so we needn't spend time on that. Thank you for having me. It was nice to meet you. Be kind to one another.

I sat there, entranced, enlightened, a little dejected. "That was an amazing interview. It seems as though there are a lot of inconsistencies surrounding God's possible existence. My family believes in God. I think I believe in God. Well, I did believe in God until all of this. How can we even have morality—right and wrong—if there's no God? There are just so many issues. And we didn't even get to the last one."

"Well, Ian, we'll get to that last issue later. We can start to see that the concept of God may just be a manmade creation. Or, at the least, He may not have the qualities that many people believe Him to have. Are you upset by all this?"

"No. No, it's fine. It's good to know, I suppose. I don't want to wager on something that's not the case. I guess I'm just surprised that no one has ever brought this up to me before."

I felt sad about this overwhelming feeling that God was not real. "But I've read that as people grow older, they tend to develop a stronger sense of God's existence. As they learn more and more, as they become wiser, they start to realize that God *does* exist. Maybe I should listen to them. They say you can learn a lot from your elders."

"I've read those surveys too. Though I draw a different conclusion. As people get closer to the end, closer to death, they *want* it to have been for something. People desperately want their lives to mean something. And, more importantly, they don't want the impending end to be the end of it all, they

"Religion is the opiate of the masses."

Karl Marx here argues that organized religion provides a vehicle with which people can find comfort in their suffering. In a sense, this allows them to be complacent regarding their place in life; religion serves as an "opiate"—a drug that sedates and eases pain.

But he goes further, claiming that people's suffering is the result of an oppressive, materialistic society: "Religious suffering is at one and the same time the expression of real suffering and a protest against real suffering. Religion is the sigh of the oppressed creature, the heart of a heartless world and the soul of soulless conditions." Thus, religion is needed to cope with the true suffering experienced at the time.

He believed that by overcoming the alienation imbedded in a capitalist, class system, this would diminish the suffering. Then, organized religion would fade because, as he wrote, "Man makes religion, religion does not make man."

want more. They want an afterlife. They want to go on to something greater. The whole concept just reduces their fear of the unknown and justifies all their struggles. People do this all the time. Some athletes put their right shoe on first before every game or they will carry the foot of a rabbit with them—this just gives them some comfort in the upcoming event. It helps them deal with uncertainty, with fear. No one really thinks that putting your right sock on first will help you throw a ball into a net. People create their reality. That's what self-fulfilling prophecies are all about. The notion of God does all this for people."

I shook my head.

Ian trampled downstairs shaking his head. "Mom. Dad. I'm sure you'll have some witty answers to all this, but this one's pretty tough. And it might be a little upsetting for you also, but I need to share it." He explained the whole interview to them, repeatedly wishing he could have taped it so they could have seen it for themselves. He told them about the problems with God's being omniscient and omnipotent. He could tell they were a little surprised, though they nodded their heads with the same confidence as with all the other dreams he had relayed to them.

"So what do you think? Pretty bad, huh?"

His parents whispered a few things to each other, nodding, smiling. His father began, "Ian, you've brought up two of the major arguments that depict God's alleged existence as paradoxical. I'll say his *alleged* existence for now, as you seem to have confidence in the claims made against it. Let's take them one at a time, as you presented them. I think the first problem was the rock-making-and-lifting you mentioned in relation to God's omnipotence."

"Yeah, that God *can't* do everything."

"Yes, let's look at that. You seem to have created a sort of 'catch-22' for *any* all-powerful being. I have a few things I want you to think about. First—and this is a major flaw with this paradox—it's logically impossible. You're asking that something all-powerful do something that can't be done by *any* being, all-powerful or not.

"Imagine that you asked God to make a round square." He paused. "Think about that. It's logically impossible. As soon as you curve a square you no longer have a square, or square a curve and you no longer have a circle. But we wouldn't imagine that the lack of ability to create a round square would really render an alleged all-powerful being not all-powerful."

Now Ian looked more content.

"Okay, secondly." A pause for suspense. "God probably *could* create a round square."

Ian flashed his *what-in-the-world* look, eyebrows raised.

"Well, first of all, the terms 'square' and 'circle' are just human terms. It's hard to imagine that squares as such would exist if we weren't around. *We* defined them. Remember how you told me that God's Agent laughed to himself about our terms for things, and the problem that 'grue' showed us—that we create words to describe the world around us? These are just human things. Finite minds. Mere mortals. But God is infinite. Even if He allowed himself to be caught up in our mortal language and logic, I bet he could find a way to make a round square."

> *"Contemplation . . .
> makes us citizens of the
> universe, not only of one
> walled city at war with
> all the rest."*
> –Bertrand Russell

---

*Logically impossible
things:*

*Round squares.
Married bachelors.
Headaches that don't
   hurt.
Four-sided triangles.
An all-powerful being
   creating a being more
   powerful than itself.*

*Aquinas explained
that an all-powerful
God doesn't "need" to
be able to perform
actions that are
inherently
contradictory: "Nothing
that implies a
contradiction falls under
the scope of God's
omnipotence."*

Can God be both infinitely just and infinitely merciful?

Fifteenth-century Bishop Nicholas of Cusa writes that not only can *this be, but that it* must *be. He applies what he calls the "coincidence of opposites." Because of God's infinite nature, He can maintain opposing qualities.*

If one were to walk along the path of an infinitely big *circle it would be straight yet simultaneously curved as well.*

Why it might *not* be a problem that God can't create a rock He can't lift:

1. *It's logically impossible.*
2. *God is not constrained by mortal language.*
3. *An all-powerful being doesn't need to be able to do this.*
4. *God can create a rock of any weight and can lift a rock of any weight.*

His mom chimed in here. "You know Ian, God has been explained as both infinitely just *and* infinitely merciful. But, with these words of ours, this is completely contradictory. If He's infinitely just, then He will always punish wrongdoers, yet if He's also infinitely merciful, then He will always forgive wrongdoers. But that shouldn't necessarily be a shortcoming of God. You see that?"

"Yeah. Yeah I do, I suppose." He seemed slightly relieved and now somewhat optimistic that his parents might be able to continue this throughout the entire line of argument. "But couldn't we say, 'Make a round square and *don't* change the meanings of *round* and *square*?' *Then* he couldn't do it."

"Funny. You're really taking this to a new level, Ian. I have three quick responses for you. One, God could just change the meaning of 'change' and 'meaning.' Two, even if our words' meanings changed, that wouldn't change the *actual* roundness of an *actual* circle. And three, it doesn't matter." He paused. "Listen. The best soccer player in the world doesn't need to be able to make a soccer ball. Likewise, an all-powerful being doesn't need to be able to make round squares.

"It's very similar to this favorite drummer of mine when I was a kid. This guy was amazing—considered the best by anyone who knew anything about music and drumming. I always joked about him saying, 'I bet he's not capable of playing poorly.' Because he'd been drumming at such a high level for so long—and in my mind *could do anything* on the drums—it turned out there was one thing he couldn't do: play poorly. He was so good that he couldn't play badly! This was obviously a joke because it was solidifying his excellence. No one really considered that a limitation of his prowess."

"Okay. I get that." He got it.

"Okay, then. Lastly, look at the logic implicit in the demand. The claim 'God cannot create a stone that He cannot lift,' is equivalent to another claim: 'Every stone that God can create He can lift.' Do you see that? If there is no stone that God can't lift, then it would also be the case that God can't create a stone that he can't lift. So it turns out that God, being all-powerful, *can* create a rock of any weight *and* God can lift a rock of any weight. You see?"

While Ian seemed proud of his father's solution, he was at the same time apprehensive about the other issue that remained. "Yeah, that all makes sense. But now what about the problem with him being all-knowing?"

His dad started right in again. "Yes Ian, let's see if we can make humans' free will and God's omniscience able to coexist. As you mentioned, once you look at the issue, it seems impossible for both," he held out his right thumb, "God to be all-knowing *and*," left thumb, "for you to have absolute free choice." Ian nodded again.

"First, I want to look at what it means for God to *know* you were going to get strawberry ice cream. I think you'd agree with me that someone's knowing that 'X' will happen doesn't necessarily *cause* X to happen." Ian looked confused. "Take the weather, for example. When the weatherman says there is a hundred percent chance of rain, and then it rains, we don't think he caused the rain. Likewise, if you went back in time and then announced that World War II would happen, we wouldn't say that you caused World War II."

"True."

"And this leads to my second point. Quite simply, God knows you well. Very, very well. So well, that He knows you're an inquisitive one who likes to push the envelope a bit. He knew you were watching the interview, and He knew that you'd like nothing more than to prove God wrong. He may even know you better than you know yourself. But that doesn't mean that He's making you do things. He can both know what you're going to do and allow you the ability to choose it. This is just one of the perks, I suppose, to being all-knowing.

"Plus, let's look at God's view of us. Because He is also eternal, he likely sees us in a different way than we see ourselves here.

How can God know everything *and* humans still choose freely?

1. *Knowing something will happen doesn't necessarily cause it to happen.*
2. *God knows each person very well.*
3. *God is outside of time and can see things more like we see a movie.*
4. *God doesn't know the future because it doesn't exist (yet).*

Predestined

John Calvin, whose doctrines are adhered to by the Presbyterian Church, wrote that God exists separately from human time. This clarified the suggested conflict between free will and God's omniscience:

"When we attribute foreknowledge to God, we mean that all things . . . perpetually remain, before His eyes, so that to His knowledge . . . all things are present, and present in such a manner, that He . . . beholds and sees them as if actually placed before Him."

He notes that God's "timelessness" explains why no one can change their destiny—God has, "determined in Himself what would have to become of every individual of mankind."

Theoretical physicist Stephen Hawking writes, "The odds against a universe like ours emerging out of something like the big bang are enormous. . . . I think clearly there are religious implications whenever you start to discuss the origins of the universe. There must be religious overtones."

One could imagine that an eternal God, who knows all, and who can see the past and the future, views the universe much like we view a film. He's outside our boundaries of time and space. He can see what we're going to do ahead of time. This doesn't mean He causes it. He just sees it. Because He's all-powerful, He's able to provide us with free will and still maintain his omniscience."

Ian then said proudly, "I think you guys covered all the problems brought up in my dream. I hope I can remember all this to share with the Old Man. And all of your suggestions actually helped me to think of one more."

His parents sat with a look of anticipation.

Ian continued, "It's logically impossible— just like the stone example. The future doesn't even exist, so how could we expect anyone to know something that doesn't exist?"

His parents nodded and smiled in reaction to Ian's thought.

"But I am a little sad that we still don't have an actual proof of God," Ian said, his tone changing a bit. "We just have arguments against arguments against Him. Is it true that scientists have proved His existence?"

"Well Ian, this is a big area of study in biology and physics. Many scientists argue that it's an amazingly small possibility that the universe happened by chance. For example, if I flipped a coin a thousand times and each time it landed on heads, the odds are *very* small that this *just happened* by chance. What would you think probably happened?"

"That something—or someone—affected the coin. Maybe you tricked us and flipped it at the last second to make sure it was heads. Or maybe someone made the coin so that it always landed heads."

"Exactly. You would think that there was some outside force and not just pure chance. That's the same with this universe argument."

Ian nodded and smiled.

"But," his dad said, pausing to let Ian down slowly, "if there *were* some explosion—like a big bang—then *something* had to result. Doing the odds this way—the odds of this *exact* universe resulting—is kind of backwards. There had to be something."

Ian frowned. A half-sad, half-confused frown.

His dad unscrewed the light bulb from the lamp in the kitchen. He looked at Ian's mom and smiled. He dropped the bulb to the floor and, with a *pop*, it broke.

He turned to Ian, "Now, what are the odds that all these pieces landed exactly where they did?"

Ian shook his head, unknowingly.

"Here's the real issue, Ian: if you had told me ahead of time that these twenty pieces of glass would land exactly where they did, in these shapes, then *that* would have been amazing. The odds of that would be astronomically low. But when the bulb broke, the pieces *had to* land somewhere. The odds that they'd land where they did are, well, 100 percent—the bulb broke and the pieces landed."

Ian nodded his head, though he had a somewhat let down look on his face. He was proud of his dad for this insight, and upset that yet another proof had been foiled.

"You know son, a lot of this results from our inability to conceptualize very big numbers and very small probabilities."

Ian shook his head, his hair bouncing along with it, awaiting the forthcoming conclusion.

"The Flip of a Coin"

The probability of flipping a coin 10 times and it landing "heads" (H) on each flip is 1 in 1,024.

The probability of flipping a coin 10 times and it landing in the following order—HHTTHTHTTT—is the same: 1 in 1,024.

The probability of flipping a coin 10 times and it landing heads or tails each time is 1 in 1: by flipping a coin, something will show each time it lands.

"In retrospect, everything is 100 percent probable. You flipped the coin once and it landed on heads—one out of one times."

–Anonymous

"Our brains were designed to understand hunting and gathering, mating and child-rearing: a world of medium-sized objects moving in three dimensions at moderate speeds. We are ill-equipped to comprehend the very small and the very large."

–Richard Dawkins

The Blind Watchmaker

World-renown biologist Richard Dawkins notes the problem with Paley's "Intelligent Watchmaker" analogy. He explains that humans result from small, cumulative changes over a very long period of time. This process involves changes that result from an organism's ability to adapt to its environment. It is thus non-random, as it is based on the organism's ability to survive.

"The analogy . . . between watch and living organism, is false . . . the only watchmaker in nature is the blind forces of physics. . . . A true watchmaker has foresight . . . [but] natural selection, the blind, unconscious, automatic process which Darwin discovered . . . has no purpose in mind."

"Let's do some speculation. Many scientists estimate—roughly, of course—that the odds of life appearing on a planet are one in a trillion. Pretty low odds, right?"

Ian nodded, his hair now bouncing forward and backward.

"I agree," his dad said. "But, what if there were a billion planets? Wouldn't that make it at least somewhat likely—given our earlier odds—that life *would* exist somewhere?"

Ian shrugged and continued nodding.

His dad added, "And it's been estimated by some astronomers that there are even more than one billion planets in the universe. So, given that our planet—and many another planet—has been around for billions of years, that seems like ample time for life to appear. Actually, given all of that, we should even expect it to appear.

"Plus," his father continued, leaning back a bit as if to suggest something a bit less technical, "What makes you think *you*—the human being—*had to* exist? What's so special about us? You know, she who writes history gets to put herself at the top. We're the ones doing the

It's Meant To Be . . .

Douglas Adams once asked his audience to imagine the thoughts of a puddle. He parodied the puddle's view of the hole that contains it:
" . . . fits me rather neatly, doesn't it? In fact it fits me staggeringly well, must have been made to have me in it!" Adams then added, "This is such a powerful idea that as the sun rises in the sky and the air heats up and as, gradually, the puddle gets smaller and smaller, it's still frantically hanging on to the notion that everything's going to be alright, because this world was meant to have him in it, was built to have him in it; so the moment he disappears catches him rather by surprise. I think this may be something we need to be on the watch out for."

writing, so we put ourselves at the top—understandably so. But it's just *our* version of the story. We think that the universe displays design and purpose because we want it to, not necessarily because it *does*. You don't want to confuse order with design. Remember back to our earlier discussion on science—we have a natural tendency to assign order to a chaotic system. But to make the jump from saying things are ordered to claiming that this order is a product of design is a big jump."

"Speaking of big jumps dad," Ian said, in a sassy tone. "What about something like the eye? I mean, how would that just appear like it is now over time? What good would half an eye be?" He was now referring to the mousetrap-theory that the eye shouldn't really be able to evolve over time. "It doesn't seem like having an eye with only half its parts would be better than an eye with half-plus-one. There's no real way for it to evolve, at least not in the way that people suggest evolution happens."

"Irreducible complexity," his father grumbled under his breath and then perked up. "First of all, Ian, don't forget about the problem we just mentioned—assigning probabilities *after* an event. Doing that, you can make almost anything improbable.

"More importantly, I'm not so sure I agree that half of a functioning eye is totally useless. Granted, it's not as good as the eye I have now, but the eye I have now also isn't nearly as good as your eye—I have to wear these glasses just to see from five feet what you can see from fifty. So, maybe half an eye could detect light sources or subtle movements that a slightly less evolved eye could not. But that would certainly give that eye an advantage, however slight. I'm just not sure that I agree that a partial eye, or a partial cilium, or a partial wing, or a partial anything is useless.

"How are we to know that these didn't serve a different purpose at one point, and then evolve to serve another purpose later? You know, the bacterial flagellum which now functions as a sort of propeller for bacteria actually evolved from a less complex form which aided in secretion in its ancestors. It served another purpose."

Ian sat, shaking his head in what seemed utter amazement.

The Purpose of the Nose

In Candide, *Voltaire parodies the notion that everything has a purpose. A character in the book points out numerous instances of purpose in the universe, the first being that noses serve the purpose of holding eyeglasses.*

"Nature has no end [goal] set before it. . . . If God acts for the sake of an end, he [must] want something that he lacks."
—Spinoza

In response to the idea that the eye can only function with all parts intact, Dawkins tells of a friend with no lenses in her eyes: "She assures me that you are far better off with a lenseless eye than with no eye at all." He relates to our experience on dark nights: that a continuum exists from, "total blindness up to perfect vision, and that every step along this series confers significant benefits. . . . The claim that 'The eye either functions as a whole, or not at all' turns out to be not merely false but self-evidently false to anybody who thinks for two seconds about his own familiar experience."

"Five per cent vision is better than no vision at all. Five percent hearing is better than no hearing at all. Five percent flight efficiency is better than no flight at all. It is thoroughly believable that every organ or apparatus that we actually see is the product of a smooth trajectory through animal space, a trajectory in which every intermediate stage assisted survival and reproduction."

He concludes, "not a single case is known to me of a complex organ that could not have been formed by numerous successive slight modifications."

"And, lastly, about this *intelligent* part of the design—I think I could have designed the eye better. As it now stands, it's completely backward. Upside down, even. Light has to travel through the entirety of the eye just to get to the light-sensitive part stuck way in the back. Then the image is flipped upside down and crisscrossed through the visual cortex in the back of the brain to be processed." He smirked, as if he were more intelligent than the purported intelligent designer.

His mother smiled at Ian's father's playful hubris. "Though," she said softly, "let's see if we can prove God simply by using logic, maybe taking a different tack from our almighty designer here." She smiled at him, lovingly. "I'm going to have you do two things. First, I want you to imagine a perfect ice cream cone."

Ian shrugged his shoulders, then nodded. After a short pause he rattled off a number of adjectives: "Ultra chocolatey; a little bit melted so it's not too hard; pretty big, but not so big that it drips everywhere and not so small that there's not very much; extra creamy."

His mother laughed, "Well, that was easy. I really just wanted you to imagine it for yourself. But you obviously know what you like in your ice cream. Okay, so now I want you to tell me if you can imagine a perfect being."

"Of course I can. He may be different than your perfect being, just like my ice cream cone might be different than your perfect ice cream cone. But I can certainly conceive of a perfect being. So now what?"

"Okay, good. Now I want to ask you one question. Do you agree that if I could add one quality to your list of qualities of the Perfect Ice Cream Cone that this would mean your list wasn't *quite* perfect?"

"Yeah, sure. If you can make a thing better, then it couldn't have been perfect to begin with."

"Good. Then I'd like to add 'exists' to your list. Surely that ice cream cone would be better if it existed. Don't you agree? Wouldn't that cone be better if it were in your hand right now instead of just in your imagination?"

Ian smiled a big smile and nodded.

"Exactly. So once we add 'exists' to your list, *then* it is the perfect ice cream cone."

Ian nodded, "Yeah, I suppose you're right."

"Okay. So since you admitted to having conceived of a *perfect* being—a being that *can't be made better*—then that being must exist. This being we call God. As you know, God differs from an ice cream cone because God is perfect *by definition*. Perfect things can't be made better—that's what makes them perfect. So it would be contrary to say that something is perfect *and* that it doesn't exist. If it didn't exist, then it could be made better and then wouldn't be perfect. But, since God is perfect, then he must exist."

Ian smiled. "A proof. Good."

His father was grumbling. It was hard to make out what he said. It sounded like, "I hardly think 'exists' is a proper predicate or adjective for something. It's not like calling something 'blue' or 'solid.' Hardly a good predicate."

Ian looked at him, trying to figure it out.

His father elaborated, "Think about it. If I had you guess what's in my pocket and I let you ask questions about it, you might ask, *Is it blue?* or *Is it soft?* but you wouldn't ask *Does it exist?* 'Exist' has a different status than other predicates." He paused, letting that point sink in. "Plus, just because you imagined a perfect ice cream cone that doesn't mean that *it* necessarily exists."

St. Anselm of Canterbury originally gave what is known as the "ontological proof" of God's existence. Descartes builds on this:

" . . . from the fact that I cannot conceive God without existence, it follows that existence is inseparable from Him, and hence that He really exists."

Anselm's Proof of God

1. *You can conceive of a perfect being.*
2. *If a thing is perfect then it must exist.*

   Therefore,

3. *This perfect being, God, exists.*

Does *It* Exist?

When we ask questions about a thing, we wouldn't ask, "Does it exist?"

Immanuel Kant overturns Anselm's "ontological proof" by arguing:

"[Existence] is evidently not a real predicate, or a concept of something that can be added to the concept of a thing."

Proving God and His Attributes . . . in Five Ways

St. Thomas Aquinas presented five attempts at proving God's existence. The fifth proof, known as the "teleological" argument (Greek telos *= "goal") is similar to the argument from design (presented earlier in this chapter): Because natural objects show purpose and function towards some goal, they must have been designed by a creator. The remaining four are often referred to as "cosmological" arguments—*kosmos *is the Greek word for universe.*

Not only did Aquinas believe that he proved God's existence, but also that his proofs ascribed qualities to God:

1. *Prime Mover—God is unchangeable and thus eternal.*
2. *First Cause—God is creator.*
3. *Necessary Being— God sustains the universe.*
4. *Moral Standard— God is all good and perfect.*
5. *Designer—God is all-knowing and directs the course of nature.*

Ian's mother clenched her teeth and crossed her arms. "Ice cream cones aren't perfect *by definition*. God is."

Ian seemed to enjoy this. It was almost like his parents had forgotten he was there for a moment. "That's good," he suggested, hoping to quiet them down. "I still wonder about a couple of things."

His mom and dad sat, mentally tired, though obviously interested as to the musings of their young son. "Yes?"

"Well. I still have four ways I think that God could be proven to exist." He paused to get his breath. "They're things I've been thinking about lately."

His parents sat nodding encouragingly.

"Okay. Well this first one seems pretty simple, almost obvious. If something is in motion, it can't move by itself. At the least, something else must have moved it. But this couldn't have gone on forever—there must be something that started it all, right? Like the first mover. That would be God."

"Well, what about a big explosion that started everything moving?" his father suggested. "A *big bang*, maybe?"

"What would start *that*?" Ian quickly responded.

"You don't think it could start itself?" his father suggested. "Current science has shown that quantum particles pop into and out of existence."

Ian nodded thoughtfully and said, "Even if they *moved* on their own—which doesn't sound right to me—what would have caused them to exist in the first place? Everything in the universe is finite and depends on something else for its existence. So something *outside* of this universe must have created it all. There had to be a sort of 'non-worldly' first cause" he said, smiling. "God."

"Thoughtful," his father said quietly. "I'm not sure that would work with the laws of physics, but I must say, it's very thoughtful."

"Yeah, so those are the first two ways: motion and cause," Ian said. "Next, I think you'll agree that all the things in the world at some point don't exist. Right? Like this mug here, or even like us. Everything that exists doesn't *have to* exist, at one point *didn't* exist, and at another point *won't* exist."

"What's the relevance here, son?" his mother asked, facilitating the argument.

Ian responded, "With everything coming into and out of existence, then at some point it's very likely that nothing existed. But since things can't cause themselves to exist—like I said earlier—then some other thing must exist all the time, otherwise there would be *nothing*." He rhetorically looked around the kitchen to show that this was not the case—things do, in fact, exist.

"You have really thought this through, son. Though I'm not sure there would really be nothing given your premise that things come into and out of existence, but it is actually worth considering," his mother nodded, smiling.

"Look at it this way, mom," Ian responded in a scholarly manner. "You are dependent on something else for your existence—your cells, let's say. Right? Without cells, you wouldn't exist."

His mother nodded, glancing toward Ian's dad. Ian's dad nodded encouragingly and stated, "One hundred billion of them."

Ian continued, "Your cells depend on 'cellular guck,' I'll call it. More simply, your cells depend on molecules. Molecules depend on atoms. All things that exist, basically, depend on other things for their existence. But this can't go on forever."

"It can't?" his mother asked rhetorically, seeming to agree but wanting to watch her son in action.

"Imagine an infinite series of mirrors" Ian said, holding his hands up, palms facing as if

The First Mover

The idea that the universe was created out of nothing is referred to as "creation ex nihilo."

Aquinas argued that a thing could not cause itself to exist. If it did then, "It would have to be prior to itself, which is impossible. But it is not possible for the series of . . . causes to go on ad infinitum *[infinitely]."*

For this reason, God is sometimes called the Prime Mover.

Can order come from nothing?

The Laws of Thermodynamics:

ONE: You can't get something from nothing—energy can't be created or destroyed.

TWO: Things naturally tend toward disorder (not order).

Ex nihilo nihil fit—
From nothing, nothing is made.

mirroring each other. "When you look in one, you see them infinitely reflected in each other. Light can reflect in them infinitely, and each is dependent on the other for that light. But no single mirror can generate the light. There must be a light source that is independent of the mirrors. That's like us and God. He's the independent source upon which all other things are dependent."

The Ultimate Good

In his "fourth proof" Aquinas relies on Aristotle's notion of how objects maintain their qualities. This derived from Plato's view of reality: there are "Forms"—the archetypes or highest standard to which all other objects relate. Given that, Aquinas writes:

"We come across some things which are more or less good. . . . But 'more' and 'less' are terms used of different things by reference to how close they are to what is greatest of its kind (for example, something is 'hotter' if it is closer to what is hottest). Hence there is something which is truest and best and noblest, and consequently greatest in being . . . just as fire, which has the greatest heat, is the cause of everything hot. . . . Hence there is something which is the cause of being and goodness and every other perfection in things; and this we call 'God'."

His mother smiled, her eyes wide with pride. "You said that you had four ways?"

"Yeah," Ian continued, apparently happy that his parents were following along. "You often say that certain things are good—ice cream is good, a movie was good, *I'm* good."

They both nodded.

"Then, there must be an ultimate good which allows for all these other levels of goodness, all these types of good."

"How so?" his mom querried.

"It's kind of like cold temperature. There is a maximum cold, right dad?"

His dad nodded, as if caught off guard for a moment. He responded, "Yes, zero Kelvin, actually. Negative 460 degrees Farenheit. This is the coldest conceivable temperature."

Ian continued, "Yeah. Now knowing that, then other things can then be cold relative to that absolute cold, but just to different degrees."

His dad smiled, "Good pun, son."

"Pun?"

"Degrees—used in two ways," his dad said, unsure Ian understood.

"No pun intended," Ian said, in a serious tone, like he was mimicking some actor he'd seen in a movie. "I'm just saying that for someone or something to be good, it's like they are a representation of the absolute goodness—God. God sets the ultimate standard for *good* just like there's an ultimate standard for *cold* which allows other things to be *somewhat* cold, *kind of* cold, *very* cold."

His mother was smiling at Ian, and looking at Ian's dad and smiling at him. Ian acted as though he'd successfully proved God's existence and could move on. "Can God have faith?" he asked, now in a more playful tone. "Because wouldn't He need to lack absolute knowledge to have faith in something? And what happens after the "Judgment Day" thing, after Armageddon? Are people then free from having to achieve salvation? Will there be another Armageddon? Has there already been one?"

As he walked off to the front door, he turned around, "I really do wonder what it would be like if there were nothing. I don't mean nothing as in no Earth, or no solar system. I mean no things. Nothing at all. We couldn't have just space, because you need something to contain that space. Like in dad's mug. There's nothing there. But we need the mug—*something*— in order to have nothing. It seems like we can't have nothing unless we have something. We couldn't even have just whiteness. Where would the white come from and where would it be?"

"You know, Ian," his mother said, "some say wisdom is often more about the questions than the answers. You've sure got that down. I'm not sure I have anything close to an answer to those. But I think that soon you won't be needing us any more."

Ian turned and smiled a curious smile. Up the stairs and out the door he went.

The Purpose of Meaning

Won't be needing my parents? And what did that broadcaster mean saying I was being trained for something? Who was he saying *sorry* to?

Jeff was waiting outside. He yelled to me as I walked out of the door, "Let's go explore the woods at the edge of town. Want to? We haven't been there forever."

I supposed I did. It's like when you're not hungry but someone suggests something that you haven't had for a while and you instantly crave it. We used to walk through those woods a lot. It's kind of fun because it seems almost like another world. Not that I had figured *my world* out, but a little vacation is always nice.

As we walked along the trail and through the trees and over-grown bushes we spotted a man up ahead, off of the trail. He had a bow-and-arrow slung over his shoulder, wearing only a little cloth around his waist and squatting down looking at something. I'd always been told that there were *people of the forest*, but I thought that was like an urban legend or maybe something to keep kids from going too deep into the forest. I looked at Jeff and we both raised our eyebrows in an affirmative way as if encouraging ourselves to speak with him.

When we got near him, he was holding a nice-looking watch in his hands. He smiled at us and said hello. We smiled, said hello. He held the watch up. In a friendly though deliberate tone he asked, "What is the meaning of this?"

I responded, equally as carefully, "It is to keep time."

"Time?" he asked.

"Yes. You know, like for example, what time do you have dinner tonight?"

"Dinner?" he responded, as if he didn't understand my question. "When is it?" he asked himself. He pointed to the sky with his arm extended and dropped his finger slowly to the horizon, "When the sun has gone away, then we eat."

It seemed that he didn't have our concept of time. How strange, to never have to be anywhere by a certain time. What could that mean, anyway? No time? You could never be late. We'd never get anything done. But it looked like he had gotten things done. He was alive, after all, and had been for what I'd guess was thirty years.

"So, *what is the meaning of this*?" he asked again, holding the watch up so I could see it more closely.

"It tells time," I said again, preparing to teach him about time.

He quickly responded, "No, not 'What is the *purpose* of this?' but 'What is the *meaning* of it?'"

I shrugged and looked at Jeff. He shrugged back at me. I asked the man, "What does it mean to you?"

He thought for a moment and then said, almost proudly, "This object has great meaning to me now. It represents the day that I met you—a person from the other world." He smiled at me, a very friendly smile. "And now, I realize that it has a very good purpose also. It has a hard and smooth surface good for cutting small berries. And it looks like it will fit on my wrist so that I can take it to the forest and use it whenever I need it."

He squatted down to fasten the watch to his wrist. Once he did, he seemed very happy about it. "Thank you for meeting," he said to us. "Now I will go to the forest and use this berry cutter." He walked off, wearing what looked like a very valuable watch on his wrist. It was a funny sight.

As I watched him walk away, Jeff motioned to me from the other side of the trail. "Ian, look at this," he said, un-crumpling what looked like a certificate. On it, it said, "*Life*. Official Certificate of *Life*."

"What does it mean?" he asked, as if I might actually have the answer. As if there even was an answer to give.

"What is the meaning of life?" I asked him rhetorically, just to make sure I'd heard him correctly.

He nodded.

"That depends, I suppose," and I thought of our recent encounter, "on what it means to you."

"Do you think that life has a purpose?" he asked.

"Does something need a purpose to have meaning? The watch had meaning to that man before he found a purpose for it. And who would decide the purpose of life?"

"Whoever created it, I suppose," he responded.

"So like you mean our parents? They decide the purpose of our life?"

"Or God. If God created actual life in general, then He decides its purpose."

"But why does the creator's purpose have to be the same as ours? What if our parents created us *just so* we could help them with the chores, or if God created us so that we would help keep the animals alive?"

Talking through this was actually illuminating. I continued, "Remember the man's watch? Whoever created the watch did it to tell time. But the man who found it gave the watch its own purpose. Was he wrong? It would have been silly to tell him that he was using the watch incorrectly."

Jeff thought through that and suggested, "So I can decide my own purpose? Whether there is a God or not, I still get to decide my own purpose—the purpose of my life. But what about the meaning of life then?"

"You can give your own meaning to life too. Just like that man did with the watch. Think of all we've been through lately. I'd say there was great meaning in all of it. Maybe our purpose is to know ourselves and our world in the best way that we can. And in doing that, we have to know others, help others, connect with others. Connect with the world. By doing that, it will certainly make life meaningful. It will give meaning to life in general."

Jeff smiled at me. *Did* I have the answer? He folded up the Life Certificate and put it in his pocket. "I know this paper doesn't have any meaning in itself, but it means a lot to me. You really made a lot of sense about our purpose and meaning in life. Because of that, this certificate really does have great meaning to me."

I realized that the watch that man found now had greater meaning to me than I realized at first. And it had certainly served a purpose.

"Okay Ian, I'm going to go get a frame for this. I'll see you after lunch maybe?"

"Yeah," I nodded. "See you then."

Chapter 6

Evil

If God didn't exist, we would have to invent him.

–Voltaire

If God does not exist, then everything is permitted.

–Fyodor Dostoevsky,
The Brothers Karamazov

The Old Man and I walked through the town. It seemed deserted. I guessed everyone was asleep. Like I was—or was supposed to be. Or was. Who knows?

"So why are you bothering with all of this?" I asked the Old Man.

"Bothering? I'm not bothering. Are you not enjoying it?"

"No, you know I enjoy it. A lot, actually. But I'm curious why you're going to all the trouble, what exactly it is I'm being *trained*

"I was not looking for my dreams to interpret my life, but rather for my life to interpret my dreams."
–Susan Sontag,
philosopher and novelist

for," I said, reminding him that I was paying close attention to the interviewer yesterday.

"Don't worry about all of that, Ian. That God's Agent, yesterday, don't let that get to you. Just look at it as a way to examine the concept of an all-powerful God. God's Agent isn't all-powerful, so he can make mistakes. Just like all of us."

I shook my head. The Old Man was obviously avoiding the question. And he was getting me off track. "Yeah, what about that—an all-good God? You know, yesterday there was an earthquake somewhere overseas. It killed 109 people. What's the point of that? How could an all-powerful God do that, or let that happen? If He's powerful, He certainly doesn't seem very good. All sorts of bad things happen all the time."

The Old Man smiled, almost as if he'd anticipated what I'd say. "Funny you should say that. Follow me."

He motioned for me to follow him into an underground tunnel. It was cold and damp, and the darkness made it a bit scary, but I had come to trust the Old Man so I kind of enjoyed it all. We walked through a corridor, and then up a flight of stairs. Then up another flight of stairs. We must have walked up twenty flights. When we got to what I assumed was the top of this building, we entered a room with one big window that wrapped around it. It was like what I imagined an air traffic control tower was like on the inside, except there were no screens, no buttons—just a big window. I walked up to the window, looked out, and saw nothing. Just black. I turned to the Old Man, obviously distraught.

"This is an unmade universe, Ian. Unmade because there's nothing there. This is *your* universe. You will be its creator. In a sense you will be its god. You can make it as you choose. If you like, you can make it the same as the universe you live in. When you're up here, in this tower, you know everything, you can do anything. You just need to decide what kind of god you want to be and create your universe accordingly."

"But I do like the universe the way it is."

"Then make it that way, except this will be *yours*. If things are good it will be because of you. If they're not good, this too will be your doing. You're the lone creator."

Instead of asking the tons of questions I had, I just took his word for it and got ready to make a universe. But before I began, I realized that I didn't have anything to begin with. "How do I start? There's nothing there. I can't make something out of nothing."

"You are an all-powerful god, Ian. You can do whatever you want. Try it."

Try making a universe? So I did. Just like that. I tried just willing it to happen. 'Let there be an Earth. Let there be planets.'

As I spoke, planets appeared all over outside. I couldn't really see them but I noticed their silhouettes. "Wow! It's that easy. I can do whatever I want. Now I've made a universe."

"Yes, Ian. You have a lot of power. The ultimate power, really. That's a nice start, but I can't really see anything."

"Then let there be light."

"But Ian, where will you get light? You haven't made a sun yet."

"It's okay. I'll make that later, in the fourth hour. I'm God. I don't need a sun in order to have light."

We looked outside. There was light. So I put water on the Earth. A sun and stars in the sky. "Pretty good so far, huh?" I was confident now in my universe-making skills. I put some grass on the Earth's ground. Some trees with fruit on them. The place looked nice. Blue and green. I sprinkled some animals throughout the Earth. Some on land, some in the water. All types of animals—I even threw in a platypus. I went back and put a little water on Mars—I knew it would evaporate but someday scientists would find evidence of it and could then devise all sorts of theories about it. This job was a little tiring. I looked at my watch. "This whole thing has taken me five hours. What do you think?"

The Old Man bobbed his head back and forth. "It's not bad. First of all, you know that you're not constrained by time. You're outside of time, so you don't have hours or days."

"True. But when this story gets recounted, I want people to be able to understand it and connect with it. They're going to want to know how long it took me. So I'll just use an increment of time that they'll be familiar with."

"Sounds good—it's *your* universe. So are you going to put people on it or just have this nice place with no one there to appreciate it?"

"Oh yeah, people. Well, I'll just make two people to start out with. I'll make them just like me, except maybe a little older." Making the people was hard. It took me a whole hour to make these two people. I was tired. After creating them I opened the window and yelled to them, "This is the best I could do, people! I hope you enjoy it and don't take it for granted! Care for it and love it and be nice to one another! Oh, and just don't eat the fruit from that little tree over there!"

I felt a real sense of pride and actually felt feelings for these two people.

"Can we rest for an hour before having to get back to work? I think this universe is good now."

"Of course. Sit back and watch the fruits of your labor. Funny that you didn't put belly buttons on those two people. Though I

Did God Use Human Time?

In the Bible, Peter writes, "With the Lord a day is like a thousand years, and a thousand years are like a day." This seems to imply that God did not concern himself with human time.

However, in Genesis, the Hebrew word used for "day" is yôm, which refers to our standard day. This is used instead of the many words for non-human time used elsewhere in the Bible. By this reasoning, some believe that the universe was created in exactly six days.

God said to Adam and Eve, "Of the tree of the knowledge of good and evil, thou shalt not eat of it: for in the day that thou eatest thereof thou shalt surely die."
–Genesis 2:17

When they came to know good and evil they were ashamed, they clothed themselves, and they were made mortal: "for dust thou art and unto dust shalt thou return."
–Genesis 3:19

suppose they don't really need them. It just looks strange.

"So why the fruit-eating prohibition, anyway?"

I shrugged, "They can't have it *all*. Something has to distinguish them from me."

That tree had the knowledge of good and evil. This knowledge was not for them. They were not God. I was. And so we watched. And these two people—who I named "Primo" and "Prima"—seemed to enjoy the landscape that I had created for them. And they enjoyed each other. I sat back and talked with the Old Man for a bit. He said that he had never created a universe before, but that I made it look very easy. It was pretty easy. There really aren't many challenges when there's nothing you can't do.

Just then he got wide-eyed. "Ian, I think there might be a problem." We looked out. Primo and Prima were sharing the fruit from the tree. This actually made me kind of angry. Couldn't they just leave that one thing alone? I couldn't let them get away with this. I had to make them pay with their lives. If they lived forever, then they would be just like me: with all the knowledge *and* with eternal life. I opened the window and yelled to them, "I saw that! You should be ashamed of yourselves. Now you will have to pay with your life! You and all future Primos and Primas!"

While they were busily covering themselves, Primo yelled back, "How can you punish us for that?"

"What do you mean!" I responded, forgetting momentarily that I could do whatever I wanted.

"Well, that's the tree of the knowledge of good and evil. If we didn't have the knowledge of good and evil then how could we know that what we were doing was not good? And if we *did* have the knowledge of good and evil, then what's the point of that tree?"

"Don't worry about that," I responded, "Just put your clothes on and behave for now!"

I turned to the Old Man. "What was I supposed to say to them? It does seem like kind of a contradiction, but I told them not to eat it."

"So you're surprised they did?"

"No, I guess not. I guess I knew they'd eat it. But I don't have to answer to them."

He nodded. "Being all-powerful might not be as easy as you thought. Let's look at the human year 2000, shall we? We can see how this is all playing out."

We walked to the left side of the tower. We looked down upon a city. There were cars everywhere, people rushing around, lots of tall buildings. It was nothing like the Earth that I'd originally created. And people were mean to each other. I saw one man run up to another, hit him in the back with a stick, knock him over, and take his wallet. I looked at the Old Man. He nodded. "It's going on all over the world, Ian. Pain. Theft. Murder. Lying. War. It happens so much in this universe of yours that people are starting to think that you don't exist."

I was hurt. This was *my* universe. Of course I exist. "There are people that think I don't exist? How could they even begin to argue that?"

"Well, while you were relaxing, I scoured the Earth for nay-sayers. I was able to find two groups: one in a little café, and another in a classroom. They are both discussing the problem of all the evil that goes on, and how they think it disproves your existence. Let's look in on a conversation going on right now."

We looked down. There was a group of four sitting at a café. One of them was writing something down. He said—or more like proclaimed—

The Problem of Evil

"Is [God] willing to prevent evil, but not able? Then he is impotent. Is he able, but not willing? Then he is malevolent."

– David Hume

The Problem of Evil was first discussed by the Greek philosopher Epicurus in 300 BC. The term 'theodicy' was introduced from the Greek words for 'God' and 'justice.' Coined by Leibniz, theodicy is an attempt to defend God's goodness in view of the existence of evil and suffering.

Letters from Satan

Mark Twain wrote a series of letters "written by Satan" to his friends. In Satan's Letter III he writes,

"The best minds will tell you that when a man has begotten a child he is morally bound to tenderly care for it, protect it from hurt, shield it from disease . . . God's treatment of his Earthly children, every day and every night, is the exact opposite of all that."

In a letter from Charles Darwin to a friend he wrote, "What a book a Devil's Chaplain might write on the clumsy, wasteful, blundering low and horridly cruel works of nature."

"Ian *can't* exist. Especially not as you say he does. I'll show you. *Either*," on the paper he wrote:

1. Ian doesn't know that evil things happen—thus rendering Him as not all-knowing, *OR*
2. He can't prevent these evils from occurring—thus rendering Him as not all-powerful, *OR*
3. He doesn't care about all the evil befalling His creatures—thus rendering Him as not all-good.

"It just seems that Ian and evil can't *both* exist. And, since Ian—namely the Western, most popular idea of Ian—is defined as all these things, then Ian must not actually exist."

"How can you say that?" one responded.

The author of this replied, "Well, look at it. We all define Ian as being three things: omniscient, omnipotent, omni-good—let's call him 'omni-omni' for short. Yet if he knowingly allows evil, then he can't be an all-good Ian. Otherwise, we'd have to say that he doesn't know about evil or can't do anything to stop it. Yet, if any of the first three statements are wrong, then Ian doesn't exist because that's how Ian is defined. And we know that evil exists. So, then, Ian must not exist. It's simple, really."

They all sat quietly. One of them patted the author on the back. The other two shook their heads.

I turned to the Old Man. "But I gave humans free will. What would be the point of making them without it? If I made them without free will, then I would basically be deciding whether they were going to go to heaven or not. If they couldn't choose what they did on Earth, then going to heaven would be out of their control. Basically My options were to give humans free will knowing they'd choose evil, or to not give them free will at all and have them be like robots. I chose the first one. Have you ever thought that they're just doing more evil than I'd planned?"

Back at the café: "Maybe Ian *did* make us and did give us free will, but we're just doing more evil than he'd planned."

I looked at the Old Man with a witty smile.

"Did you do that?" he asked. "Did you have him say that?"

God's Options in Making Humans

1. *They have free will and so they'll sometimes choose to do evil.*
2. *They won't have free will so they won't be able to choose to do evil.*

A third option?
They have free will and *they can't choose to do evil.*

I just smiled. Of course I did. I can do anything.

But one of the members of the group replied, "Are you suggesting that things didn't quite happen as Ian planned? That He made a mistake or things didn't go as He hoped? That's a pretty big inconsistency for an *all-powerful* being."

The Old Man glared back at me, realizing this was not an option: things couldn't work out differently than an all-powerful God intended. I winced, scrunching up my nose.

Then another one spoke up. "I have another concern about this 'free will defense.' Do you think that evil and free will have to go together, like in a package? Isn't there a way that we could have free will and yet *not* be able to do evil? We supposedly have free will now and we can't choose to bend our elbows backward—just because we can't do that doesn't mean that we don't have free will. Does that mean there's no free will in heaven? If not, then it doesn't seem like a very nice place to go. And if there is then, as you say, there must be evil in heaven too. Kind of strange."

Then another jumped in. "Listen, I don't think that free will is the way out of this problem. Even if it explained evils such as murder, jealousy, rape—what I'll call moral evils—where does that leave us with *physical* evils such as earthquakes, tsunamis, and tornados? Maybe Ian just isn't finished with making the universe."

They all shook their heads. "Of course He's finished. An all-powerful being doesn't leave things undone. How would He be all-powerful if He couldn't complete a universe?"

Now they were all nodding their heads. "Geez, that's a real problem for Ian," one of them said—the same one that was defending Me earlier. "I thought that our free will would solve the problem, but it doesn't. It seems like there's either more evil than Ian planned on, or that Ian could have given us free will without the ability to do evil, or that Ian's not finished with things yet. Either way, that makes Him not the god that I once thought He was."

I looked at the Old Man. "This is ridiculous! What was I supposed to do? How do these people think they can possibly discuss Me like that? They don't understand Me at all. I'm going to go down there and scare them to death. Figuratively, I suppose. But I'm going to prove my existence. Then we'll see how that changes things!"

> *"I shall never believe that God plays dice with the world."*
> –Einstein

> *"How would man exist if God did not need him, and how would you exist? You need God in order to be, and God needs you."*
> –Martin Buber

"Ian, if I may lend a humble word." He paused. Was he really deferring to me now? I guess so. I *was* God, after all. Maybe I should have silenced him just because I could. I nodded to him to continue. "There are many different religions down there. And in a number of these religions, the main tenet is faith. In order to achieve salvation, to participate in the religion, one must have faith in You. *Faith*. You set this up Yourself, so I'm sure You understand. Faith maintains a slightly different status than knowledge. When people say that they *know* that Ian exists, they don't know it in the way that they know *there is a cup on the table*—they know it with faith, something very different. So, if You went down there and showed yourself—if You went floating down to Earth throwing lightning bolts at all the nonbelievers, healing the sick, dancing on water—then people's belief in the status of Your existence would be transformed from faith to knowledge. That's the irony: in Your showing Yourself, religions would be overturned. Uprooted."

Wow. I guessed he was right. Though, I knew that. "You don't think I've thought of that?"

"Of course, Ian. I just wanted to show you that I was capable of this thought as well."

He must have known by now that I realized he was capable of good thinking. After all, I knew everything. "Yes. So I won't go down there. Where's this other group of non-believers?"

"First of all, Ian, it's not necessarily that these people don't believe, it's that there are logical problems with their belief. I think part of the trick for people believing in you is belief without proof. That's faith. This other group is in a philosophy class. They're right over here."

I looked down and saw a class of about fifteen students. One of them had her hand raised. The professor called on her. She suggested, "Maybe the issue with this whole 'Problem of Evil' is our concept of evil."

Proof Destroys Faith

Contemporary philosopher Alisdair MacIntyre argues that if God were somehow proven, then people would no longer be "free" to believe because they would be forced to. This would undermine faith—believing when there is no proof—which is a main principle of many religions.

"Suppose religion could be provided with a method of proof. . . . Since the Christian faith sees true religion only in a free decision made in faith and love, the religion would by this vindication be destroyed. For all the possibility of free choice would have been done away with."

"'I refuse to prove that I exist,' says God, 'because proof denies faith, and without faith I am nothing.'"

–Douglas Adams
Hitchhiker's Guide to the Galaxy

The professor encouraged her, "And how would that tie in? How would that solve the Problem?"

"Well, the argument says three things:

1. Ian is omni-omni.
2. Evil exists.
3. An omni-omni Ian *and* evil can't exist.

Therefore, Ian doesn't exist."

"Sure. But how does our concept of evil disprove the argument?" the professor asked.

"Well, if statement number two is wrong, then the argument doesn't hold, so Ian *could* exist."

The professor nodded. He motioned with his hand as if he were inviting her ideas to continue flowing out of her.

"Okay, well, instead of evil being an actual thing, maybe it's just the absence of good. Like evil is really a *no-thing*, instead of a *some*thing. It could be like a shadow. A shadow is really just the lack of something—light. It's not really a thing the way that other things are things. So, evil *doesn't* exist."

"Insightful. Though I think you may have sidestepped the issue. Let's agree, momentarily, that evil is just the absence of good—that it's a lack of something. The question is then just rephrased, 'Why does Ian allow the absence of good?' Call it what you will, it's *not* good."

"But don't we need evil to have good?"

"Well, you tell me. It's purported that, after Ian created the universe, on the seventh hour He said, 'And it was good.' So how could He say that? According to you, there would have to have been evil at the time of Ian's creation. That He created evil. How could an all-good Ian create evil? More importantly, how could Ian create good without having evil?"

She was silent, as if ready to withstand a whole bunch of questions.

"And on top of that, if evil's not real, then we've been deceived into thinking it is, which itself is a sort of evil. Either way, it seems that evil is here to stay."

More silence.

"Anyway, it would be illogical to say that evil wasn't real or that we couldn't understand evil. It would be illogical because, if for no other reason, you say that God is *good*. You have to be

---

Evil as a 'No-Thing'

"Whatever [exists], is good; and evil . . . is not a substance, because if it were a substance, it would be good."

– St. Augustine, fourth-century theologian

"The spread of evil is the symptom of a vacuum. Whenever evil wins, it is only by default."

   "The evil of the world is made possible by nothing but the sanction you give it."

–Ayn Rand

"The lesser of two evils is still evil."

–Attributed to Winston Churchill

If Evil Doesn't Exist . . .

1. *Things still happen or exist that are "not good."*
2. *How could God create good if there was no evil?*
3. *We have been deceived to think there is evil, which is a sort of evil itself.*
4. *The concept of good (evil's opposite) becomes meaningless, so God can't be good.*

able to distinguish between good and evil in order to claim that something's good. You can't say both, 'God is good' *and* 'I have no idea what evil is.' You'd be contradicting yourself."

She spoke up again, "But do you really think we need evil or bad things in order to have good things? What about smells? Do you think that roses smell good only because we have things like rotten garbage and sulfur? It doesn't seem like we really need bad smells to have good ones. It seems like an all-powerful being could have made *everything* that way." She stood up and started walking toward the chalkboard. "Can I use the board for a sec?" The professor extended his hand with the chalk.

"I'll make a short list of things that smell, both good and bad. I'll put roses at the beginning of the 'good' column. Then perfume, freshly baked bread, then after that, maybe the smell of a crisp new morning. You can have your own ranking of smells, but let's just imagine this one. Then there is the zero-point, like right now, where I don't smell anything. After that are the bad smells. An old shoe, maybe. Garbage. Then a skunk's smell—even though some people say they like that smell. Then sulfur, okay? So it looks like this:

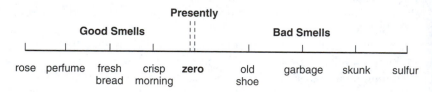

"Now," she continued, taking on the attitude of a professor, "according to the idea that *we need bad to have good*, if we were born into a world where none of these bad smells existed, then some of the current good smells would become bad. It would look like this:"

The Ultimate Good

Thirteenth-century Christian theologian St. Thomas Aquinas borrows an idea from Plato and Aristotle. He claims that for there to be a certain quality there must be something that maintains that quality maximally. For example, the quality "hot" is contained maximally in fire. The quality "good" is contained maximally in God.

If we need bad to have good:

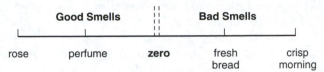

She looked at what she wrote as if it were some revolutionary discovery. It was actually a pretty interesting point. She continued. "This seems wrong to me. I argue instead that the good smells would still smell good." And she finished, writing:

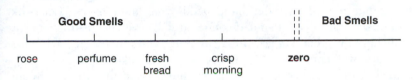

As she walked back to her seat she commented, "I just don't think it's *always* necessary to have bad in order to have good. Would freshly baked bread really smell bad, just because there was nothing that smelled worse than it?"

The professor nodded his head in an approving yet contemplative way. "Very thoughtful," he began. "This will give us something to think about. My only concern here is that you just don't want to make the concept of *goodness* meaningless. You don't want to contradict yourself. And the forces of good and evil are much more complex than smells. Anyway, if Ian exists, he *didn't* make things that way. So we're stuck here on Earth with all sorts of evil."

She nodded appreciatively and smiled. She seemed to appreciate the professor's remarks.

The Old Man turned to Me. "Looks like you've got some problems on your hands, Ian. You've created quite a conundrum. Doesn't seem like there's really a way out of this one. How do you expect people to believe in you with all of this going on? Faith is one thing, but you need at least a mustard seed's worth of faith to start with—it doesn't seem like you've even given the people that."

"Okay. Would you like me to explain this all to you?" I said to him, acting exasperated. "I know I shouldn't. I know that I should let you figure this out on your own. But I'll just let you see for yourself."

> *"When all in the world understand beauty to be beautiful, then ugliness exists. When all understand goodness to be good, then evil exists."*
> –Lao Tzu

I went to the side of the tower that we hadn't looked out. It was dark. "You see the lack-of-anything over there? I'm going to make a universe for you. Except this time, I'll make it without anything bad. No evil. We'll see how that plays out."

In Orson Welles' Time Machine, *the characters experience a utopia where no one works, everyone is immortal, everything comes easily.*

I went through the creation process again. Now that I'd already made a universe, this one was much easier. It took me only about a half an hour. "Okay. So let's fast-forward like we did last time to the year 2000." We did. It looked almost exactly like the last time we did this. There was no pollution in the air though. The Old Man called out, excitedly, "Look, Ian, here's that same robbery that happened in your first universe. Looks like there's still some evil." I smiled confidently. We watched as the man ran up behind the other like last time. He went to hit him on the back but as the stick was about to strike his back it turned to paper. The victim smiled at the attacker. The attacker politely asked that the victim surrender all the money in his wallet. The victim did. And as soon as the money left his wallet, his wallet refilled. They both walked away happily.

Then a little girl walked into the street. As a fast-moving car approached her, she had no time to get out of the way, and the car went right through her. She continued on to her soccer game.

We watched the game. As the referee blew the final whistle signaling the end of the game, both teams jumped up in elation proclaiming, "Yeah, we won!" In this universe, there was no losing. Just winning. No F's, only A's. No death. No sorrow.

"First of all," I said to the Old Man, "you should see their physics books. They're a mess. *Nothing* happens according to any sort of regularity—sticks turning to paper, cars becoming non-physical. And their logic. What a wreck! Both teams winning? Everyone getting 'A's?' But let me show you something else. Look at this dictionary of theirs." I flipped through the pages to where *courage* would be. Nothing there. We looked

The Worst of all Possible Worlds?

Contemporary philosopher John Hick imagines a world without evil. He concludes, "It would be the worst of all possible worlds."

for *compassion. Fortitude. Determination.* Nothing there. "These words aren't there because there's never any chance to be courageous. There's nothing to fear, no obstacles to overcome. They don't even have a concept of courage, of determination. None of it.

"You see, without any evil, without any bad things happening, without any suffering, there would be no real important goods. This,

No Pain: No Gain

*Many religions emphasize the importance and the value of human suffering.
The crucifixion of Jesus Christ, for example, is not meant as a mere symbol but
as a way to live one's life: not until one has suffered and experienced the
"death" of the worldly self can one grow and know God. Luke (17:33) writes,
"Anyone who wants to preserve his life must lose it." And likewise in Jeremiah
(1:10), "Your job is to take apart and demolish, and then start over building
and planting anew." In this sense, one can truly be 'reborn.'*

> *"This is how we grow:*
> *By being decisively defeated by even greater forces."*
> —Rainer Maria Rilke, poet

I call the 'Greater Goods Theory.' With evil, people can achieve greater
goods.

"Come to think of it, my soccer team experience was a lot like this.
We really felt a great sense of accomplishment when we won the third-
place game last season. When we went to the end-of-the-year banquet,
my coach didn't talk about all the games we won; instead he talked
about all the sacrifice we made. He talked about all the difficult—and
sometimes painful—training, the early-morning workouts, running
sprints in the soft sand, losing that tough game early in the season. He
talked about the struggle to get to where we did. I know these are all
relatively small types of evil, but without them—without the pain, sacrifice, defeat, sadness—the richness of our feelings of accomplishment
would have been greatly diminished. Thank God for evil!"

"Or in this case, thank Ian," the Old Man added. "Very good. It
looks like You just may exist after all!"

"Funny. But I really learned a lot here, creating this universe.
Thanks for letting me do that."

"You're welcome, Ian. You know, very soon you won't be needing
me anymore. You're progressing much faster than I'd imagined."

Ian's alarm clock went off. He woke up. As he walked down the stairs he grumbled, "Now *that's* an evil I could do without. Couldn't God have made getting up in the morning less evil? Couldn't He just wake us up when we need to get up?" He stood on the bottom stair a moment and seemed to ponder that seemingly rhetorical question he had posed. He mumbled to himself, "No, no I suppose not. Must be a reason for it somewhere.

"*And now it's the Old Man I won't be needing anymore?* What could that mean—*need* him? Progressing? Toward what?"

He walked into the kitchen with an odd look on his face. It was a mix of anxious-yet-calm, confident-yet-uncertain. His parents looked at each other. His mother spoke up first, "Judging by the look on your face and all the mumbling, this looks like a tough one, Ian. You must have some difficult questions for us."

Defending God

In his defense of God, St. Thomas Aquinas writes,

"As Augustine says: 'Since God is the highest good, He would not allow any evil to exist in His works, unless His omnipotence and goodness were such as to bring good even out of evil.' This is part of the infinite goodness of God, that He should allow evil to exist, and out of it produce good."

Ian just walked up to the breakfast table and sat down quietly. He folded his hands on the table, looked up, and said, "I actually have some answers for you this morning." He paused. "Answers."

They both raised their eyebrows and looked at each other unknowingly. "Answers to what?"

"Well guys, if there is a God, He's got a pretty tough job on his hands. *That* I can tell you. How I know this I won't bother you with for now. But I'll tell you one thing I realized regardless of whether or not there is a God."

"A realization? Let's hear it."

"There is good in all evil. In a funny way, evil is good. Not that evil *equals* good in the way that Ian *equals* your son, but evil is good in the way that Ian is a boy. Evil allows us to achieve much greater goods. I suppose I'd say now that I really appreciate the struggle much more than I used to. I've always appreciated it but have steered away from it."

His parents raised their eyebrows at him, nodding slowly, smiling an unfamiliar smile. "How so, Ian?" his mother asked.

He tilted his head towards his mom, as if to defer to her, to let her figure it out. "How so, mom?"

She was initially taken aback, but then began, "Well, I think I may have an idea. You know, when I look back on our marriage the past fifteen years, some of my best memories are of when we struggled. Your father was between jobs, we were trying to buy a home, I was working evenings. We'd play board games with friends at the café or the park as our weekend entertainment. You were born, and we moved to a more affordable area for a while. And we made it through. I think your point is that when people look back at events, it's not the parties, or the expensive dinners, or any of that that they remember. It's making it through the struggles, doing it together, showing fortitude."

> "The marvelous richness of human experience would lose something of rewarding joy if there were no limitations to overcome. The hilltop hour would not be half so wonderful if there were no dark valleys to traverse."
>
> –Helen Keller

> "Need and struggle are what excite and inspire us; our hour of triumph is what brings the void."
>
> –William James

Ian smiled. He hugged her. During the hug his parents looked at each other with a tear in their eyes, shaking their heads at the apparent maturity of Ian's recent revelations.

His mother continued, "You know, many people argue that there is the perfect amount of evil in the world, the perfect amount of struggle. Take your father, for example."

"Dad's evil?"

"No, not at all. But he's not perfect. He's not perfect in the sense of having absolutely no imperfections. He *does* have those. But, to me, he is perfect. He has the perfect amount of imperfections. Perfectly imperfect!"

The Best of all Possible Worlds?

Leibniz argued that, despite the amount of evil in the world, this is the "best of all possible worlds." In the 1759 novel Candide, *Voltaire's main character, Dr. Pangloss, suffers through many unfortunate, often painful experiences which illustrate that it seems like this world* could *be better, though Pangloss rationalizes it all as serving a purpose. When a friend falls off a boat into the water, Pangloss says, "the bay of Lisbon had been formed expressly for him to drown in." At one point after being beaten, Candide says:*

"If this is the best of all possible worlds, then what are the others?"

Ian smiled. His dad smiled. "Thanks, honey . . . I think."

"It's kind of like that term, 'a necessary evil'—evils we need to achieve certain goods," she added.

Ian was smiling—a coy smile, as though they were preaching to the choir, so to speak. "I like to think of it in terms of two people getting to the top of Mount Everest. One spends a year planning and training and then goes through the struggle of getting to the top, and the other takes a helicopter to the summit. I would have to imagine that the one who struggled to reach the top will have a much more meaningful experience and will really feel a strong sense of accomplishment."

His mom smiled, nodding her head thoughtfully, "A very good point, son. And I feel like I should comment on another important point relating to all of this."

Ian sat up in anticipation.

"Well it's just that we need the possibility of evil in order to even have free will. Can you see why, Ian?"

"Well Mom, I'll first tell you that it *is* possible for humans to have free will under an all-knowing God. Because God created us with free will, then we must be able to choose *anything* that is at least logical and humanly possible. Otherwise, it wouldn't be free will. So, when God created the world, he had to choose between two things. One," right thumb out, "humans get free will and evil exists. Or, two," left thumb, "humans don't get free will and there's no evil." The second one seems silly and like a much worse choice. What would be the point of putting us here on Earth if we were just robots or puppets? In giving us free will, the downside was that sometimes we'd choose to do evil."

Ian smiled modestly as if it were *they* who were somehow helping *him*—a once-all-knowing god—to resolve this issue.

His parents looked at each other and nodded proudly. "Son," his mother said, "I couldn't have explained it better myself. You have access to some very genuine insights."

Condemned . . . or Not?

In Albert Camus' "The Myth of Sisyphus," the main character is condemned by the gods to repeatedly roll a rock up a hill and then upon reaching the top, he must let it roll down and then again roll it back up, for eternity. Camus writes, "The struggle towards the heights is enough to fill a man's heart. One must imagine Sisyphus happy."

<u>Another logical impossibility:</u>

A person who is not a person.

John Hick writes, "creatures who lack moral freedom, however superior they might be to human beings in other respects, would not be what we mean by - persons."

Ian smiled a proud smile, as though he had solved one of the major issues throughout time.

"But dear," his father suggested cautiously, "are you sure that all of this isn't just humans' way of making sense out of things? I certainly appreciate the positive outlook, but I have to wonder just how legitimate it all is, especially this so-called 'greater goods' point you and Ian are suggesting."

Ian's mother motioned for him to continue and Ian leaned in towards him attentively.

He began by shaking his head before he spoke. "A tsunami resulting in 200,000 seemingly unnecessary deaths. I say *unnecessary* because I happen to think they are. But by your position, you would say this is all part of a loving god's plan. Or let's take an even simpler example: a human dying alone, unknown, by burning to death in a forest fire. Or a deer even. A slow, painful death which no one even knows occurred. Where is the smidgen of *good* there?

"Sure, doing wind sprints makes your soccer experience more rewarding and yes, honey, that struggle early in our marriage proved to be joyous, but it's a bit trite to compare these so-called evils to something like anonymous death, torture, and mass annihilation." He shrugged his shoulders, almost embarrassed, like he had shattered their whole view.

"But dad," Ian responded, "how can we know the true good that results from these examples? How can we really know it's not somehow good in the long run?"

George H. Smith explains an inconsistency of the "greater goods" argument—if one claims that large-scale, seemingly pointless disasters are compatible with an all-good god, then it leaves no possibility for any sort of event that could disprove God's goodness, no matter how horrendous. Smith argues that this then becomes meaningless dogma:

"Some theologians argue that evil exists for the sake of a greater good. . . . Although something may appear evil to man, we are assured by the Christian that God is able to view the overall perspective, and any apparent evil always turns out for the best. These approaches share the premise that man cannot understand the ways of God, but this simply pushes us into agnosticism. It will not do for the Christian to posit an attribute of God and, when asked to defend that attribute, contend that man cannot understand it."

"I will call no being good who is not what I mean when I apply that epithet to my fellow creatures."

–John Stuart Mill

"Son, if a person burning to death alone and 200,000 people dying in one place at one time are somehow good and a result of love, then we can throw the words *good* and *love* out the window."

"Yeah, I guess," Ian responded dejectedly. "And there are some things I wish I'd looked into last time I dealt with all of this—it would have been much easier to figure all of this out then." They nodded, as if they understood what he meant. Ian continued, "If our nonphysical selves go to heaven, can heaven really be an actual *place*? It's been said that heaven's not a place in the way that we know places. But if we do go to heaven then we have to go *somewhere*—we can't go to heaven *and* go nowhere. And what about people who have married more than one person in this life? Will that create problems for them in heaven?" he asked, pausing. He answered his own question, "I guess not—no jealousy in heaven. That actually might work out well for them," he suggested, smiling.

"But more seriously, when I go to heaven, I wonder if I will get bored. Everyone always talks about heaven as running through green fields and playing under fresh spring waterfalls with all your friends. Maybe there needs to be some evil and pain in heaven. Maybe I'll lose the perfect amount of games to make the wins that much better. Maybe *this* is heaven? Maybe our conception of heaven is really hell, where everything goes exactly right all of the time and there's never any chance to struggle and achieve anything."

"Well, honey, I don't know about that. Who knows what heaven will be like? That problem can be reconciled, maybe, by considering Earth a testing ground and heaven a final home."

Ian smiled. They hugged him. As Ian ran off, his mother said, "I've been warned that there comes a time when a child's intelligence supersedes that of his parents. I just never thought it would happen so soon."

Is There Evil in Heaven?

"The saved, once glorified, will no longer sin throughout eternity."

This quote from the Bible denotes that the answer to the above question is "no." It explains that once we die, we inherit a divine nature that allows free will yet also leaves us with an inability to sin.

Earth: A Testing Ground for Souls

This concept was the focus of Dante's greatest work, Divina Commedia. *He wrote that in Purgatory, a sinner's soul would be purified by suffering before ascending to Paradise or would be damned to Hell. The final fate of the soul was decided based on the behavior of the soul while on Earth. This concept is prominent in Western religions as well as in the Eastern notion of reincarnation.*

The Price of a Paper and a Paper for a Price

As I walked down the street I noticed the pretty color of the trees. I thought about how amazing it is that I live in a world where everything goes on forever and ever. It was strange—a strange world to live in.

Though how could it be strange? Strange compared to what? It's the only world I know. We don't know any other worlds. It would be like seeing a 20-eyed monster and thinking, "What a strange 20-eyed monster." That wouldn't be right at all. It would be the only 20-eyed monster I'd have ever seen. So, I take that back, it's not a strange world we live in. It's just where we live.

I saw Jeff walking down the sidewalk towards me, and on a bike behind him was the paperboy that had been on our block for a long time, probably the last four years. He nearly ran Jeff over on his bike, snickering to himself, his eyes hiding behind his straight black hair. We never thought that he was the nicest kid, but he certainly seemed to be a diligent paperboy. I didn't know him, but Jeff did. I only knew about him through the family that lived down the street.

"Hi Jeff. Looks like Mike almost ran you over."

"Yeah. He's very efficient. He tells me that his record for completing his paper route is 42 minutes. He always tries to beat that but he said that it's gotten harder because he's had to throw the papers further as the years go by."

"Yeah. I've talked with the mom of the family down the street about that for years."

"Oh, and what does she say about him?"

"Well, three years ago, Mike would just set the paper down at the end of their driveway. So, every morning, the parents would have to put on their slippers and walk all the way down the driveway to get their paper. That's a long driveway too. For the whole year this happened. Christmas came and she didn't even give Mike a tip—no Christmas bonus. And the papers stayed at the edge of the driveway for that whole next year."

"Yeah, I remember Mike complaining about not getting a tip from them."

"Then the following year, even though the papers still landed at the end of the driveway, the family gave him a small Christmas tip. Starting January 1, the papers consistently made it about a third of the way down the driveway. So, that Christmas, the family gave Mike an even bigger tip. And that next January, the papers made it about two-thirds of the way down the driveway. Finally, last year, at Christmas, the family increased the tip even more. And now, the newspaper lands on their porch every morning."

Jeff nodded. "Yeah, that's exactly what Mike said about it."

I continued, "Well, I talked with the mom about it yesterday. She seemed pretty proud of herself. The one comment I remember her making about Mike was, *Good to see that he finally caught on.*"

"That's strange," Jeff noted. "When I talked to Mike yesterday he said the exact same thing about that mom—*good to see she finally caught on.* I can remember him snickering."

We shook our heads. Maybe they were both right. "Funny how people work sometimes," I said. "There really is no *science* to it. It's so much a matter of perspective.

"So, Jeff, do you think this is a strange world we live in?" Now he was not only thoughtful, he was smiling a bit. This conversation would consume our next few hours.

Chapter 7

Going East

You must unlearn all that you have learned.

–*Yoda (from the movie* Star Wars)

The fish trap exists because of the fish; once you've gotten the fish, you can forget the trap. The rabbit snare exists because of the rabbit; once you've gotten the rabbit, you can forget the snare. Words exist because of meaning; once you've gotten the meaning, you can forget the words. When can I find a man who has forgotten words so I can have a word with him?

–*Chuang Tzu*

As I dozed off, I heard the Old Man say, "Let's get back to more of the usual, shall we?"

"Could we not? Could we just let sleeping boys lie?" I liked that one. "Really. Could we not?" He shook his head, grinning. Apparently we couldn't . . . not.

"Ian, I know I'm giving you a lot of information to process."

"Not just information," I quickly responded. The information was fine with me—I liked information. "It's all the other stuff. It's that these ideas are changing the way I see things. Literally changing the way I see things. Changing the way I feel. It's the *ideas* that I'm trying to get a hold of, not the information."

"Learn from your dreams what you lack."

–W. H. Auden, Poet (1907–1973)

"I know it's a lot. But you're going to need all of this eventually. Very soon, actually. We could do this at a slower pace—usually more like once a week instead of every night. But we just don't have that time now. There is a great need for people like you."

"People like me?"

He nodded, obviously not wanting to explain what it even means to be *like* me. "Over the past few years there has been such an increase in information for people to deal with. People are being inundated with information. With the technological advances in television—if those really are *advances*—and a surge of information from Web sites, billboards, evangelizing, movie and literature themes pushing the envelope. Not only are people forced to organize it all, but they're starting to need to make sense of everything around them. The need for people like you is greater than ever. You're handling the pace very well, whether you like it or not."

I guess I did like it, though I still didn't quite understand the need to hurry the process. As we were walking and talking, we had approached a large courtyard, surrounded by an old building, with trees and thick bushes peppering the patio.

"What are we doing here?" I asked. I assumed that I had gotten all I could out of him about our meetings and their quick pace.

"We're going to visit a sage, Ian. A wise man of the East. An ancient Chinese philosopher. Or maybe *philosopher* isn't the right word. A thinker. A mystic. A Zen Master." As we walked into the open courtyard, a man was sitting with his back to us, dressed in a plain white T-shirt, short hair, medium build, very nondescript—except for *nondescript* being a kind of description itself. He wasn't quite what I'd expect from a master of anything, though this lack of anything extraordinary kind of added to the uniqueness. Strange.

When we got closer, I saw that he was sitting in front of a globe. Without turning to me, he asked me to sit down. He instructed me to put my finger on North America. As I sat down, I saw his face, also ordinary, though somehow comforting. Yet, again, I felt a contradiction: in the comfort of his face I also now felt more *dis*comfort, like I had expected something different from him. I put my finger on North America as he'd asked. It landed on

**Religions/
Philosophies/Mystics
of the East and the
Time and Place of
Their Inception**

- *Hinduism: India,
  1500 BC*
- *Buddhism: India,
  sixth century BC*
- *Taoism: China,
  520 BC*
- *Confucianism: China,
  500 BC*
- *Zen: China, late
  fifth century AD*

Denver, with Salt Lake City just to the west. The Old Man stood off to the side, as though he too was a little uncomfortable. He couldn't be uncomfortable, though. Could he?

"Now, Ian," the sage spoke softly, "drag your finger eastward. Do so slowly. Feel the ridges of the mountains. Drag it east until I instruct you to stop."

I did. I dragged it slowly. I focused on the globe and watched my fingers go over the little mountains. All I could do now was look at the globe. What could be the point of this? What kind of a test was this? Was I doing this right? Now my finger was spilling into the Atlantic Ocean. Though the globe was small, this trip across the ocean seemed like it would take a long time.

"Very good, Ian."

I was doing well. That was good to know. That actually gave me a little confidence. I was ready to look at him again, to nod a grin of approval. He smiled. A comforting smile. I could see his wisdom in his smile. I bet he was going to have some great things to say. Though I bet he'd really be able to stump me. Now that I had reached the end of the ocean, I left my finger there and started spinning the globe on its axis, slowly. My finger continued to go east. The sage put his hands together, he hummed, he nodded his head approvingly. The humming was somehow soothing. I smiled. My finger traveled. He smiled.

"Stop."

I did. I stopped. My finger felt like it was almost stuck to the globe. He smiled. "Very good, Ian. Now, where is your finger?"

I looked down and immediately returned to my feelings of inadequacy. I was in Salt Lake City. "Salt Lake City."

"Yes. I see. You went east. Yet you ended up west. I can tell that you've been in the west to begin with."

"How?"

"You want to put everything into words. To discuss it. Argue it. Solve it."

"How else can you do it?" What in the world could he be getting at here?

"Talk without speaking. Hear without listening. See without being."

That wasn't terribly helpful for me. So I sat silently, waiting.

"It's ironic, isn't it? You have spent all of your life living the Western way—accumulating things, gathering knowledge, living by the

"The instant you speak about a thing you miss the mark."

–Zen proverb

"He who speaks does not know. He who knows does not speak."

– Lao Tzu

A Taoist Proverb

Chuang Tzu and a friend walked along a river. "How delightfully the fishes are enjoying themselves in the water!" Chuang Tzu exclaimed.

"You are not a fish," his friend said. "How do you know whether or not the fishes are enjoying themselves?"

"You are not me," Chuang Tzu said. "How do you know that I do not know that the fishes are enjoying themselves?"

strict constructs of logic. Yet, you come to me, a man of the East, and you travel east, and yet you end up in the west."

I sat silently, waiting. My eyes wide open. Waiting. Wondering what the point could have been for me to drag my finger from Denver to Salt Lake City the long way.

He brought out a small thatched tube of some sort and held it up.

"Chinese handcuffs," he said.

They didn't look too much like handcuffs.

"Place each of your pointing-fingers in either end." I did. I didn't see how they could be handcuffs in any way. Once inside, he helped me pull my fingers away from each other and the thatching tightened preventing my fingers from coming out of the tube. I pulled and pulled, trying to pull one finger out at a time, both at once—I even used my teeth to hold the tube while I pulled with each finger. I started to panic a little bit—the harder I pulled, the tighter this trap became.

"So much in your world is done by force. Yet sometimes, instead of pulling as hard as you can, all you need to do is push. Push," he said.

"Push?"

"Push."

I pushed my fingers together, just to appease him. The tube became loose. I took my fingers out one at a time.

"In our martial arts, very often it is not *our* momentum that we use to defeat the opponent; instead we use *their* momentum against them.

In Dellatre's Tales of a Dalai Lama, *he writes of a conversation between the Dalai Lama and a Western philosophy professor both viewing a group playing volleyball. The Dalai Lama expresses concern, asking, "Why should anyone be playing against anyone else? Everyone tries to keep the ball in the air. That's all there is to it. When the ball hits the ground, it's a sad moment for everyone and you'll notice how they take a moment to console the person responsible."*

The professor responded, "In our country . . . we divide into opposing sides and then we try to make the others miss the ball."

Confused, the Dalai Lama commented, "But the ball must hit the ground all the time." He began to weep, concluding, "Such a way to play with the human spirit."

In your game of soccer, you all try to kick the ball all the way up to the corner where the goalie has trained countless hours to defend. Yet, very often, the best shot is right to him, between his legs. The toughest shot of all to stop." He paused for a moment. "Why are you always trying to *beat* people in these games anyway? Another Western habit, I suppose— always needing a winner and a loser. It's very combative. It's sad, actually.

"Like with your Western way of war. You know, very often it is *non*violence that gets things done most effectively. If there's no one to fight, then no fight can occur. Without waging war, no war will be waged.

"Yours is a world of opposites, Ian. For you, things are black and white, right or wrong, big or small, good or evil, east or west. And for you, this creates problems. Yet for me, it does not. Going east and landing in the west is just part of the *Tao*. Everything is connected. The world is not black and white. Yet, you make claims that because a god cannot create a rock that he cannot lift, he is thus not a god. You have even put spirituality on a par with logic. There is so much more than logic."

I sat silently for a bit more, nodding slowly as if trying to understand. He raised his eyebrows. I asked, "The 'Tao'? What is this?"

He slowly looked to the Old Man, raising his eyebrows towards him as if to ask, "Would you care to answer this?" though he said nothing.

The Old Man nodded, confidently. "Certainly. The Tao is a rather complex and historically rich concept, dating back to the sixth century BC. It is the basis for one of the two schools of Chinese thought, known as 'Taoism.' It is literally translated as 'The Way.' It is the ultimate reality: the cosmic process that represents the continual flow of the universe. *That* is the Tao." He was nodding, somewhat boastfully, as if I and the sage were impressed. I wasn't, as I'd already seen enough of this

"Action by Non-Action"
This Taoist phrase is translated, "wei wu wei."
Gandhi put into practice the Hindu ethic known as "ahimsa," or, nonviolence. His government won independence from the forceful British colonists through such passive methods as boycott, peaceful protest, and fasting. Martin Luther King, Jr. successfully used similar nonviolent methods in his fight for human rights.
"The softest thing in the world rides roughshod over the strongest."
–Tao Te Ching

"The fundamental idea of Buddhism is to pass beyond the world of opposites, a world built up by intellectual distinctions . . . and to realize the spiritual world of non-distinction, which involves achieving an absolute point of view."
–Buddhist scholar D. T. Suzuki

from the Old Man. Though I was somehow proud of him, knowing how seriously he took all of this. It was nice for him to have a chance to be onstage. I imagined the sage was pleased with his answer.

"If one asks about the Tao and another answers him, neither of them knows it."

–Chuang Tzu

I looked to the sage. He shook his head slowly. "In your answering the question, you failed to answer. In speaking of the Tao, you admit your lacking. To explain the Tao, is to explain your failure to know."

I sat in silence. The Old Man now sat in silence. I came to his defense.

"That wasn't fair. You tricked him."

"Not a trick," the sage replied. "No tricks. Just the quest for enlightenment."

That was definitely a trick, but I moved on. "Enlightenment?"

"Yes, Ian. The mutual interrelation of all things. The breaking away from pure logic. To silence your thinking and awaken your intuition. To *be* without thinking. It is at *this* point that you will know yourself. You will resolve your Earthly opposites and experience the interconnected cosmic process that interpenetrates all of nature."

"The true seeing is when there is no seeing."

–Shen Hui, Chinese Zen Master

I still felt like he had been avoiding answering my questions, like he was just full of riddles. Though, there was something peaceful about his demeanor.

"When you came to me, Ian, you felt conflicting feelings. You felt like I was *extraordinary* and *ordinary* at the same time; that my disposition was simultaneously *comforting* and *discomforting*. And this created angst for you.

"Your mind is clouded, Ian. It's clouded by habit. The habit of your society: your schooling, your language, your paradigm. It's also clouded by your self, your ego, your *being*. Lucky for you, this has only been a habit for a few years. You can break this habit through becoming enlightened."

I supposed there was something to this—my conflicting feelings, my eastward travel bringing me west. "So how can I do this? How do I break these habits?"

"This is not easy. It takes time. It will not happen today. Nor tomorrow. Yet every day will be like this one."

That must have been a riddle of some sort. "So it's impossible?"

"No, it's possible. It just requires you to forget everything you've learned. It will happen in the same way that you remember things that are on the 'tip of your tongue,' as they say. You remember these things, not when you focus directly on them, but when you turn your focus away. You will have to turn your focus away from this goal, and in doing so, you will achieve it."

"It will only happen if I ignore it?" This couldn't be right.

He sat silently for a moment, then continued, "I want to help you with this, Ian. I will help quiet your mind. It is only when you have a quiet mind that you may become enlightened. I will ask you a number of questions, and I want you to let them permeate you. These questions are not riddles—not like the ones you're used to. There's no answer. There's no lesson to learn. There is just a question. Let the question consume you. And in this consumption, your mind will clear."

I couldn't wait to hear this. So I sat silently, cooperating.

He spoke clearly, crisply. "You know the sound made by two hands clapping. What is the sound of one hand clapping?"

I sat.

He sat, though his sitting seemed so much better than my sitting, as if he actually got something out of that question. One hand clapping? It wouldn't make a sound. But what would *that* sound like? Does he mean the rushing of the air? Or maybe it was half of the sound that two hands made. But one hand doesn't make *any* sound. Then, out of impulse, I raised my right hand off of my lap so that my palm faced me and my fingers were outstretched. I looked at the sage and, as I did, I swiftly brought my four fingers down to my palm. I did this repeatedly. It made a soft clapping sound. I smiled. I figured he'd be very proud of this answer.

His face showed anything but pride. He shook his head. "That is the Western answer. That is your habit." He sat silently.

"Okay. I will try again," I said.

"There is no *try*, Ian. Don't fight it. Let the question consume you."

> "Empty your mind of all thought."
>
> –Lao Tzu

> "In clapping both hands a sound is heard. What is the sound of one hand?"
> –Hakuin Ekaku
> Japanese Zen Master
> (1686–1769)

Koans

The Buddhist term "koan" refers to the seemingly non-rational puzzling statements or anecdotes aimed at helping in meditation. The idea is not to solve them, but for them to help clear the mind. Many examples are given in the text. One other:

A monk saw a turtle in the garden of Daizui's monastery and asked the teacher, "All beings cover their bones with flesh and skin. Why does this being cover its flesh and skin with bones?" Master Daizui took off one of his sandals and covered the turtle with it.

I sat silently. There seemed to be a lot of silent sitting going on and this was my way of saying, "Okay, I'll do that."

He answered my silence, "What is your original face before you were born?"

More silent sitting. My face? Before I was born I didn't have a face. Okay. That was it. Let the question just be a question. I nodded to him. I definitely didn't understand this exercise yet, but I played along to see what would happen.

"Change change," he said.

I nodded.

"Describe an apple without thinking of one."

Now my head was starting to feel light. It was different than I'd felt before with the problems given by the Old Man. It was a good feeling, but strange. Not strange—unique.

"If you meet a man of the Tao on the roads, greet him with neither words nor silence."

The questions now were starting to feel right. I didn't fight them. They just consumed me, in a way. I think I understood what he had been saying. I was starting to feel it. Yet as I started to feel it, I ignored the feeling. It was enlightening. But I was still trying to actually solve these things. It was nice, though.

"That is what you need to do to become enlightened, Ian. It takes great patience. It takes time."

"Yes. Yes. I think I understand." I was a little disappointed that we didn't go further. That he didn't let me sit in that state for a while.

"When you get to the state of enlightenment, then you recognize your part in the action of the universe. The universe is part of you."

I smiled and sat silently.

He continued, "It is in this way that you can eliminate evil—the evil that you and your

---

Karma *Means "Action"*
Fritjof Capra explains, "It is the active principle of the play, the total universe in action, where everything is dynamically connected with everything else."

Zen Master Suzuki Roshi writes that before birth, we are one with the universe. Once born, we develop feelings and perceive ourselves as separate, "[just] as the water falling from the waterfall is separated by the wind and rocks. . . . When you do not realize that you are one with the river, or one with the universe, you have fear."

He concludes, "When the water returns to its original oneness with the river, it no longer has any individual feeling to it; it resumes its own nature, and finds composure. How very glad the water must be to come back to the original river!"

Realizing this connectedness, Suzuki writes, "Our life and death are the same thing. When we realize this fact we have no fear of death anymore, and we have no actual difficulty in life."

Western cohorts are so concerned about. You can do this not by fighting outwardly, but by looking inward. What you must do is eliminate your desires. It is only from desire that evil springs. You desire money, and when you don't get it you experience despair. You desire pleasure, and without it comes despair. And, when these desires *are* satisfied, you become bored and anxious, looking for more desires to fulfill. It is an endless cycle that subsists as a universal human condition. And it's destined to fail. Destined for sadness, pain, evil."

I thought about this. It was kind of a scary thought. And getting rid of desire—that seems impossible. What could be a way to even apply this to my life?

"Let me give you a way to apply this to your life," he said, knowingly. "Think of a time when you needed a good night's sleep— the night before a big game or an important test, for example. You go to bed early and you lie there telling yourself to go to sleep. You basically lie there and *desire* to be asleep. But your desire gets in the way of your sleeping— as long as you are lying there thinking to yourself, *I want to fall asleep, I want to fall asleep,* you don't fall asleep. You only attain your goal of sleeping when you stop desiring it.

"Or, if you want to stop thinking about a green apple, you first have to eliminate that *want*. As long as you *want* to stop thinking about a green apple, you'll be thinking about that green apple. So, just do this with everything—eliminate desire.

"Not only will this allow you to eliminate evil and achieve enlightenment, but it will help to release the hold on you of material objects. If you don't desire them then they can't control you."

Practical, yes. But it didn't seem like I could do this with everything. After thinking

---

Buddhism has no word that directly translates to the English "evil." While there are evil actions, there is no "force" of evil as we know it. Instead, there is akusala: *a state of mind opposite to that of* kusala, *which is a state of mind that leads toward doing things intelligently, skillfully, beneficially, which is our synonym for "good."*

Happiness and Desire

"Perfect happiness is the absence of striving for happiness."

–Chuang Tzu

"In this world there are only two tragedies. One is not getting what one wants and the other is getting it."

–Oscar Wilde

In Anna Karenina, *Tolstoy describes Count Vronsky after finally winning the hand of the woman (Anna) he long desired. Vronsky realizes that he is not nearly as happy as he had expected: "It showed him [Vronsky] the eternal error men make in imagining that happiness consists in the realization of their desires."*

Eliminate Desire . . . Gain Control

"We are possessed by the things we possess. When I like an object, I always give it to someone. It isn't generosity—it's only because I want others to be enslaved by objects, not me."

—Jean-Paul Sartre, Existential philosopher

In 1964 Sartre refused the Nobel Prize for Literature. He said, "I don't want to be a prisoner to my status . . . I consider that the greatest honor I can have is to be read."

about this for a moment, I *did* come up with a problem in his 'desire-elimination' scheme. I asked him, "If I want to eliminate desire, isn't that just a desire itself? The desire to eliminate desire?"

He shook his head slowly—obviously not as interested in my suggestion as I was. "I have two responses for you, Ian, and then I must go. First of all, to solve your supposed problem, you can just take your desires one by one. First, get rid of the desire for material goods. Then, the desire for fame. Go through the list of all your desires until there's only one left: the desire to not desire. Once you eliminate this one, you're left with no desires whatsoever," he said, shaking his head, as if disappointed in my suggestion.

"My second response for you," he continued, as if he had recovered from his first response, "is to just eliminate desire. Don't reason through it. Do it. Eliminate desire. This will take work. Though once you achieve it, you will eliminate your sense of self and achieve nirvana."

I sat peacefully, watching him talk. I wanted to thank him. I didn't feel totally enlightened or anything like that, though I did feel like I got a small glimpse of what it might be like. There was nothing left to argue

---

The Noble Eightfold Path

Laid out by Siddhartha Gautama (the Buddha), this is the Buddhist guideline to proper development mentally and ethically. Through this, one may break free from suffering thus attaining the truth in all things.

<u>*It involves having the correct . . .*</u>

1. *View—understand oneself and the purpose of suffering.*
2. *Intention—be free from ill-will.*
3. *Speech—speak no lies, nor harsh words.*
4. *Action—act mindfully of others.*
5. *Livelihood—earn a living which does not harm other beings.*
6. *Effort—work to promote good.*
7. *Mindfulness—have awareness of one's actions and thoughts.*
8. *Concentration—practice proper focus, often through meditation.*

about with him. Nothing. I sat silently. I sat for what was probably minutes, or hours, or however long. It didn't feel like minutes, though. It just felt. It was. I sat. I never did thank him.

He got up. "You are welcome." It was sincere. He realized my gratitude. I smiled at him. He picked up his globe and headed east.

Nirvana

Literally translated as "snuffed out." In the same way that a fire is extinguished, the elimination of desire "extinguishes" the self. It is this state of emptiness—known as "sunyata"—that the Buddha is said to have passed into upon his death.

Ian woke up on his own. No alarm clock. No parents calling to him. He put on his jeans and an old T-shirt, his sneakers, and a baseball cap. He walked downstairs and seemed surprised to see that his parents were not at their usual spot, sitting perched and ready to discuss the evening's events. He announced, as if still speaking to the sage, "Of course. What could we have talked about today? What words could I have used to examine these issues with my parents? Then again, what issues are there to examine?" He seemed almost cheerful about it.

But as he sat down at the table and began to peel an orange he got that pensive look on his face. As he focused on the orange he almost started to look troubled in a way.

"Ian," his mother said as she hurriedly walked into the kitchen. "Sorry, dear. I didn't know you'd need us today." She motioned with her hand for his father to follow from an adjacent room.

"Need you?" Ian asked, unsure.

"Want us," she corrected herself nervously, shrugging her shoulders. "Or just like to speak with us, maybe?"

"How well we live—that is, how thoughtfully, how nobly, how virtuously, how joyously, how lovingly—depends both on our philosophy and on the way we apply it to all else."

–Lou Marinoff, from *Plato Not Prozac!*

Here Marinoff explains that many people's troubles come not from past psychological issues but from presently lacking a consistent philosophical doctrine.

"You'd like to speak to us, son?" his father asked encouragingly as he followed Ian's mom to the kitchen table.

Ian crinkled his nose a bit and responded, "Yeah. Yeah, I guess so. I mean, I didn't think so at first but, yeah." He assumed his now-comfortable, usual practice of retelling the dream and all that happened in it. His parents assumed their now-usual calm, caring demeanor as they listened, and maybe even learned a little.

After Ian took a final breath and paused long enough so that it was obvious the story had ended, his father raised his eyebrows as part of the conversation ritual. Ian nodded in return.

"Well, son. I must say, I find the way that you—or this sage—deal with language and with suffering and evil to be very intriguing. It's funny though: I think we can come to the same conclusion, yet with a totally different approach."

Ian nodded for him to continue.

"Well first, I too can see the power behind the view that we are all connected by and to nature. And I think that achieving happiness requires practice. And I understand how getting rid of desire—or more specifically, of emotion and passion—can help eradicate much suffering. The *difference*, though, is that I think we can use reason to do so. Actually, I think it *requires* that we use reason and logic, whereas your experience showed otherwise."

"Two paths to the same summit," Ian's mother interjected, in her witty way.

Ian looked at her and smiled and then directed his motion-detector-like eyes back to his father. "How so dad? I mean, from last night's adventure it does seem like reason and logic might create more problems than it solves."

His father smiled, "Okay. Before I talk to you about your fears," he said slowly, raising his eyebrows, "I want to play a quick game or two with you." He reached into his pocket and pulled out a silver dollar. "If I tell you that to guess ten times which hand holds the coin *and* I tell you that it will be in my right hand seventy percent of the time, how many times will you guess that the coin is in my right hand?" he asked Ian, matter-of-factly.

After a quick shrug of his shoulders, Ian responded, "Seven."

His dad made a discerning *tssk* sound with his lips. "If you're interested in guessing correctly, then you should choose the right hand every time. By choosing it only seven times, the odds are that you'll be wrong some of the times and have very little chance of being right that it's in my left hand. Counterintuitive, but true."

Then he placed the coin under a napkin on the table, placed two other napkins on the table, and mixed them up, so as to conceal which one hid the coin. "I'm going to have you guess which napkin has the coin under it. After you point one out, I will lift up one of the other napkins to show that the coin is not there. Then I will give you the option to change your initial decision, okay?"

Ian nodded.

"Will you change your initial decision?" his father asked.

"We haven't started yet," Ian responded.

"True, but think through it. Given the situation, will you change your decision?"

Ian shook his head, "It shouldn't matter. It's still the same odds. No, I wouldn't change. I would be confident with my first choice."

"Ahh, the ol' confidence in guessing something that is totally left to chance," his father said, shaking his head. "If you used reason, logic, you'd see that it is more beneficial to change your answer. Twice as much, actually."

"How could it be, dad?"

"When you first choose, your odds are one in three that you choose the coin. And they are two in three that you choose the empty napkin. So, when I reveal an empty napkin, the coin will be under the remaining napkin two out of three times. That's much better than one in three. Relying on *reason* would make you considerably richer," he said, staring at Ian, as if waiting for it to click. Ian stared at the napkins momentarily until the rationale washed over him and manifested itself in a smile and an intellectually satisfying giggle.

Ian added, "Yeah, you're right. If I choose the empty napkin first and then switch, then I will win the coin. I have a two-thirds chance of choosing the empty napkin first, so I should switch every time," he said, still giggling a bit with excitement.

"It's counterintuitive at first," his father suggested. "There's a lot of 'counterintuitive' out there. *Counter*—against; *intuitive*—intuition. Reason clears it all up. Just think about why computers are so efficient—they

Now known as the "Monty Hall Dilemma" (see the three-napkin-and-coin example in the corresponding text), it was initially posed in 1959 (in a slightly different way) by Martin Gardner in Scientific American. When Parade columnist Marilyn Vos Savant wrote in 1990 that the game-player should change his decision once the incorrect option was revealed, more than 10,000 people responded, a large majority saying she was wrong, though probability theory, logic, and experience show that she was correct.

" . . . every error is due to extraneous factors (such as emotion and education); reason itself does not err."

–Kurt Gödel

don't have all those emotions and feelings and what-not getting in the way," he said, taking a deep breath.

His father smiled, "So I want you to think for a minute about why we fear something, son." He continued without allowing even a second for Ian to think about it. "Because we lack understanding. We can't reason through it. When you were much younger you were afraid of the dark. Some nights you even slept with your bedroom light on." He paused to smile. "Do you remember being scared of the dark?"

Ian nodded, somewhat embarrassed.

"Follow where reason leads."

Founded in 300 BC, the school of philosophy known as "Stoicism" held that we should live in strict accordance with reason. Now the term "stoic" has come to mean "unemotional." The original term derived from the Greek stoa, *or "porch," in reference to the porch on the agora in Athens where stoic philosophers met.*

"Virtue is nothing else than right reason."

–Seneca, Roman Stoic

"If you are distressed by any external thing, it is not this thing which disturbs you, but your own judgment about it. And it is in your power to wipe out that judgment now."

–Marcus Aurelius, Roman Stoic

His father continued, "But then you learned about the rotation of the earth and the cause of night and day, about all of the amazing animals that are nocturnal, how nothing really changes in your room when the sun goes down. Your ability to reason totally eradicated your fear of the night.

"I was kind of like this with tarantulas at one point. I was scared to death of those things. But a friend of mine who is a zoologist and expert in spiders taught me about them. They're really very tame creatures. And some don't even have the capacity to bite. So, once I learned all there was to learn about them, I met him at his office and actually let a tarantula crawl on my arm. I even pet it. They're surprisingly soft," he said, smiling. "With the help of reason, I overcame my fear."

Ian nodded.

His dad added, in a more serious tone, "I happen to think this sort of irrationality is what drives the fear behind racism. But maybe we can revisit that once I get my point across. Do you get it?"

"Yeah, it definitely makes sense," Ian said. "But I still don't think that I could get rid of my fear of tarantulas just through reason."

"You haven't had the practice, son. You haven't had the time to reason things through.

Think about death, for example. Talk about *the unknown*," he said, shaking his head. "I too have heard logic that attempts to squelch this fear and reason it away, but that fear is still there for me a little. As you know, many cultures have created myths to help explain away the unknown of death. This will always be an unknown, though. It all comes back to practice."

"Practice? You mean practice reasoning? Thinking?"

"Yes, exactly. It is very much a way of life—to never stop questioning, to learn how to reason better and better. That's the thing we do best, you know. Reason. Logic. It's what humans were made to do, really. Part of the natural order of things. If we ignored that, we'd be ignoring what it is to be human. Any creature can follow its desires, but humans have the unique capacity to reason—no other animal uses logic, mathematics, abstract reasoning. Ignoring our capacity to reason would be like an eagle walking everywhere all of its life. Not much of an eagle."

"So all of this reasoning helps solve the problem of suffering? I mean, we should just be purely logical about it all?"

His dad nodded and looked at his mother who was bobbing her head back and forth a bit as if in slight disagreement, though wanting to hear more from him.

> "Death is one of two things. Either it is annihilation, and the dead have no consciousness of anything; or, as we are told, it is really a change: a migration of the soul from one place to another."
>
> –Socrates

Natural Law

A theory that sets moral guidelines on the grounds of our essential human nature—it renders morality not as human-made but, instead, as something discovered as a result of examining human nature.

Stoics relied on this in determining that we ought to follow reason and logic, as this is what nature intended for humans. It was also posited by Aristotle as a means for determining how one ought to live. Natural law has since been applied by religious scholars as far back as Thomas Aquinas as a means for grasping divine law. The Roman Catholic Church has applied this to sexual morality to argue that the natural purpose of sexual intercourse is procreation and any other intent would be outside of the natural order. There are Natural Law overtones in the Declaration of Independence as well: "We hold these truths to be self-evident, that all men are created equal, that they are endowed by their Creator with certain inalienable rights."

"Passion" = suffering?

Stoics believed that reason would free one from the troubles of passion and emotion. By following reason, one develops apatheia—*apathy or detachment. In doing so, they avoid the pitfalls of passion, defined by Stoics at the time as "suffering."*

"Freedom is secured not by the fulfilling of one's desires, but by the removal of desire."
–Epictetus,
Greek Stoic Philosopher

He answered, "I know it doesn't sound like the most romantic view, but you do see the point, right? Emotion and passion can be great one day, yet miserable the next. Logic and reason are hard and true. I mean, passion is referred to as a 'fire in the belly' for a reason. And crimes of passion are so different from all other crimes. Handled differently in court too. Allowing our emotion to come into play when trying to determine the way of the world may not be the best idea.

"If you are suffering, it is a product of not reasoning properly."

He paused for that little morsel to sink in and then continued, "For example, think of that friend of ours, Mr. Belzden. He smokes almost a pack of cigarettes a day yet he won't go in the ocean for fear of sharks. The number of people who die from cigarette smoking is about a billion times greater than those who die from shark attacks. He's just seen those movies with sharks, and heard the sensationalized reports on the news and attached an emotional component to his fear.

"Or that friend of yours, Anatol."

"He's not really my friend," Ian responded, almost feeling bad for "de-friending" someone.

"Okay, well he's scared of flying, right?"

Ian nodded.

Psychologist David Myers suggests four factors that account for irrational fears:

1. *innate fears passed down from our ancestors; e.g. fear of spiders*
2. *things out of our control; e.g. plane flights*
3. *immediate, present dangers*
4. *dangers most available to our memory*

Fear doesn't deter many smokers even though it is estimated that smoking causes 3 million deaths per year. Myers suggests that if cigarettes were harmless, except that 1 in every 50,000 packs were filled with dynamite, while they would result in considerably fewer deaths, they would be outlawed immediately and certainly more feared.

Despite a reported 67 deaths due to shark attacks since 1876, people still fear them in greater proportion to other considerably more dangerous things.

"Yet he'll go anywhere in a car without making a fuss. But the odds of dying in a car are considerably greater than in a plane. He's just heard more about plane accidents, or maybe it's the fact that they're more out of his control, or maybe because they're sensationalized by the media as well. Regardless, his fear is a product of something irrational, illogical."

"Geez, dad. That really is two paths to the same summit. Eliminate passion and desire and emotion—but do it by totally embracing reason instead of ignoring it."

His dad smiled while Ian winced thoughtfully.

"And through the use of reason, son, we can not only make informed decisions for our own lives—such as how to choose rationally, what to fear, etcetera—but also for the greater community as a whole—such as how to run a political state, what to fund, and whatnot. All by employing our naturally-rooted logic and reason." He finished as though he had said the final word on the topic.

> **To Fly or Drive . . .**
>
> *According to a Gallup poll survey (taken before the September 11, 2001 terrorist attacks), 44 percent claimed they were fearful of flying. This, despite the National Safety Council's report that in the second half of 1990, Americans were 37 times more likely to die in a car crash than a plane crash, mile for mile. David Myers alludes to this in what may initially seem a counterintuitive statement: "When I fly to New York, the most dangerous part of my journey is the drive to the . . . airport."*

"But dear," Ian's mother began, in an inquisitive tone, "How is it that we can really determine what it is that's natural for humans to do? I mean, what if one human just doesn't like to rely on logic? What if humans are naturally inclined to do something else—like love? Why can't *that* be the *natural order* of things?

"I love the approaches that you and Ian have taken to this—it's actually been somewhat illuminating for me. I think next time we might want to spend a little more time on the positive side of passion and of love. It may be just a bit more powerful than you both are suggesting. Powerful in a positive way, I might add," she said as she stood up from her chair with an almost preemptive *I told you so* look on her face.

"I would *love* that, honey," his father responded, smiling, standing up with her. "And I was sort of playing devil's advocate here you know." This also seemed to be a preemptive response to her forthcoming *I told you so.*

"We need to run, dear," she said to Ian as she rustled his hair and kissed the top of his head. "We'll be back this afternoon." They walked toward the door, his father looking back sheepishly over his shoulder at Ian sitting at the kitchen table.

Ian sat for a moment staring at the front door. He stood up and walked towards the door, putting on his sweatshirt.

No Thing

I yanked on the door and was amazed at what I saw: nothing. I saw nothing. I saw it in a way that I'd never imagined. I quickly closed the door. I pinched myself to make sure I was awake, as if that would help. I said "ouch" just because I thought I should, though I didn't pinch myself very hard. I opened the door again. I stood at the edge of the doorway, looked out, and saw *nothing*. I didn't see a blank tablet. I didn't see white. I didn't see black. I didn't see something holding nothing. I saw no things. Not one thing. I didn't much like it.

So, I closed the door and sat in the entryway, right there against the front door. I grabbed the book that was always there—the one about the history of art and how, like science, it too seemed to go through paradigms. Though these weren't truth-seeking paradigms— more like stages, or fads even. Yet they did seem to mirror what was going on with the science of their time. For example, at the time that science conformed to religion, art also conformed and was very non-confrontational; at the time of the scientific revolution, the art was very rule-based; then art started to ignore any sort of rules, and then it tried to make statements, and then it would say nothing at all. Nothing at all. A plain red canvas, for example. Nothing more. Maybe this artist painted something really amazing but he just used the same color red to paint it all. Was that art? What is art? Does art improve on itself? Who decides if something is art? Art can't include just anything. But if there are guidelines, then who chooses them? I know there's some government organization that funds art, but how do they choose? Do *they* somehow know the standard of art? Or do they just get to define what that standard is?

Art that is nothing, though. Now *that's* something.

Just then there was a knock on the door. It kind of shocked me as I had gotten used to the idea that there might be nothing outside my door. I stood up and opened the door. Jeff stood there jutting his head out towards me, raising his eyebrows as if to say, "You ready to go?" I had forgotten about our field trip.

The Problem with Solutions

This field trip was part of a mandatory program that our school ran called, "Grown-ups and the Workplace." Each student has to visit a person at his job for a day to see what he does. It was supposed to help us realize that our education serves a purpose and to encourage us to set goals for ourselves. Jeff and I chose to visit the "Solver of all Problems." This woman's job was to visit with people and solve their problems. She's not a psychologist. She actually refers to herself as a "Perspective Changer." We were actually looking forward to it.

As I walked out the door and down the street with Jeff, I still felt a little uneasy from my earlier trip outside. "Jeff, did you happen to see nothing on your way here?"

He looked at me as if this was some sort of riddle.

"Never mind," I said. I figured it would be too hard to explain—seeing nothing. I chalked it up to my maybe being "enlightened" at the time or something.

After a short walk, we entered the office door. It seemed sort of like a doctor's office. It had that sterile smell and a bunch of couches with month-old magazine subscriptions on the tables—the addresses on the magazines were all scratched out so that after a patient's meeting with the doctor, he or she couldn't go to her home and steal all her stuff.

The secretary noticed us. "Ian and Jeff?"

We nodded.

"You're right on time. Dr. Curtis is expecting you. First door on your left."

We walked up to the first door on the left. On it a sign read:

The hardest door to open is the one that is already open.

No name, just the sign. I looked at Jeff and shrugged. He nodded like he understood the sign's significance and opened the door. We walked into the room and Dr. Curtis, we presumed, was sitting behind her desk reading a file.

"Hello, boys," she said, standing up to shake our hands. She looked very smart. Very neat. Perfect glasses. Perfect hair. Perfect smile. Wearing plain white clothes—pants and a shirt—they were perfect. She seemed very nice. She seemed smart and she had hardly said anything. "You're just in time. I have a number of patients coming in back-to-back. They should all be relatively short meetings. I just need to give them a quick new perspective and they're on their way."

Jeff and I nodded.

"It's like math," she continued. "If you want the answer to be *six*, and you don't like *three plus three*, then you can change it to any number of formulations: *twelve divided by two* for example. Or you could write a *nine* on a sheet of paper and turn it over."

We both smiled.

Just then the door opened. A man entered, somewhat nervously.

"Hello, Jim," Dr. Curtis greeted him. He immediately became more comfortable. "Have a seat."

He sat down, his hands folded in his lap.

"What can I help you with today?" she said.

"Well, I'm just nervous lately about flying. It's just that I don't trust the other passengers."

"What exactly are you afraid of?" Dr. Curtis asked.

"Well, I know the chances of this are very low—exceptionally low—but I'm still afraid of one of them bringing a bomb on to the plane. Research shows the odds of someone doing this are one in fifty thousand. I guess it's just not low enough to keep me from worrying."

She nodded, "So if I can lower the odds even more, would this help?"

He nodded hesitantly. I wondered how she could have any control over this.

"Okay," she continued, "all you need to do is bring a bomb on the plane."

He shook his head to signify that he didn't follow her solution.

She explained, "The odds of one person having a bomb are already low. But just imagine how low the odds are that *two* people on the *same* plane have a bomb. So if *you* bring a bomb, the odds that *another* person has one would be astronomically low. You're free to fly without fear."

He smiled. This seemed to help him. "Thank you so much."

"You're welcome. Good luck."

And he left. Jeff and I wanted to talk to her about this but another patient came in the door. He looked like a college guy. She shook his hand, he sat, she asked for his problem.

He began, enthusiastically, "I was with a friend of mine and I found a rare silver coin. He wanted it and started saying that it was his. This obviously isn't the case—there is no way that this coin could be his. Now he says he's going to steal it from me. So that's my problem—how can I prevent him from stealing this coin from me?"

She nodded slowly and, in her thoughtful way, responded, "I've got two answers for you. First of all, if it is his he *won't* steal it."

He raised his eyebrows in anticipation.

"My 'Principle of Stealing' states, *You can't steal your own property*. It's a self-evident truth of stealing—no one has ever accomplished it. So if it's really his, then he can't steal it."

His raised eyebrows crinkled thoughtfully.

"Now, secondly, if it is *not* his and you really want to prevent him from stealing it, then just follow that principle and *give it to him*. This is a surefire way to prevent him from stealing it from you. Problem solved."

He nodded. She stood up and shook his hand. He left.

Then another knock at the door. In came another man. He was bigger and looked like he lifted a lot of weights or something. She shook his hand, and asked for his problem.

"I'm a police chief," he began. "And we have had a huge problem with people breaking the speed limit law on a certain residential street. It seems like the more tickets we write, the faster people drive. I just want this to stop—I want people to obey the laws on this street."

"What is the posted speed limit on this street?" Dr. Curtis asked.

"Thirty-five."

"And what do people tend to drive there?"

"Most of the tickets we write are for fifty."

"Okay," she paused, "raise the speed limit to sixty."

She stood up and shook his hand. He walked out.

As he was going out, a boy who looked to be about our age walked in. He smiled at us and sat down. He began, "My mom told me to come see you. I have a problem with the boys on my street."

"Go ahead. What's the problem?" Dr. Curtis asked kindly.

"Every time I go out to play, they bring these big squirt guns out and drench me with water. Now it's like they have this power over me to get me to do what they want when I go out to play. I guess I could try to fight back but I don't think I could take them all on. There's like four or five of them."

Dr. Curtis smiled, "This is simple, Noah. Just take a big bucket of water with you next time you go out." When she said this, the boy started to smile, like Dr. Curtis was giving him the permission to drench *them*.

"Then," she continued, "when they come to bully you," his eyes widened even more, "just dump the water all over yourself." He immediately hunched down in confusion. "By doing this, you'll take the power out of their hands—if you're already drenched, then what force will a little water from a squirt gun have? I call this *disempowering*. Okay? Does that make sense? Disempower them. Good luck."

She turned to us. "Four for four this morning. Pretty simple stuff, really. I've got one more quick one before our break—that is, unless one of you has a problem to work through."

The door opened. A nice-looking high school-age girl came in. She immediately looked at us, obviously concerned we were there. Dr. Curtis shook her head as if to say, "They're no problem." The girl shrugged and smiled. Problem solved, I supposed. The girl started talking before she sat down, "I have been dating the same boy for two years and we haven't even kissed. My parents tell me that premarital kissing is wrong and that I could go to hell for it. 'No premarital kissing,' they say every day, 'no matter what.'"

Dr. Curtis held up her finger, announcing that she had heard enough. I wondered how she could possibly solve this one. "Just don't get married," Dr. Curtis said, assuredly. "That makes premarital *anything*—including pre-marital kissing—impossible. Nothing can precede marriage if you don't ever get married." She stood up and shook the girl's hand and she left.

"That's my profession," Dr. Curtis said, turning to us. "It's all in your frame of mind. If you don't like something, you can either change yourself or you can change that thing. Every problem has a solution. Even if your problem is that you want to find a problem that doesn't have a solution. I'll let you two solve that. It's time for my break. Good luck, boys."

"Is there a problem with no solution?" I thought. And if so, is *that* a problem? I supposed it would be if you're a "Solver of Problems" whose motto is "Every problem has a solution." Though I had one problem that had always bothered me. I did think it was unsolvable—and a bit depressing—a problem of life and death. Actually, it was really just a problem of death.

"Do you have a question before I leave, Ian?" Dr. Curtis asked thoughtfully, apparently sensing my body language. She was an expert, after all.

"Well, yes," I responded, nervous about giving her an unsolvable issue. "I don't think there is really anything that you can do but I'd at least like to share it with you."

She smiled and nodded encouragingly.

"It deals with the fact that I am dying," I said sternly. She widened her eyes, obviously concerned. I continued, "Ever since I was born, I have been getting closer to death. So *by definition* I am dying. Right? There's really no way around it."

She nodded caringly, almost as if she'd heard this before. "Tell me, Ian. When you walk into a store an hour after they have opened, would you say they were closing?" She continued without my answering. "Of course not. But if you walk in five minutes before closing time, and the shopkeeper is sweeping up the store, locking the back door, and organizing the shelves, you would say he's closing, right? It's much more a state of mind—they're not closing until they start getting ready to close."

I nodded, grinning. She had done it. Solved the unsolvable, and in a very uplifting way.

"So, are you dying?" she asked.

I shook my head, smiling still, "Not until I decide I am."

She smiled and patted me on the back. We thanked her and left her office.

"What time is it?" I asked Jeff.

"It depends," he said.

"Yes, I suppose it does."

"I'm hungry," Jeff said.

"Then you should eat," I responded.

We nodded. Some problems were easier to solve than others.

Chapter 8

Faith and Reason

The heart has its reasons, of which reason is unaware.

–Blaise Pascal

A person with faith needs no explanation; for one without faith, no explanation is possible.

–Msgr. O'Sullivan

"Are you rested after our last meeting?" the Old Man greeted me as we climbed down the ladder and out the tube.

"Yes, I guess so." I was really brimming with questions now. Questions about what exactly was going on with all of this. But also questions about what he and I had done so far. I was really starting to see things differently. I felt like I was more a part of the universe, like I was more connected to it. It was like I had previously been living in a big magic show and was being given the explanation for all the tricks.

"You?" I asked him.

"Well yes, Ian, I'm always rested. Thank you for asking. I'm just going to stop by the teachers' lounge for a minute before class. I'll see you there shortly."

" . . . it is in our idleness, in our dreams, that the submerged truth sometimes comes to the top."
–Virginia Wolfe

Instead of going straight to class, I figured I would go by Alexis' homeroom class. I peered in through the door's window and saw her talking to a woman. From behind, the woman looked older, probably some teacher, or maybe a substitute because I didn't recognize her. Alexis was smiling and chatting away. She wasn't typically a chatterbox—not with adults,

195

at least. And her smile wasn't a big smile—big enough that I knew she was happy, but small enough that I could tell she was probably talking about something serious.

I got so she could see me through the window and obviously startled her. The teacher turned and looked at me. I'd never seen her before but she looked familiar. Alexis came running through the door.

"Ian, it's so good to see you." She hugged me. "But what are you doing here? You shouldn't be here. I shouldn't see you outside of the ladder-tube for another week probably, at least not without the Old Man here."

"What do you mean, 'outside the ladder-tube'? What's wrong with seeing you here?"

"Because I can't. We just can't. It sounds like you're doing so well, though. I'm so glad I get to see you just for a little bit at least." She paused to smile at me. "I really shouldn't even be talking to you here. It could mess everything up, you know?"

"No, I don't know."

"That wasn't meant to be answered. I know you don't know. But you don't need to. You're doing fine."

"Doing fine?"

She hugged me and smiled. "I'll see you soon."

"Do you want to come over to Jeff's with me tomorrow?"

She hesitated. "I want to but I can't. I'm busy then."

"How about next week? We could go to the fair."

"I'm busy then too. I can't wait to see you soon though." And she hugged me again. Lots of hugging, at least.

But don't *I* decide when I see her in my dreams? I guess I just did decide that. There she was—in my dream. But then I really *don't* see her during the days.

"Ian, soon we'll really be able to just go out and do stuff again. Things are so different now. It's like I had been living in a big magic show and then I was given the explanation for all the tricks. You'll see—if you already haven't."

What? That was *my* magic show analogy. But I never actually said that.

"Bye, Ian." She went back through the door, locking it behind her. I peered back in and the old woman looked at me, nodding a sincere nod as if everything was okay. They got back to talking. I went to class.

The Old Man was teaching today. As I glanced around at the classroom, I supposed today was yet another day when my classmates' parents opted not to sign the consent form. I was beginning to wonder if my parents even read the forms they were signing. Though I must admit, I was actually enjoying my recent schooling—much more interesting, much more active than the typical sit-listen-memorize-regurgitate method I'd gotten used to. Not that that method is bad—I suppose they need some way to judge us kids. Good thing for me my brain can function that way; some friends of mine just seem to learn in different ways: they have a different brain composition or something. Like in football: not everyone can be a linebacker—some are designed to run quickly, some to block, some to kick, some to pass, and some not to play at all. But in school, despite our differences, we're all treated the same and the same is expected of us. We all have to play by the same rules. It seems kind of unfair in a sense because . . .

My daydream-within-a-dream was cut short as my glance over my left shoulder continued throughout the room. In the back corner was a student—a student?—I'd never noticed before. A person—a person?—like I'd never seen. He looked somewhat human-like, but it was as if he—it—was wearing a mask. A human mask. The same way that humans wear monster masks, though however real these monster masks are, we always know there's a human under them because we don't believe that monsters just roam the streets. As a matter of fact, if I were a monster and wanted to disguise myself, I think I'd just go out as myself: people would think I was a human in a monster mask. Instead, I got the feeling that this person—monster?—was really a monster (are there such things as monsters?) disguised as a person. It was very unsettling.

Old Man to the rescue. "Ian, today is your lucky day. Today you have a chance to win some real cash. All you have to do is make some choices. One choice, really." He glanced towards the big table in the front of the room. On it were two boxes. One was clear, and in it was a stack of money. The other was opaque—its blackness prevented me from seeing if there was anything inside it. I figured it was going to be one of those pick-the-for-sure-thing-or-take-a-chance games. I was wrong. It was much more complicated—though in a strangely simple way.

"Ian, this person," and he gestured to the monster-thing, "this *being* in the back of the classroom has brought with him a game for you to play. This being is like none other that you've ever encountered. He is a tremendous *predictor*. I told this being what a strong desire you have for that new science set, amongst other things, and that you would do whatever you could to obtain the maximum amount of money in his game. Okay?"

"Of course. Geez, there are so many things I could do with some extra money. How much are we talking about? What do I need to do?"

"This *being*, whose name is Damus, assessed you as you walked to school today. Before you got to class, he placed 1,000 dollars in the clear box, as you can clearly see. Also, he *either* placed 100,000 dollars in the black box *or* he placed nothing in it. He acted on the black box in the following manner:

If he predicted that you would open both boxes, then he put nothing in the black box.

If he predicted that you would open *only* the black box, then he put the 100,000 dollars in that box.

"Damus has played this game a great many times. He is so good that his current 'successful predictions' statistic is 99 percent. He correctly predicts a person's choice 99 percent of the time."

"So all *I* have to do is predict what *he* predicted and then act accordingly?" I asked and he nodded, assertively. I continued, "Why don't I look under the black box and then, if there's nothing there, I'll take what's in the clear box?"

"That's not an option. You need to announce your decision before you choose. Your options are either:

Open the black box only, OR

Open both boxes."

The Problem of "Newcomb's Problem"

This paradox was originated by physicist William Newcomb. Robert Nozick brought it to the public in his 1969 paper, "Newcomb's Problem and Two Principles of Choice." He wrote:

"To almost everyone, it is perfectly clear and obvious what should be done. The difficulty is that these people seem to divide almost evenly on the problem, with large numbers thinking that the opposing half is just being silly."

I thought through this: if Damus predicted that I would choose both boxes, then he put no money in the black box, but if he predicted that I would pick the black box only, then he put the money in it. So, if I choose the black box only then I seem to have a better chance at getting all the money.

So that was it. I was in this game to get the maximum amount of money, so I would choose the black box and hope that Damus was right. I will choose just the black box.

But I felt a strong inclination to pick both boxes—the money in the clear box was guaranteed. And the money in the black box was unsure.

"Does Damus make the money appear or disappear the instant that I pick? Is he waiting to teleport the money the moment that I choose?"

The Principle of Expected Utility
(Choose the black box only)

When confronted with a choice of actions, one should choose that which provides the maximum value (utility).

In this version of Newcomb's Problem, this principle guides one to pick the black box only:

Picking the black box only provides a utility of $99,000 (99% × $100,000).

Picking both boxes yields a utility of $2,000 (1% of $101,000 + 99% of $1,000).

"No. Damus has *already* acted on the black box. He has already predicted what you will do and then acted accordingly."

"Can I use the chalkboard to figure this out?"

He nodded.

On the board I constructed a sort of payoff table which included my two options—to choose one box or both boxes—and the two outcomes of the black box—it will either have money or no money:

		Outcomes	
		Black box has money	Black box has no money
Choices	Open black box only	$100,000	$0
	Open both boxes	$101,000	$1,000

"It seems, mathematically at least, that I ought to choose to open both boxes. Since the money's already been placed, I may as well get the guaranteed 1,000 dollars. In either case, I have the opportunity to get more money.

The Dominance Principle
(Choose both boxes)

If a particular action always leads to a more optimal outcome in a given situation, then one should choose it.

In this version of Newcomb's Problem, this principle guides one to choose both boxes. Regardless of whether there is money in the black box, choosing the clear box will always result in gaining $1,000 extra.

"I'm a *Two-Boxer*," I announced.

"Very interesting," the Old Man remarked. "Though you failed to account for the predictive abilities of Damus. Remember, if you pick both boxes, then there is only a one percent chance that there is money in the black box. Right? And if you pick the black box *only*, then there is a 99 percent chance that the money is in there. So, looking at it that way, you really ought to pick the black box only."

I had walked back to the other side of the room. The table was now separating the Old Man and me. I was proud of my shrewd calculations on the board, though the Old Man seemed to have a point too. I felt stuck. Damus must have figured that I would realize the best option was to choose both boxes so he would have placed no money in the black box. So, maybe all I need to do is *become* a *One-Boxer*. If I can some-how be inclined to "one-box" then that will make me a One-Boxer and Damus will have placed the money in the black box. But how can what I do *now* affect what Damus did *earlier*? Or was it Damus' action earlier that affected me now?

How could I convince myself to one-box? Would this even be enough for the money to end up in the black box?

The Old Man suggested, "Imagine that your best friend Jeff were here and that he knew the situation and had the opportunity to gamble on it. Knowing that Damus is 99 percent correct, wouldn't Jeff be smart in bet-ting that, if you choose the black box *only* there will be money in that box? And since that seems such a smart bet, isn't it best that you one-box?"

That's what I needed, some real convincing. Of course it made sense for Jeff to make that bet. Actually, even though he hates betting, I believe he *would* make that bet. I felt like I was becoming a One-Boxer. And, being a One-Boxer, there would be money in the black box, and I'd be justified in choosing that one alone, despite the more rational choice I'd decided on moments ago.

"I'm a One-Boxer!" I exclaimed.

"Before you do your one-boxing thing," the Old Man said, with a smirk on his face, "I just want you to imagine one more scenario."

"What scenario?" I responded.

"Just imagine that *both* boxes are transparent—made of glass. Just try this and see if it helps with your decision."

I played along, looking at the boxes as if they really were both transparent. Again, there were only two possible situations, and I thought through them both:

If there were no money in the black box, then I would certainly choose *both boxes*. This way, I'd at least get $1,000 and not miss out on it by choosing only the black box.

If Damus placed the money in the black box, then I would certainly choose *both boxes*. This way, I'd get the money that was placed in the black box as well as the extra $1,000.

I had solved it. If I did have access to what was in the black box then regardless of the situation, I would choose both. I was definitely a Two-Boxer.

"I'm a Two-Boxer," I said proudly to the Old Man.

He replied, "It seems that you've chosen the rational option. I saw your gears turning as you thought through the glass-box scenarios. And, along with your little calculation on the board, it seems as though the *rational* thing to do is to choose both boxes. But, Damus rewards only those who choose the black box. So, could it be that Damus rewards *irrationality*? In that case, it seems that the rational choice just may be the irrational one. It is rational to choose irrationally. It's irrational to choose as you have: rationally. So what is it that makes an action rational?"

Rational is irrational? Irrational is rational? How could that be?

I didn't care. The Old Man was trying to confuse me. I had thought through both sides long enough. This was the rational choice and, in being the rational choice, it was the rational thing to do.

"I'm ready." I opened the clear box and took the 1,000 dollars out of it. I smiled, knowing this meant all the ice cream and CD's and science sets that I could want. But the big money was about to come. I started out as a One-Boxer. Damus likely picked up on that as he observed me walking to school and put the money in the black box. This, I believed, would not only get that science set, but would also get that new car for my parents. I went to the black box. The Old Man raised his eyebrows—are those "yippee" eyebrows or "bad choice" eyebrows? I started to lift the box.

> **"Why Ain'cha Rich?"**
>
> *David Lewis explores the issue of rationality as it relates to Newcomb's Problem. In doing so, he answers the above question (which is also the title of his essay). He writes that the person in this situation who chooses rationally is not rich—i.e., he chose both boxes thus getting only $1,000. It is only the irrational person who achieves greater sums in this situation.*

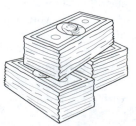

"We accept the reality of the world with which we are presented."

–"Christof" from the movie *The Truman Show* in which the main character is born into a Hollywood world for the sake of a TV show. This becomes the only reality he knows.

"Ian!" his mother yelled from downstairs.

"Mom? What, mom? Hold on. This is important!"

"What is, honey? *What's* important?"

"Mom! But the money in the black box! The money in the black box!" Ian was yelling to her as he walked downstairs. "Mom, some of that money would have been for you. I have no idea if there was even money in that box! Couldn't you wait just two more seconds to wake me up?" Ian was frustrated. He was genuinely interested to see the outcome and was now left guessing. He seemed to still be bothered by his decision. Now that she had woken him up, he was curious to see what she would have done. What will she possibly have to say about his rational irrationality? He sat down at the kitchen table and told her of his predicament.

"Son. Even though this was just a dream, I think there's an important lesson here. First—and this is not the main lesson, though it's directly tied to it—it's a lesson in prefixes. You spoke of *ir*rationality and you spoke of plain ol' rationality, but you left one out—a very important one that has a lot to do with the whole human experience."

"But it seems that something is either rational or it's not. What else is there? Pre-rational? Re-rational?"

She laughed. "Well, this is kind of a tricky one." She paused, "A."

"*A*rational?"

"Yes. Arational. Something that is neither rational—reasoned through logic, mathematics, etc.—nor *ir*rational—reasoned through *poor* logic. We act outside of reason all the time. You know, I married your father for 'arational' reasons."

Ian raised his eyebrows hesitantly, awaiting a potentially mushy response.

"Love." She smiled. "You often hear people say that something just *feels* one way or the other. This is romance. This is love. Oftentimes this is your *conscience* speaking to you about ethics—right and wrong."

Ian looked confused still, though his interest seemed completely piqued.

"Breakfast, Ian. I've made pancakes—with chocolate chips."

Moral "Reasoning"

In the 1970's Harvard professor Lawrence Kohlberg established the three stages of moral reasoning. In the third and most advanced stage—"Post-Conventional"—mature adults act morally due to an internal conscience and not for external reasons such as reward or punishment.

He smiled, his eyes big. He tried to retain his enthusiasm a bit, as he was still left unsatisfied about his premature wake-up. "Chocolate chip pancakes! Yum!"

His mom grabbed two plates of steaming hotcakes, fresh off the griddle. "Have a seat, Ian." He sat down. "Okay. Both of these plates have exactly one pound of pancakes on them, each with 20 chocolate chips. They are equally far from you. Also, they were taken off the griddle at exactly the same moment. Go to one of the plates and start eating."

Ian looked back and forth. He started to lean toward one and then looked at the other. After some deliberation he realized that there was absolutely *no* perceivable difference between the two plates. So he went to one and sat down.

"How did you choose?" his mother asked, knowingly.

"How could I explain that, mom? There was absolutely *no* difference between the two plates. I'm glad I chose, though. Great pancakes."

"So?" Her head tilted.

"Mom. I just chose. I just went towards one. There was no reason."

"Would you say that you chose irrationally then?"

"No." Mouthful of pancakes, shaking his head as if it were starting to hurt from all this verbiage. "Mom, if I were older and liked coffee, I feel like now would be a perfect time to drink coffee. I could take a sip as though it was the ultimate life force—that it had cleansed me, oiled any rusty joints, and sped through my brain as if to clean it out just like those plumbing liquids that you see on TV commercials removing all the guck from the pipes. Coffee, though. Yuck."

She smiled. Then continued more sternly, "Ian, would you say that you chose rationally?"

"Ohh." He seemed exasperated. "No. There was no rhyme or reason to my choosing. Nothing rational, reasonable, logical about it. No choice tables. Nothing to possibly factor into a rational decision."

"You chose *a*rationally."

"Okay. I get the point. But, having gotten over my excitement about the pancakes, I'm

The Death of a Donkey

Medieval philosopher Jean Buridan tells a parable of a donkey—a donkey that stands exactly between two equally sized piles of hay. Given his situation, the donkey has no rational basis for choosing one pile over the other—while it may be rational to choose to eat versus not eat, there is nothing to distinguish eating one pile of hay versus another. Unable to rationally choose between the haystacks the donkey remains in the middle, undecided, and dies of starvation.

Man Versus Donkey

Seventeenth-century philosopher Benedict Spinoza substitutes a man for Buridan's Donkey. He argues that the man will choose one over the other, thus proving that he has free will. He writes:

"If I concede that he will [starve to death], I would seem to conceive an ass, or a statue of a man, [but] not a man. But if I deny that he will, then he will . . . have determined himself, and consequently have the faculty of going where he wills and doing what he wills."

"There has never been, nor will there ever be, enough time to be truly rational."

–Robert Ornstein
The Evolution of Consciousness

interested to see the *real* point." He perked his head up and smiled. "Thank you for the pancakes. And I understand your point now too. But what do we do with that?"

"Well, we let our 'passional' nature become a legitimate part of our decision-making process. Growing up, my mother always said to me, 'Listen to your heart.' If you relied *only* on reason, then you would still be sitting here looking at the two plates of pancakes. You might have reasoned that eating pancakes is better than starving to death—and that would certainly be a rational choice. But then you would have no way to solve which plate to go to—reason alone would prevent you from making a choice. A *purely* rational being in your situation would have died."

Ian nodded, smiling a bit now. "So how can this help in real life, mom? Like in other situations besides pancake-choosing?"

"Well, for example, we know that God either exists or He doesn't. These are the only two options, even though we may not be able to prove it either way."

Ian nodded, encouraging her to continue.

"And, either you believe in God or you don't. It's not really a decision one can avoid.

Forced Options

Early -twentieth-century psychologist and philosopher William James examined the role of the passions in decision making. He explored the forced *option: one that cannot be avoided by just ignoring it. For example, a man stuck on a snowy mountaintop has the option to take a path that may lead to the bottom, or to remain on the top. He must pick one or the other. To not decide is a decision—he will remain on top, unsure which option to choose.*

James argues that the "religious option" is one such "forced" option. Being overtly skeptical and waiting for more information does not allow one to escape the religious option. Skepticism, "is not avoidance of option; it is option of a certain particular kind of risk." That risk, he notes, is the risk of missing out on the truth of God's existence.

"If you choose not to decide you still have made a choice."

–Rush, Musical group, from their song "Freewill"

By saying that you'd rather not decide or by avoiding the matter altogether, you've really just chosen to not decide, which is a choice in and of itself."

"Okay."

"So, let's make one of those little decision boxes that you talked about in your dream." She got a pen from near the telephone and wrote on a napkin:

	Outcomes	
	God exists	God doesn't exist
Believe in God	Eternal happiness	Life has religious purpose. But you lived according to false doctrine.
Don't believe in God	Eternal damnation	Life has no religious purpose. You avoid living according to false doctrine.

Options is labeled on the left side.

"Here we can see that it's logical to believe in God. Seeing as how eternal salvation is on the line, it certainly seems reasonable—*rational*. Can't you see why it is rational to believe in God?"

There was a lot of head-nodding going on.

His mother continued, "Imagine that you were on a hike and came across a rope bridge over a canyon. If you weren't very sure that the rope on this bridge was very sturdy, and this bridge presented a shortcut of thirty minutes, would you take it? What kind of wager would you make?"

"Well, I probably wouldn't. Though I'd study the bridge and maybe ask others what they thought about it. But risking my life wouldn't seem worth the time I would save."

"Good answer," she responded, as if she were worried that Ian would risk his life for a mere thirty minutes. "You would not risk dying in order to save thirty minutes. So imagine if we were talking about an *eternal* life. It certainly seems like it would be worth potentially wasting a relatively small amount of time at church, or believing something false. The rewards for wagering correctly would literally be *infinitely* good. And the

Wagering on God

Seventeenth-century mathematician Blaise Pascal provided what he believed to be rational grounds for belief in God. Known as "Pascal's Wager," he showed that belief in God is the prudent thing to do. "There is nothing to ponder," he wrote, "because one has little to lose and an infinite amount to gain."

A Third Option?

"Pascal's argument only looks persuasive if we take our options to be just two: Christianity or atheism. A third possibility is belief in a jealous non-Christian God who will see to our damnation if and only if we are Christians. . . . So Pascal's argument is of no help in deciding whether or not to accept Christianity. For we may be damned if we do and damned if we don't."
–Stephen Stich

"We are what we repeatedly do."
–Aristotle

"We are what we pretend to be, so we must be careful what we pretend to be."
–Kurt Vonnegut

"Just as no one can be forced into belief, so no one can be forced into unbelief."
–Freud

punishment for wagering incorrectly would be infinitely bad."

Ian smiled at the idea of infinite rewards.

"So, in a sense, people must make an arational decision on grounds of something rational."

"Is that bad?"

"Well, look back at your predicament with the black box. You felt in your heart that you were a Two-Boxer. Because of evidence and a feeling you had, you noticed that you just weren't a One-Boxer—even though you wanted to be. You *wanted to want* to One-Box. This brings up the question of how much control you have over your beliefs and inclinations. For example, grab that glass of water. Try to believe that it's cold."

The water was cold. "I do believe it's cold," he said.

"Good. Now, I'll give you that 100,000 dollars that you missed out on if you can believe that it's hot."

"Okay," Ian smiled, awkwardly. "Wow. This water's hot."

"*Really* believe it," she said sternly. "Don't just act it out. Don't put your finger in it and say to me, 'Oh, whew, that's some hot water.' I want something more meaningful than that— I'm paying you a lot of money here.

"Let's try something else. I'll give you that money if you can get yourself to believe that there are invisible gremlins hiding under the kitchen table."

Ian looked at her quizzically, "Are you saying that invisible gremlins are like God?"

"No, son. I'm trying to get you to perform an exercise of believing in something that you can't prove. Maybe I should add a punishment to your disbelief, to give you an even greater incentive?"

Ian raised his eyebrows in anticipation.

"I'll give you that money, dear, if you can believe that Alexis is reading a comic book right now. But if you don't believe it, you will be on restriction for the next four years, never allowed to leave the house. Can you see how it is in your best interest to believe this?"

Ian cringed at the thought of four years of being grounded. "But how can I believe something that I," he paused, mumbling, nodding slightly, "don't believe?"

"That's exactly the point. And it's somewhat illuminating. Regarding belief in God, for example, some just don't have faith. People make this accusation against scientists and philosophers all the time; they assume that because God is not provable through science or logic that these academics can't believe. We now realize that this is not necessarily true—while a scientist can't *prove* God, he could certainly believe. What's important here is the concept of this arational faith. For many religions, faith is the key. Yet, it is posited that one gets the gift of faith from God. Quite a tight little circle."

"A circle?" Ian asked.

"Yes. Basically, God gives you what you need to meet him."

She continued, "But people convince themselves of things all the time. You hear the phrase, 'That person can rationalize anything—and believe it.' It's a whole area of study in psychology on the phenomenon of self-deception. People really can lie to themselves. If you lie to yourself about something enough times, you'll start to believe it. Kind of like property and 'squatters' rights.'"

Ian flashed his confused look.

"It's a legal notion that if you inhabit a piece of land that is not yours for over seven years, it legally becomes yours."

Intellectually satisfied look. Head nod.

"So the point here is to really delve into yourself and try to recognize just what control you have over your beliefs. Some people really do think that they can control their thoughts. That's actually one of the thoughts they think they can control."

Agnostic—*coined by T. H. Huxley (1825–1895). It derived from the early Christian gnostic, meaning "knowing." (The prefix, "a" means "opposite.") The agnostic holds that the assertion or denial of God's existence cannot be proven either way, and thus cannot be known.*

"I seek not to understand in order [to] believe; but I believe in order that I may understand . . . unless I believe, I cannot understand."
—Anselm of Canterbury

"If you don't believe it, you won't understand it."
—Augustine

"The madman is not the man who has lost his reason. The madman is the man who has lost everything except reason."

"You can only find truth with logic if you have already found truth without it."
—G. K. Chesterton

Queer Philosophical Idols

William James explains that ignoring our "passional" nature and instead wait-ing for "enough" evidence would be irrational—doing so would cause us to miss out on certain truths which cannot be known by reason alone.

"When I think of . . . this command that we shall put a stopper on our heart, instincts, and courage and wait . . . till such time as our intellect and senses working together may have taken in evidence enough—this command, I say, seems to me the queerest idol ever manufactured in the philosophical cave."

Confused, yet intellectually appreciative look.

"And a final point regarding all of this, son—maybe the most important point of all—something I mentioned earlier when we talked about letting the passions become a legitimate part of our reasoning. You know, even the most hard-headed skeptic makes his decisions and formulates his philosophies based on his passional nature."

Ian remained with the confused, intellectually appreciative look.

"In the same way that the arational person is passionate about find-ing the truth, the skeptic is passionate about avoiding error. The reli-gious zealot follows a desire to know God, even though that knowledge is never certain and is based on faith. The skeptic constantly claims we can't know things—especially regarding the existence of an eternal being—and, because of that, he follows a desire to avoid error. The skeptic may never be wrong, but he risks missing the truth and in this case, eternal salvation. The religious person risks being wrong about his faith, but he also may be right and achieve great things. They're both wagering something. And they both wager it based on their passions:

The believer, or *faith-affirmer*, is passionate about finding God, but risks being in error;

The skeptic, or *faith-denier*, is passionate about not being in error, but risks missing the truth.

The Ethics of Belief

W.K. Clifford writes, "It is wrong always, everywhere, and for anyone, to believe anything upon insufficient evidence." This is contrasted by James who writes, "Our passional nature not only lawfully may, but must, decide an option between propositions, whenever it is a genuine option that cannot by its nature be decided on intellectual grounds; for to say, under such circumstances, 'Do not decide, but leave the question open,' is itself a passional decision—just like deciding yes or no—and is attended with the same risk of losing the truth."

"And they both take a leap of faith to know what they claim it is they know. Think back to how it is that we know things: there's something required outside of reason. Pure reason sells us short—whether we're talking about what we lack in our senses, or the inconsistencies of reason, shortcomings of induction, or all the thought experiments of brains-in-jars, evil geniuses, and the more obvious notion that we can't distinguish dreaming from waking. Pure reason can only get us so far—and then we must leap. Look." And again she provided a diagram to help explain:

Fideism—*the notion that reason and logic are irrelevant to belief in God.*

"For since, in the wisdom of God, the world did not know God through wisdom. . . . For the foolishness of God is wiser than [the wisdom of] men"
—Paul, Corinthians 1:21–25

Senses + reason + logic + science ⟶ **Leap** ⟶ Earthly knowledge

Senses + reason + logic + science ⟶ **Leap** ⟶ Divine knowledge

"There's a leap required for all knowledge. Our senses and reason can only take us so far—that's why we have the capacity to transcend them. We have faith. Without that, we really would miss out on *any* sort of reality.

"The challenge for you, son, is to try to really examine your beliefs. Which are you proud of? Which would you like to change? Take a conscious role in trying to change those beliefs of yours. Many people believe that prayer or meditation can help do this. Yet many believe these things are unchangeable. And, for those beliefs you can't change, how do they affect who you are?"

Overwhelmed look. Though kind of excited too.

"I knew you'd choose the 'rational' choice in that strange box-picking situation you presented. You have such a good mind for those

---

A Leap of Faith

Søren Kierkegaard coined the above phrase. The impetus behind it was his belief that "Truth is subjectivity." A leap of faith is required because of the lack of objective certainty. He writes, "If I am capable of grasping God objectively [then] I do not believe; but precisely because I cannot do this, I must believe."

Because he cannot know—*with absolute certainty—he relies on faith to help him "leap" over the gaps in logic and objectivity.*

The Faith of Atheists and Believers.

" . . . atheists are my brothers and sisters of a different faith, and every word they speak speaks of faith. Like me, they go as far as the legs of reason will carry them—and then they leap."

"Reason is excellent for getting food, clothing and shelter. Reason is the very best tool kit. . . . But be excessively reasonable and you risk throwing out the universe with the bathwater."

—Yann Martel, *Life of Pi*

"Reason's last step is the recognition that there are an infinite number of things beyond it."

—Pascal

Knowledge Through Intuition

Psychologist David Myers shows that intuition is as important to one's framework of knowledge as logic. He defines intuition as, "our capacity for direct knowledge, for immediate insight without observation or reason."

Likewise, in Malcom Gladwell's book, Blink, *he defends the subtitle of his book, "The Power of Thinking Without Thinking." He references numerous examples and studies in which our intuition provides us with "truths" not available to our rational mind.*

things. I just hope this great ability to reason doesn't overshadow the richness of the ability to feel and to utilize your intuition."

His mother smiled as she kissed Ian on the forehead. Ian smiled back at her.

Why He Loves Her

I'd had enough of this. No rest in the kitchen, no rest in my bed. Jeff's house was rather restful. So it was off to Jeff's.

When I got to Jeff's I knocked on the door. I prefer knocking to the doorbell: so much more personal.

"Hi Ian!" Jeff yelled from inside. "Come on in!"

I always felt a little weird just *coming on in* to people's homes. What if a normal occurrence in their house was not a normal one in mine, and I just *came on in* to it? What if not everyone inside was ready for me to *come on in*? And what if I knocked something over when I came on in because the people who put things in the walkway on Saturday mornings weren't ready for other people to start coming on in? I poked my head in the front door. "Hello." I always felt like I was breaking in to someone's house when I just came on in. "Jeff?"

"Ian. Hey. Down here." Another successful coming-on-in. I walked down the basement stairs and Jeff was holding a thick black wire, showing it to me. One end had a video screen on it and the other end extended into a mouse hole in the base of the wall.

The hole actually looked like it was made for mice, almost like the holes in cartoons. "Are you trying to get rid of the mice?" I asked.

He grimaced at me as he shook his head. "No, this is amazing. You'll love this. This gadget is the 'View of a Lifetime.' That's what it's called. I've just gone through one series with it. It's amazing. Look. Through this screen you can see perfectly into this mouse home. And you can actually hear what they're saying to each other through this ear-piece. The last family I watched was really cool. And that's the thing. This device speeds up time like crazy—you can watch the lifetime of a mouse in like a half hour."

"That's kind of sad. How does the mouse feel living for only a half-hour?" I responded.

"The mouse doesn't know. This gadget functions on some new relativity principle. The pamphlet explains it all, but I couldn't really understand it. I was actually hoping that your dad could explain it. But that doesn't matter for now. You've got to see this."

"So what do you do?" I asked.

He handed me the tube. As I looked at the screen I saw a newborn mouse and his mother. Both very cute. "Here, put the ear-piece in. You can hear what they're saying to each other." I put it in my ear. "Good morning, Fester," the mother mouse said. Fester opened his eyes and smiled. He obviously couldn't talk yet. As I watched, Fester soon began walking, then reading, then even playing soccer (except they didn't have a hand-ball rule because they just have feet). It was amazing. It was like Fester was five mouse-years old already.

"Ian, you've got to tell me what's going on. I can't see it or hear it. Tell me what's happening."

"Like a play-by-play? What do you want me to do? Tell you everything?"

"Yeah, everything. Pretend you're narrating for a kid's book or something. Hurry, the mice are getting older."

"Okay." As I looked back to the screen, Fester had just come home from school. Second grade. Geez, talk about time flying! Just then his mom said to him, "My, you look so grown-up today . . . time just flies by." Strange.

"Ian, what's happening?"

"Okay. Fester just got home from school."

"And? What are they saying? What's going on?"

"Okay. Okay. Hold on." Then Fester's mom continued. "You know, son, I'm so proud of you."

"Yeah, mom, I know. Why, though? Why are you so proud?"

"Well, you're a very hardworking student, you're polite, and you're so adorable."

Fester smiled.

"You know how much I love you."

"Yeah, mom, I know. Why, though? Why do you love me?"

"Because you're a beautiful person."

"What's that mean? A beautiful person?" He paused to clean his whiskers. "You must love me for a reason. Like because of my good grades? Or my nice white coat? Or the way I play soccer?"

"No, son. I just love you because you're a beautiful person. You really are. It's been so fun to watch you grow up and become this person."

"That's weird, mom. I don't see how you can love me for no real reason."

Time went by. Quickly, though. The mice didn't seem to notice it, except on occasion when they'd say "My, how quickly time flies." But Fester never really said that. Only his mom. Maybe she noticed it because, in a way, she was watching Fester from the outside just like I was watching her.

And time certainly was flying. Fester was now graduating from high school. As they came home from the ceremony, his mom scratched his head with her claws and told him how much she loved him. "Now I know why. Because I graduated. Right? Is that why you love me?"

She sighed, "No, Fester. I like that you're smart. But I love you because you're a beautiful person. You really and truly are. I can't put my claw on it any better than that—you really are a beautiful person."

Fester shook his head out of frustration. "You know, mom, this whole love thing of yours really doesn't make sense. I know that you love me, but I think there are reasons that maybe you just don't realize. If there *aren't* reasons, then how could you love me? How could you love anyone? And when you did, it would just be some haphazard reason, or no reason at all. Just seems strange, that's all."

She smiled.

"Thanks for a great party, mom. I can't believe I get to go to college now." He hugged her. "Good night. I'm tired. I'm going to sleep."

College went fast. Really fast. A matter of about two minutes for me. Fester did very well in college. Looked like he had some fun. Visited home quite a bit. And now, three years after college, he was getting married. A very cute wedding. The wedding party looked great in their tuxedos and light blue dresses. At the toast, his mother stood up, with a fine piece of the sharpest of cheddar cheeses, and toasted, "To my son and his bride, both of whom I love, simply because they are beautiful people." To this, they all raised their cheese and there was a loud cheer and they all ate. Fester's mom was showing signs of age, and Fester himself looked a little more dignified. After the toast, Fester's wife thanked his mom for such a heartfelt toast and a wonderful wedding. "Heartfelt?" Fester asked. "But she didn't say anything, really. Just her usual thing." He looked at his mom, looked at his wife, looked back at his mom, saying, "You know, you both have the same twinkle in the red part of your eyes." He smiled. They smiled at each other. He continued, "I would just hope that you figure out someday why you really love me. So that it means something. So that it has some sort of consistency to it."

His mom nodded, kissed his forehead, and went to check on the other guests to make sure that all was well with them. Fester's wife smiled at him, "Your mom really is amazing."

So, Fester and his wife had kids, built a cute little mouse home in a wall just two blocks away from Fester's mom, and continued the daily routine. Then, one day, Fester got a telegram regarding his mother's health. She was not doing well. Fester's wife was with the kids all afternoon and evening, so he went to her home immediately, by himself.

His mom was lying on her back when he walked in. She lay in bed, with the covers pulled up to her little nose. Even though she obviously wasn't doing well, she had a little smile, and her eyes twinkled a bit as she saw Fester come in the room. There was a flower at her bedside, and nothing else really. "Mom, why are you smiling? Are you better? I got the telegram. Are you okay?"

"Fester, I am glad that you could come be with me. I don't think I have much time left. All this time goes so quickly anyway, especially my time with you. You have been such an amazing son and such a treasure to watch grow up. I love you."

Her head was now nodding off to the side, her whiskers on that side folding under her head as she looked at Fester. She smiled. He felt a lump in his throat. He felt, though, that she would finally share with him this secret of love that she'd had for so long.

As she looked at him for what he thought might be the last time, her eyes twinkled at him, and she closed them. "Mom. Mom." She opened her eyes. "I love you."

She smiled. Her eyes twinkled. She nodded slowly. She closed her eyes.

Fester's eyes were now watering. "That twinkle in your eye. Mom. I love you. You truly are a beautiful person. I'm sorry that I never noticed it before. Or that I could never express it. It's just that, when you said . . . "

She opened her eyes again, for the last time, "Shh, Fester, I know. It's how I've loved you all along. It's how you love your wife, and your children. And it's how you have loved me. You don't have to put it into words."

As her eyes closed, Fester put his paws around her and kissed her soft white cheek. He was smiling now. Crying and smiling.

Chapter 9

Free Will

I am firmly convinced that a man has no more to do with his own conduct than a wooden Indian. A wooden Indian has a little advantage for he does not even think he is free.

–*Clarence Darrow*

"You sound to me as though you don't believe in free will," said Bill Pilgrim.

"If I hadn't spent so much time studying Earthlings," said the Tralfamadorian, "I wouldn't have any idea what was meant by 'free will.' I've visited thirty-one inhabited planets in the universe, and I have studied reports on one hundred more. Only on Earth is there talk of free will."

–*Kurt Vonnegut*, Slaughterhouse Five

So there we were, my friend and I. I guessed he was a friend by now—it would seem silly that we spend so much time together and I not consider him a friend. He was taking me to get ice cream at lunch. Kind of odd, too, that he was treating me to ice cream—getting ice cream is sort of a normal outing. Yet, in its normalcy it was strange. Strangely normal.

I had a real craving for ice cream. Chocolate ice cream. Maybe even a double scoop—I felt like I could eat a whole gallon of it.

"A dream is an answer to a question we haven't learned to ask."
–Dana Scully,
The X-Files

As he chuckled to himself for some reason, we turned to walk into the ice cream shop. He perused the selection, stroking his beard as if deciding what to get. I had a brief moment of wanting strawberry—it would actually be a pleasant change from my standard. I like the mix of creamy and fruity—almost like I'm eating something healthy even though I know it's not, but that's how I rationalize it. I finally decided to go with strawberry but, at the last second he says to me, "You ready for that double of chocolate?" My mouth watered. "A double scoop of chocolate, please," I tell the server. Great decision.

"You know, that sounds good to me too—just make it a single though," he said. We walked out of the store gleefully eating our ice cream cones.

"Thank you. That was nice. What's so special about today? Why the treat?"

"No reason. Just figured it would be nice to get off of school grounds for a bit, let you make some choices of your own."

And here was the catch. "Choices of my own?"

He smiled, subtly. "Free will."

"What's that?" I asked, not sure if I heard him correctly.

"Free will—that we're free to make our own decisions, to decide freely, to choose between one thing and another. It's somehow liberating to choose freely."

"Yeah. Free will, I guess. It's nice."

He laughed again. "Have a good rest-of-day at school."

I got to class and there he was, up in front. "I'm your substitute for the rest of today," he said. "Your teacher is at a conference." No one else was in the class. I knew the ice cream treat was too good to be true. I've heard it said that there's no such thing as a free cone.

He took roll, which struck me as preposterous seeing as how I was the only person in the room. Nevertheless, he read off all 26 names in the class, and I responded "here" to "Ian Pinkle."

Once he figured out who was *here* he asked, "Would you say that you freely choose something if you couldn't have done otherwise?"

"What do you mean?"

"If there was no other choice to make, could you choose freely? Would you call it a choice if I dragged you outside of the classroom and threw you in a pool of water? Would you agree with the statement, 'Ian *chose* to go swimming'?"

"Of course not."

"Why not?"

"Because everything that happened there was out of my control. I really had no choice whatsoever in the matter."

"Did you freely choose chocolate ice cream today at the store?"

"Of course I did."

"I argue differently."

"How could you possibly say that? I almost chose strawberry, but, at the last second, chose chocolate. I could have picked any number of flavors."

"I want to show you two things." He pulled out a big sheet of paper with some strange symbols and numbers on it. "This is a computer printout of your genetic code. Your DNA was scanned as you walked in the room today. None of the other parents agreed to this, only yours. I suppose the others were worried about insurance matters, or privacy rights. Or maybe they just didn't want to know."

"Wow, really?"

"Yes. I want to show you something very interesting about you. You're very flexible, aren't you? You've always been able to touch your toes."

"Yes, I am."

"A result of your genetics. Both of your parents have very resilient muscle fibers.

"Your earlobes are connected to your head. Here's that part of the readout right here—could have told you that without even looking at you."

"Geez. This has everything."

A Part of Human Nature

- *"I am convinced that anyone interested in winning Olympic gold medals must select his or her parents very carefully."*

  –Sports physiologist Per-Olof Astrand

- *" . . . studies imply genes account for about 50% of the difference in intelligence from one person to the next."*

  –Wall Street Journal, 6/20/03

- *Compulsive stealing known as* kleptomania, *is related to low levels of serotonin as well as actual design of the brain. Often, the kleptomaniac steals just for the sake of stealing, not for profit or other gain.*

- *Rousseau and Kant wrote that we all inherit an established human nature.*

- *Noam Chomsky argued that humans have a biological predisposition for learning language.*

- *An article in* Time *(6/2/03) reports that one's environment may "turn on" genes for many traits, including: the ability to fall in love, anti-social behavior, fear of snakes, and homosexuality.*

"Yes. And, as we come to know more and more about human DNA, we realize just how much is determined about us, both physically and psychologically, before we're even born. It's pretty amazing. And here's a rather pertinent one: you have a strong natural affinity for cocoa—the main ingredient in chocolate. You're a *chocoholic* if I've ever seen one."

"You can tell that from my DNA?"

"Yes. And it's all out of your control, wouldn't you agree?"

"Well, I suppose. Yeah. I had nothing to do with the body and genes I was given. Completely out of my control."

"I agree. And here's the second item I wanted to show you."

He dimmed the lights and started the film rolling. It was an old film of my mom and dad with a baby. They were in my home—with different wallpaper—and my mom had a baby in her arms.

"That's you, Ian. Age five months. Pay attention to your parents' conversation. It's slightly misguided, but with all the right intentions."

"Honey," my dad said, "he won't stop crying. Let's put chocolate milk in his bottle and see if that helps. I've read that the more palatable something is, the more of a soothing effect it has on the child. And milk is milk anyway." They poured chocolate milk into the bottle and I immediately quieted down. I drank the whole bottle and then went to sleep. Obviously content and comfortable wrapped in my *blankie* and mother's arms, belly full of chocolate milk. My dad then went to the refrigerator and put the carton back. I could see, from the film, that the whole bottom half of the refrigerator was filled with chocolate milk. The film showed me, three times a day, every day for my first years, drinking chocolate milk while my mom rocked me, and my parents said soft, tender words to me.

"Your dad read about that in a magazine he saw one day. Kind of silly, but it did seem to do the trick for you."

"Where'd you get these films?"

"Never mind that. Would you agree that your upbringing—your parents, home, conditioning, education, basically the whole environment in which you were brought up—was completely out of your control?"

Francis Crick, co-discoverer of DNA in 1953, writes in his 1994 book, The Astonishing Hypothesis: The Scientific Search for the Soul,

"The Astonishing Hypothesis is that 'You,' your joys and your sorrows, your memories and your ambitions, your sense of personal identity and free will, are in fact no more than the behavior of a vast assembly of nerve cells and their associated molecules. As Lewis Carroll's Alice might have phrased: 'You're nothing but a pack of neurons.' This hypothesis is so alien to the ideas of most people today that it can truly be called astonishing."

"Sure. That's obvious."

"And would you agree that your decisions are based *only* on factors related to your *genetics* and your *environment?*"

"I suppose. It seems like that's all there is. In school we've talked about the nature-ver-sus-nurture controversy. Most people seem to think that they both have a major effect on people. So, yes, my decisions are based on either my nature or my nurture."

"Well, then here is my proposition for you: *You, Ian Pinkle, have no free will.*"

"What?" I exclaimed.

"I only use the statements that you have made. Look." And he wrote on the board:

1. Your genetics are completely out of your control.

2. Your environment is completely out of your control.

3. Your decisions are based only on your genetics and your environment.

4. If you act based on things completely out of your control—like the swimming example from earlier—then you can't be said to act freely.

5. *Therefore*, you can't be said to act freely . . . ever.

Hard Determinism (No Free Will)

This is the position that every human action is determined by forces outside of human control. It is the antithesis of free will. Baron d'Holbach summarized this stance:

"[Man] is born without his own consent; his organization does in no [way] depend upon himself; his ideas come to him involuntarily; his habits are in the power of those who cause him to contract them; he is unceasingly modified by causes, whether visible or concealed, over which he has no control. . . . Nevertheless, in spite of the shackles by which he is bound, it is pretended he is a free agent."

This argument sure appeared flawless, yet I *feel* like I make free choices all the time. "But when I decide to write something, in my back-pack I have a pencil and a pen. I could choose either, or both, or choose not to choose at all."

"Then choose one."

I pulled out the pen.

"So, you picked the pen over the pencil, but that doesn't mean you picked *freely*. It's always going to fall back on the argument I gave just a second ago. What you're really saying is:

If I had different genetics and/or a different envi-ronment, *then* I would have chosen differently.

"There is no such thing as free will. The mind is induced to wish this or that by some cause and that cause is determined by another cause, and so on back to infinity."

–Spinoza

"But you *didn't* choose differently. You chose what you chose."

"But I *could* have chosen the pencil. It was right there in my back-pack next to the pen. I've chosen it lots of times before."

The Old Man pointed at a big rock in the corner. Then he went to the VCR and pushed *play*. The film showed a car driving on a winding road. As it rounded a curve, a boulder came crashing to the ground, inches behind the car.

"That was a *close* one," I heard, in a somewhat deep voice behind me. I turned toward the rock that the Old Man had just pointed to. "I guess I was just in a good mood that day—I didn't feel like hurting anyone."

A talking rock?

"Listen to what he has to say, Ian. He's giving the same argument you just gave." The Old Man then turned to the rock. "*Could* you have fallen earlier?"

"Of course. I saw that car coming around the corner and I just fell close enough to scare the driver—maybe give him a greater appreciation for his life. You know, after near-death experiences, people are consider-ably happier than before them."

"Insightful," the Old Man responded. "So you could have fallen earlier? You *could have done otherwise?*"

The rock rocked forward and backward—its way of nodding, I supposed.

The Old Man rewound the film. We sat closer now, and he whispered. "It is true that the rock *could have* fallen earlier," and he leaned in to me, very closely, "*if*," and he took a breath, "if it were just a few ounces heavier. Or *if* that branch it was leaning on were just a millimeter thinner. Or *if* gravity were a tad stronger. Or *if* that gust of wind had blown a second earlier. It certainly *could have* fallen earlier. But it didn't. It fell when it did. It's a good thing too.

"The rock could have done differently *if* its physical make-up or its environment were different." He paused. "So, I will repeat—whatever you choose, it will be based on your genetics or your environment, both of which are completely out of your control. They are

---

The "Free-Falling" Rock

In Spinoza's correspon-dence to Schuller, he wrote that if a falling stone were able to think, "Such a stone . . . would believe itself to be com-pletely free, and would think that it continued in motion solely because of its own wish. This is that human freedom, which all boast that they pos-sess, and which consists solely in the fact, that men are conscious of their own desire, but are ignorant of the causes whereby that desire has been determined. Thus an infant believes that it desires milk freely."

the way they are. You *could* choose differently, just as a rock *could* fall at a different time. You just don't."

"Okay. Wait. If it really is these two things that lead to our decisions and thus our actions, then all we have to do is to be able to consciously change one of them and then we *could* have free will."

He raised his eyebrows in anticipation.

"I know I can't change this body I inherited. But I *can* change my environment. My parents actually did that. They chose to move to this town when I was young because it was safer and had better schools. And I could choose to change the friends I spend time with, or the TV I watch. So, given that, I *do* have control over my environment and so I have free will."

"Your attempt is crafty, but it really just sidesteps the problem. Look at the way you phrased your argument. Your parents *chose* to move. You could *choose* to change friends. But how would you make that choice? You'd make it based on your un-chosen genetics and *current* environment. *Those* two factors would determine that you change your environment."

"You mean that my choice to change my environment is a choice like any other? That it's a product of my genetics and environment? That this choice is out of my control?"

He started right in with his example. "Yeah. Listen, Ian, your parents are either *naturally* caring people—i.e., influenced by genetics—or they've been affected somehow by their environment. Their environment could affect them in a way that they think it best to be in a safe neighborhood, a place where their son can be sheltered and go to a good school. A place where he can best be indoctrinated in what we believe it is important that people know. Each decision is determined. Even the decision to decide.

"And, you know, there are things going on in you that you probably don't even realize."

"Like what?"

"Well, aside from your genetics and your upbringing, which we've already touched on, there's what I call the 'Iceberg Effect.'" He paused as if I were expected to show an outward sign of my intense intellectual curiosity—which I admit I was feeling. So I raised an eyebrow somewhat indifferently. I actually thought we might be off to interview an iceberg.

Can I control what controls me?

Psychologist B.F. Skinner writes, "We are all controlled by the world in which we live, and part of that world has been and will be constructed by men."

"We cannot make wise decisions if we continue to pretend that human behavior is not controlled."

The Inner Struggle
Id vs. Ego vs.
Superego

Austrian neuroscientist and founder of psycho-analysis Sigmund Freud suggested three levels of the mind: the conscious (in which we are aware of our thoughts), the pre-conscious (where the memories and thoughts that are easy to recall are stored) and the unconscious.

It is in the unconscious that a majority of the memories lie, unavailable to the conscious realm yet greatly affecting it. Here the id (instinctual needs) and superego (the conscience) "battle" each other and are then sorted out by the ego.

He continued, despite my reaction. "Did you know that an iceberg's mass is about 80 percent underwater—whatever you see above water, there's a lot more that you don't see. This is similar to human consciousness. There is so much that we don't even realize is going on. And your nature and nurture, these things all have an effect on your subconscious, which, by definition, you're not aware of. You have your '*id*'—your primitive desires and instinctual needs; your '*superego*,' which serves as your conscience and is derived from rules taught by your parents and society; and your '*ego*,' which rationalizes between the two. This ego helps to balance what's going on *behind your own back*, as they say—it serves as a sort of mediator. This mediation often results in a defense mechanism such as denial or rationalization which protects the ego from certain uncomfortable feelings like shame and anxiety. But people aren't in control nor are they even really aware of their unconscious. Yet this unconscious has a great effect on what you do and how you do one thing versus another."

I nodded slowly, wanting to conceal how interested I really was.

"Look at you now, sitting there as if your interest level is low. But your back is upright. You're sitting on the edge of your seat. Your body language—of which you're totally unaware—shows that you're interested in the conversation. There's so much going on with your actions that you either aren't aware of or just don't recognize you do. That's hardly freedom to act: you don't even *know* you're acting, much less choosing to do so. I want to do something with this group in the next room. Come with me."

"Our very acts of volition . . . are but facades for the expression of unconscious wishes, or rather, unconscious compromises and defenses."

–John Hospers, 1950

We went to the room next door and there were twenty kids sitting quietly, like they were ready for an exam. The Old Man announced, "Welcome to the 'Un-Scramble-A-Thon.' On your sheets you will see ten scrambled words. All you need to do is unscramble them to form an actual word. When you're done you may bring your papers forward and leave the room." He passed out the tests. I sat at his desk and looked at the tests. Then the Old Man came and sat down. We sat there quietly, watching the students work. The first person who finished brought her paper to the Old Man. He reached out to get it from her and, in doing so, knocked his pen to the ground. She smiled and picked it up for him and left the room. On a sheet of paper, under column "A" he put a little mark by "Yes." Then another student brought her exam to him. Again he knocked his pen to the ground, though this girl did not pick it up; she smiled at him, and walked out of the room. Then, under column "B" he put a slash mark next to "No." This went on for the whole exam. He knocked his pen on the ground every time someone turned his or her exam in. After the last person left the room, he looked at his paper, then looked at me smiling, nodding his head.

"Yes?" I sat, anxious to learn what the lesson could possibly be.

"Well, Ian, just as I thought. There were two different tests handed out today. The first, 'Test form A,' contained words that all relate to being helpful, such as: helpful, nice, courteous, kind, friendly, caring. And the words on 'Test form B,' didn't have any connection with anything: hand, cloudy, fighting, water. These students thought I was testing their ability to unscramble words. I was really testing the involvement of their unconscious on their decision to pick up my pen. It turns out that eight of ten who took Test A picked up my pen for me, while only three of ten who took Test B did so. I've got a lot more studies like this one too, if you need to see them. The unconscious plays a major role in one's decisions, and we're not even aware of it. Some free will that is!"

The Will is Like a Flashlight

"We cannot be conscious of what we are not conscious of. . . . How simple that is to say; how difficult to appreciate! It is like asking a flashlight in a dark room to search around for something that does not have any light shining upon it. The flashlight, since there is light in whatever direction it turns, would have to conclude that there is light everywhere. And so consciousness can seem to pervade all mentality when it actually does not."

–Julian Jaynes

"Choosing" to Walk Slowly

An unscrambling experiment was done in which the subjects unscrambled words related to aging such as retired, old, wrinkled, etc. After unscrambling these words, the decrease in walking rate of the subjects was considerably greater than the "control" group's. They later reported that they were unaware of the elderly stereotype and its subconscious effect on their behavior.

Lying to Yourself—Unknowingly

Current psychology holds that when someone makes an observation, the information goes to his or her "first memory system." Only a small amount of the information makes it to the conscious awareness. The rest resides in our subconscious and, when this information is viewed as threatening or undesirable, it is either ignored by the conscious awareness or it is actually changed by certain defense mechanisms to more accurately "fit" what the observer wanted to see.

I sat there, amazed at his ability to throw experiments together like that. But his conclusion just didn't sit well at all. It didn't *feel* right. "But doesn't the fact that I *feel* as if I freely chose have any relevance?"

"You tell me. Call that ice cream store and ask them. Here's the listing." The phone book read, "31 Gallons." Strange name for an ice cream store. So I called them. A woman picked up.

"What do I ask them?"

"Ask if they really have thirty-one different gallons of ice cream."

I did.

"They do."

"Ask what flavors they have."

"The woman is just repeating *chocolate* over and over."

"How many times did she say it?"

"Well, she's on 26 right now. 27. 28. 29. 30. 31. All they have there is chocolate ice cream." She hung up.

"So, could you have chosen otherwise? Could you have chosen anything other than chocolate?"

Does "I feel like I acted freely" mean "I acted freely"?

"All theory is against the freedom of the will; all experience is for it."

–Samuel Johnson

"No, I guess not."

"But did it feel like you could have?"

"Yes." It did.

"Let me show you something else." He took out a deck of cards. "I want to show you some magic. First I'll have you choose a totally

Freedom Under Hypnosis?

Hypnosis creates a situation in which the subjects feel that they are freely choosing to act, yet are unknowingly compelled by outside forces. One method of hypnosis embeds a key word in the subject's psyche—they are told that when they hear this word, they will perform an action. Later, when they do so, they typically verbalize a reason for acting, despite the fact that they are actually acting out of obedience to the hypnosis.

random number between ten and twenty and then we'll add the two numbers in that number together and subtract that sum from the number." He then wrote something down on a sheet of paper and put it inside a book.

"I choose fourteen."

"Fourteen it is. So, we'll add 1 and 4, which is 5, and then subtract 5 from fourteen. That leaves 9. So, you put your hand out and we'll see what the ninth card is."

I put my hand out. I watched his hands very closely for any trickery. As he counted and placed the first eight cards in my hand, I watched as he placed the ninth card in my hand. It was the Six of Diamonds. "So? What's so special about this card?"

"Look at the sheet of paper on the desk." On it was written, Six of Diamonds. "How did you know? I picked that number after you wrote that down. I chose that number. I chose that card."

"That's just it. You *feel* like you chose that card. But *any* number between ten and twenty manipulated in that way gives the answer, *nine*. So, you actually did *not* choose the ninth card. Yet, you yourself admit that you *felt* like you were choosing. We've already encountered this problem. You feel like you're seeing water in the road, bent sticks in water . . . yet you're not. What you *feel* is the case isn't necessarily the case. It's not enough to say 'I have free will because I feel that I have free will.' And now we're back to our original position."

"But why do people say they're free to choose?"

"Quite simply, they say that because it fits. People want to cause their actions. They *want* to have meaningful things in their lives like intentions, wants, desires, plans. It's very similar to the way that having the Earth as the center of the universe *fit* at one time. People wanted to be God's creation in the middle of it all. Just think about how often people mold reality to fit what they want to see. We've already talked about this in regard to perception. People are very active perceivers. Just

> *"I'm determined that there's free will."*
> –"M. S.," Philosophy Student

> *"Do I believe in free will? Of course. I have no choice."*
> –Isaac Bashevis Singer, 1978 Nobel Laureate in Literature

Self-Fulfilling Prophecies

People have more control over how they feel or what they do then they often realize. This is often portrayed in positive-thinking slogans such as Henry Ford's, "Whether you think you can or you can't, you're right," as well as the oft-noted placebo effect, in which taking a pill that one believes will cure him often does, even if it's made of non-medicinal (e.g. sugar) ingredients.

last week at your soccer game, the parents of *both* teams walked away convinced that their son's team was shortchanged by the referee and that the *other* team played unfairly. Humans are fragile. They often see what they hoped to see simply by their hoping to see it."

"But why is this feeling so strong then—in everyone? It must be more than just psychological."

"Well, actually, it is. I just want you to do a quick exercise for me. I want you to raise your pointing finger. Pay attention to what happens when you do this. Then, write out the chain of causes that lead to this."

Without inquiring, I lifted my finger.

"Okay, so what caused your finger to lift?"

"Well, some muscles in my forearm contracted."

"Good. What caused that to happen? Work backwards."

"Well, I know some ATP was broken down so the muscle could contract. Synapses firing caused the ATP. Brain activity caused the synapses to fire. And," I paused. What caused my brain activity? "My *will*, I suppose, caused my brain to work."

"Interesting." He nodded. I'd supposedly answered his question just like he wanted me to. "I've brought something that will help you to see what's actually going on in your head during this process. Don't worry, your parents signed the consent for this too."

Of course they did.

"This is brain dye. I'm going to insert this in your head and then we'll get some real empirical answers to this question."

So I sat there. He injected the dye into my brain through a little needle that he put into my temple. I could hardly feel it. He nodded, assuredly. And so I sat, waiting to feel something, waiting for the next instructions. He sat and looked at me for a moment, saying nothing.

"Good," he said, out of nowhere, "you lifted your finger. Well done. Now, let's watch in slow motion what happened here." There was a graph that showed activity in parts of my brain. I couldn't quite understand what was going on. He explained, "That first activity is the onset of brain activity for your moving your finger. Something in your brain is getting you ready to move your finger. This

Which comes first: the will to move or brain activity?

This study was carried out in 1983. Harvard University psychologist Daniel Wegner writes, "It seems that conscious wanting is not the beginning of the process of making voluntary movement. . . . The position of conscious will in the time line suggests that the experience of will . . . might just be a loose end—one of those things, like the action, that is caused by prior brain and mental events."

begins to happen 535 milliseconds before you move your finger. Next, you'll see another big surge of dye movement. This is your awareness of wanting to move. *This* is your 'consciousness-of-moving.' *This* is your will. It chimes in 204 milliseconds before the motion—300 milliseconds *after* the onset of brain action! Then, at 86 milliseconds before movement you become aware of your finger moving and, at the zero-point, your finger moves.

It turns out that your will actually occurs *after* you begin the process of moving your finger. Look." A chart appeared on the screen:

1. Brain starts movement $\longrightarrow$	2. Ian is aware of wanting to move $\longrightarrow$	3. Ian is aware of moving $\longrightarrow$	4. Finger moves
535 ms	204 ms	86 ms	0

I was somewhat dumbfounded. I had him repeat the experiment. It was hard for me to grasp that my will is not the first link in the domino effect that results in my moving.

He could tell I was a little shaken up. "People don't bother to think about it," he commented. "And it has some pretty serious implications."

"Yeah?"

"Let's go spy on one of the other classes across the hall." We went to watch the algebra class. They were working on a project in groups. He tilted his head as if to direct my attention to the left side of the class. Then we watched Ashley take Logan's hand and, before Logan could realize what was going on, she slapped Mike on the back of the neck. It made a very loud slapping noise and Mike yelled out from the surprise of it all. The teacher came over and asked Logan if she had slapped Mike. Logan didn't know what to say. She just sat there. The teacher asked, "Was it your hand that slapped Mike—that made that loud noise? That left these marks on his neck?"

Keep your eye on the ball?

John Searle explains how the brain often tricks us in regards to time. He references a study (similar to the one noted here) in which it only appears that our conscious will precedes the beginning of an action. Also, he talks about reaction times in high-speed sport actions such as hitting a baseball:

"The batter—when the pitch is coming at him at ninety miles an hour— he's got to start his swing before the brain can register the conscious inflight of the ball. . . . As far as your feeling is concerned, you think you saw the ball consciously and then swung at it. . . . What we find is that the guy's brain starts to activate before he has made the conscious decision."

"Yes." Logan's reply was confused, and it came across to the teacher as expressing apathy.

"You need to go to the principal right now."

Logan seemed perplexed. As she left the classroom, tears welled up in her eyes. I felt how unfair it was that she should be punished for something out of her control.

"I had a feeling we might see something like that," the Old Man claimed, proudly. "Do you think she deserves to be punished?"

"Of course not."

"And why not?"

"Because her actions were beyond her control. She did slap Mike, but only because something outside of her will compelled her to do it."

"Exactly," replied the Old Man, as if I'd walked right into something that he'd laid out for me. "Basically, our punishment system is based on what one *deserves*—if you choose to act against certain rules or laws, then you will have deserved a certain punishment."

"Okay. So why is this a problem?"

"Well, look at Logan. She hardly deserves to be punished—yet she *did* do the act. She certainly broke a school rule and the law. But we don't really hold her morally accountable. It's hard to imagine that anyone would say that Logan acted immorally. If we say Logan *ought* not have acted that way, then it implies that she *could* have *not* acted that way. In this example, though, that doesn't seem to be the case. But there are many other, less obvious examples of this happening in courtrooms every day. Turn on the TV."

I turned it on. A man was being sentenced to life in prison for murder. The judge said that because they had film of the man in the act and because the man admitted to it, it was an easy case.

In Michael Shermer's book, The Science of Good & Evil, *he cites cases in which determinism has been used as a successful criminal defense:*

- *Twinkie Defense: high blood sugar caused someone to murder San Francisco's mayor.*

- *Abuse Excuse: two brothers murdered their parents due to their abuse as children.*

- *PMS Defense: a woman's assault of a police officer was caused by premenstrual syndrome.*

- *Insanity: John Hinckley was diagnosed with Schizophrenia Spectrum Disorder and Paradoxical Rage and so not held responsible for the attempted assassination of President Reagan.*

"I have no problem with that," I said. "That's the law."

"Yes, but I want you to look at this man's DNA and family history. I got his read-outs when he was shown on TV." We looked at the DNA sheet. It seemed that he had a very strong natural propensity for violence. It was almost as if he was somehow *wired* to act violently. "And look at *this* part of his brain." The Old Man pointed at the top front part of it. "This is called the 'frontal lobe'; it's where a majority of people's decision making goes on—such as the decision whether or not to act morally, or even *be able* to determine right from wrong in the first place. This man's frontal lobe activity is extremely low. He may not have even been aware of what he was doing."

Then we watched the film of his upbringing. He had three different father figures, all very abusive. His mother was never home because she worked all day and night. He had been out on the streets fending for himself ever since he was eight years old. His life was about as different from mine as it could have been.

"Listen, Ian. This is the sad truth. This guy was doomed from the start. His actions were beyond his control. Not only was he genetically disposed to act violently, but this is the world in which he lived his whole life. He's probably never heard the words 'I love you,' or, 'How about a nice bottle of chocolate milk.' He was born and raised a scavenger.

"It all comes back to my original position: this man's actions were determined by his genetics and his environment. How can we say that

"Ought" Implies "Can"

In claiming that someone ought to or should do something, then at the very least, that person should be able to do that thing.

For example, "You ought to continue living yet stop growing older." This is impossible, because one cannot do this—it makes no sense to tell someone he ought to do this. Likewise, if one's actions are determined—i.e., if he can't do otherwise—then he cannot be held morally accountable.

The "Seat of the Will"

Railroad worker Phineas Gage survived an accident in which a metal rod shot up through his cheek and out the top of his head, destroying his left frontal lobe. He survived, but without this part of his brain he was unable to carry out basic voluntary actions, leading neuroscientists to believe that our ability to will an action lies in this part of our brain.

Findings like these—that the brain controls what was initially ascribed to the mind or soul—are often referenced as evidence against an immaterial mind or soul.

In 1924, attorney Clarence Darrow applied determinism to help his client—who admitted to committing a murder— successfully avoid the death penalty. In his closing argument he stated that his client's actions were a result of his biological composition and his environment, both out of his control:

"If there is responsibility [for this crime] anywhere, it is [in the] back of him; somewhere in the infinite number of his ancestors, or in his surroundings, or in both. And I submit, Your Honor, that under every principle of natural justice, under every principle of conscience, of right, and of law, he should not be made responsible for the acts of someone else."

"It would be very [strange] that all nature, all the planets, should obey eternal laws, and that there should be a little animal, five feet high, who, in contempt of these laws, could act as he pleased."

–Voltaire

he *deserves* to be punished? It totally goes against our paradigm of punishment. And certainly seems problematic in holding someone morally accountable."

"So you're saying that this man's actions were out of his control in the same way that Logan's were?"

"You tell me. They had no control over their actions. Neither of them acted freely. If their circumstances had been different—if Logan's hand hadn't been grabbed and if this man's genes and environment hadn't been as they were—then they would have acted differently. Their actions, *like all actions*, are not free. They're all determined."

"Determined?"

"Well, sure. Like we've been discussing. Open up that science book in your desk. Look up Newtonian Mechanics."

I flipped through the pages until I found Newton. "Now what?" I asked.

"What does it say?"

"It says that we can successfully predict the behavior of an object if we know enough about it. Every event has a cause."

"Yes. Good ol' science. So knowing that, and knowing that human actions are events, then they are all results of a causal chain. We may not be able to predict human events with great success yet, but that doesn't mean that we're somehow outside the realm of everyday physics. What makes us so special that we can somehow avoid the laws that the rest of the universe abides by?"

"So you say that my actions are caused by other factors, just like a rock's *actions*?"

"You say *actions* in jest. But as a rock falls to the ground, we don't think of it as somehow free, do we? Remember our chat with Rock?

Same goes for us. We're just physical things in the universe, subject to all the same laws as other things. And every action of yours results from actions before it. So if you say you act freely, then you must have had a first free act. Yet, when in the chain of actions could you all of a sudden just start acting freely?"

"But you can't predict what I'm going to do. So what good is this scientific account?" I asked, assuming he had a good answer.

"There was a time when we couldn't predict what a ball would do on an inclined plane, too. That didn't mean that the ball acted freely *then*. We knew that the ball acted with respect to physical laws, we just couldn't figure out how to apply these laws properly. Likewise, while the weather is almost always successfully predicted, when the Weather Man gets it wrong, we don't say that the weather acted freely.

"You're just another determined entity."

He had really hit me hard with all this. It was kind of disappointing. No free will? That just didn't sit well. I thought of the paintings I had made recently, the poetry I had written. While it wasn't "A + " material, it was original. It was mine. Yes, it was original. Mine. That was it. Creativity. Creativity! That was proof enough of free will. How authors, painters, sculptors, come up with original works throughout history—things that resembled nothing that existed at the time of their creation. They *must have* acted freely to create original art works.

"An interesting point," he said, as if he'd been reading my mind—or maybe I was actually thinking out loud. "But it doesn't solve the problem so much as it just side steps it again. Think of a woman having a baby."

"Okay." *Is this guy for real?* I asked myself, somewhat rhetorically and somewhat literally. "I don't see how there's any similarity."

"Well, what does she have to do with what comes out—with the offspring?"

"Have to do with it? Well, everything? What do you mean?"

"Yes, she has everything to do with it in the sense that, if it weren't for her, there would be no baby. But what does she have to do with the *content* of that baby? What *say* does she have?"

I sat there, perplexed, so he continued.

"Nothing. She is the locus. She is responsible for half of the genetic makeup of the thing, but she certainly doesn't play an active role in that. She basically provides a place

Poetry . . . and Childbirth

In B. F. Skinner's article, "How Having a Poem is Like Having a Baby," he compares giving birth with writing a poem. In the first case, the mother has very little to do with the child that is born: she is merely a "locus" for it to grow. Likewise, he argues, for the poet. He is just a "locus" for a poem to grow and he really has very little to do with what comes out.

Control over Our Ideas

Albert Einstein recounts how he conceived the law of gravitation. The thought seemed almost totally out of his control:

"I was sitting in a chair in the Patent Office at Berne when all of a sudden a thought occurred to me: 'If a person falls freely he will not feel his own weight.' I was startled. This simple thought made a deep impression on me. It impelled me toward a theory of gravitation."

"Painting is stronger than I am. It can make me do whatever it wants."

–Picasso

where the thing can mature and be born. That's it. Likewise a poet. Through the poet's environment—which is out of your control—and genetics—out of your control—the poet's body and brain provide a locus for the poem to mature. Sure, the poet *feels* like it's his *creative juices* but that's just a metaphor that allows us to give credit to the poet. This is true of all supposed *original* ideas, whether they're artistic, scientific, philosophical. Even Einstein's major theories: simply a result of things totally out of his control. The thought just *popped into his head all of a sudden*. Not much *will* involved there."

I was exhausted, and a little disappointed too. The day was somewhat distressing. I'm not free. So, everything I do from now on, because I'm not free, is determined to happen. It doesn't really matter what I do. It doesn't really matter. It doesn't really matter . . .

"Son? Are you okay? What is it that doesn't matter?"

"Mom? What do you mean?"

"I can hear you mumbling and grumbling from all the way down here!" She was yelling from the kitchen. "Come downstairs. It's Sunday morning. I thought you'd like breakfast. And I want to hear the new poem that you just finished. I'm also curious to hear what doesn't matter."

Ian straggled into the kitchen, "Geez, mom. I don't think anything I do matters anymore. *Especially* that stupid poem I just wrote. I'm just a vehicle, a canister for those words. I'm not sure I'm really free to do anything. It's bleak, but I think it's the way things really are."

"Why don't you sit and have breakfast and you and your father and I can talk about all this. You've been gallivanting with that friend of yours, haven't you?"

"Yes. Okay. Breakfast." He sat down for breakfast. A mere robot following orders.

"Now, son, explain what you meant by all this *nothing matters* talk, and you being a vehicle with no freedom. How in the world could you think that *you*—a smart, creative young boy—aren't free to choose?"

"Well . . . " and Ian retold the dream from the very beginning: the trip to the ice cream store, the DNA readings, the family films, card tricks, discussion of punishment, brain experiments, involvement of science, poetry writing. His dad lifted his finger to test his own will.

His mother started in, "Ian, the debate of free will and determinism has been an issue ever since the beginning of time. It has importance regarding a great many things. As you've mentioned, it's important to ethics, and we've talked about its importance to religious doctrines. Psychology has become involved in the debate as has computer science and neurophysiology.

"I'm really happy to hear you even begin to think about this. There really are so many forces working on us as people, many of which we don't even realize. This is one reason I always mute the commercials on TV—partly because it's a great time to chat with you, but partly to avoid the expert brainwashing that goes on. I happen to think that advertising not only forces products on us unnecessarily, but that it

---

The "Freedom" of the Consumer

"The purpose of advertising is to destroy the freedom of the market."

-Unknown

Advertising experts rely on results from MRI brain imaging, pulse rate, and skin temperature to determine people's responses to given images, sounds, colors, etc. They use this data to create effective advertising ploys.

A famous case of advertising strategy involved Freud's nephew, Edward Bernays. He used psychology theory to help Lucky Strike cigarettes gain popularity by organizing a charity event to promote green—the color of the cigarette carton—under the guise of a charity ball (sponsored anonymously by the American Tobacco Co.) and staging what he called a "women's liberation march" in which well-known women carried Lucky Strike cigarettes as "Torches of Freedom."

He remarked, "[those] who understand the mental processes and social patterns of the masses . . . pull the wires which control the public mind."

portrays societal values in a not-so-sophisticated way. And they're very good at it. So good that, while we all realize advertising's affect on people, we simultaneously think it only affects *others* and not *me*. That obviously can't be true though," she said, rustling his hair.

"But getting back to your original point, it turns out that there are just certain things that we can't do. But, these things aside, we *are* free."

Ian sat, hopeful that there would be some sort of resolution to this—for his own sake. For the sake of humanity.

Free . . . and in Chains

"Man is born free, yet everywhere he is in chains."
–Jean-Jacques Rousseau
Eighteenth-century Swiss-born social philosopher

Rousseau was a proponent of the "Social Contract" which held that, while people are basically free, they should give up certain freedoms for the good of the majority.

The Freedom to Choose
How "coerced" are we to act?

In the 1999 Columbine High School shootings, a terrorist pointed a gun at 17-year-old Cassie Bernall. According to eyewitnesses, he asked her if she believed in God, threatening to shoot her if she did. She answered in the affirmative and was subsequently shot.

"Listen. We can't fly through the air like birds can. This is just a limit. We're not *free* to fly."

"Okay. But that's just a result of gravity, not our will," Ian responded.

"Then imagine someone who is in jail. We don't typically think of them as free. But that's only relative to our freedom. While I am free to go to the movies, the condemned prisoner is not. But he certainly is free to think about what he wants. He's free to write letters. He's free to talk. So, in a sense, he is free—just as free as you and I—he just has more worldly restrictions placed on him."

"So am I free to ditch school?"

"Sure. You're free to do whatever you want," his mom responded sincerely. Ian's look showed that there was an obvious catch. "You know, I had a teacher in high school who, when we asked if we could go to the restroom during class would reply, 'You can do whatever you want.' We'd ask, 'Can we just leave now and not come back?' 'Yes,' he'd reply. This confused us. We asked him to explain. 'You can do whatever you want,' he responded. 'If you leave class, you will miss material that you need to know if you want to do well on the exam. Likewise, I will mark you as absent and your parents will get a note and you'll be in trouble with the school. Lastly, because you know how much I value education, I will be disappointed in you. You just

---

Why We Punish

Two prominent paradigms exist to justify punishment by a government:

1. Utilitarianism: *for the greater good—even if people don't necessarily "deserve" a particular punishment, it serves to deter others from committing similar crimes and to create social harmony.*
2. Retributivism: *the person has "earned" the punishment because they knowingly committed a crime and, thus, deserve the punishment.*

---

need to decide how much all those things matter to you. Once you do, then you're free to act on that decision.'"

"Sounds like kind of a cool teacher," Ian said, smiling.

"Well, he was: very challenging in the sense that he gave us a lot more responsibility for ourselves than did other teachers. It was, as you mentioned earlier, kind of empowering."

"But what do we do about the whole problem of punishing people? I mean, if they're not wholly free, how can we give out moral praise or blame?"

His mother glanced at Ian's dad who was somewhat preoccupied with what looked like a calculator or computer game of some sort. He looked up at her and nodded for her to continue. "Son," his mom started back in, now realizing the genuinely serious tone of his Ian's concerns, "when you were three months old, and you crawled over and knocked down our nice crystal vase breaking it, we didn't say that you acted immorally. You weren't an unethical person for doing that. Likewise, when a dog does something even as drastic as violently attacking an innocent human being, we don't think of the dog as unethical. While we may put the dog away, or even put it to sleep, we don't do so because the dog somehow *deserved* it, but in order to protect humans from that in the future—for utilitarian reasons. But if you *now* walked over to that vase and pushed it to the ground, causing it to shatter, then you *have* acted unethically. You broke something that was not yours and you did it intentionally. You *deserve* a punishment. There's a difference between *your* action and the action of a three-month-old or a dog. That difference we ascribe to free will."

"Okay Ian, ready for some tic-tac-toe?" his dad asked, playfully. "Do you think you can beat this computer game at tic-tac-toe?"

"I don't know if I can beat it, but I know it won't beat me. That game always ends in a tie," Ian responded, referring to having played one hundred games with Alexis one day and neither winning any of them.

Can Computers Cheat?

In a conversational piece, Trudy Govier explores whether computers can cheat. One character notes,

"To cheat, you have to know the rules and deliberately break them to try to get a better result. You also deceive other people, making them think you got your result the right way. Computers can't do all this. They don't know rules, they can't aim at results, and they can't pretend. Therefore they can't cheat."

Another responds that computers do "know" the rules: "The rules have got to be in there somehow, or else the computer couldn't play the game at all."

His dad placed the hand-held game in front of Ian and pushed "New Game." The computer placed an X in the top left square. Ian nodded and placed an O in the middle. The computer placed an X in the middle left and Ian placed an O in the bottom left. Then Ian looked in amazement as the computer placed an X in *both* the top right and top middle and flashed, "I win!—You lose!" repeatedly. A beeping noise alerted Ian's parents that the game had ended.

"Who won?" his dad asked.

"It says it did. But it cheated."

"The computer *cheated*?"

"Yeah. It put down two X's in one move. That's illegal."

His mother smiled, understanding the purpose of the game.

His father asked, "Don't you have to act with intent—that is, *freely*—in order to be morally blameworthy?"

Ian nodded suspiciously.

"So are you saying that computers have free will?" his dad asked.

Ian shrugged, "No, I guess not. But that doesn't feel right either. Did *you* cheat?" he asked his dad, "since *you* programmed it?"

"I didn't cheat. How could I cheat at a game I wasn't even playing?

"Because you programmed it."

"Well aren't you programmed too? Isn't this what you explored with the Old Man? I hardly think that you thought up this language you're using all by yourself," his dad added, now smiling a bit.

The Importance of Intent . . .

"An ant is crawling on a patch of sand. As it crawls, it traces a line in the sand. By pure chance the line that it traces curves and recrosses itself in such a way that it ends up looking like a recognizable caricature of Winston Churchill. Has the ant traced a picture of Winston Churchill? A picture that depicts Churchill? Most people would say, on a little reflection, that it has not."

–Hilary Putnam

"Existence precedes essence."

This is the core tenet of existentialism. It holds that we first *come into existence and* then *we determine our essence or self. This view opposes the notion that we get our nature from a creator or from a predetermined nature. Thus we are completely responsible for creating our* self *through the choices we make.*

Jean-Paul Sartre writes, "Not only is man what he conceives himself to be, but he is also only what he wills himself to be after this thrust toward existence. Man is nothing else but what he makes of himself."

"That's my whole problem with this to begin with," Ian said. "If I *do* have free will then how? What would that even mean? And why wouldn't computers have it too?"

His mother reentered the conversation. She rubbed Ian's dad's back as if to congratulate him on his example of which he was obviously very proud. "You know, an interesting analogy can be made with this. When someone writes a novel, she starts out with a character sketch. For example, if you were a character in a book, the author would probably have pages written on you: how inquisitive you are, that you're extremely creative, very friendly, though somewhat shy around people, very loving—you'd be a great character in a book." She ruffled his hair and kissed his forehead. "But, in the beginning of the book, instances arise which the character sketch doesn't explain. It just doesn't seem that there's an obvious action consistent with the sketch. So the author makes that decision, which builds the character even more. That's kind of what we do. We're creating our own character sketch. While some of it has been done for us—the body and home we're born into—the rest is up to us. So, we can actually act freely in a determined world. There's a sort of happy medium between having absolute free will or *hard* determinism. We could call it *soft* determinism."

"I like that. But I feel like whatever we author our character to do in these supposedly free instances is also determined."

"Well son, it sounds like the determinist in you has set up a pretty unrealistic demand for free will."

Author Your Own Life Story

Contemporary philosopher Robert Kane explores the book-character analogy. He writes, "Agents who exercise free will are both authors of and characters in their own stories all at once. . . . They are . . . 'making themselves' out of past that, if they are truly free, does not limit their future pathways to one."

Two roads diverged in a wood, and I—
I took the one less traveled by,
And that has made all the difference.
　　　–Robert Frost,
　"The Road Not Taken"

SOFT DETERMINISM—a compromise between Hard Determinism and Free Will. The term was coined by William James as he found that hard determinism led to a hopeless view of life.

1. *All actions are caused and determined by prior conditions.*
2. *Voluntary behavior is free as long as it is not constrained by outside forces.*
3. *Where there are no constraints, voluntary behavior is caused by the desire and volition of the agent.*

COMPATIBILISM—free will and determinism are compatible, i.e., they are not mutually exclusive. Hume championed this view. He argued that one can be said to have free will when: one could have acted differently in a situation if one had different beliefs at the time. Thus, while our beliefs may be caused by outside or unknown forces, our actions based on those beliefs should be considered as free.

"How? It seems pretty clear."

"Well, it seems like the determinist camp has defined a *free act* as: an action that results from something completely random or unplanned. Yet this is hardly a notion of free will at all. Things happening for no reason at all, caused by nothing?" He shook his head. "If we acted as a result of something completely unrelated to us in any way—something totally uncaused—that would hardly seem free."

She continued, "Exactly. And this is the compromise I was talking about. You do have freedom, even though some things are out of your control. Free will and determinism are actually compatible."

"So does that help us get around the problem of the whole physics thing? Newton and particle prediction? It does seem that there's some validity to that—if all particles obey the laws of physics and everything results from cause and effect, then it seems like it would be the same for us. Maybe we just aren't good at predicting yet."

"Son, that's a very advanced point you bring up. Your science teachers would be proud. But one thing you probably haven't gotten to in your class is something called the 'Heisenberg Uncertainty Principle.'"

Ian nodded as though he'd heard the words but couldn't recall the meaning.

Richard Taylor describes the notion of totally uncaused *motions of his right arm—motions that don't seem to be determined by any cause at all:*

"This is no description of free, voluntary, or responsible behavior . . . I can have no more to do with . . . the uncaused motions of my limbs than a gambler has over the motions of an honest roulette wheel."

"This is a much more advanced idea. But on the surface, it's very simple. It states that you can't know *both* the position *and* velocity of a moving particle at any given time. In order to test one, you affect the other. But even more interesting and pertinent than that are the recent findings in quantum mechanics. Basically, scientists are finding that there are particles that *do* act outside of any sort of cause-and-effect mechanism. Newtonian mechanics doesn't seem to apply to all particles. This is a really big deal in physics now. And you can see already what a broad application this will have."

"Plus, Ian," his mother added, "you've forgotten about the one thing that differentiates humans from all other things."

"Impossible thumbs?"

"Nope." They laughed proudly at his attempt to incorporate some of his recently acquired verbiage. "Not opposable thumbs."

"That we feel emotions like jealousy and envy?"

"Hmm. That's true, but not quite what I was looking for."

"We experience boredom?"

"Again, true, but not what I'm looking for."

Are Particles "Free"?

Recent theory in physics shows that, at best, we can only know the probability *of a particle occupying a particular point in space. Since the 1930's, the Schrödinger Equation has become widely accepted. Schrödinger basically claims that a particle's position can only be described as a function of probability. It turns out that quantum physics may* not *be able to determine and predict particles' positions after all.*

Physicist Paul Davies writes, "In the quantum microworld, energy can appear and disappear out of nowhere in a spontaneous and unpredictable fashion."

"That we're the only species which participates in mass destruction of itself?"

They glanced at each other as if to say, *you can learn a lot from a kid*. "No, not quite that either, though these are all very good answers. We actually talked about this a bit last week."

"That we have minds or souls?"

"Exactly. And these things are outside anything in your physics book—I can't imagine a physicist *ever* being able to analyze the properties of someone's soul. And because of this, we *can* act outside of the notion of particle prediction and determination."

Ian sat silently. He had an uncomfortable-looking smile on his face, his brow furrowed. "I think that I think I have free will," he said. "No, I *do* have free will. After I woke up from that dream I felt like I was doomed. There seemed no way out of that whole scenario. But it does seem like certain events are determined and within those events I have the chance to assert my free will—to author my character a little bit.

"I'm free."

The Power of the Hill

I went up the stairs to the front door and off to the soccer field. When I got to the field, I saw a strange-looking person walking a dog. As we passed each other we caught eyes. I tried my best to smile and not show my awkwardness at his appearance. He had tall shoes on: not high heels but like the whole sole was tall, and very skinny—they looked very uncomfortable; I couldn't believe how skinny his feet must have been. He had a big thick metal neck band on too—not really a necklace, but just a metal band. And then his forehead: kind of big and lumpy—it really stuck out. Strange. He looked at me with the strangest look. Me? I felt that the feeling was mutual but was somewhat scared of him so I just smiled.

When I got to the soccer field, *everyone* was wearing those shoes, that neck thing, and had that forehead. Everyone. I walked past it from afar. I had never seen anything like it—like there was some dress code or like it was Halloween and I had somehow missed the announcement. I went to the library instead of staying. As I approached the door, everyone coming out of the library had the same shoe/neck/head thing. I walked past everyone in their costumes—they must be costumes. I rushed to the magazine section to see if I could find any explanation. There on the cover of every magazine were people dressed like this. Headlines on the covers reading, *Forehead Maintenance, How can I get my feet skinnier and still be able to walk?*, and *Neck bars so heavy you'll need to lie down every hour.* The store "In" was advertised in each of these magazines, so I quickly left the scorn of library-goers and went to the mall.

At "In" a man approached me with a "where-in-the-world-have-you-been" look. I told him I needed a new pair of shoes. And a neck plate. And a forehead? He quickly fitted me. First with a pair of extra-wide shoes. Extra wide? I felt like my feet had been folded in half. Next, I got a size one neck plate, the smallest possible. It felt cold, and the weight of it on my collarbone was already a little uncomfortable, but he nodded his head approvingly. He told me it went well with my complexion. Of course. I wondered if any employee in *any* store had ever spoken the words, *That one doesn't look too good on you.*

Lastly, I got the "Starter's Kit for Forehead Beautification." After having the molds fitted to my head, I already felt my forehead drooping onto my eyebrows. Though again, more encouraging head nodding from him. I was accepted. I paid the man and clumsily walked out of "In." I walked into a world of "hellos," smiles, and playful greetings. I was one of them.

As I walked down to get a burger, I saw one of my dad's friends going to the same burger place as me. He treated me to lunch and we talked for a while. He was actually pretty interesting—I could see why he and my dad were such good friends. He invited me to go for a walk after lunch. Seeing as how I didn't really have anything to do, I agreed.

We drove to the base of a big hill at the edge of town and parked the car. "You'll need to change shoes—no way you can make it up this hill in those." He handed me a pair of sneakers. Ahh, sneakers.

"You might want to take that neck bar off, this hike's pretty tough." Ahh, my neck.

"You might want to dislodge those forehead skins, it gets pretty sunny up there and you'll need to wear a hat that can fit over your head." What if we see other people on the way up there? "Nah. They're new. I don't mind the sun."

Just then another man walked up. He was wearing regular old shoes, no neck bar, no forehead. Weird. He shook my dad's friend's hand and introduced himself to me. "Nice to meet you, Mr. Pax." They were obviously friends. "Shall we?" he said. And we started the walk.

It really was a nice area. I usually didn't much like hiking—it always strikes me as plain old walking but much more tiring. But the scenery was beautiful and even after walking for just twenty minutes, we could already see so much of our little town below. The next twenty minutes was harder, though, and I was starting to get out of breath. The sweat on my forehead was starting to irritate it. I did feel my face getting burned a little. We came around the bend at the top and sat down on a little bench. There seemed to be another valley behind us, and we looked out over the town.

From this spot I noticed something very peculiar. Everyone was walking in lines. It looked like a big snake. Everyone was following everyone else. After watching for a minute, I voiced this observation to the other two. My dad's friend turned to Mr. Pax. They nodded at each other. Mr. Pax turned to me. "They all follow each other all the time. They can't see it because they're in the middle of it. They don't have this vantage point that we have. None of them know about this hike. Access to this hike is actually one reason I'm so good at what I do."

I hesitated to ask. "What do you do?"

"I'm a Need Creator. Companies hire me to create needs for their products so that they can sell them. Take those shoes and neck bands that you see everyone wearing. Totally senseless—actually they're bad for your posture. But two years ago, our company got a multi-million dollar offer to create this need. Shoe companies as of today have made millions on this. It's quite easy to do. We pay good-looking people to wear these things, we pay magazines to showcase them, and within three months, superficial needs become *actual* needs.

"As a challenge, we tried the forehead implants. This was part of an eight-year plan. For the first two years, we created the need for them. Next we take six months to phase these out and instead promote forehead wrinkles. This will involve pictures of Einstein and a promotion of something like, *Forehead wrinkles mean you've been thinking, thinking is sexy, blah blah blah*. Something like that. That phase will last a couple of years. And then, two years after that, we can release the product we've been working on which gets rid of wrinkles. We'll have a campaign against wrinkles showing how ugly they are: *Wrinkles mean you're getting old, getting old is bad, thinking means you haven't been playing, so use our product and play and be young, be free, blah blah blah*. Geez, when I hear these campaigns all I really hear is *blah blah blah*. But since everyone follows everyone else so mindlessly, it works out quite nicely."

"So don't you feel bad about that?" I asked as I began to peel the patches from my forehead. My face was burned so the whole thing was a little uncomfortable. Plus I felt a little embarrassed that I was a part of this whole scheme.

"Well, there's really not much to feel bad about. People want to feel good and I give them a way to do that. Did you know that human beings are the only creatures that blush? They're very aware of their *selves*. And this is all we need: unsure, emotionally needy, ego-driven things—*human beings*. As Need Creators, we use information about people's psychological makeup and we *create* their needs and fears, we make them feel unsure, emotionally needy. Then, we give them solutions—we convince them that their ego can be saved by a certain product. It's kind of a self-perpetuating cycle—perpetuated by us, I suppose.

"You know, anything sold is sold to make money. That's the bottom line. You think Need Creators and their employers are looking out for the customer? They're trying to make money. Whether it's a clothing company, an artist, a vitamin maker—they just want your money. So they act like they care. Come on, you really think that the corporation that runs 'Burger Mania' wants to see you smile because they care about you or do they want to see you smile because when you smile you give them money? And do you think that the clothing company 'Space' really wants you to Be *Original* as they say in their ad? How can you Be Original if *everyone* is wearing Space jeans? If you really want to Be Original, you'll watch for the ads and then do the exact opposite. And one of my favorites—that recent ad for the clothing store 'Bangledon and Nash.' We were selling their new line of clothes, yet every model was practically nude. Imagine that—selling clothes for people by using models with no clothes on. I guess people actually believed that if they bought Bangledon clothes their bodies would somehow morph into the bodies in the ads."

He was kind of laughing to himself now, as though he forgot he was letting us in on the almost embarrassing root of his profession and of human nature.

"Actually, you don't even need to *watch* for the ads—we'll force them on you. You know, by the time the average person is 18 he's seen 750,000 commercials. That doesn't even include radio, magazines, billboards. By 45 you'll have seen 2 million. A person spends *3 years* of his life watching T.V. commercials—3 years of experts in human nature telling him what he wants, how he should look.

"Pretty girls standing next to cars so men will buy them. Actors telling you that one toothpaste is better than another. What could *they* know? But it works. You know, companies spend considerably more money on need-creation than they do on the actual product. They do it because advertising works. It works so well that no consumer ever admits, 'Yeah, I'm trying to look like the models in Space.' But why else would they spend five times more on their jeans than another store with products of equal quality? It's very subtle and, for us, it's better that way; and good for me, I suppose.

"But people are free to think for themselves if they want. They don't have to throw out all their mauve-colored clothes from last year just to buy the pea-green-colored clothes that are being sold at places like In this year. But thinking for one's self is hard. So I do it for them. If I can think for them, then I create their needs. We produce the supposedly-needed objects in bulk for cheap, and then sell them for a lot. Don't quote me on that, though. At least not in this world."

Chapter 10

Selfishness (and Science Revisited)

It is impossible to understand the science of shoes until one understands what science is.

–Plato

"When I use a word," Humpty Dumpty said, in rather a scornful tone, "it means just what I choose it to mean—neither more nor less."

–Lewis Carroll, Through the Looking Glass

And there we were, looking over the school grounds below. We had sneaked up to the school's top floor made up of one room with small windows that looked out over the grounds and the nearby street. The Old Man had taken out a book and started to read. The title on the cover read, "Amazing Scientific Discoveries That Few Know About Which Are Impossible to Disprove."

Because he knew that I'd be immensely curious about the book, he sat, ignoring me, with his nose in the book. As I was anxious to get on with it, I appeased him. I flashed the curious/intrigued look, asking nonchalantly, "What's that?"

"The trick is to combine your waking rational abilities with the infinite possibilities of your dreams. Because, if you can do that, you can do anything."

–Waking Life, movie

"Well Ian, we don't have much time, but I think you'll find some of this pretty interesting. Listen to a few of these hypotheses which have yet to be disproved. Better yet, they're *impossible* to disprove."

I sat. I listened.

"It turns out physicists have discovered that,

Every day, everything doubles in size.

And this has been happening since the beginning of time."

"That can't be," I responded immediately. "I wear the same size shoes today that I did yesterday. And my hands and my pencils are the same size."

"How do you know that?"

"Well, they look the same. I could even measure them for you if you'd like."

"That's just it, Ian. Of course they look the same. You're viewing your hands with your eyes—when your hands double in size, so do your eyes, your visual cortex, and the rest of your body. Likewise with the pencil you hold. They *both* double. So, *relatively speaking*, they appear to be the same size. Even if you use a ruler to prove it—the *ruler* has doubled in size as well! So, what was once a foot-long ruler is now a two-foot-long ruler. But it's just that the things that were once a foot long, such as your shoes, are now two feet long. So, both yesterday and today, your shoes have been the same length as your ruler. There's no way to disprove it."

"Is that really the case? It seems like a pretty difficult theory to overturn. What's the other one?"

"Yeah, it's the case. Until someone can find a way to disprove it. The other hypothesis is:

Everything was created five minutes ago."

He paused for it to sink in and then nodded his head.

"That's ridiculous. I can remember having cereal for breakfast yesterday morning. And playing baseball yesterday. So *there*."

"Well it turns out that you were created five minutes ago *with those memories*. It

Would it matter if . . . ?

Leibniz argued that space was relative. This was in direct contrast to Isaac Newton's model of space as an absolute (i.e., not relative). Leibniz imagined that there were two worlds, exactly alike, except in one everything had been shifted to the left by exactly three feet. He argued that there would be no difference between the two and, therefore, that space was nothing more than relations amongst objects. He made the same claim regarding time.

certainly seems feasible that, if you and this Earth and this universe could be created, that you could be created with certain memories."

"Maybe so. But look at my shoes, they are worn down at the toe because I always drag my left foot. That's a lot more than five minutes of wear."

Bertrand Russell presented the "Five Minute Hypothesis" in support of skepticism and whether we can really "know" things—especially from memory.

"Yes, they too were created in just that way, five minutes ago, along with everything else. There's no way around it, Ian. Many people have tried to disprove it and it can't be done. It looks like this hypothesis holds. It has some pretty serious implications too, which we won't get into for now."

I sat, somewhat dumbfounded. Everything doubles in size every day? Everything was created five minutes ago? I wondered why I'd never heard of these? These were great theories—totally unable to be proven false.

"You know about the concept of 'survival of the fittest,' Ian?"

"Yes." I'd heard of that. "That organisms have some sort of biological drive to live, to reproduce themselves, create fit offspring."

"That's it. To reproduce their genes. Not only that, but people have insatiable—and very fragile—egos. Currently, big names are paying millions of dollars to clone themselves. The clone won't be anything like them, except for looking like them and having their DNA. They'll be dead just like the rest of us. When it all comes down to it, people are really just selfish. Everything anyone does is done for purely selfish reasons; there's no such thing as true honor, sacrifice, and certainly no *selflessness*."

Philosopher Herbert Spencer coined the phrase, "survival of the fittest." He derived it from Darwin's principle of natural selection: individuals with "favorable" traits will survive and thus pass those traits on to their offspring, while individuals without them will die off and thus cease to produce more individuals without those traits.

"How can you say that? I can think of many selfless people."

The Old Man then pointed down to the cafeteria. "Look. Look right now, at the lunch line." We really could see a lot from this room.

I looked down at Billy, a classmate of mine. He reached in the cookie jar that had only five more cookies. Even though there were about twenty people left in line, he took three of them for himself—started eating one, and put two in his pocket.

"That's pretty selfish, wouldn't you say?"

I agreed. "But that's only one person. One action."

Selfish Genes

Contemporary biologist Richard Dawkins takes the idea of survival of the fittest to the micro level. In his book, The Selfish Gene, *he argues that it is the gene that is responsible for reproduction and not the individual. Thus, our selfishness is rooted in our DNA. Genes use us— their "survival machines" —to live and reproduce.*

He writes, "The gene is the basic unit of selfishness."

"Look again. Out *that* window." Carter, a neighbor of mine, was helping an elderly woman across the street and carrying her bag for her.

"How could you call that selfish?" I asked, thinking of how easy it was to find one example of selflessness. "He's doing that for *her* not himself."

"Look again."

I looked to see Carter glance over his shoulder at Alexis. He'd had a crush on her for a while. She was talking to friends and hadn't noticed him. He walked slowly, dragging the woman's bag on the ground, waiting for Alexis to glance his way. Then, as her head motioned toward his seemingly honorable act, he turned to the woman, said something, they laughed, and he led her to the curb. Alexis smiled to herself, pointed it out to her friends, and they all tilted their heads in admiration as if to say, "Wow. What a guy. He's so giving. I'd want to go out with a guy like him."

"Pretty selfish, huh?"

"Yes, I suppose. It didn't seem so at first, but it turns out it was a pretty selfish thing. But, still, that's only two instances."

"All our acts, reasoned and unreasoned, are selfish."

–Mark Twain
(Whose birth name was Samuel Langhorn Clemens.)

"Okay," the Old Man said, "then you pick one of these *many* which you mentioned earlier."

"Well, a pretty easy one is Mother Teresa. She helped who-knows-how-many people. She lived in poverty. She made the lives of everyone around her better. She totally gave of herself so that others could be better off. That's about as selfless as one could be."

"Ahh, well that's a pretty obvious answer." He thought to himself for a moment.

"Yes, I agree," I responded. I had actually shut him up for once. That was a first. This one was pretty easy though.

"Mother Teresa could be the most selfish person I've ever known about. She, and maybe Gandhi."

Could he be serious? Should I even ask him to defend this? It was the most ridiculous thing I'd ever heard. "Defend that claim. That's the most ridiculous thing I've ever heard."

"Okay." He took in a breath. "Tell me, have you ever helped someone *less fortunate* than yourself—how ever one determines that one is more fortunate than another."

"Sure. I suppose I have. Our family works in a homeless shelter every Christmas."

"Cute. Well, how do you feel after you've done that?"

"Very good. It's a really good feeling. I even did it on my own over Easter. You should try it some time."

"That's okay. I'll save the martyrdom for some other time."

"Martyrdom?"

He took another deep breath as if he knew this would be a long, though interesting one. "Imagine feeling your Christmas Eve feelings *every* day. Why do you think Mother Teresa helped those in need: because it made her feel miserable, or because it made her feel good? Look at how accomplished one feels after helping others. It's a natural high that you can't get anywhere else.

"And, on top of that, she gets the constant affirmation from others. You know, when people donate to charities or other programs and their name is announced or, worse yet, they announce it to others—why do you think they do that? They want others to think, 'What a guy.' Just like your friend Carter did with Alexis.

"And what's more, Mother Teresa became famous. Look, she's being talked about in the tall tower of some small middle school years after her death. She lived on the other side of the world and *everyone* knows her name. Her name will live on. She's achieved the worldly immortality that we all want, deep down.

"And lastly, her actions led to her achieving spiritual immortality. As far as she's concerned, she goes to heaven for eternity—forever. A few years doing good deeds pales in

Looking out for Number One

"Can I honestly say that I believe Gandhi was acting selfishly when he 'sacrificed' himself for the freedom of the Indian people? No, I can't say that I believe it. It would be more proper to say that I know it for a fact . . . . Whatever Gandhi did, out of rational or irrational choice, he did because he chose to do it. . . . Martyrs are selfish people—and the same as you and me—but with insatiable egos."

–Robert Ringer,
Looking Out for #1

Reasons Why Mother Teresa Was "Selfish"

1. *Helping others made her feel good about herself.*
2. *She liked that people respected her and viewed her as a good person.*
3. *Her name lived on after she passed away.*
4. *She believed that she would achieve infinite happiness in heaven.*

The Ethics of Selfishness

Moral Egoism is a moral code that accounts for the supposed selfishness inherent in humans. Because people cannot help but be selfish, when they encounter an ethical dilemma, they ought to do that which they believe to be in their best interest. Both political philosopher Thomas Hobbes and eighteenth-century economic theorist Adam Smith based their respective theories on this notion of inherent selfishness.

"You will find as you grow older that the first thing needful to make the world a tolerable place to live in is to recognize the inevitable selfishness of humanity."
–Somerset Maugham,
Of Human Bondage

comparison to eternal bliss. How much more selfish could someone be?

"You see now? You have any other good examples for me?"

Amazing. "I guess not. So everything that anyone does is always selfish?"

He nodded.

"That's depressing."

"That's life, boy. Get used to it. And since people can't help but act selfishly, we can't expect anything more from them. Even in looking at right and wrong, what people ought to do is that which promotes their *self* the most."

"So I ought to kill everyone on my track team so that I can be the star?"

"No. That wouldn't promote Ian Pinkle. Everyone would look down on you. You'd get no respect. Plus, the people in your society would put you in jail. Not much reproduction of genes going on in there. You'd be better off helping the team in any way. In giving of yourself to the team you'd be *perceived* by most as *un*selfish, and then people would want to help you more than if you were otherwise. It would be a seemingly unselfish move guided by selfish desires. *That* is what you should do. Promote yourself. It's how we're wired as people; you might as well realize that now."

We're all selfish. Every act is selfish. We're all selfish. Every act is selfish . . .

Enough. He was awake. Awake at six a.m. "Is every act really selfish?" he mumbled.

It seemed that this time, instead of confusion, there was maybe some enlightenment. Ian walked down to the kitchen at what sounded like the same time as his dad. As he entered the kitchen he heard his dad say to his mom, "You look lovely this morning, honey. Let me help you with your things."

"How selfish of you," Ian exclaimed.

"Excuse me?"

"Well, whatever the reason you just said that to mom, it was merely for selfish reasons."

"What could you possibly mean by that, son?"

"Well, either you did it because you want to make her feel good, which actually makes *you* feel good. Or maybe you want to *do unto others as you would have them do unto you* and you say that to her just so she returns the compliment sometime, making *you* feel good. Or maybe *you* want to appear as a caring guy, which will make your lot in life somehow better. Your being perceived as a good guy will eventually get you something. I heard one of the teachers at school say to another, 'If you bring her flowers for no reason, she'll be yours forever.' It's all selfish."

Yossarian, the main character in Joseph Heller's Catch 22, *remarks that he is a "collector of good questions" so that he may "wring knowledge out of people."*

A catch-22 places one in a "no-win" situation. In Heller's novel, a fighter pilot requested that he be grounded (not permitted to fly) for reasons of insanity (a good reason for grounding). Yet, as soon as this pilot asked to be grounded he was declared sane as no sane person would really want to fly a plane in wartime. So, whether he declared himself sane or not, he still had to fly.

His father dropped his head a bit, raising his eyebrows, looking up at Ian, as if to wonder from whence the cynicism for such a young kid. "Well, son, that's a pretty dismal view of life, a pretty sad way to view things. First of all, I think your mother is the most beautiful thing I've ever laid my eyes on—that's the honest truth, since the moment we met. We sat on the school lawn that day and discussed what in the world dogs must think when they're in a car zooming past objects at over sixty miles per hour. Plus, she has a glowing face."

"Humph."

"But son, not only is your view dismal, it's logically incorrect."

"If you must be selfish then be wisely selfish, not narrow-mindedly selfish."

"When we act to fulfill our immediate desires without taking into account others' interests, we undermine the possibility of lasting happiness."

–Fourteenth Dalai Lama, Tenzin Gyatso

The Dalai Lama is the spiritual ruler of Tibet. In fifteenth-century China, the emperor named two Buddhist monks to positions of spiritual and secular rule. Both Lamas are believed to embody spiritual beings.

What's Right for Me Is Right . . .

Wittgenstein wrote extensively on words and their meaning. In numerous instances he examined the notion of words being used with no criteria and, thus, losing all meaning:

"One would like to say: whatever is going to seem right to me is right. And that only means that here we can't talk about 'right.'"

Translation: *One can't use "right" simply to mean whatever one wants it to mean, because without establishing an agreed upon meaning, a word becomes meaningless.*

"How could that be? I've found a way to use the word *selfish* so that it includes *all* actions. So how could you say that I'm wrong?"

"Well, that's just the catch. In including *everything* the word excludes *nothing* and in turn loses all meaning."

Ian gave him the *confused look*.

"Look at it this way. I used to use a similar trick on my father—your grandfather—when I wanted to eat sugar cereal for breakfast. He'd always tell me there was something wrong with my reasoning, though he couldn't quite express it in words. Here's how it worked.

"I would begin by asking him if I was allowed to eat cereals that were 100 percent natural. I knew he'd allow this, and then I'd have him hooked. Once he inevitably agreed to this, I continued. And I continued by going to my room and getting the box of 'Super Sugar Explosion' cereal. I'd then ask him, 'So I can have this every morning?' This resulted in the obvious response, 'Absolutely not!'"

Ian too seemed a little unsure of his dad's reasoning. "Why did you think he'd let you have that?"

"Funny, that's what he'd ask me too. And I'd respond: 'Look at the ingredients and find something that's not natural. Take sugar for example; it couldn't be more natural—it's taken straight from the sugar cane that grows naturally all over the world.'"

"Of course. Well, what about 'Artificial Colors'?"

"Okay, let's take those. Let's look at 'Yellow #5' specifically."

"Yeah, that's hardly natural."

"Well, funny that you say that; I've actually made Yellow #5 in the lab. It consists of nothing more than some basic chemicals mixed together in a specific way. Now, we both know that the elements found on the periodic chart are the building blocks of all of nature. So, myself—a *natural* human—just mixed these natural elements in a lab which I composed out of things taken from nature to make Yellow #5. Thus, Yellow #5 and all artificial colors are natural. I went through

What Is Used to Make Yellow #5 . . . and Is It Natural?

Ingredients	Natural?
Water:	
Hydrogen	Yes
Oxygen	Yes
Carboxylic Acid:	
Carbon	Yes
Hydrogen	Yes
Sodium Nitrate:	
Sodium	Yes
Nitrogen	Yes
Chloride	Yes
Lead	Yes
Arsenic	Yes
Mercury	Yes
Fire	Yes
Human in a lab	Yes

In 2000 the United States Food Standards Agency drafted the following definition for "natural":

"'Natural' means essentially that the product is comprised of natural ingredients, i.e., ingredients produced by nature, not the work of man or interfered with by man."

every ingredient on the box and explained how they were all natural. And since every ingredient in the box was from nature, then the cereal was in fact 'all-natural.'"

"Hmm, well did he let you have it?"

"Nope."

"Why not?"

"He'd just say, 'Because I'm your father.'"

"Oh. I've heard that one before."

"But there is a real problem here—something obviously wrong. It's very similar to what you did with your use of 'selfish.' Basically, when you use a word, it needs a criterion. There must be a way to use the word incorrectly. It can't be the case that *everything* is selfish, or that *everything* is natural. If that were the case, then the word would become meaningless. If *everything* were considered natural, what would be the point of asking, *Is this thing natural?* It's sort of paradoxical in a way: I create a word that means everything and, in doing so, it means nothing."

The Humpty Dumpty Theory of Language

The speaker can use any word to mean whatever he wants it to mean. Lewis Carroll's character, Humpty Dumpty, employed this practice and Carroll used it to parody this use of language in order to show how illogical it would be to use words with no criterion for correctness.

"[The phrase] 'I am awake' is suspect . . . its proper negation (I'm asleep) is meaningless."
–Norman Malcolm, *Dreaming*, 1959

"I suppose that makes sense. There's a song by a band that I like and in it they say, 'Without dark, there is no light. With no wrong, no right.' Isn't that the same kind of thing?"

"Yes, son. That's exactly it."

"I think I understand. But what about the actual word, 'everything'? Doesn't that mean *everything* sort of by definition? So does that mean that it loses its meaning also?"

His dad paused for a moment. "Well, that one seems tricky. But look at the definition of 'everything': 'all things pertinent to a specific matter' or just, 'all things.' So, the word 'everything' can't mean 'just some things' or 'nothing.' And that's just it—there's a criterion for the word."

Ian pondered this. He nodded his head approvingly, smiling. "Dad, I just remembered the book that the Old Man was reading, and those crazy theories. Would this apply to things like scientific theories too?"

"It could, yes. Like what, for example?"

Ian relayed the two theories to him, one on things doubling in size, the other on the Five-Minute Hypothesis.

"You know, son, there's actually a technical word for those theories: they're 'unfalsifiable.' They're incapable of being proven false. No possible piece of evidence or theory would undermine those hypotheses. So, while at first glance that seems to be a strength, in the end it is actually a weakness. A theory that can't possibly be proven wrong is useless."

Science Versus Pseudoscience

"A theory which is not refutable by any conceivable event is nonscientific. Irrefutability is not a virtue of a theory (as people often think) but a vice."
–Karl Popper, Philosopher of Science

Popper is best known for suggesting a way to distinguish science from nonscience. He argues that the theories of Marx, Freud, and Adler are all nonscientific because nothing conceivable could disprove them. He explains that to be considered scientific, theories must make "risky predictions," and that, "the more a theory forbids, the better it is."

Ian shook his head. "That can't be right. It doesn't make much sense."

His father crumpled up a piece of paper and threw it in the direction of the trash can. It hit the side of it and landed on the floor. "Perfect shot!" he exclaimed.

Ian differed, "*Perfect*? You missed."

His dad shook his head, crumpled up another piece of paper, and threw it. Again, it bounced off the side and landed on the floor. Again, he exclaimed, "Perfect!" Ian shook his head. His dad explained, "Ian, both of those throws landed where I wanted them to. *No matter where* they land, it's where I want it to land. So every shot is perfect. There's no way for me to throw a bad shot. Pretty good, eh?"

His mom was now engaged in this discussion. "Ian, it has actually been argued that a very well-known psychologist's theory was unfalsifiable. We've talked about Freud. It looks like he devised a theory such that he could never be wrong. Take his Oedipus Complex. In any given situation, regardless of what happens, his theory is confirmed. For example, imagine a boy who sees his dad drowning. If he *doesn't* save him, then, *according to Freud's theory*, he has given in to his subconscious will and Freud is right. If he *does* save him, then he has subverted his id-wish and his superego has won out. Again, Freud is right.

Perfect Shot . . . Every Time

Homer Adkins makes the point in a clever manner when he writes,

"Basic research is like shooting an arrow into the air and, where it lands, painting a target."

What's the harm in pseudoscience?

" . . . isn't it all—crystal ball gazing, star signs, birth stones, ley-lines and the rest—just a bit of harmless fun? If people want to believe in garbage like astrology, or crystal healing, why not let them? But it's so sad to think about all that they are missing. There is so much wonder in real science. The universe is mysterious enough to need no help from warlocks, shamans and 'psychic' tricksters. These are at best a soul-sapping distraction. At worst they are dangerous profiteers."

–Richard Dawkins

Numerous maladies have occurred in the name of pseudo-science, such as the death of a 10-year-old girl in 2000 resulting from treatment with "attachment therapy" (in which therapists verbally abuse, violently shake, bang the head of, and eventually suffocate the patient by lying on her). In 1976, priests performed an exorcism on a girl who had experienced serious shaking fits, verbally and physically abused her family members, and stopped eating. In lieu of giving her a feeding tube, the month-long exorcism left her with pneumonia, broken knees (from the 600 daily genuflections), and death by starvation.

Whatever happens, Freud is not proven wrong. And he uses all these as *confirming instances* to support his theory. *Of course* it's going to be confirmed, though. There's no way to dis-confirm it. It's unfalsifiable. No criterion whatsoever."

She continued, speaking rapidly. "A theory like that would have no predictive power. Imagine watching from afar as the father falls into the water flailing and the son notices him. Then the following conversation ensues:

IAN: Dr. Freud, what will happen? According to your theory, what will the boy do?

FREUD (scratching his chin): Either the boy will try to save his father or he won't.

Science *and* Religion?

In the 1998 Newsweek *article "Science Finds God," Michael Shermer comments that science and religion are, "such different things, it would be like using baseball stats to prove a point in football."*

Pseudoscience researcher James Randi writes, "Religion is based upon blind faith supported by no evidence. Science is based upon confidence that results from evidence." He continues, "Science approaches truth, closer and closer . . . . Religion already has it all decided, and it's 'in the book.' It's dogma, unchangeable, and unaffected by . . . whatever facts we come upon in the real world."

"I could have told you that," his mom suggested encouragingly, smiling at Ian. "But imagine that a coin is dropped off of a tower. With the use of science, you can *predict* exactly what will happen."

His father started back in, after flashing Ian's mother a look of loving pride. "This actually becomes useful in trying to distinguish between pseudoscience and real science. Real science is falsifiable. It's progressive. It improves on itself. Pseudoscience doesn't. Like art. Artists don't necessarily *improve* on past artists, they just invent new techniques. So astrology is a pseudoscience. Psychics. Mythology. Do you think someone's going to come up with some new finding about Zeus and his lightning bolt throwing—that a recent study will show that when Zeus throws lightning he's not angry, and that it's just his way of showing love for the people? No. It's like saying that invisible, undetectable Martians are responsible for all motion, yet when you go to test it, the theorist says, 'They're completely undetectable, by any method. They're just there.' How can you progress there? What could possibly show that to be false? It's very unscientific. This isn't to say that science is necessarily better than pseudoscience—though I happen to think it is—but that there's a difference. There's a criterion."

"It's actually somewhat counterintuitive," his mother interjected. "If a word's meaning includes everything, then it means nothing. If a theory can't possibly be proven wrong, then it is actually useless. But it all makes sense—*criterion*."

"Think back to our discussion the other day, about confirming a hypothesis. Remember—no matter how many times you confirm it, you still can't *prove* it? You just strengthen it. People sometimes try to attack a scientific theory by saying that it is 'only a theory.' But some theories are *highly* confirmed. If we went around saying that induction and science are *not really true*, then we'd hardly know anything."

Ian smiled and looked to his dad as if they were both enjoying the same intellectual ride.

His mom continued, "So we should also look to *dis*confirm a hypothesis too. Let's try a little something." She leaned over to Ian's father and whispered something in his ear.

"Okay, Ian. I want you to guess the rule I just told your dad. The sequence of numbers—two, four, six—follows this rule. If you'd like, you can suggest other three-number sequences and I'll tell you if they follow the rule. When you're confident enough, tell me the rule."

Ian nodded. "Okay. Eight, ten, twelve?"

"Yes," his mother responded immediately. "That follows the rule."

"Ninety, ninety-two, ninety-four?"

"Yes."

"Okay, I know the rule—three consecutive even numbers from smallest to largest."

His mother shook her head.

Ian was taken aback for a moment. "So, does zero, two, four follow the rule?"

She nodded.

"And the rule isn't: even numbers that increase by two?"

"No. No it's not."

Ian pursed his lips and suggested another number sequence, "How about one-hundred-eleven, one-thirteen, one-fifteen?"

She nodded.

"Three, five, seven?"

She nodded.

"Oh, okay. The rule is: *any* three numbers that increase by two."

She shook her head and turned to Ian's father.

Confirmation Bias

This "2-4-6" task was presented to numerous subjects in 1960 by psychologist Peter Wason. Eighty percent guessed the wrong rule on their first attempt as they typically looked only to confirm their hypothesis. This came to be known as "confirmation bias"— the tendency to seek out data that supports one's hypothesis, and to ignore data that refutes it. It is relevant not only to testing scientific hypotheses, but also those in psychology as well as other areas of people's interests such as politics and ethics.

"The moment we want to believe something, we suddenly see all the arguments for it, and become blind to the arguments against it."

–George Bernard Shaw

"The general root of superstition is that men observe when things hit, and not when they miss, and commit to memory the one, and pass over the other."

–Sir Francis Bacon

"The rule is," he said in an official tone, "any three numbers ordered from lowest to highest."

Ian looked dejected.

"You never tried to *dis*confirm your hypothesis, Ian," his mom suggested. "You developed a hypothesis and then tried to find confirming instances. But all it would have taken was *one* disconfirmation to show your hypothesis wrong. You should have tried to *falsify* your hypothesis. You fell into the trap of induction—imagine if you just kept suggesting even numbers that increased by two: fourteen, sixteen, eighteen; twenty, twenty-two, twenty-four. All you'd get was confirmation. But that's never enough for proof."

"But all my suggestions *did* work," Ian noted, half-heartedly.

"True. All of your sequences followed the rule," she responded, pausing for a moment. "Let's imagine for a moment that I didn't know about the law of gravitation. That it was hidden from me just like the rule I just hid from you. So I test it by dropping things. I walk all throughout the house and drop thousands of different types of objects, noticing how they behave. Finally, I conclude: 'All objects fall towards the floor of the Pinkles' home.' They all did, right?"

Ian nodded, laughing at the thought of the Pinkle Law of Gravitation.

His mom concluded, "If I never tried to disconfirm my hypothesis I may have a very short-sighted law."

Ian shook his head, half out of intellectual amazement, half from mental fatigue. After all, he'd already been working on this in his sleep, and on top of that it was only six in the morning. "Guys, this is making my head tired. I'm going to walk down to the doughnut store and get a doughnut. Then maybe I'll go back to bed for a couple of hours. Good very-early-morning."

The Power of the Quill

I didn't really feel like a doughnut. I left the house with nowhere really to go. Too bad there's not a place called Nowhere, because then I would go there. And when people asked me where I was going I could reply, *Nowhere*, and then ask them if they wanted to come along. Well, maybe that wouldn't be so great after all, plus it would be really confusing. And that thought brought me to an elderly woman sitting on a park bench, knitting. She greeted me. I said *hello*. She smiled and I asked her what she was knitting. "It's a sweater for a porcupine," she answered. "Porcupines get cold too. Do you know any porcupines?" she asked. She asked with such a straight face that I thought I should know some, but I obviously didn't. "No, I suppose I don't." "Sit down here, then. Let me tell you about one porcupine that I knew years ago."

As I sat, the woman put her knitting down in her lap and looked off into the sky. She smiled. She shook her head to herself and smiled. Then she began, in sort of a storybook way. . .

It was recess time again, everyone's favorite. All the young porcupines strutted out to the playing fields to get their energy out. Will especially looked forward to this time, seeing as how he was new to the fifth grade and really only talked to other fifth graders during recess. He left his last all-porcupine school because his mother has to move from city to city a lot for her job. He also has struggled a bit in the past year because he had started to lose some of his quills prematurely. While about twenty-five percent of porcupines lose a majority of their quills in later life, about 5 percent start to lose them early, just around the time of fourth or fifth grade. And, unfortunately for Will, this age-group really notices any differences—and they let you know about it.

Today at recess the porcupines were going to play kickball. Two of the porcupines picked their teams and Will was again the last one chosen for the team. (Though Will was delighted, as he told his mother later that night, "Kenneth chose me for his team today, mom!") Kenneth announced, "I've got the fifty-year-old porcupine on my team. He's the last one there. I suppose I choose him." The other porcupines laughed, and Will assumed they were all happy to get the game going, and he was happy to be a part of it. Every now and then, kids would come up to him and make some remark regarding his quills—or lack thereof—and would then pat him on the back. It was nice for Will to finally have the others actually come up to him and talk to him.

Immediately after recess that day, Mrs. Jeffries, their teacher, took three of the porcupines aside and spoke with them. Will watched from afar—though he could not hear their conversation, he could see them chatting. She said to them, "Boys, I see no reason why you need to make fun of Will for his quills. For one thing, I see no reason to make fun of anyone for any reason—it only hurts their feelings. But secondly, you're making fun of someone for something completely out of their control. This is ridiculous. It would be like making fun of the grass for being green. Doesn't that seem strange?" And she walked away.

That next day at school, during the second recess, the boys came to Will again. He wondered why they hadn't been able to talk earlier, but figured they must have other things on their minds. "Hey Will, can we borrow a quill, looks like you've got next-to-nil . . . still!" They all laughed. Will laughed. He tried to put the pieces of their little poem together, but just assumed it was a sort of funny poem that sounded nice. He'd never had a poem written about him, so he just laughed with them and enjoyed the moment.

During lunch, while Will sat and read, he saw Mrs. Jeffries sit down with the group of friendly poets, again out of hearing range. "You know," she began, "Will is a very talented artist, and he reads a lot. You three do nothing like that—you spend no time on your creative, intellectual endeavors. Yet, I don't see him make fun of you for that. Why is it that having a full set of quills is somehow better or worse than creating great works of art or becoming an avid reader? You should think about what you're saying about yourselves before you speak." And she left.

The last month of school that year went along about like this. Will would be teased for his quills—and he did seem to lose more and more quills as the year went on—he would enjoy the interaction with the other boys, as he couldn't imagine someone making fun of someone else just because of the number of quills they had, and then Mrs. Jeffries would sit down with the boys and try to talk some sense into them, though unsuccessfully.

Unfortunately for Will, his mother's job required that they move again. Because it was the end of the year, she waited for the move until the next-to-last week of school so that Will could take his last tests and finish fifth grade, just a week early.

That Friday, after school, Will came to Mrs. Jeffries' office. He was carrying a paper bag filled with papers. Mrs. Jeffries was gone for the day, so Will left them on her table so she would get them when she got to school Monday morning, for the final week of school. Will was sad he didn't get to see her, but very happy about being able to deliver this for the class before leaving that weekend.

When Mrs. Jeffries arrived at school that Monday morning, she saw the bag and opened it. There was a huge stack of thick papers and, on the top, was a letter. It read,

Dear Mrs. Jeffries,

Now that I will graduate from the fifth grade, I want to thank you for being my teacher. All my other teachers in all the other towns were not like you. Your class was fun and I liked learning in it. I know that you are the person that got all the other boys to talk to me. I didn't really care because I just liked that they would be friends with me. And I liked that you cared so much to tell them to talk with the new guy, and even pick the new guy for their kickball teams. Because I like this class so much, I made everyone a drawing. Each drawing is supposed to bring out the nice part of every person. I know the drawings aren't like all the ones in our art book, but all I had were my quills to draw with and they are not as good as the paintbrushes in class. Before this year, I used to think that how we dressed or how I combed my quills were the most important things about us. Because of you, I see that this was silly—but I was just a kid! From your class I learned how important it is to see the good things in everyone. It was very fun doing this for my classmates. Thank you for being such a good teacher.

Love,

Will

The letter moved Mrs. Jeffries to tears. She pulled out the first painting and it was a painting of a flower. In the middle of the flower was a heart. And in the middle of the heart was a face. While it was not so clear that the face was hers, she knew it was hers. It was the most amazing painting she had ever seen. It was her favorite. She framed it and hung it above her desk in the classroom.

That week, the class went on their end-of-the-year field trip to the big art museum in the city. They each decided to bring the painting that Will made for them so they could compare their paintings with those in the museum. They were all very proud of their paintings, they were proud of Will, and they were all a little more aware of what qualities in porcupines were most important to them. While at the museum, one of the curators came to a group of them and marveled at their personal artwork. She asked which artist they were representing. As none of the children understood her question, one said, "Will. These are by Will." After a long discussion with the teacher as to how they acquired the art, the museum collected all the paintings and created an exhibit of Will's work for the following month. The exhibit was entitled, "The Power of the Will." Because the paintings were so unique—as most painters were simply using paintbrushes to paint—they quickly became popular and were soon known nationwide. When Will arrived at the exhibit, he had even fewer quills. And the students knew what that meant. And they all complimented him on it.

Then there was silence. The woman was knitting again. I felt like I had been there, with Will. She looked at me and I smiled. She smiled back. "Thank you," I said, sincerely. "Thank you for sharing that story. I really enjoyed it."

She smiled at me, she reached over and patted my knee and then went back to her knitting. I didn't know how long I'd been gone, but it felt like much longer than one round trip to the doughnut store. So I went back home, up the stairs, and back to bed for a very-early-morning nap.

Chapter 11

Heaps and Eggs

A hen is only an egg's way of making
another egg.

–B. F. Skinner

It is . . . easy to be certain. One has only to
be sufficiently vague.

–C. S. Peirce

Finally, some rest. Since I'd already had my nightly encounter with my friend, I could actually get some sleep. Maybe I could just dream about . . . well . . . whatever kids dream about—running through fields, walking hand in hand with Alexis, falling through the air. Something other than my usual.

Enter Old Man.

Okay. Why rest? Why rest when there are more important things to deal with like yellow-number-five? Selfishness. Science. Yes, that did seem important. I wondered what he'd have to say about that.

"I can never decide whether my dreams are the result of my thoughts, or my thoughts the result of my dreams."

–D. H. Lawrence

I started in, "And, by the way, your 'everyone's selfish' thing doesn't work. If everyone's selfish, then no one's selfish and *selfish* loses all its meaning. Every word we use must have a criterion for incorrectness. Criterion. Pretty important. Need it for scientific theories too you know."

"Interesting indeed, Ian. Do you understand a word you just said or are you simply repeating what you've been told?"

Before I could answer he continued, "I am interested in your idea of assigning criteria to words. Let's go downstairs."

I got up to follow him out my door. He waved to me to follow him down the ladder-and-tube path. "Why don't we just go this way?" I asked, thinking it not out of the question that we take the stairs *downstairs*.

"We can't," he responded. Although I knew that we could, I just followed him down the ladder and into the kitchen that way. My parents had maybe gone for a walk, or gone back to sleep . . . or I suppose they could have just up and flown away. The Old Man pointed to a small pile of sand, noting, "Watch out for that heap of sand."

"A *heap?*" I thought, chuckling to myself.

"Watch out for these few heaps of sand on your way out."

Again, these sand piles were hardly visible to me. Probably fifty grains of sand in each little pile—a very strange way to use the word 'heap' but inconsequential nonetheless. He's a funny man.

> "*The invariable mark of wisdom is to see the miraculous in the common.*"
> –Ralph Waldo Emerson

We went out back and there were two pretty big piles of sand, one next to the other. Next to each pile were two official-looking people wearing tight blue jumpsuits, latex gloves, and glasses with magnifying glasses attached to them.

The Old Man turned to me, "So, Ian, look at these two collections of sand. Are these heaps?"

"Yes, sure. One would certainly be correct in referring to *those* piles of sand as *heaps.*"

He turned to the official-looking people, "Expert Sand-Grain-Counters, how many grains are in each of these piles of sand?"

One replied, "There are 407,003,739 grains in pile A and 407,003,738 grains in pile B."

"Are you sure?"

"Yes. We're the *most expert* Expert Sand-Grain-Counters in the world, and we've counted both piles twice and come up with the same numbers each time."

"What could possibly be the point of this?" I asked. "One grain of sand would never make a difference between calling a collection of sand a heap or not."

"Yes, I agree," responded the Old Man.

We both stood there, in silence—it was kind of an uncomfortable silence. I felt like I was supposed to be reading between the lines or something. But all I could see was an absurdly obvious statement.

Then he got going. "So, to put it more clearly, it sounds like you'd agree with the following statement:

(1) If you consider a specific collection of sand a *heap*, then subtracting just one grain would not cause it to be a non-heap.

"Yes, of course." This hadn't made this blatantly obvious situation any less blatantly obvious. But now I was sure there was a catch. I had hoped to find a flaw in his statement as I expected that he'd use it against me at some point in the future. But the statement seemed too obvious to be flawed.

"That said, you must agree that *this*," and he held out his hand which held one grain of sand stuck in the middle of his palm, "is a heap."

"No." I shook my head. "No, I do not agree with that."

"You do not think this is a heap of sand?"

I shook my head. "I don't know how anyone could possibly argue that it is."

"Well, it's a very simple argument, really. Taking Statement One, we are forced to conclude that no matter how many times one removes a grain of sand from a heap, it does not cease to be a heap. This, then, leads to the conclusion that one grain of sand is a heap."

"That's got to be some pretty bad logic you're using. *No one* would believe that one grain of sand is a heap."

"Look at it with me. Let's assume that you and everyone we interview refers to a 10,000-grain pile of sand as a *heap*. Now, by your statement—with which I totally agree—if we remove one grain from this collection, thus reducing it to 9,999 grains, we still consider that to be a heap. Again, using Statement One, 9,998 grains is a heap, don't you agree?"

> **"Statement One" Applied**
>
> If *100 grains of sand is considered a heap, then 99 grains is also a heap.*
>
> If *10,232 grains of sand is considered a heap, then 10,231 grains is also a heap.*

I nodded.

"And then again for 9,997 grains. You know, we could do this exercise all the way down to a two-grained heap, or, for simplicity, we could just jump to there right now."

"Sure, I suppose."

"Of course. So once we are at our two-grained heap, we again apply Statement One, and get down to one grain. A one-grained heap."

"So what's the catch?" I asked.

"Well, it appears that there is no catch. I used a statement that you and, from what I've gathered, *everyone* agrees with, and arrived at the conclusion that *every collection of grains of sand—even one-member groups—constitutes a heap.*"

> *The "Paradox of the Heap" was initially posited by Eubulides of Miletus in approximately 400 BC. It is known as the "Sorites Paradox," from the Greek word for "heap," sôros.*

"There's no way. I don't care if I agreed with everything you did and said, I do not agree with your conclusion. One grain of sand is not a heap."

"Hmm. Well, if you think that to be the case, then what if I add another grain to this one grain I hold in my hand?" He dropped a second grain into his palm. "And then there were two."

"This isn't even an issue," I responded. "Everyone in the world agrees that one grain of sand isn't a heap of sand. That being said, *I* will now make another little rule, or postulate, or whatever you call it:

(2) If you consider a specific collection of sand as *not* a *heap*, then adding just one grain would not cause it to become a heap."

That felt right—like my own little postulate. This would at least halt the course of absurd reasoning. That way I could go back to counting sheep—instead of sand grains—like the rest of the sleep-deprived world.

"Interesting, indeed. Though it seems that your point—or postulate—is rather obvious. I don't think you've stated anything that anyone in their right mind would disagree with."

"Yeah," I agreed. "So that should keep you from going on in the way that you are: asking if adding one grain of sand to something that's not a heap makes the new collection a heap."

"Statement Two" Applied

If *10 grains of sand is not a heap, then 11 grains is not a heap either.*

If *10,232 grains of sand is not a heap, then 10,233 grains is not a heap either.*

The Old Man tilted his head, looked away, and then looked back at me with his sneaky grin. "Ian, tell me, if I add this third grain to the collection in my hand, will it make a heap?"

"No. We just went over this. By my postulate, Statement Two, adding one grain will never make a non-heap into a heap."

"So, by *your* postulate, it sounds like you're saying, even if I add 1 grain of sand to a non-heap 10,000 times, I will never make a heap. Is this what you're saying? That, if you start from a non-heap you could *never* construct a heap?"

It seemed like he'd trapped me once again. "I suppose my postulate was wrong, then. But it seemed so obvious. It seems like we have two obvious postulates and they both conclude that there is no such thing as a heap of sand."

"They *both* conclude that?" the Old Man asked.

"Sure. As it turns out, vague terms, such as the term 'heap,' apply to all or nothing. Statement One—the 'all' of the 'all or nothing'—says that no matter how many times you take a grain of sand away from a heap, it will still remain a heap. *But* this means that *all* collections of grains of sand are heaps. Yet, if the word *heap* refers to *all* collections, then the word *heap* loses its meaning. It's the lesson from the meeting I had with you last night, or earlier this evening . . . or morning . . . or whenever that was."

The Old Man nodded thoughtfully, so I continued. "So, we're left with Statement Two—which is the 'nothing' of the 'all-or-nothing'—which states that no matter how many times you add a grain to a collection of sand, it will *never* constitute a heap of sand."

"Exactly, Ian. You're learning well. And this argument applies to a lot of other things also."

I raised my eyebrows in anticipation.

"People being rich. If someone's not rich, giving them a penny won't make them rich.

"A color changing from orange to red: if a bucket of paint is red, adding one part per million of orange will not make that paint orange. Think of all the vagueness in our language: child, game, toy, tall, large. It turns out that almost any term actually has no meaning at all."

Numbers: Neither Large nor Small

There can be no large numbers: *Adding one to any non-large number will not make it large.*

There can be no small numbers: *Subtracting one from a non-small number will not make it small.*

There must be a way out of this. It seemed like there were just what we call *"gray areas"* when it comes to these problems. One grain is obviously not a heap. A man with ten billion dollars is obviously rich. Maybe that was the key.

"I think I've found a problem with this issue. Or a solution to this problem."

"I'm all ears," replied the Old Man.

"Okay. Well, let's look at some obvious examples. We can use the example you just mentioned of a man being rich." I paused to get ready for this. "A man with one cent is definitely *not* rich. While a man with a million dollars *is* rich. Agreed?"

"For now, yes, I would agree to that."

"Okay. There is an obvious problem that comes up somewhere between these two amounts of money. This problem is kind of hard to define—it's like a thing that we're not sure about, something that's unknown, at least for now."

"Quite an enigma," he said to himself.

"A what? An enigma?"

"Yes. An enigma. Something slippery, hard to pin down. Somewhat elusive."

What it Means for a Word To Be . . .

Vague: *A word has essentially no meaning. If someone says he is "tall," if he isn't speaking relative to something else, it doesn't mean anything.*

Relative: *A word has meaning only in comparison to something else. For example, the average height of a group of people is precise. And you are either taller or shorter than the average.*

Ambiguous: *A word has a meaning but you're not sure what it is. If someone says, "He is closer to his mom than his dad," we wonder, "Is he standing closer to his mom?" or "Is he more emotionally open with his mom?"*

"Yes. An *enigma*," I said, nodding my head to affirm him as he had done for me so many times. "So, at some point, it seems like it's not so clear that a man is rich, or that a pile is a heap. You yourself admitted that there are an excruciating number of steps that would lead us to getting at the unacceptable conclusion, 'A man with $1 is rich.' Remember? But, somewhere we would come to a point where it wasn't so clear. Maybe that a man with $100,000 is rich, though that's not important. Yet, it would again become clear that a person with a certain amount of money would *not* be rich, maybe someone with $5,000, though I would think that any friend of mine with that much money was rich. This kind of confuses relativity with vagueness, which isn't the concern here."

"Very insightful."

"Thanks. So, what I propose is that between $100,000 and $5,000 there lies an enigma—an area of statements that are neither true nor false."

"And how does that help us?"

"I'll diagram it for you here," and I scribbled on a sheet of paper:

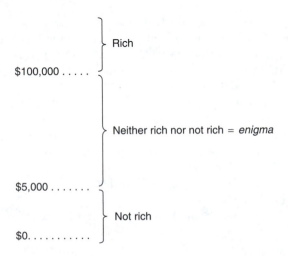

"As you see, if I say that someone with the amount of money in the enigma is rich, then that is neither true nor false. In other words, it is neither true nor false that people who have anywhere from $5,000 to $100,000 are rich. But it *is* true that people with more than $100,000 are rich and people with less than $5,000 are *not* rich, though they're not necessarily poor. This way, it allows for the word 'rich' to have meaning, which avoids the problem of vagueness. In a way we can have our cake and eat it too—there's both vagueness *and* exactitude."

Super Truths

The diagram with the "enigma" is known as "supervaluation." We can say that the segments above the enigma are "super true" and those below it are "super false."

The Old Man furrowed his eyebrows and, scrunching his lips up, announced his momentary approval. "Thoughtful, Ian. Somewhat convincing," he paused, as if the moment of approval had ended. "Though I'm afraid that you've just sidestepped the problem a bit—you've hidden it in your wording. You've really just created a 'meta-vagueness' or higher-order vagueness."

"I'm not sure I understand what you're saying," I said, feeling a little dejected.

"Initially we had the problem of deciphering just when someone became rich. We agreed that 1 cent didn't make a difference. Though this led to the seemingly unacceptable conclusion that either everyone is rich, or no one is rich. Now you've created what you call an *enigma*. Though here's my question for you: Couldn't the upper-end enigma start at $100,000-and-one-cent instead of $100,000? Or, put another way, does giving a man a single cent really remove him from the *neither-rich-nor-not-rich* category and place him in the *rich* category? With your enigma you've just re-created the problem. We could create a new challenge—instead of trying to define something as a heap or someone as rich, we could try to define something as *definitely a heap* or someone as *definitely rich*. In doing so, we would just be creating new enigma cases, and new levels of vagueness. Either way, there's going to be some vagueness."

"But I believe in heaps," I pleaded. "I have always believed in heaps. There must be heaps. Heaps of heaps, even. Please let there be heaps."

"Ian. Ian," his mother called down to him.

"Of course. Of course. No heaps, mom. No rich people. No children. No people, I imagine." He spoke rapidly as he meandered into the kitchen so as to get it all out. "No toys. No games. Either that or no logic, no language." He paused for a breath, drumming his fingers on the kitchen table. "So where does that leave us?"

"You want to talk about this? I'm interested to hear what you're struggling with. Sounds pretty serious."

He calmed down a bit. "Yeah, let's talk. Let's have cereal and talk."

"Good morning," his father hesitated, "again. Sounds like you hardly had a restful nap."

> *"He . . . who can no longer pause to wonder and stand rapt in awe is as good as dead: his eyes are closed."*
>
> –Einstein

"No such thing as naps, dad."

"Hmm," he seemed to prepare himself mentally. "Curious to hear about this."

And so Ian told them. He told them all about the heaps, or what were formerly known as heaps, or what we'd read about in books as heaps.

His father started in, "And so it sounds like the overall problem is that, according to simple logic, there is no such thing as heaps. No such thing as rich people. No color red. No children." He paused, nodding. "Interesting."

"See, dad. So something has got to go. If we don't want to accept that conclusion, then either we have to deny the supposedly sound reasoning *or* we have to reject the supposedly true steps."

> *"We should have a great fewer disputes in the world if words were taken for what they are: the signs of our ideas only, and not for the things themselves."*
>
> –John Locke

"Well, let's see. I did like your attempt at solving this—through your idea of an enigma—though I also see the new problem it presents, or how it just frames the old problem in a new way.

"You know, one possible solution relates to your proposed solution. It relies on the overturning of something called '*verificationism*,' which was a very popular theory in the mid-1900s."

"I remember reading about that somewhere. How would it help us?" I asked.

"Well, verificationists basically held that every comprehensible sentence is necessarily *either* true *or* false. We've talked about this before. But as we see, this isn't at all the case. For example, the sentence, 'Pizza is good,' is neither true nor false. As is the sentence, 'What time is it?'" Yet they're both comprehensible."

"Okay, and so that allows for certain vague sentences, like mine in the enigma, to be legitimate?"

"Yes, it does. But it quickly returns us to the problem introduced by the Old Man earlier."

"Yeah, so now what?" Ian asked, somewhat impatiently.

"Well, think back to an earlier discussion we had regarding our shortcomings as people seeing the world as it *really* is. Remember? Humans require a slight margin of error in deciphering the world. We see shorter lines as actually longer, white shirts as orange under light, straight sticks as bent, big stars as small. To say that we *know* what's going on around us, we must allow for a slight margin of error."

"And same goes with *knowing* a heap?"

"Yes Ian, that's right. Let me tell you a funny story about the first time I met your mother. We were playing a game of darts and the object was to first throw three darts in the number 20 slot and then, after doing that, to throw one in the bull's-eye. Your mother commented how difficult getting a bull's-eye must be. Then, on her first attempt at getting her dart in the '20,' her dart went straight in the bull's-eye. She thought I'd be very impressed with this. But I wasn't impressed—not with her ability to throw darts, anyway. And why do you think that was the case, Ian?" he asked, smiling lovingly at Ian's mom.

"Because she wasn't aiming for the bull's-eye? Because it was just luck—an accident?"

"Exactly. And it's the same with knowledge. You can't claim to *accidentally* know something. You already know this. If you say, 'I know the Giants won only because I'm wearing blue socks,' *and* the Giants *did* win, that wouldn't count as knowledge. Your socks and the outcome of a baseball game have nothing to do with each other."

"So how does this relate to the heap?"

We can't know the world exactly as it is.

R.M. Sainsbury remarks on the imperfection of human perception: "Our cognitive mechanisms . . . require a margin of error."

Black-and-White . . . and . . . Gray

In 1965, "fuzzy logic" was introduced to deal with partial truths as opposed to the binary system of classical logic, which expressed things in the "black and white" terms of 1's and 0's. Instead, fuzzy logic presents truths in shades of gray. While classic logic may say that someone is rich or poor, or that something is cold or hot, or that something is or is not a person, fuzzy logic may hold that something is 0.6 hot, or 0.2 cold or 0.8 a person.

"*Because our perceptual system has a margin of error,*" he emphasized slowly, "there are certain things we just can't know. We develop a language that allows us to navigate through the world very successfully; however, there are facts about the world that we can't know. And we have to accept that."

"That's not very satisfying, though. There are just things we can't know?"

"I agree, it's not a pretty view. But it's realistic. There's really only one other way to get out of this dilemma you've posed."

"And what's that?" Ian asked, hopeful.

"Well, it falls again on our use of language. Tell me, Ian, did the Giants win yesterday?"

"Yes, they did."

What Is "Certain Enough"?

Statistical theory has three criteria for determining when enough certainty about an event's occurring is enough.

1. Probably: 95% sure
2. Definitely: 99% sure
3. Certainly: 100% sure

When we act on these confidence intervals we can make two types of errors:

Type 1: We wrongly believe the probability of a desired outcome is too small.
Type 2: We wrongly believe the probability of a desired outcome is too high.

"How certain are you?"

"Pretty certain. Jeff has a friend who was actually at the game. He told us."

"Would you bet five dollars on it?"

"Yeah, of course."

"Would you bet all your money on it?"

"Well, I'm not sure. Maybe."

"Maybe? I thought you were *certain* of it. Would you bet your life on it?"

"No way. I'm not certain enough to bet my life on that."

"Certain *enough?* So you admit to there being levels of certainty? Or, maybe degrees of knowing something."

"Yes, I suppose there are."

"Well, then we can accept the statement, 'The Giants won yesterday' as true, and say that we're *pretty darn sure*, or, in scientific terms, true with a 99 percent confidence interval."

"Yeah, I'm 99 percent sure of it."

"Okay. So, this all comes back to the options you gave earlier: we deny the seemingly sound reasoning *or* we have to reject the seemingly true steps taken. In this case, the two are connected. As we've seen, vagueness may just alert us to the fact that we rarely attain *absolute* certainty for anything. So then, the steps aren't *wholly* true, and thus we *can* reject the reasoning."

The Trouble with Categories

Richard Dawkins explains our natural inclination to categorize. With words like "tall" and "short," we tend to try fitting people into those categories. He suggests that if you say a woman is 5'9" and ask him to classify her as tall or short he would respond, "She's five foot nine, doesn't that tell you what you need to know?" He then mentions the pre-apartheid courts in South Africa that forced people into categories of white, black, or "coloured," and the negative effect that had. He also suggests that this problem of classification wrongly takes rights away from non-human animals as they are not put in the same category as humans despite very few relevant differences.

"Now that makes some sense, dad. This way, if the logic doesn't hold because of the way we're speaking about the world, then it's not the world that's vague but, instead, it's our way of speaking about it."

His dad nodded slowly, as if awaiting the conclusion of Ian's reasoning. Ian continued, "So the statement, *This is a heap,* is true in the same way that many true statements are true. They all have a level of uncertainty. And, since we can't *really know* these things, then we can't use pure logic to help us decipher it."

"Very good, son," his mom chimed in. "I'm very interested in your statement, *it's not the world that's vague but, instead, it's our way of speaking about it.* That's very insightful and may actually help us look at some real-life issues—something a little more pertinent than heap-designation."

"Really?"

"Yes. We probably don't have time to go into it much now. But one major issue this relates to is abortion."

"Oh. I hear people argue about this all the time."

"Yes. For the most part, people believe that it's morally wrong to kill innocent humans. So the real crux of the issue is determining when a certain conglomeration of cells becomes a human—when does a fertilized egg actually become a human? If the fetus *is* an innocent human, then it would be wrong to kill it, even if the pregnant woman didn't feel like carrying it around. For many people, a collection of 32 cells is not a human, yet most

When does a fertilized human egg become a human person? Some common answers:

1. *It is fertilized (day 1).*
2. *It acquires a soul (40–90 days, according to Aristotle).*
3. *Its brain starts to function (weeks 8–10).*
4. *It can feel pain (week 14).*
5. *It is viable—able to live outside the womb (week 24).*
6. *It is born.*

everyone also agrees that a fetus which is 1 second from being born *is* a human. So, again, we have your problem of the heap, though here it's drastically more important."

"Honey," Ian's father interrupted, "before we go to lunch, can we finish on a brighter note? I think your point is extremely important and very pertinent, but not something we can solve in the next few minutes. I, on the other hand, do have an age-old question that I think we are now able to answer."

"Of course. And what is that? Is this your whole 'trying to define what a *game* is' problem?" she asked.

"No, hon."

"Game?" Ian questioned. "That's easy."

"Okay then," Ian's dad immediately responded, "Is Frisbee a game? What about boxing? Ring around the roses?" He was rattling these off as though he'd already spent some time thinking about it. "Bull fighting? Olympic ballroom dancing? Russian roulette? War?"

"Let's not get into this," Ian's mom interjected, as if preventing an hour's worth of discussion over games. "What is this perennial question which you suppose we can now finally answer?"

He sat up proudly, "Which came first, the chicken or the egg?"

"How, dad?"

"Well, son, it's like this. We can even use your enigma suggestion to help us solve it."

Ian smiled.

"The problem lies in the vagueness of the term *chicken*. Given the widely received theory posed by Charles Darwin that organisms evolve," he paused to see that his small audience obviously accepted this, "we must start with the notion that the chicken was preceded by very chicken-like organisms." They nodded. "So, then, there must have been a time when chickens were *not* chickens. Likewise, at the present time, we *do* believe that there are chickens. So, there is an enigma—a time when we weren't quite sure if there were chickens. You agree?"

As they agreed, he began scribbling something on a napkin. He continued, "Mutations

What Is a Game?

Wittgenstein examines games such as board games, card games, ball games, chess, "noughts and crosses," patience, and ring-a-ring-a-roses. He argues that games are not defined by any general features, such as amusement, skill, luck, etc. Instead, he asks us to simply "look and see" what we call games as opposed to saying, "there must be something common, or they would not be called 'games.'"

Wittgenstein implies that no class of objects has an "essence" or common denominator.

can't happen within one organism's lifetime. So the change from non-chicken to chicken must have happened between the egg-layer and the egg. So, at some point there was a mutation and a chicken first appeared. It's not important *when* this happened just that, theoretically, *it happened*. The *egg came first*." He turned the following diagram on the napkin towards them so they could read it:

Non-chicken →	**Egg** →	**Chicken** →	**Chicken egg**
(Can't mutate into a chicken in one lifetime.)	(Mutations happen between offspring. So, *this* was first.)	(Now a chicken may be born, as the mutation happened in the egg.)	(*Then* comes the chicken egg.)

Ian smiled again, until his mom spoke up.

"Honey," she said softly, as if announcing a disagreement. "I hate to be the one to fine-tune the biology, but I think it's actually very important here."

"How so, dear?"

"Well, first of all, I have a question for you: Can an alligator lay a pigeon egg?"

He chuckled. "No."

"Why not?"

"Because an organism of a specific species can only be produced by a member of that species."

"Exactly. So the thing that laid the egg which then became the first chicken wasn't a chicken, correct?"

"Yes, theoretically, that's true."

"Well, then, the egg that was laid was not a *chicken* egg."

"True."

"So, then, if the question is, what came first, the chicken or the egg, then the answer *is* the egg. But I think the question we're really concerned with is, *What came first, the chicken or the chicken-egg?* And this being the case, the *chicken* preceded the chicken-egg. The chicken came first. The egg that produced that chicken was not a chicken egg: it was a non-chicken egg with a chicken in it."

"The daughter of a crab does not give birth to a bird."

–Confucius

"'Chicken' Is Vague"

Roy Sorenson explains, ". . . Charles Darwin demonstrated that the chicken was preceded by borderline-chickens so it is simply [unknown] as to where the pre-chickens end and the chickens begin. . . . Contemporary evolutionary theory favors the egg."

Though applying Mendel's "theory of inheritance," Sorenson argues the chicken came first.

His dad nodded an approving nod at Ian's mother. "See how fruitful this discussion has become, son? From heaps of sand, to rich people, to human beings, and finally to chickens and their eggs. Oftentimes in a dispute, people are talking about the exact same thing—like in our egg example—yet call it something totally different."

Ian smiled. "Mom, Dad. Tonight, instead of my bedtime being 10:00, can we make it 10:01?"

"Oh no, son," his dad laughed. "The bedtime for eighth-graders is set by Mother Nature at 10:00. That's just an absolute truth of nature."

"How about 10:00 and one second?"

"If you're good, then 10:00 and one second is fine, I suppose," his dad said, jokingly.

Ian smiled. "Where did you guys go when I took a nap?"

His parents looked at each other. His mother responded, "We went for a walk. We were just out and about, looking for maybe a new slice of sky to hang in the living room."

"So you weren't here while I was asleep?"

"No," his mother responded. They seemed a little confused or even worried as to why Ian would ask. "We got back just before you woke up."

"Okay," Ian said and went up the stairs and out the door.

The Hanging Town

That was enough of that. I must admit, I was kind of proud to have such smart parents. They make a lot of interesting points.

Today I was excited. It wasn't just a go-outside-and-see-what-you-can-stir-up kind of day. Jeff and I had a plan. We were going to the Hanging Town. Jeff had told me about this place last week. He said that they have a great baseball card shop there, along with some other pretty weird things. He wouldn't tell me much, but it definitely piqued my curiosity and, at the least, I could hopefully find some cards I was looking for.

I met Jeff outside with my bike. He rode up and we were off. He said it was only a ten-minute bike ride. So we wove in and out of the street markers, up and down the curbs, and I thought of how odd it was that there were never cars in the street. Never. Not one. I wonder why we even have streets? To ride our bikes? So the word *street* means something? Would we have the word *street* if there were no streets?

"There it is," announced Jeff. Just like that. I could tell already that there was something unique about this place. The whole town was fenced in. I could see a grand entrance, sort of old-western style. Two big trees framed the entrance and tied to each tree trunk was a rope that held a big wooden sign. Carved into the sign in big capital letters was "Hanging Town." I looked at Jeff and shrugged my shoulders as if to say, "Looks good to me." He nodded, grinning.

As we approached the entrance, I could see a man sitting in a big leather chair, reading. He greeted us upon our arrival and wished us a good day. "Good day," Jeff responded. Then the man spoke in an official, though friendly tone:

You must now say your plans here today,

And when you do, you're on your way,

If truth you say, you'll leave alive today,

If false you say . . . you'll hang, you'll hang.

I wanted to be frightened about this but something wouldn't let me—whether it was his matter-of-fact tone or just the fact that if I told the truth, I would be allowed to leave. What a strange practice—to hang people just for lying about their business. I did feel confident, though, in what I was there to do, so I said to the man, "I have come here to look for baseball cards." I said *look for* instead of *get* because what if I didn't see any that I liked, or what if they all cost a million dollars or something? So, all I had to do was look for baseball cards and I'd be okay. I could still buy them if I wanted to. The man nodded. I stood and waited for Jeff. Why *did* Jeff want to come here today?

"I have come here to be hanged," he said, confidently. The man wrote these responses down and nodded. "Enjoy your day here," he said, and we walked off, with our bikes in our hands.

"Jeff, what were you thinking? These people are serious. There were two coffins next to the entrance! This is not a good time to joke around." He just smiled, saying, "Don't worry about it. I'll take care of everything. You just make sure that you don't forget to look for a baseball card or two." I shook my head.

Following that little glitch, the day proceeded as expected. We rode our bikes through the dirt, got some ice cream, and went to the baseball card shop. I made sure that a lot of people saw me there, greeting everyone, asking them how they were doing. It turned out that the cards there were not a million dollars, and I bought three that I wanted and they were only four dollars altogether. So I had proof.

As we walked out of the card store, there was some commotion next door at the barber shop. A group of people were talking outside the shop and after watching them discuss whatever it was they were discussing, Jeff walked up to the group to ask what was going on.

"Well," responded an elderly woman, "we're trying to figure out who shaves the barber." Jeff looked at me with a "they're crazy" look on his face. Funny. The woman continued, "Every day, people visit the shop to figure it out. No one really has yet. It's quite a problem. Who shaves the barber?" Again, the crazy-look from Jeff, though this time more animated.

We stepped back into the street to look at the sign on the shop. It read:

The Barber Shop Where the Barber Shaves

All and *Only* Those Who Don't Shave Themselves

"That's quite a name for a barber shop. I wonder why they didn't just name it *The Barber Shop* or maybe *Hanging Town Hair Salon* or something," Jeff said.

"But Jeff, don't you see the problem?" I waited, now able to connect with the confusion of the townsfolk. Jeff raised his hands, signaling that he did not see the problem. So I asked him as he had been asked already, "Who shaves the barber?"

He responded, "He does. He's a barber. He can shave himself."

"But obviously he doesn't. This barber shaves only those who don't shave themselves. If he shaves himself, then he doesn't because he only shaves those who *don't* shave themselves."

He responded, "Okay, then, someone else does."

"But that can't be right either." A pause to let him see why. I was impatient, though, so I continued. "He shaves *all* those who don't shave themselves. So, if he's one of those who doesn't shave themselves, then he must shave himself." Jeff nodded approvingly. I continued, "But that *can't* be the case as I just explained."

The people continued discussing. Occasionally, someone would have an *aha!* moment, only to be quieted down by another of the townsfolk. Quite a dilemma they were in. Quite a dilemma.

Just then I heard Jeff calling my name from across the street. "Ian, check this out. This shouldn't be weird but it is."

As I got to Jeff he was walking around a tree, in little spurts, like he was chasing something. In the ground a sign that read,

The squirrel is on the tree.

Walk around the tree.

Did you walk around the squirrel?

I wasn't quite sure why *this wasn't supposed to be weird*, as Jeff had said. "Ian, watch this. Whenever I move to the right, the squirrel moves to the left. And after I have gone all the way around the tree, the squirrel has gone all the way around the tree too; he was just on the opposite side from me the whole time. So, even though the squirrel is *on* the tree, and I've gone *around* the tree, I don't feel like I've gone around the squirrel. It's very strange." I watched him walk quickly around the tree. The squirrel did, in fact, walk equally as quickly around the tree, at all times keeping the tree between him and Jeff.

"Is it possible that you walked around the tree but you didn't walk around something *on* the tree?"

"No. Of course not. But it's also the case that I didn't walk around the squirrel either. He was opposite me the whole time."

"Jeff, this whole place is a little weird. And we've got to get back home. By the time we get out of here we'll have just enough time to get home for dinner. Plus, we have to deal with the man at the gate too."

So, we picked up our bikes and rode off to the gate. I had my cards in my pocket, but I was a little nervous about what we were going to do about Jeff. As we approached the gate, the man took out his clipboard and looked us up. He nodded as we came to a halt. I could see the hanging gallows now on the inside of the gate. I felt a lump in my throat.

He looked at me, "Did you look for baseball cards here?"

"Yes, sir. I even bought some. I looked for them and then I bought a few." I held them up for him to see.

"That's fine. Looking for them would have been enough. You're free to pass."

I smiled and waited along side Jeff.

"And you? Were you hanged?"

Jeff looked quizzically at the man, raised his eyebrows awaiting the man's realization that, on account of Jeff being alive, he obviously wasn't hung. No response. "No sir, I was not hanged."

The man called out toward the gallows, "We've got one here, boys!"

"But sir," Jeff said, confidently, "If you hang me then I will have done what I came here to do. And so, it will have been an unjust hanging."

The man's eyes widened, he nodded, he yelled, "Cancel that, boys! My error!"

Jeff smiled at him. He smiled at me. I couldn't really smile as I was still a little upset and also nervous that the man would realize the results of his present decision. "Thank you, sir."

The man nodded. As we walked away, he yelled, "Wait! If you leave without being hanged then you will not have done what you set out to do here. So you must be hanged! Boys!"

"But sir, respectfully, remember that if you hang me, it will be done unjustly."

The man nodded and yelled, "Cancel that!"

Jeff smiled. We again began our journey home.

As we turned to walk away I heard the man yell, "Boys!"

Jeff turned to him and raised an eyebrow. "Cancel that!" the man yelled.

"Boys!" Pause.

The man nodded and yelled, "Cancel that!" Pause.

"Boys!"

"Cancel that!"

This went on for as long as we could hear him. I imagine it will still go on for a long time.

Chapter 12

Society, Politics, and Money

Man is by nature a political animal.

–Aristotle

When people learn no tools of judgment and merely follow their hopes, the seeds of political manipulations are sown.

–Stephen J. Gould

"Today you're going to take on some *real* responsibility, my boy," the Old Man said, his arm resting on my shoulder.

My boy? That was unusual. "How can I have responsibility in a dream?"

"You created a universe, didn't you? That took some responsibility. This will be similar, just not to as great an extent." He paused a moment and then continued in a more playful tone, "And you're still convinced this is *just a dream*, eh?"

As we came out of the portal, we landed on what seemed to be the outskirts of a town or a village of some kind, though there was really no sense of structure. I could see small gatherings of people huddled together but no stores, no sign of electricity, nothing that showed any sign of a civilization.

> *"Judge of your natural character by what you do in your dreams."*
>
> –Ralph Waldo Emerson

We looked toward one of the groups as we heard a yell. One of the villagers—a boy about my age—had taken a piece of fruit from another. They were shouting about it, but there wasn't much for the victim's group to do.

281

"Strange. What are you supposed to do if there are no rules, or authority, or laws? I would say they should go tell someone but who would they tell?"

The Old Man rested his chin on his hand with his elbow braced by his other arm, crossed over his abdomen. "Quite a responsibility," he said, nodding toward me.

"*Me*? They're going to tell me?" I shook my head with my hands in the air as if to say, *why would they tell me?*

"Even better, Ian. *You* are going to tell *them*."

"Tell them what?"

As we talked I noticed another group of kids. They were all kids. Some were sitting and playing with each other but most were arguing and pushing about one thing or another.

"I was here first," I heard one girl yell.

"This tree can't be *yours*. It's in nature, it doesn't *belong* to *anyone*," another exclaimed.

"Don't tell me what I can or can't do. You're not the boss of me."

It was like all these kids had memorized the *Me-First Guide to Getting What You Want*. It was sort of playful in a way, but I saw how it could really escalate if nothing changed.

"This could really escalate if nothing changes," I heard a woman whisper from behind us. We turned around and I saw a familiar older woman—that's the only description I could give, because next to her was Alexis. I felt a strange sensation of fear and happiness, like when you have something you really want yet you know it could be taken away at any moment. So instead of greeting Alexis, I looked to the Old Man. He smiled at the woman and they shook hands in a very familiar way.

The woman turned to me, "Ian, I presume."

I just nodded at first. "Yes ma'am." We shook hands. I stood there with my left hand in my pocket. I waved to Alexis. I wanted to hug her but felt uncomfortable and I didn't want to shake her hand because that's for grown-ups. She waved back. Her wave forced a smile out of me, like my body reacted to it without my even knowing.

The moment was interrupted as the woman yelled to everyone in a booming yet controlled voice, "Stop this nonsense!" I went back to being scared, or maybe intimidated was more like it. The arguing and fighting stopped, more out of curiosity in us, it seemed, than from obedience to her command. She walked towards the groups of kids while motioning for us to follow her. The Old Man nodded in encouragement and Alexis and I shrugged our shoulders and followed, leaving the Old Man behind.

As we approached, more kids came out from little crevices in the landscape. They surfaced from places I hadn't noticed. When we finally encountered the initial group, there were probably over fifty kids there. They all looked like they were our age, like they could even go to my school at home.

"Hello, everyone," the woman said, in an official tone. "I want to introduce you to Ian and Alexis. I know you may not want to be here, but you are. So together you all are going to sort things out here. You're going to figure out a way to govern yourselves, form a society, and live in a more civil manner."

She turned and smiled at us. She nodded to the group, waved to the Old Man and left us. I wanted to watch her to see where she and the Old Man would go, though one of the boys immediately asked, "What makes you think we want that?"

I had hoped they would have been a little more receptive to this, and would also realize that none of this was really our idea. "You just do. Trust me," I said, not able to think of why they would want this.

"I don't think so," the boy continued in a sort of educated way. "Look. As humans we have the capacity to reason. Right? And we have the freedom to do so—autonomy. Without these things—reason and autonomy—what's the point? If you try to impose some government that restricts my personal freedoms, it infringes on my humanity. It's

Creating a State

Nearly every society throughout history has formed what is called a state—*a community in which a recognized person or group has the authority to impose laws, taxation, and punishment, even through force.*

There are exceptions. The Mbuti people, in the forests of Africa, have no semblance of political organization. While they maintain religion, morality, language, and customs, they do not have any political structure and thus no formal punishment or governing body.

Defending Anarchy

In Robert Wolff's book, In Defense of Anarchism, *he writes,*

"The autonomous man, insofar as he is autonomous, is not subject to the will of another. He may do what another tells him, but not because he has been told to do it. He is therefore, in the political sense of the word, free . . .

"The primary obligation of man is autonomy, the refusal to be ruled. . . . Insofar as a man fulfills his obligation to make himself the author of his decisions, he will resist the state's claim to have authority over him . . .

". . . anarchism is the only political doctrine consistent with the virtue of autonomy."

like how life without worldly freedom would be sad—you know, if we were mere puppets of some playful god—life without total personal and political freedom would be sad too. Don't think that you're going to turn any of us into your puppets."

I nodded. That seemed well thought out. Actually, I wondered how it is that *we* are even governed? Why do we allow ourselves to be governed? I turned to Alexis assuming that she would agree with my intuitions.

She squinted her eyes at me as if to say this boy really hadn't thought things through. "Is this life the most ideal life you can imagine?" she asked. She had always been a little more confident in these sorts of situations. "With all the fighting, the solidarity, the lack of schools, arts, paved roads? Given that we are, as you say, *rational beings*, wouldn't it make sense to give up certain less significant freedoms so that, in the end, we can attain even greater freedom?"

A lot of the kids whispered to each other. The boy glared at me as if he'd wished I were the one to speak up instead of Alexis. Though he wasn't yelling, as if there was some sense in what she had said. It made sense to me. Without government, the lack of resources would put a strain on the people and with everyone looking out for themselves, it would result in a life that was not the quality that it could be.

The boy responded, "Okay, since I am rational, I'll listen to what people have to say." He looked around at the rest of the crowd and everyone nodded in agreement.

While I agreed with most of it, I didn't think life would be *that* bad.

"First of all," I started in, "I must say that I have a little more hope for us than what we saw initially. I don't believe that people left without any government would kill each other, would be nasty, or would cheat each other. I'm sure we'll always have disagreements, but I don't think people are naturally bad. I know of lots of selfless, altruistic acts."

"The State of Nature"

Thomas Hobbes wrote that humans, left without political governance, would experience a life that would be, "solitary, poor, nasty, brutish and short." In this "state of nature," all people would have similar wants and an equal ability to satisfy them, and thus: "If any two men desire the same thing, which nevertheless they cannot both enjoy, they become enemies; and in the way to their end, which is principally their own preservation, and sometimes their enjoyment only, endeavour to destroy, or subdue one another."

On the other hand, Jean-Jacques Rousseau held a more romanticized view of mankind, claiming that in the absence of a formal civilization (i.e., in a "state of nature") man would be a "Noble Savage" and essentially good.

"I agree with him," another boy spoke up. I felt a sense of relief as if this were actually going to be a reasonable conversation. "We are all God's creations," the boy continued, "and thus created out of goodness."

I immediately became a bit tense as he presented his reliance on God. He continued, "We all have *rights*. Natural rights." He paused again, as if thinking this through. "Because we each are our own person, we *own* that person, and have complete rights to that person. We each have the right to life, which no one can take away from us."

"But where do these rights come from?" one of the boys shouted out in a genuine tone. "How do you know we have these rights?"

"We are born with them. It is part of being human. Humans everywhere have them—not just this group here. They are the basis of any sort of morality and sense of treating others. You each have the basic right to life, to liberty, to property."

"What does that mean for us though?" a girl shouted. "What about liberty?" another shouted. "What is that?"

"Well," the boy started, as if he had all of a sudden become an expert in the area, "it means that you have the right to personal thought, to religion, to speech."

"We can say whatever we want? Whenever we want?"

The Myth of Nobility?

Steven Pinker explains that the idea of a "Noble Savage"—that humans are inherently good—is a myth: " . . . homicide rates among prehistoric peoples are orders of magnitude higher than those in modern societies—even taking into account the statistics from two world wars!" Though he claims that this in no way justifies violence, as he quotes Russian writer Anton Chekhov, "Man will become better when you show him what he is like."

"Nature, Mr. Allnut, is what we are put in this world to rise above."
    –Katherine Hepburn to Humphrey Bogart in
    The African Queen

Seventeenth-century philosopher John Locke's writings on liberty and political authority greatly influenced the writing of the U. S. Constitution and Declaration of Independence. He wrote, "Political power I take to be a right of making laws with penalties . . . only for the public good. . . . The state of nature has a law of nature to govern it, which obligates every one."
    –Second Treatise of Civil Government

"We hold these truths to be self-evident, that all men are created equal, that they are endowed by their Creator with certain inalienable Rights, that among these are Life, Liberty and the Pursuit of Happiness."
    –United States Declaration of Independence, July 4, 1776

Rights: Rand vs. Locke

While Locke believed people have rights granted by God, Ayn Rand held that these rights were instead part of the nature of humans. The society was to support the people, and not the people to support society. She writes,

"A 'right' is a moral principle defining and sanctioning a man's freedom of action in a social context. There is only one fundamental right . . . : a man's right to his own life."

"Fire!"

In a 1919 decision, Supreme Court Justice Oliver Wendell Holmes wrote, "The most stringent protection of free speech would not protect a man falsely shouting fire in a theater and causing a panic."

This analogy of yelling "Fire!" has been applied since this ruling relating to other freedom of speech issues. Regarding pornography, for example, many argue that the harm done to both women and men— physically, psychologically, and socially— outweighs their freedom of speech to distribute pornographic material.

"Not quite."

"Then how is that a right? What's the point of saying we have a right to free speech if we can't speak freely sometimes?"

"As long as your speech does not lead to the harming of another person, then you can speak freely." He paused. "For example, right now you are not free to yell, 'Wild boars are attacking! Run!'—unless, of course, there are wild boars attacking—because this will cause unneeded chaos and will likely lead to the injury of others. So you don't have the right to speech and expression when it directly harms others. Your speech is limited in that way.

"I just think we do have rights and that this allows us to have rules. Like if we're playing a game. There are rules. And we can't play the game unless everyone agrees. It's almost like a contract that everyone signs in order to live here. We play by the rules and then we get to experience all the good that comes from it."

"But I never signed a contract. I won't sign one," another boy yelled out.

"No one signs it. It is implied. It's unspoken. If you make the conscious decision to live in this state and benefit from all the goods it provides, you *imply* that you agree to give certain things up.

"Think about when you play soccer. Before a game, no one signs anything saying that they won't use their hands. It's *implied*. By agreeing to play soccer, you agree that you won't throw the ball around. Why do you play soccer?" He asked the group. "Why do you do it?"

"It's fun, I guess," one boy responded. "Because it's fun."

"Anyone else?"

"Good exercise," another boy responded.

"I like the competition," remarked one of the girls.

"Exactly," the leader responded as if ready to make his point. "You wouldn't be able to do all of that if no one played by the rules. If someone picked the ball up and threw it in the goal and were then chastised for doing so, it would be ridiculous for them to respond, 'Well, I never signed anything.' By playing the game, you imply that you'll follow the rules."

They were nodding their heads in agreement. I was pretty impressed with his point.

"Same goes here," he continued. "It would be wrong to think that you could drive on our roads, go to our schools, enjoy our community, and simultaneously ignore your duties to obey the laws and pay your taxes. By living here and enjoying the fruits of the community, you have agreed to play by the rules. It's implied."

> *"Every man that hath any possession of enjoyment of any part of the dominions of any government doth thereby give his tacit consent, and is as far forth obliged to obedience to the laws of that government, during such enjoyment, as any one under it."*
>
> –Locke

"So the government that we establish can do whatever it wants to us?"

"No. The government is designed to protect its people. Once the state begins to infringe on the rights of the people, to take their property, to enslave them, then revolution is legitimized. Until then, and assuming that the government is for the people, you are bound to this contract."

Everyone started in on the collective whispering. I assumed it was a good thing—almost like what they had heard made some sense and they were contemplating it. And it was a lot better than collective yelling.

Sport Philosophy and Tacit Consent

Many argue that simply by playing in a game, participants agree to abide by the rules, thus limiting what they can do (i.e., soccer players cannot use their hands to score a goal).

"Locke's minimal condition for the legitimacy of the contract is tacit consent. That is, similar to the analogy of sport, that nobody actually signs a contract before 'playing,' but they would if there was one to sign as is (purportedly) evidenced by the fact that they freely engage in the game."

–Simon Essom

Warren Fraleigh writes about two people who decided to play badminton:

"In reaching that agreement, they did not say such a silly thing as, 'Shall we follow the rules of badminton?'"

All is fair in . . . war?

Just War Theory dates back to Thomas Aquinas and continues through today. It puts forth the following criteria to suggest when going to war is justified:

1. *just cause—war can only occur for good reason*
2. *must be declared by a proper authority*
3. *must be carried out for the right intention*
4. *must be a reasonable chance for success*
5. *the objective of the war should be proportional to methods used.*

It also suggests what types of actions are permitted within the context of war, namely, that:

- *civilians should not be targets*
- *the methods (i.e., force) used should parallel the need*
- *certain weapons are outlawed (flattening bullets, types of gas)*
- *rules exist regarding treatment of prisoners.*

One of the girls asked, "So if we do set up a state here, what will we do about other states that hear about us? If we become so successful here, won't others want to be a part of it, or take it from us? And what about other states that we hear about—can we take *them* over? Could we intervene if we don't think they have created a fair state? I'm just curious what we're going to do with all of this power that we will have as a group."

Another girl nodded in agreement, but added, "Wait, first of all, how will we set our own state up? I mean, how will we decide who gets what? What will be fair? Like who gets to claim that tree over there as their own? And how will we tax people? Who will get to vote? There are so many decisions to make."

This was an area that I had thought much about. Before I started in I asked Alexis to run back to the Old Man and ask him for "the veils." She gave me her best *what are you up to* look and then ran back to him. "The main problem with determining fairness," I suggested to the group, "is that we really have no impartial judges. Anyone who determines who should get what will always include themselves in the equation. Think of slavery, for example: white people determined that black people should be slaves. Before women's liberation, men distributed jobs and education to other males; they even determined that women shouldn't get a vote. These two situations were obviously not *fair*.

"So maybe we could start from the start, so to speak. We will begin in what I will call the 'Original Position.' This position assumes that you have basic knowledge of economics, psychology, and other areas of general knowledge. It also demands that you think rationally about what it is we will do and that you actually make decisions purely out of self-interest. The catch here is it requires that you view

The Tyranny of the Majority?

Democracy—derived from the Greek words demos *(the people) and* kratos *(strength): a system of government in which the people elect representatives to make decisions on their behalf.*

In theory, democracy gives a "voice" to the people. Yet some have argued that this leads to problems such as people not knowing what's best for them, and the majority always getting what they want at the expense of others. Lord Acton, the first baron of Aldenham, referred to democracy as, "the tyranny of the majority," claiming that the majority (or party in power) often succeeds by either force or fraud.

"Were there a people of the gods, their government would be democratic. So perfect a government is not for men."

—Rousseau

"Democracy is a pathetic belief in the collective wisdom of individual ignorance."

—H.L. Mencken

"Democracy is the worst government, except for all the others."

—Winston Churchill

yourself from behind what I call the 'veil of ignorance.'" Alexis' timing couldn't have been better (as usual). She walked up and handed me a stack of small square pieces of slightly transparent cloth.

"I'll take the three of you in the front," I suggested to the two girls—one in a green top and the other in blue—and one boy in the front row. They eagerly approached. My teachers always took the kids in the front row, and now I see why. When you're standing in front of a group, you don't want a lot of dead time, and kids in the front row tend to be more receptive to this kind of stuff.

Justice according to John Rawls

Rawls introduced his hypothetical "Original Position" and "veil of ignorance" as a way to determine a concept of justice. He writes:

"Among the essential features of this situation is that no one knows his place in society, his class position or social status, nor does any one know his fortune in the distribution of natural assets and abilities, his intelligence, strength, and the like. . . . This ensures that no one is advantaged or disadvantaged in the choice of principles by the outcome of natural chance. . . . This explains the propriety of the name 'justice as fairness': it conveys the idea that the principles of justice are agreed to in an initial situation that is fair."

The Original Position

Criteria for making fair judgments:

1. Maintain basic understanding of general areas of knowledge.
2. Rational
3. Self interested
4. Behind the veil of ignorance: Your acquired traits (i.e., sex, race, etc.) are unknown to you.

I tied the veils around their faces. Each was immediately shocked as they looked at themselves.

"What do you see?" I asked.

The girl in green responded, "Oh my gosh. Nothing."

"Nothing?"

"Well, I mean I can't tell if I'm a boy or a girl. I can't see my skin color."

"How about you?" I asked the boy with the veil. "What religion are you? What's your race? What's your sexual orientation?"

He just stood there shaking his head, shrugging his shoulders.

"And you?" I motioned to the girl in blue. "Do you come from a wealthy family? Are you big and strong?"

"I can't really tell," she responded. They each seemed to have calmed down a bit, possibly realizing the purpose of the exercise. "I can't see any of that. Only that I am a human being."

"Good. So, taking that into account," I asked my veiled group, "should we have slavery? Should we say that black people should be slaves? Or maybe that white people should be slaves?"

"No. Not at all," the boy responded. "That wouldn't be rational. When I take off this veil I don't know what color skin I'll have. I don't want to be someone's slave—that's not in my best interest."

"Good. What about taxes? Should we tax the rich more than the poor or tax everyone the same?"

"Well, that's hard to tell," the girl in green responded. "I don't know what category I am in so I would say that we should do what it takes to make things better for the least well-off. If I take off this veil and realize that I am poor, I will want help, but if I'm rich, I won't mind being a little less rich."

The other two with veils nodded.

"So what sort of rules should we make from behind the veils?" I asked, now looking for a little *cash value* in the exercise.

"I think everyone should have equal rights to basic liberties," the boy responded. "As long as they are consistent with the same rights for everyone."

"That seems fair," I responded. "Anything else?"

The girl in green suggested, "Like I said before, I think that any inequality that does arise should benefit the worst-off."

The girl in blue added, "I like that rule. I think that in conjunction with that rule, any inequalities that are created—whether it's a better-paying job, or a position on a sports team—should be available to everyone. There should be no sort of caste system."

"That sounds very good," I responded. "Could you two maybe provide an example of how your principles would work?"

"Okay," the girl in blue began, "everyone who is smart enough may train as a doctor. Not everyone, obviously, can be a doctor. So, while a doctor may earn more money than a teacher, the teacher benefits from having doctors and so, in this case, the slightly disadvantaged teacher—in terms of income—is provided with the advantage of health care. What we would *not* do is allow doctors to earn more money while not providing health care for teachers."

The girl in green then added, "Imagine that you were to cut a cake for this group. If I tell you that you are going to cut the cake and that you'll get the final piece after all others have been selected, you'd be silly to cut some big pieces and then some very small pieces—assuming you want as much of the cake as possible. You'd cut them all the same." She nodded and smiled.

I thanked them and took the veils off. Each of them immediately looked at themselves, realized they were back to normal, and smiled. The group clapped for them.

"Now we just need to decide on what kind of economic system you want to establish," one of the boys in the back of the crowd yelled. "How will we set up our stores and factories?"

Application of Rawls' Two Principles

After specifying his two principles of justice, Rawls summarizes:

"All social values—liberty and opportunity, income and wealth, and the bases of self-respect —are to be distributed equally unless an unequal distribution of any, or all, of these values is to everyone's advantage. Injustice, then, is simply inequalities that are not to the benefit of all."

Any collective whispering that was going on stopped immediately. It was silent and Alexis and I stood there looking at each other. I didn't know a single thing about economic theory.

"Don't know a single thing about economic theory, eh?" the Old Man asked, knowingly, from a few yards behind. "Good thing. There are prototypes set up for you." He pointed to a road that immediately came to a fork.

"At the end of each fork is a town. Each town utilizes one of the two most popular economic systems."

This was apparently all he was going to tell me. I walked off with him and Alexis went down the other fork in the road with that woman. We arrived at the first town, the fork on the left. Arching over the entryway was a big wooden sign that read, "Marxington." At what seemed like a toll booth, a middle-aged man stepped out and greeted us. He was a big, jovial-looking fellow with a long black and grey beard.

He greeted me in more of a serious tone, not very jovial. "Greetings, young man. What is it that you do for your wages—for a living?"

I looked at the Old Man then back to the toll booth man, not really knowing what to say. "I did sell lemonade all last summer," I said. "It was very good lemonade and I made it fresh."

Toll booth man nodded his head, "Well, we do have one spot left for a lemonade stand."

I smiled a smile of relief as I had an initial feeling that he would want something more than lemonade from me. I started to envision all of the things I could do to make my lemonade stand appealing to my customers and ways of growing lemons (organic maybe) and different options like sugar-free or even extra-sugar depending on what the customer wanted.

As I was daydreaming, the man had gone back in the booth and returned with a large sack. "Here you will find the recipe for lemonade. We have included all the ingredients you will need. Last month we decided that there should be a lemonade stand every six blocks and we still have one vacant—it is already constructed, four blocks down and two to your right. Please don't make any changes to it. We need two people to work each stand so I'm sure your friend here"—he motioned towards the Old Man, and they each nodded confidently at each other as if they knew what was going on—"can work with you."

We took the bag and walked with it to our stand. We were both pretty quiet—me not knowing what to expect and him being quiet

Karl Marx and Socialism

Marx is considered the most influential socialist thinker. Born in 1818 in Germany, he is best known for his economic analysis of social structures resulting from a class system which he believed to be inherently unfair. He co-authored the Communist Manifesto *with Frederick Engels.*

Socialism is an economic system in which the "means of production"—i.e., land, factories, mills, etc.—are collectively owned by the people. The goal of socialism is to provide necessities for people versus to make a profit.

probably to create excitement or something. I wasn't terribly happy that I had no say in how the lemonade stand was to be run.

When we arrived at the last stand—*Ian's last stand*—I was somewhat let down. It was built with plain wood, no paint, and had a counter. Across the top piece of wood was the word "Lemonade" in white paint. It was nothing like the dream lemonade stand I had envisioned. We dutifully made the lemonade and turned the "closed" sign to "open."

In the first hour we sold three lemonades. Not bad for nine o'clock, but I still felt like we could do much better. The next hour we only sold two, and the hour after that only one. At the noon hour, as we were nearing the end of peak lemonade hours, we sold six. That was pretty good, I supposed, but I was anxious to go to the other town.

"You ready to go?" I asked the Old Man, as if I couldn't tell who was leading who at this point.

He nodded. "Have you had enough of this?"

"Yeah, I've got it. I'm ready to see what the other system is like."

We packed everything up and took a different route out of town. On our way, about six blocks from our stand, was another just like it. I could see from the distance that this stand was exactly like ours.

"We should really get to that other town before the sun gets too low," the Old Man urged.

I nodded, looking over my shoulder at that stand. We dropped everything off at the toll booth and the Old Man and the old man shook hands. The man in the booth got my address and said he would send the paycheck that day. He had to see if we sold more than expected, though. If so, he would have to apply a heavy tax. "You only need so much to live on," he explained. "Any more and we'll have to tax it heavily to provide for everyone else."

"That's fair," I thought, and I thanked him.

"Well what did you think?" the Old Man asked.

Turning back to him I responded, "It was actually better than I thought it would be in the beginning."

"And why is that?" he responded.

"When they gave us all the materials and told us what to do, how to do it, where to do it,

---

Abilities and Needs

Marx is well known for summarizing a central tenet of socialism with the remark, "From each according to his abilities, to each according to his needs." He believed that socialism would best suit everyone in that each person would be fulfilled through his work and also receive enough to satisfy his basic needs.

I was a little disappointed: I wasn't going to get to create my own stand. But having everything laid out like that makes things a lot simpler. I know—and the customer knows—that there is a standard for lemonade. I don't have to waste money and time advertising, and it makes things fair for everyone. And I know that I'm going to get paid, when it will be, and what I'm going to get. I suppose if everything is standardized like that and run by the state then it really makes things fair and easy on everyone."

We arrived at the entrance to the next town. It too had a sign above it, just like the last one, and it said, "Smithsville." There was a similar toll booth and a man came out to greet us. He was a bit taller than the last man, with shorter hair and no beard. He looked more like a polished salesman than anything.

"Hello there, what is it that you do to earn wages?"

"I sell lemonade," I responded, proudly, knowing that this was, in fact, my current profession—my means of earning wages, to be more precise.

"Great. Good luck with that." And he waved us through.

The Invisible Hand

Eighteenth-century economist Adam Smith laid the groundwork for capitalism. He believed that an economically free society in which everyone pursued his own self-interest would result in the greatest common good. It is as though an "invisible hand" would create that common good as a byproduct of the interest of its individuals.

He wrote, "It is not from the benevolence of the butcher, the brewer, or the baker, that we expect our dinner, but from their regard to their own interest."

I felt a little nervous. "That's it?" I said to the Old Man. "Now what?"

"You get to work," he said.

We walked down the first three blocks and saw two lemonade stands—the first painted a bright yellow, advertising "The Freshest Lemonade in Town," and the other looking more new-age and advertising twelve different species of lemons to choose from.

We found a place that had a nice little hut for sale. It was painted green and had a big lime tree in the back yard. The Old Man offered to pay the first day's rent to get us started. "A little capital can go a long way," he said. I shrugged in agreement.

After we cleaned up a bit, I thought out loud, "Why don't we make *limeade*? Everyone else is already selling every kind of lemonade imaginable."

The Old Man smiled proudly, saying, "Yes. You know the old saying. When life gives you limes . . . "

I waited.

"Make limeade," and he laughed to himself. "I'll go get everything we'll need."

While he was gone, I cleaned up and made a sign.

By three o'clock we were open for business. Because of the novelty of it, we had almost fifty customers in the first hour, many of them ordering multiple glasses. It was very exciting to see success like this so quickly.

At four o'clock we raised the price just a bit and the Old Man hired a boy to work for us, bussing tables and restocking the sugar and glasses when needed. The increase in cost didn't slow business at all—it actually seemed to make people think that our limeade was somehow *more* special. It was like, "If it cost that much then it must be *really* good."

After serving over two hundred glasses in that hour, we saw the owners of the lemonade stand down the block come in. "Great place you've got here," they said, somewhat solemnly. "We actually had to close our shop down. We sold it to a woman who is going to open a jewelry shop. No one seems to want lemonade anymore. Do you have any openings for us here?"

We desperately needed some people, so we hired one of them to slice and squeeze the limes and another to measure the sugar and the water. We had three people working for us. They did their jobs very well for the next two hours and we sold over six hundred glasses of juice.

At the end of that hour I noticed one of the past owners eying our cash register. "You know, for the past two hours I have been sitting here cutting limes in half," he said to me, somewhat agitated. "I feel completely alienated from this whole business, and certainly don't feel very fulfilled. On top of that you're paying me eight dollars an hour while you're bringing in something like fifty an hour for yourself."

Little did he know that we had bought the lemonade stand on the other side of town as well and were going to convert that, thus bringing in more money and continuing to grow.

Battle of the Classes

Marx believed that capitalism would result in a two-class system:

bourgeoisie—*the ruling class who own the means of production.*
proletariat—*the worker-slaves.*

Eventually, he argued, the proletariat would revolt as they became more aware of being exploited:

"The worker is related to the product of his labor as to an alien object. The object he produces does not belong to him, [it] dominates him, and only serves in the long run to increase his poverty. Alienation appears not only in the result, but also in the process of production. . . . Finally, nature itself is alienated from man, who thus loses his own organic body."

"You have complete control of this situation," he continued. "I can't really leave to go anywhere, and if I do, I'd just be working at a similar job. You just got lucky because your old man here had money to get you started. If I leave, you'll just find some other person to slave for you cutting limes at these slave-wages you're offering. *You're* getting rich and *I'm* losing my identity."

The other two workers had heard this and had come over to us. The customers had filed out of the store as it was likely a little uncomfortable for them. All three of the workers seemed to share the feelings of the one. They even looked angry, like they wanted to pick a fight with us.

"It is actually time for closing," the Old Man said to the group. "Here's the deal. You three can take over this business for us. We need to go home."

Rich Get Richer

The Guardian *reports that the 356 richest families in the world have a combined income greater than that of 40% of the annual income of the world's population.*

Marx believed that capitalism creates a "surplus value" because the wages earned by the workers were considerably less than the worth of the product. This, he argued, allowed the factory owners to increase their capital and thus their profit, while simultaneously lessening the value of the working class.

"The rich have become richer and the poor have become poorer."
   –Poet P.B. Shelley writing at the same time as Marx (1792–1822)

They looked to each other, smiling. I heard one of them say, "Now *we* will go and hire someone to cut the limes for *us*."

"So much for it being unfair," I thought to myself.

As we walked away from our budding enterprise, the Old Man asked, "So how did you like that?"

"Much more exciting," I responded. "I felt like we did all we could to make money and, in doing so, we created a new product that everyone could enjoy. It was a win-win situation."

"Well, your workers didn't seem to *win*. They seemed upset."

"They could have come up with that idea," I suggested. "Everyone is free to do as they choose—to earn wages in the best way they see fit. And with everyone trying to make a living like that, it results in a system that's best for everyone."

"But you got a bit lucky, wouldn't you say?" He paused. "How would you have gotten started without my initial investment, without the capital I provided?"

I nodded in agreement.

"And not everyone can run a business. The people with all the capital control everything—

we already owned three stores and were going to buy more if we had more time. And the more we owned, the more of those workers we'd need. I agree there are a lot of benefits, but you just don't want to look at things from your perspective only."

I stood and thought about what he had said. Then he added, "It was a real pleasure working with you today, Ian. A real pleasure." He held his hand out and we shook hands, as if we really were in business together. He shook my hand so hard that . . .

. . . Ian woke up. And he went immediately downstairs.

His mother was reading a book and drinking tea, awaiting the ritualistic discussion with her son.

"This was a strange dream, mom," Ian began as he sat down at the table. He crossed his right leg under him, sitting on his foot and leaning on the table. He seemed to be arranging his hair, though it ended up more messy than it began. "It was different from the others." He paused, as if to decipher its differences. "Though every dream has been different. So I guess in their being different they were all the same that way."

His mother nodded an exasperated nod as though she was afraid the whole discussion would converge around this type of banter.

"It's not like there was something to argue, unless that maybe *having* a government is better than the alternative of anarchy. I'd never thought about rights before.

"So what is it with rights, mom? How do I have a right to an education?"

"Well, you have a right to an education because the state maintains a duty to provide you with one—until you're eighteen, at least. Then you're on your own."

"It was philosophy that inspired men like Martin Luther King and Booker T. Washington to fight against racial prejudice. Philosophy formed the basis of Jane Addams' efforts to make a better life for the poor at Hull House. And it was philosophy that fired up Simon DeBeauvoir to demand equality for women. Philosophy is the starting point for making society more just."

–Read by John Cleese for the American Philosophy Association's "Celebrating 100 Years of Thought"

Rights and Duties

Rand and Locke both held that rights exist apart from duty, that one's rights should not force another's actions. Rand writes, "If some men are entitled by right to the products of the work of others, it means that those others are deprived of rights and condemned to slave labor."

Most philosophers disagree, claiming that rights do impose duties of another. They claim that there are "negative" duties which involve non-action such as a duty not to take another's life, and "positive" duties such as a duty to provide an education.

"Observe . . . the intellectual precision of the Founding Fathers: they spoke of the right to the pursuit of happiness—not the right to happiness."

—Ayn Rand

"But can I have a right to be happy? Or to play baseball?"

His mother smiled, "Well, no. You don't have that right because no one has a corresponding duty. Imagine if it were everyone's duty to make sure everyone was happy. It would be impossible. And it certainly can't be anyone's duty to provide you with the opportunity to play baseball, or have a car, or get a job. That's *your* responsibility."

"So if rights don't come from God, and they don't come from society—whatever that would mean—then where do they come from?"

"Well, as you recalled from your dream, they could result from human reason—from the basis of this notion of a social contract that you mentioned. This way there's some actual foundation, versus having rights just given out haphazardly or based on something that not everyone believes."

Ian nodded thoughtfully and then began to explain the veil of ignorance.

"Minimizing the troubles of the worst off seems like a pretty smart way to do it," Ian suggested. "Though the second town I went to didn't really seem to do that. But I kind of liked it more."

Dear Santa . . .

Regarding the idea of "natural rights" (i.e., rights granted by God or by "nature") former United Nations ambassador, Jeane Kirkpatrick, likened this to "writing letters to Santa Claus."

"Why is that?"

"I guess I liked it because I was in charge of my own success—or my own failure. The Old Man and I owned the store and we hired people to work for us. It was better than having the store owned by the government and then being told what to do. Plus, in that first town, there wasn't any real incentive like there was in the second one. The second one was competitive, so we had to be creative and actually make a better product."

His mother nodded and suggested, "But that first town was fair, wasn't it? I mean, regardless of how much money you had—or inherited, in your case—you still worked as much as the next guy. Plus, no one felt alienated—there were no people in charge of people like at your store; much less chance for any sort of rebellion."

"Yeah, and that is a good point in favor of Marxington. It just seemed like, in the second town, the harder you work and the more successful you are, the more money you make. It just makes sense. Harder work leads to better products."

"Very insightful. Though think of the advantages that you, Ian Pinkle, have over a boy your age in a poorer neighborhood, whose family cannot send him to a private high school, or to college, who doesn't have a computer or who even has to work 20 hours a week at a grocery store during high school just to help pay for food. It makes you question just what you meant by *fair* when you recounted your dream to me."

"How, mom?"

"Well there are really two types of fairness. Let's imagine a simple case like flying on an airplane."

Ian nodded.

"Think of that airline that we fly with only one class of seats. Each seat is the same. In one sense, the seating is very fair—every person has the same amount of space. But your father is considerably taller than the average person. So, in another sense, the seating *isn't* fair: your father has two inches of leg room, while others may have six, yet we all pay the same price.

"But imagine how difficult it would be for airplanes to have moving seats to accommodate everyone with exactly, say, five inches of leg room. It would be almost impossible, and not very realistic."

"Yeah, I get that. So the rest of society is kind of like that airplane?"

"Certainly. Do you know what affirmative action means?"

"It's a way to make things fair for everyone."

A Village of 100 People

If the world's population were shrunk down to the size of a 100-person village, with all the current ratios kept intact, here is what that village would look like:

17 unable to read

25 live in substandard housing

2 have a college education

4 own a computer

13 suffer from malnutrition

20 would earn 89% of the entire village's income, while the poorest 20 would earn just 1.2% in 1998. (In 1960, these numbers were 70.2% and 2.3%, respectively.)

Racism and Affirmative Action

Racism results when certain humans are classified as biologically unique and judged morally based on that difference. This occurred in Nazi Germany as Jews were considered a weaker "race," and in the United States at one point with black people. As recently as 1857, the Supreme Court ruled against slave Dred Scott who sued for his freedom. At the time, the Court interpreted the Constitution as claiming that black people were, "altogether unfit to associate with the white race," and that slaves were "property in the strictest sense of the term." It wasn't until 1954 that the court ruled school segregation to be unconstitutional in Brown v. Board of Education.

The first affirmative action legislation in the United States occurred in 1959. In 1978, Allan Bakke sued the UC Davis Medical School because his application was rejected while a less qualified minority applicant was admitted. The Supreme Court ruled in favor of Bakke claiming that he was wrongly discriminated against.

"Well, it's a little more complicated than that, but essentially, you are like I am on the airplane—you're *lucky*. Your father is unlucky in regards to sitting on airplanes—though his height certainly gives him advantages in other areas. But a seat on an airplane for three hours isn't too important in the grand scheme of things. The education you receive and the job you hold—now *those* are important things.

"So, affirmative action takes into account *how* you got where you did, not just *that* you got there. For example, if you have all B's on your report card and that boy working 20-hour weeks that I described has all B's, wouldn't you say that he may be more deserving of entrance to a certain school than you are?"

"Why is that?"

"Because he overcame more obstacles. He didn't have all the good fortune you had—the extra time for studying, the best teachers and tutors, nutritious foods. In a sense, affirmative action tries to account for the sociological and economic differences between people and reward them for things that we value more like hard work and determination. Not only that, it tries to erase the discrimination aimed at minorities that still remains. It does so in one sense by helping to provide certain opportunities for minorities in education and in the work force. It does so in another sense by integrating minorities into schools and thus into the workplace at higher level jobs so that they can become more respected by everyone."

Ian nodded thoughtfully, though not convincingly.

"The trick becomes what to do if you have half A's and half B's and this other boy has all B's. If we let the other boy into college and not you, then it seems that maybe we are lowering the standards a bit."

"Yeah, that would be like discriminating against *me* because I'm in the majority. That would be like *reverse* discrimination. Is that really fair?"

"That's what you need to figure out," she said, nodding. "One other way to look at this is through the notion of taxation. Did you decide what to do about taxing people? Should everyone be taxed equally?"

"That seems fair," Ian responded. "Why would you tax some people more than others?"

"To compensate for the misfortune of others, maybe?" she suggested. "You've heard of Robin Hood—steal from the rich to give to the poor?"

"Yeah, and I understand that. But then the poor could just sit back and let the rich do all the work and then cash in on it."

"That's an awfully jaded view, son. I'm surprised that with your open-mindedness and all that you know, that you think that would be such a grand view of life. Not everyone has the good fortune that you do."

"So you mean it would be fair to tax the rich *more* heavily than the poor?"

"Arguments can be made both ways, son. The challenge is determining what sense of fairness you want to achieve and then how you can go about doing that. Not everyone agrees on what taxes should even pay for."

"Isn't that easy?" he paused. "I mean, they should pay for things that benefit everyone. Like schools. And defending the country. And things like transportation and roads."

"Certainly, but what about something like art? Should the government use a portion of people's taxes to subsidize artists?"

Ian nodded his head in thought as if he recognized that matters of taxation were not always so easy. "In theory, yes."

"In theory?"

"Free" Versus "Equal"

Contemporary philosopher Robert Nozick argues against taxation for the purpose of redistribution. He believes that taxing some to give to others treats people as a mere "means," i.e., just as a source of money. He likens this to "forced labour." He differs with Rawls who argues that we must do what it takes to make things better for the worst off.

Nozick promotes the political philosophy "libertarianism" which advocates a more limited government—it is often referred to as laissez faire *which is French for "let things alone." This in contrast to the notion advocated by Rawls, known as "egalitarianism," which seeks to achieve equality even if it involves taking from the more fortunate.*

National Endowment for the Arts (NEA)

The U.S. government established the NEA in 1965 to provide funding for the arts and to preserve the cultural heritage. It not only funds specific artists but also public television stations, national book awards, museums and the opera. In 2004 the agency maintained a budget of $121 million. In 1989, the French government spent $560 million on the arts and German government spending on "culture" reached $4.5 billion.

"Well, yeah. I mean, art is good for the public—it's something that benefits everyone. It's a very important part of our culture, you know. So it would be good to have the government sponsor artists so they can do their art."

"Yes, son, but if everyone is already paying for art, then what's the point of the government paying for it? Think about that band you like."

"The *No Names*?"

"Yes. Now they're pretty good, right? A lot of people buy their music?" she asked him, knowingly.

"Yeah, they're pretty popular."

"Well, then they *deserve* that money—they've created art that people like. They don't need money from the government, do they?"

"No, I guess not."

"And if no one bought their music, then it would be silly for the government to use people's taxes to pay for music they're not willing to buy to begin with, right?"

Ian nodded, somewhat dejectedly. "But what if the band that no one paid for was really good? Like what if they had invented a style of music that was new and nobody was used to it? There would be no incentive for artists to produce anything new—to push the envelope, as they say."

"Market Darwinism"

U.S. Senator Jesse Helms argued that the government should not fund art that is obscene, offensive towards any religion, or denigrating towards any race or sex. He also notes, "I have fundamental questions about why the federal government is involved in supporting artists the taxpayers have refused to support in the marketplace."

In response to this, Time *magazine art critic Robert Hughes writes, "This was exactly what the NEA was created . . . to do. . . . Lots of admirable art does badly at first; its rewards to the patron are not immediate and may never come. Hence the need for the NEA. It is there to help the self-realization of culture that is not immediately successful."*

He sat, smiling, and continued, "You know, a lot of the greatest artists weren't even appreciated in their time because people didn't recognize their greatness. Not until they were dead, at least."

His mom now seemed to recognize Ian's real concern with this issue.

"Very thoughtful, son. But I have a feeling I know why you clarified *in theory* when you touted your support of the government's subsidizing art."

He raised his eyebrows in anticipation.

"How do we choose which art and artists to fund?"

Ian nodded, his lips pursed, obviously realizing the rhetoric in the question.

She continued, "Once we start doing that, we have to assign criteria to art. You have to determine what makes some art better than other art. How in the world can you do that?"

"Just have the experts choose," he suggested. "Like museum workers, art historians, professors of art."

"And who is going to choose them?"

He shrugged.

"At some point in this process, *someone* is going to have to make an objective decision based on art, which is subjective. If you like the *No Names* that's one thing. They may be *your* favorite band. But you shouldn't then say that *I* should pay to buy their music. You shouldn't believe that because *you* think one band is the best that that band then *is* the best. Remember, you're saying that the government should use people's money to pay for certain art.

"And in a way, son, this could result in a subtle form of censorship."

"Censorship?"

"Imagine two artists, 'A' and 'B.' If the government gives Artist A a bunch of money and its stamp of approval, who do you think is more likely to be seen? They're not saying 'Artist B is bad and shouldn't be seen,' but

---

Can art be good without people thinking it is? And what would that mean?

"Wagner's music is better than it sounds."

–Mark Twain

"When the mode of the music changes, the walls of the city shake."

–Plato

What Is Art?

Economist Robert Samuelson writes on the difficulty of classifying genuine art: "By definition, it is undefinable. Standards are always subjective."

He then examines the legitimate uses of national taxes, suggesting that the government is the, "mechanism by which we tax ourselves to meet collective national needs. Subsidizing 'art' fails this elementary test."

National Endowment for Rodeo?

Samuelson wittingly suggests the "National Endowment for Rodeo" as an analogy to the NEA, asking if rodeo riders should "merit special treatment" or if they, "create some public benefit." He argues that they do not, just as artists do not. In doing so, he also hopes to show that funding art basically subsidizes the activities enjoyed predominantly by the wealthy—such as opera and museums—who don't need the subsidy in the first place.

Artist A is sure going to have an advantage out there. I guess the question is, who do you think is more likely to *not* be seen?"

"But *some* art is better than *none*. Think of how bland life would be if there were no art of any kind. I think it would be a good message for the government to sponsor art. It would be like they were saying, 'We don't just want you to live, we want you to live *well*.' We need art for that."

"I agree dear, though this is just another personal value judgment. What if someone hates painting and the opera, but loves skateboarding? She believes it embodies all that is good with humanity—living on the edge, maybe, in balance with everything yet totally on your own."

Ian smiled.

"Should the government then fund skateboarding?"

He quickly shook his head.

"Plus, I'm not saying that art isn't valuable—I happen to think it is. Very much so. There will still be art even if the government doesn't subsidize it. And people say that the best art comes from struggle—that very few great artists come from very well-off families."

Ian nodded, "I guess these are all the reasons I did say that I liked it *in theory*. I see your point."

His mother, though, didn't seem as confident as she did initially. "I see your point too, son." She pulled his head towards her and kissed his forehead.

If Only

Jeff and I were simply walking down the street. That's all. Walking down the street. Maybe we'd jaywalked or dropped a gum wrapper on the sidewalk, I don't know, but if we did, it was an accident. Just walking down the street. Jeff decided that he wanted to get the new rookie baseball card that had just come out, and I already had it, so he went into the baseball card shop and I stood outside to wait for him. As I waited, Anatol walked by. He was looking around, suspiciously. He's always like that, like he's done something wrong. He stopped to talk to me for a minute about the science test we'd had that week. As he began to explain his recently-acquired cheating technique to me, a police car pulled up behind us, two policemen jumped out and grabbed us, and threw us in the backseat. I was shaken up a little, but mostly just in shock.

The policemen sat in the front and didn't say anything. They just drove. The tint in the backseat windows was very dark, too dark to see much of anything. I had trouble seeing through the metal mesh separating us from the policemen. So we sat there. I asked Anatol if he knew what was going on and the man in the passenger seat yelled at us to be quiet. So we sat quietly. We got to our destination, I supposed, and the car stopped. The policemen got out and grabbed us, and, while they were firm with us, they also treated us gently—not the way I usually see bad criminals treated in movies. I told them I thought they had us mixed up with someone else. All I got was them telling me to be quiet. They took us into the building. As we approached a hallway, one of the men took Anatol down a separate hallway. While I had a small feeling that this was some sort of joke, I was also scared. Afraid that something bad could happen and no one would know about it. The man unlocked a jail cell, led me inside, and then locked it behind him.

It was a strange cell. Not that I'd ever really been in a cell before. Nothing really to compare it to. There was a refrigerator, a piano, a coffee-and-hot-chocolate maker, and a small library of books. But it was definitely a cell. Concrete floor. Small bed. Locked bars to keep the criminal in. Criminal? What had I done?

I sat, wondering how long I would be here. Minutes? Hours? Days? Weeks?

About ten minutes later, another man came to the cell. He was thin and wiry, wore glasses and had a bow tie on. He sat in a chair outside the cell and began to speak to me.

"Hello. My name is Nigel. You and one other boy have been taken in for littering the streets of the town. I want to be clear about your options. I will state them explicitly for you and then you can decide on your course of action.

"You can either confess to the crime or not. Here are the consequences of your and the other boy's decision:

1. If neither of you confess, then you will each remain behind bars for one hour, as we will have no evidence for littering, though we will hold you for possession of gum wrappers.
2. If you both confess, then you will each remain behind bars for five hours.

3. If one remains silent while the other confesses, then the silent one will remain behind bars for *ten* hours while the one who confessed will be set free.

The following chart may help explain." He pulled out a cardboard sheet with a diagram on it:

	Anatol confesses	Anatol doesn't confess
I confess	Me: 5 Anatol: 5	Me: 0 Anatol: 10
I don't confess	Me: 10 Anatol: 0	Me: 1 Anatol: 1

"You should also know two final things," he continued. "First, you are each concerned with getting the shortest sentence, though that should be obvious. We happen to know that in one hour, you're each having lunch with your grandparents. We know that, in three hours Alexis' pool party starts, and you're both invited, and it's only a two-hour party. And in eight hours it will be considerably past your curfew and your parents will punish you for coming home any later.

"Secondly, you both have been told the exact same things, and we consider you both to be rational people. I will need your response in five minutes." With that, he slid the cardboard diagram through the bars of my cell and left.

So I began my thinking . . . I obviously wanted to get the smallest jail time possible. I had a strong feeling that all of this was Anatol's fault anyway. He's always causing trouble, but never getting caught for it. And he's certainly a rational person, no need to make that distinction for me. I'd really like to see my grandparents. And I've been waiting for that pool party all week. Alexis will be there.

So, it looks to me like the rational thing to do is to confess: that way, I either get five hours or, hopefully, zero hours. Because if I didn't confess, then I'd either get ten hours or one hour. Confessing seems rational. And I'm rational.

It seemed easy at first.

But what will Anatol do? He's rational too. And, if he's rational, then he'll have figured it out the way I did. And he'll confess. I looked at the cardboard sheet under "Anatol confesses." Very interesting. Given that Anatol will confess, I should then also confess. That way, I avoid the biggie: ten hours in jail. Aha! I'd solved it. I will confess.

But, if what I'm doing is the rational thing then, because Anatol's rational, he'll do the same thing. He'll confess. And, since he'll confess, then he knows that I will also confess, because he knows I'm rational. But if he does that and I do that, then we'll both be stuck here for five hours. That's the third longest option and clearly can't be right. So given that we both want to minimize our time in jail, we should both remain silent. *That's* the rational thing to do.

But, if he knows that, then it would be rational for him to confess, because then he would get zero hours in jail. So, maybe the rational thing to do is to confess after all.

At that point I realized that this was the second time around. I'd already decided it was rational to confess. Then rational to *not* confess. Then rational to confess again? And I only had a minute and a half left to figure this out.

It was a good thing that there was only so much time to think about this, otherwise, I could complete this circle over and over.

Then I figured, "I'll just reason the way a rational person would reason until the five minutes is up. And, since Anatol is rational, I know that when the five minutes is up, we'll both have reasoned the same way and so we'll both have come to the same conclusion. Then, at the last second, I'll switch my answer—I'll change my rational answer and answer irrationally."

So, for the next ninety seconds I continued the back-and-forth reasoning of confess/not-confess, rational/irrational. I went through a sort of I-know-that-he-knows-that-I-know thing as I'd done the previous three minutes. It was kind of fun, actually, to let my brain do the reasoning, knowing that I was just going to do the opposite of what my brain came up with. It was almost like I was sitting and watching, and my brain was hard at work. Like sitting and watching a computer run a program.

Then I saw Nigel coming down the hall. "Five seconds," he announced. I could hear the same announcement coming from Anatol's hallway. I was confident that I would be right. I was just going to give him the opposite answer of what my brain came up with. I was doing the rational thing by acting irrationally. "Three seconds." But wait, Anatol is also rational. He's going to do the *same thing*. Too late, I couldn't make any changes at this point. "One second." I went to my brain. It had decided that the rational thing to do was to confess. Okay, so now I just switch that to *not confess* and I'm done. But that's what

Anatol will do. *That's* the rational thing. What would be irrational, then?

It would be really irrational to switch it *back*. Or would it be more irrational to not switch it at all? Wait, those were both the same things. But I didn't have time to think about this. I was thinking totally irrationally.

"Your answer please, Ian."

"I confess."

"You are free to go."

Chapter 13

Ethics and Morality

There is nothing either good or bad, but thinking it makes it so.

–Shakespeare, Hamlet

What good fortune for those in power that people don't know how to think.

–Adolf Hitler

"You look like the cat who swallowed the canary, Ian."

"No, my mom's mad at me for letting Jeff steal Anatol's pen."

"For *letting* him?"

"Well I was with him and I didn't stop him. But Anatol's not that nice of a guy anyway."

"I'm not sure I see the point," the Old Man responded in what seemed a sincere tone. Though at this point I knew it was really just a way to force me to explain something that he'd probably have an issue with.

"I didn't actually *do* anything. And Jeff likes the pen. And Anatol kind of deserves it. He's pretty much mean to everyone."

"What did your mom say?"

"That it was *wrong* of me to do that."

"And what do you think?"

"Well, Jeff and I talked about it. He doesn't think it's wrong—not to steal from Anatol, anyway. And I didn't really do any-

"The visible world is no longer a reality and the unseen world is no longer a dream."
–Arthur Symons (1899), referring to a style of literature rich in symbolism (i.e., poet W.B. Yeats).

Morality vs. Ethics

Morality—*principles and systems used to determine actions as right or wrong.*

Ethics—*the study and application of moral principles and how they are used to evaluate actions.*

Actions are typically classified as immoral, morally praiseworthy, or non-moral (e.g. walking on a public sidewalk).

"Man prefers to believe what he prefers to be true."
    –Francis Bacon

"Morality differs in every society and is a convenient term for socially approved habits."
    –Ruth Benedict
American anthropologist

thing. We both decided it was okay. It's not like anyone can actually prove to us that it was wrong. Just because *you* might think it's wrong, or my mom does, doesn't mean that it *is* wrong."

The Old Man nodded slowly, as if he agreed with me. "So whatever you think is right and wrong *is* right and wrong? Is that your position? What's right for you is right?"

That was pretty much what Jeff and I had decided. How could anyone else tell us what was wrong? It may be wrong for them, but it wouldn't be for us. I nodded. "Proving that one action is better than another is like trying to prove that steak is better than shrimp," I suggested, smiling.

He put his arm around my shoulder. "Keep in mind your position, Ian. We are going to take the portal to go look at a few different situations throughout history. I just want you to use your statement—that whatever one thinks is right *is* right—and evaluate these instances. Judge their moral status. Remember, these things have already happened, so there's nothing you can do to stop them—that is, even if you think you should."

He had a very calm, yet serious tone, like he was trying to comfort me, to prepare me. As we came out of the portal, I saw a girl about my age tied to a stake in the ground. A man dressed in a colorful though eerie costume was announcing something to the crowd of onlookers. The Old Man leaned over to me and whispered, "He says that he is going to cut her chest open and take her heart out. He's doing it as a sacrifice to the god of the sun."

I stood in disbelief. I just shook my head back and forth, rapidly, pointing my palms toward the sky wondering why no one would stop this.

"Let's go over here," the Old Man motioned, as if to shield me from seeing anything horrible. I felt a little short of breath.

As we walked a hundred yards or so, we saw a man in the distance speaking to a group of people in uniform. As we approached, it looked like the pictures of Hitler that I had in my history book. While he talked the Old Man translated, "He's saying that they must continue exterminating the Jews because he says their existence continues to dilute the purity of their Aryan race. They are going to gas them to death—six million of them."

I felt sick. I had read about this in my textbooks, but when you saw a person actually say this to a crowd of people who then cheered in support, it was hard to stomach.

"Just two more to show you, Ian. Let's go over here."

Another few hundred yards away, we saw a black man standing up on a wooden platform. As we got closer, I could see that his hands were tied together by some rope. There was a white man standing near him holding what looked like a leash around the other's neck. People were yelling at him and the white man was whipping him. He yelled out, "This is a good slave. You will not need to feed him much yet he can work fourteen-hour days. He responds well to whipping and could serve you well for five years before you get rid of him. Let's start the bidding."

I had a similar feeling as with the last two scenes. Reading about them is one thing, but when you realize that these are *people*—when you see their eyes—it means so much more. My eyes even watered a little bit, partly out of empathy for this man, but mostly, I think, out of an overall sadness for human beings, that they could do things like this to each other. I looked up at the Old Man—he too was solemn.

The Inca Empire in South America made a practice of sacrificing children to the sun god. It was considered a sign of prestige towards their parents. Likewise, when a king died, they often sacrificed his servants and concubines to accompany him in the afterlife, or they would sacrifice a community member in hopes of appeasing the gods, thus avoiding the wrath of natural disasters such as earthquakes and volcanic eruptions.

During the early 1940's in Germany, the Nazi Party worked to implement what they called "The Final Solution." After establishing the Aryan race as the top of the "food chain," they went on to "purify" their race, by not only murdering approximately 5,800,000 Jews, but also blacks, homosexuals, mentally disabled, Jehovah's Witnesses, and other races and religions as well.

" . . . Today I believe that I am acting in accordance with the will of the Almighty Creator: by defending myself against the Jew, I am fighting for the work of the Lord."

—Adolf Hitler

> "There is nothing more frightful than ignorance in action."
>
> –Johann Wolfgang von Goethe

> "Irrationally held truths may be more harmful than reasoned errors."
>
> –Thomas H. Huxley

> "Men will cease to commit atrocities only when they cease to believe absurdities."
>
> –Voltaire

"The last one is right over here." As we walked, I could see what looked like *my* house in the distance. I looked at the Old Man, curiously. Outside the house were men with ski masks covering their faces. They had guns. I started walking quickly to the house, yelling to them. I looked back at the Old Man and he stood there just shaking his head. None of the men even looked towards me, as if they couldn't hear me. I could see my parents inside, in the kitchen. Alexis was with them.

"Let's move in, kill the three of them, and take any jewelry we can find," one of the men said, in a gruff voice. I was screaming as I approached them. I didn't know what I was going to do as I neared the closest man. I ran at him and shoved him in the back as hard as I could. At the moment I contacted him, he disappeared. The house, everything, disappeared.

I looked at the Old Man. He had obviously set this up. I felt angry. My emotions from it all were so high and I focused them all on my anger towards the Old Man.

"Ian, this last one never happened. You needed to learn a lesson, though. Tell me, were any of these instances you just witnessed immoral? And don't tell me if they were wrong *for you*. Tell me if they were *wrong* at all?"

I glared at him, nodding my head, gritting my teeth, wanting to scream at him, though also seeing his point.

"I agree," he continued, calmly. "But if you took your initial position—that what is wrong is determined by individual taste—then none of these situations would be wrong. And if you blindly let a specific culture determine what is right and wrong, then you'd have to argue that human

Shockingly Amoral

In one of the most renowned human behavior experiments, Stanley Milgram put subjects in a situation where they believed they were electrically shocking a cohort when the cohort failed to memorize word pairs read to them. Of the 40 who participated in the 1960 study, 37 completed the incremental increase in shocks, until the cohort went silent and there were no stronger shocks to administer (cohorts were actually part of the experiment, and not really being shocked). Milgram relates this to the mindless obedience observed by people in a group who often ignore responsibility for morally atrocious acts (i.e., wartime, Nazi Germany).

sacrifice, genocide, and slavery were all morally permissible—that having slaves was *right* at the time. That hardly seems correct.

"On top of that, you would have no justification for even assigning moral blame to those bandits outside your home. If they thought that what they were doing wasn't wrong, then according to your position, it wasn't wrong. If people think they can kill others just because they don't like their skin color, or because they don't think it's wrong, that doesn't make it right."

I took a deep breath. My mom always said to take a deep breath when I felt like I was angry, because that would help me to calm down. The Old Man had made a pretty convincing point.

I shrugged my shoulders, "So how *do* we show what is right and wrong? I mean if it's not just a matter of taste like you just pointed out, how do we determine what someone *ought* to do?"

"*That* is a difficult question, Ian. On the surface level, it's basic. We can devise an argument which contains both factual and moral statements, and then see how it plays out. Let's take a simple one first."

I nodded.

"*Hitler killed innocent people*. That's a fact. We won't argue about how many, but it's confirmed that he did this.

What I think is right is right?

"One would like to say: whatever is going to seem right to me is right. And that only means that here we can't talk about 'right.'"

Wittgenstein argues that we can't use "right" to mean whatever we want it to mean. In doing so, the word loses all meaning.

"Truth does not change because it is or is not believed by a majority of the people."

–Giordano Bruno

James Rachels enumerates the pitfalls of Cultural Relativism—*the notion that morality is merely what a culture deems it to be:*

1. *"We could no longer say that the customs of other societies are morally inferior."*
2. *"We could decide whether actions are right or wrong just by consulting the standards of our society."*
3. *"The idea of moral progress is called into doubt."*

He goes on to say that just because there is disagreement amongst people or cultures does not necessitate that no objective morality exists. People didn't agree on the shape of the Earth at one time yet that didn't change the Earth's shape. He believes there are some moral rules that societies can agree upon, such as prohibition of murder and rules against lying.

Approaches to Ethics

Nihilism—*there is no truth in ethics: moral statements are neither true nor false.*

Subjectivism—*ethics are a matter of taste and cannot be determined objectively.* Two versions:

Ethical Subjectivism: *ethics are a matter of individual tastes.*

Cultural Relativism: *ethics are decided by particular cultures.*

Objectivism—*universal ethical standards exist regardless of personal tastes and can be discovered:*

Divine Command Theory: *God determines morality.*

Utilitarianism: *morality is determined in relation to what results in the greatest good.*

Deontology: *doing one's duty, determined through reason, is the foundation for morality.*

Virtue Ethics: *development of character determines moral actions.*

"*It is immoral to kill innocent people.* That's the moral statement. It denotes the rightness or wrongness of an action."

"So the moral conclusion is, *Hitler acted immorally.*"

"Yeah," I concurred. "That does seem pretty simple."

"In this case, I agree."

I felt somewhat relieved. After our last little exhibition, I was worried that this really would be difficult. Though I thought about the moral statement that he made. I looked to the Old Man now as we walked down the main street of town, which was practically deserted. "But your moral claim can't be true just because I think it's true. That's the whole problem we just discussed."

He nodded more emphatically now. "Exactly. The difficult part, Ian, is to determine *why* the moral statement is true."

Then he smiled, laughing a bit to himself. "Tell me, do you think incest is immoral?"

"Incest?" I responded, scrunching up my face in disgust.

"Yes," he answered, now more matter-of-factly. "Consensual sex between a parent and their adult child—over eighteen, of course."

"Yes, definitely immoral," I said without thinking much about it.

"Why is that?"

"Well, it's gross. I mean, think about it. I mean, I can't even think about it." Just the topic made me feel a little uncomfortable.

"So are you suggesting that anything that anyone finds gross is immoral? Look at this in our formula:

1. *Fact:* Ian thinks incest is gross.
2. *Moral Claim:* Anything that someone thinks is gross is immoral.
3. *Conclusion:* Incest is immoral.

"Is eating liver and onions immoral?" He asked with his Devil's Advocate face on. "I find that to be gross."

"Well, no. But I do know that incest can lead to offspring that have a higher chance of being handicapped in some way."

"So now are you suggesting that anyone who has sex that may have a particular chance of creating a 'handicapped' offspring is unethical? That seems a little scary. Plus, most sex does not produce children anyway—a majority of people who have sex do not procreate."

"Is there a point to this? Are you saying that incest is totally moral?" I asked, trying my best to change the subject.

"The point is that morality takes some real thought. Determining the moral status of actions and formulating moral principles is difficult. You can't go around saying that people's actions are unethical just because you think they're gross. But as you can see from those instances we just witnessed earlier, morality is worth thinking about.

"And, no, I'm not saying that incest is morally permissible, though it is common practice in certain cultures. Maybe we can talk more about that later," he said, smiling a bit, knowing that I probably wouldn't be the one to bring it up.

After a short pause he asked, "Taking something a bit more obvious—*why* is it immoral to kill innocent people?"

At this point there was a man with a beard standing on the corner where we were standing. He held a sign that said, "The End is Near" in big red letters. "Because God says so," he whispered to us.

The Old Man turned to me, his eyebrows raised in their upside-down-U shape of anticipation. "This is one very popular attempt at determining moral status. Let's look at that in our framework:

1. *Fact:* God forbids killing innocent people.
2. *Moral Claim:* What God forbids is immoral.
3. *Conclusion:* Killing innocent people is immoral.

"What do you think, Ian?"

That actually seemed pretty simple to me. I bobbed my head around to communicate that it made sense.

A Need for Religion in Morality?

"For the preservation of the moral order ... religious authority must enter in to enlighten the mind, to direct the will, and to strengthen human frailty by the aid of divine grace."

–Pope Pius XI,
December 31, 1930

If human beings (and their beliefs) really are the mindless products of their material existence, then everything that gives meaning to life—religion, morality, beauty—is revealed to be without objective basis."

–John West, creationist advocate

Differences in Religious Views

Christian Science—
Prayer cures illness
and injury, not
doctors; thus,
Christian Scientists do
not utilize medicine.
"Matter, sin, and
sickness are not real,
but only illusions."

Hinduism—The cow is
considered sacred and
thus given special
treatment (and thus
not favorable to be
killed and eaten).

Judaism—Prohibits
eating "swine" (pork),
camel, coney, and
hare.

Rastafarian Church—
Regards marijuana as
a "wisdom weed" thus
encouraging its use.

"Which God should we listen to?" the Old Man started back in, to show that it wouldn't be this easy. "You know, there are hundreds of different religions. Many of the gods in these religions are assumed to say different things. Think about the gods in our first excursion above, who demanded that the hearts be ripped out of children."

My head bobbing turned to more of a thoughtful nodding. Initially I thought we were done with this exercise as it seemed to be solved by religion. Then I suggested to him, "Yeah, that is a good point. And what about things that no god ever talked about, like cloning or affirmative action? How would a religion determine if those things were right or wrong?"

"Yes, Ian. There are a lot of complications with this method. And oftentimes, even within certain religions, they seem to make claims that conflict with each other or are left up to our interpretation."

"And what about people who don't believe in God? Then how could they be moral or immoral?" I asked.

"Very true. Though remember, believing something doesn't make it so. Yet it does seem odd to demand of someone that they follow the commands of a god that they don't think exists.

"There is one interesting dilemma that remains with this issue: *how* does God determine moral actions? There are really only two ways.

"The first, that God has perfect knowledge of right and wrong. Things aren't right and wrong because God says they are, but instead, God says

---

"Men have authority over women because God has made the one superior to the other. . . . Good women are obedient. . . . As for those among you who fear disobedience, admonish them and send them to beds apart and beat them."

The Koran

The Koran is believed by Muslims to be the word of God. Even today, women are beaten, jailed, and killed for having sex before marriage. Known as "honor killing," this results even in the case of rape, or in a few reported cases, if a man dreams that a woman has had sex.

What Makes an Act Good?
Divine Command Theory

Plato poses the question in one of his dialogues, "Is what is pious loved by the gods because it is pious, or is it pious because it is loved by the gods?" In other words:

Are actions good because God says they are, or does God say they are because they are good?

A character in this dialogue named Euthyphro argues that these are the only two options and that both are unacceptable. The first is a form of moral dogma and could lead to moral atrocities, and the second suggests that God uses some outside moral criteria independent of God.

things are right and wrong because they are—because He knows. Though this assumes that there is right and wrong independent of God—that right and wrong exist separately from God and He just happens to know it.

"The other option is that things are right and wrong *because* God says they are. This view holds that morality stems only from God—that He makes things right and wrong just by saying so. It's rather dogmatic, as you can see, and assumes that there would be no morality separate from God. Imagine the consequences of people going around and behaving in ways *just because* some certain god is said to have commanded them."

Numerous passages in the Bible show apparent contradictions:

- *"A life for a life. An eye for an eye." In contrast with: "If someone strikes you on one cheek, turn to him the other."*
- *Abraham was commanded by God to kill his only son and was praised for attempting to do so.*

Our talking and walking had brought us to a drug store, with an ice cream counter inside. We sat down at a table outside and I let everything we had just discussed sink in. I was a bit frustrated with what we had concluded so far. "If there are so many problems with determining morality through religion, then how else could we do it?" I asked the Old Man, knowing there probably wasn't a very easy answer to this question. "If morality isn't determined by personal taste or by culture, and if not by religion, then how?"

He sat there shaking his head. So I sat too, shaking my head. This was one of those "Ignorance is bliss" moments, only because I realized I was a bit more blissful before all of this. I continued the subtle head shaking modeled by the Old Man.

At the bank across the street, a limousine was being loaded up with bags of money. The Old Man glared at the car, frowning slightly,

> *"I consider ethics to be an exclusively human concern with no super-human authority behind it."*
>
> –Albert Einstein

exhaling through his nose, continuing his head shaking. "Pete 'The Great' Miller. Richest man for miles," he said, with disdain. "Gave himself his own nickname. Hasn't donated a dime to charity—says it's not his responsibility." The car pulled away, doing a U-turn right in front of us. The trunk had been left open and a bag of money fell out and rolled up to the curb right where we were sitting. Our head shaking stopped and instead, the Old Man began a more thoughtful head nodding.

He motioned for me to get the bag. I looked around and didn't see anyone else on the street that would have seen it. I grabbed the bag and returned to my seat next to the Old Man. The bag had "$10,000" painted on it. I raised my eyebrows and grinned at the Old Man.

"What should we do?" he asked.

"We have options?" I thought to myself. "Return it to the owner," I suggested, after a momentary consideration of all the things I could do with this much money.

"And why is that?"

"Because it's the right thing to do. Because we *ought* to." I paused. "I'll even use one of your little formulas that you mentioned earlier.

1. *Fact*: This money belongs to someone else.
2. *Moral Claim*: I have a moral duty to return other people's property.
3. *Conclusion*: I have a moral duty to return this money.

"See there," I said proudly.

He chuckled a bit. "I agree with your factual claim—that the money is someone else's. But now we're back to defending the moral claim. How do you have a duty? What does *that* mean? Where does a duty come from?"

"From reason. You can determine duty through reason. It's like I make up a rule for myself and then see if I can realistically—*reasonably*—apply it to everyone. If I can, then it's a duty. If not, then it's not."

The Importance of the Will

Kant wrote that the highest moral action is one that is motivated by doing one's duty. To be motivated by anything else—such as consequences of one's actions, or because one is simply inclined to do so—is not as praise-worthy:

"Without the principle of a good will [people] can become extremely bad. ... The good will is not good because of what it effects or accomplishes or because of its adequacy to achieve some proposed end [goal]; it is good only because of its willing, i.e., it is good of itself."

Who Has Greater Moral Worth?

Two people walk by a wallet that could easily be stolen as no one is around. Each person desperately needs money and sees the wallet as she walks past. Person A stops and deliberates, considering all that she could do with the money, but eventually decides that she has a duty not to steal. Person B sees the wallet and walks by it without the thought of stealing it. Kant values Person A because she acted out of duty alone: to rely solely on one's natural inclination may lead one to do something morally abhorrent just because they "feel like it."

"So it's kind of like the Golden Rule: do unto others as you would have them do unto you?"

"Like that, yes," I responded hesitantly. That seemed easy.

"So, what if I like listening to loud music at two in the morning? Should I play loud music for my neighbors too?"

"Well, no. That's the thing—this isn't *just* about me. It involves what *everyone* would want."

He nodded as if expecting me to expand on this.

"Okay, in our case right here I figured, 'I will return another's property whenever possible.' Okay? That's like my own little rule."

"Like a maxim?" he suggested. "A personal principle to guide you."

"Yes, a maxim. So then I see if it can rationally be applied to everyone: '*Everyone* will return another's property whenever possible.' Now *that's* a good law. You see?"

"So what's an example of a bad law?" he asked.

"There are two ways for a proposed law—a universalized maxim—to fail. First, if it would be irrational to implement it. Imagine the opposite of the one I just gave: 'Everyone will *not* return another's property whenever possible.' That would be silly. If I ever lose something, I would never want someone to keep it if he could easily return it to me. So that's one way—it could fail because it would be irrational.

"The other way it could fail would be if it created a contradiction. Like if we took the law, 'Every person should own a slave.' This would be impossible because only half the

> **Kant's Method for Determining Duty: The Categorical Imperative**
>
> 1. *Develop a personal maxim.*
> 2. *Universalize that maxim by making it applicable to all people.*
> 3. *Test it:*
>   a. *Could I rationally instate this as a law?*
>   b. *Does it result in a logical inconsistency?*
> 4. *If it passes both tests then it is a duty.*

people can be slave-owners; the other half would be slaves. It totally contradicts itself.

"So if you can rationally impose a universalized maxim without either of these contradictions, then it becomes a moral law, a duty. I acted out of duty."

"So the consequences aren't important for you? Just the motive?"

"Yeah, that seems right. Like if I have a duty to tell the truth, then the consequences don't matter. The truth hurts. Doing the right thing isn't always easy," I said, proudly.

"And the road to hell was paved with good intentions," the Old Man retorted, obviously hoping to make sure I didn't get too confident.

"The road to hell is paved with good intentions."

This proverb is attributed to Saint Bernard of Clairvaux (1091–1153), as "Hell is full of good intentions or desires." In 1670 John Ray added, "Hell is paved with good intentions," and this became popularized by Samuel Johnson.

At that moment, a man walked out of the drug store. He was holding his head in his hands like he had a headache though it seemed like he was maybe even crying. He sat down at the table next to us, with his back to us.

"Sir," the Old Man said, in his most comforting voice. "Are you all right?"

He turned to us, his eyes red, nose runny. "My wife," he whispered to us. "She's dying of a rare strain of cancer." He sniffled. "This druggist has invented the cure for this cancer. Even though it only cost him fifty dollars to make, he's charging five thousand. *Five thousand dollars.* I've asked my friends and family members for money and all I have come up with is three thousand. There's not much more I can do at this point and she's near the end. I just can't believe that my wife could live for another twenty years with the aid of a fifty dollar medicine only ten yards away from me."

The Old Man looked at me. He looked at the bag of money. I looked up at him. I looked at the man.

I reached into the bag and took out about half of it. I put my hand on the man's shoulder. "Sir. My grandfather here just won the lottery. He and I would like to help you and give you the money you need for this medicine."

The man looked at me and took the money. He started crying more now than he was before. "Thank you!" He hugged me. "Thank you!" He hugged the Old Man. "I must run now. Thank you. Thank you." He was yelling "Thank you" as he ran into the store.

The Old Man and I sat for a moment. I could almost anticipate what he was going to say.

As the man ran back out of the store, still crying, still yelling "Thank you," the Old Man turned to me. "You just gave away someone else's money. You also lied to that man. I thought you had a duty to return people's property? A duty not to lie?"

"*You* know the money would be better off spent on that man's wife. The rich guy probably won't even notice it's gone. And the lies were white lies—what did you want me to tell him, that we'd basically stolen the money, that you weren't my grandfather but were instead," I paused, still unsure of his relation to me, "a dream mentor person, or whatever you are?"

"Isn't lying wrong? Don't you have a duty to tell the truth? Isn't it wrong to use other people's money without their knowing?

"You just told me that you have a *duty* to tell the truth. That the consequences don't matter, but that instead you must act according to your duty. In this case here, you *did* act according to the consequences—you didn't want that man's wife to die." He smirked in a way that embodied his earlier "road to hell" comment. "I think you did the right thing."

I thought I did too. "But if I did the right thing, then there must be something more to morality then just doing one's duty."

"It does seem that way, doesn't it?" he responded.

Lawrence Kohlberg presented the "Heinz Dilemma" to different age groups to determine their method of moral reasoning.

Heinz is unable to afford a medicine needed to cure his wife's illness. Kohlberg asked subjects to determine what Heinz should do and, more importantly, why he should do so. From the responses he devised six stages of moral development (stage 6 being the highest):

1. *Obedience—act in order to avoid punishment.*
2. *Individualism—act to satisfy one's needs; there may be more than one view of "right."*
3. *Interpersonal Relations—act according to societal norms so as to receive approval.*
4. *Maintaining Order—do your duty out of respect for authority.*
5. *Social Contract/Individual Rights—follow the rules out of a concern for the general good.*
6. *Universal Principles—regardless of what the majority wants, we should seek universal, impartial moral rules.*

"If there aren't rules like that—duties—then what else is there? Imagine a sport without rules, there'd be nothing to play. No way to even start playing a game. There must be rules of some sort."

"Well, look and see how you acted in that last situation. What motivated you?"

"I guess I tried to make the consequences work out in everyone's favor."

"Not everyone's," he corrected me. "Pete the Great didn't get what he wanted—he didn't get his ten thousand dollars."

"True. But his loss was totally outweighed by the gain of that man and the life of his wife."

"Why don't you put this into our little formula so I can see how it works."

"Okay.

1. *Fact*: The life of the wife is a greater good than Pete the Great having another $10,000.
2. *Moral Claim:* We ought to do whatever results in the greatest good.
3. *Conclusion:* We ought to use the money to save the wife.

"Makes sense, doesn't it?"

The Old Man nodded.

"It gives us an objective way to determine morality, we don't need to involve religion, and it's easy to figure out. Don't we want morality to lead us to goodness, to happiness? This does that for us. Obviously, a woman's life is more important than some rich guy's money. You can't put a price on human life."

"You can't?" he snapped. "Hospitals do it every day. Practically *no* hospital does *everything* they can—running every test, administering every drug, and consulting every expert. They'd run out of resources. They can and must put a price on human life."

He continued nodding.

Utilitarianism

The doctrine of utilitarianism holds that we ought to act to promote the greatest amount of happiness for the greatest number of people.

Jeremy Bentham provided the initial formulation. He defended a view known as "ethical hedonism": Because humans seek pleasure and avoid pain, we ought to do that which creates the greatest amount of pleasure.

In contrast to Bentham, John Stuart Mill based his theory of utilitarianism not on bodily pleasure, but on the "higher faculties," arguing that humans are more than merely pleasure-seeking beings. He wrote, "It is better to be a human being dissatisfied than a pig satisfied; better to be Socrates dissatisfied than a fool satisfied."

Kill One or Let Twenty Die?

Bernard Williams provides a dilemma to show the appeal of utilitarianism:

Out exploring, Jim has stumbled across a group of 20 Indians tied to trees in a small town. The captain of the town's army, who was moments away from killing all 20 of them, offers for you to kill one of them. If you choose to do so, he will let the remaining 19 go. You realize that killing the captain is of no use as there are many soldiers nearby, and that killing yourself (another possible solution given in this dilemma) would still result in the 20 deaths. What do you do?

"What?" I asked him sharply, realizing that his nodding wasn't an *agreeable* nodding but was instead an *I-know-something-you-don't-know* nodding.

"How much money did you spend last time you and Jeff went to the movies?" he asked.

"I dunno. Probably about twelve dollars for the movie and a licorice."

"Then I'd argue that, by *your* moral claim, you acted immorally."

"It's wrong to go to the movies?" I responded, knowing this obviously couldn't be true.

"Yes. While I do believe you enjoyed yourself—i.e., that some good was created—I think a greater good would have resulted had you spent that money to feed an entire family of four who hadn't eaten that day. Don't you?"

I shrugged my shoulders. "I guess so."

"Your theory—maximizing the good—requires too much of people. It makes going to the movies immoral.

"Plus, I'm curious," he said before pausing. This pause of his began to make *me* curious as well. "You were so adamant about helping that woman—giving that man $5,000 to save her life. Do you know how many lives you could have saved in any number of impoverished countries? There are people dying everywhere, Ian, people in great need of basics like food and clothing. If you're morally obligated to save her life, then why not someone in the next town, or next city, or throughout the world?"

Two Trolley Car Scenarios

1. You are alone on a runaway trolley car with no brakes. It is heading for a group of five people on the tracks and will surely kill them. You can turn the car to a fork in the tracks where one person stands. Do you turn it or let it run its course?

2. You are standing next to a very large stranger when a trolley car with no one on it comes racing down the street. There are five people up ahead who will die if it continues, or you can push the one person onto the tracks, killing that person, but stopping the car from continuing. What do you do?

The Global Village

Every day *an estimated 24,000 people die from hunger or hunger-related causes.*

Peter Singer writes, *"if it is in our power to prevent something bad from happening, without hereby sacrificing anything of comparable moral importance, we ought, morally, to do it."* *He gives the following analogy: upon seeing a child drowning, one ought to wade into the water to save the child even though it will dirty one's clothes.*

He notes that this principle holds true regardless of the proximity of those to whom we have a moral obligation: "we cannot discriminate against someone merely because he is far away from us. . . . From the moral point of view, the development of the world into a 'global village' has made an important . . . difference to our moral situation."

His point almost made me want to cry. A little out of frustration, I suppose, but more out of helplessness. He again had made a good point, for which I had no response, yet which had pretty sad consequences. The only upside, I supposed, was the feeling of connectedness I once again felt—not just to him, but to people, to the world, I guess. Like I wasn't just responsible for the little bubble I lived in.

He caught me by surprise as he continued, "It also ignores any semblance of duties. If your father promises to take your mother to the airport, but on his way home to pick her up his friend calls and asks him to come work at a homeless shelter, he'd be morally obliged to go to the shelter if he believed it would create more good."

What he said made sense, but I still felt like I was on to something.

So I suggested, "Okay, how about this moral claim: it is morally wrong to do anything that *decreases* the overall good. So now you don't have to act in order to do the greatest good, you just have to act so that you don't reduce total good."

"I still have a problem with both of these," the Old Man responded. "How can we determine what creates *more* good in certain situations? This all comes back to subjectivism. Think about the death penalty for example. I may think that the government killing murderers sends a message to society that life isn't valuable, and someone else may think that it sends the message that life is so valuable we're willing to kill to protect it and to hopefully deter others from killing. Then we have to judge between which we value. There's no right answer."

I shrugged my shoulders again.

"Plus, I'm not so sure how realistic this all is. Imagine that two people need an immediate kidney transplant—your mother and a famous scientist studying a cure for cancer. You are the only one at the hospital who can provide a kidney. It would create more good if you donate it to the scientist and let your mother die—not doing that might actually result in more bad. But does that seem realistic?"

"But couldn't we just use this process of maximizing good to make rules?" I asked. "So, instead of looking at each action itself, we could look at classes of actions."

He motioned encouragingly.

I continued, "It would create more good if we had the rule, *Don't lie.* That way, everyone would tell the truth and it would create more good in the long run."

"Yes, Ian. But if your goal is to increase the total good, and you realize that when your aunt asks if you like her new hair when you really don't like it, don't you think it would create more good to lie to her and tell her you like it? If you do, then this solution just breaks down to your initial position, which has its obvious flaws."

"Well now I'm really stuck," I said, frustrated. "Morality isn't just what I want it to be, or what a culture says it is—it's not just relative, I get that. But if there is a morality, it can't be determined by religions, or by duties, or by consequences. So what else is there? How can we determine morality?"

"That is certainly one question, isn't it?"

"Yeah, it's one. There's another?"

"Yes, almost more difficult. If you ever do figure out which acts are moral, then you must answer why you should do what's moral in the first place. Why be moral?"

My eyes widened.

"If you do determine that it's wrong to lie, then what motivation do you have for acting morally—for not lying?

"Why be moral?" he asked again.

"Why be moral?" I asked myself. "Why be moral?"

The Happiness of Peeping Tom

James Rachels gives an example which he believes shows that utilitarians (who are only concerned with creating the most good) ignore the relevance of respect for individual rights:

A "Peeping Tom" spies on a woman ("Ms. York") in her home, taking photos of her only for his enjoyment. She never detects him and he enjoys taking and viewing the photos. Rachels writes, "It is clear that the only consequence of his actions is an increase in his own happiness. No one else, including Ms. York, is caused any unhappiness at all. How, then, could utilitarianism deny that the Peeping Tom's actions are right?"

"Why be moral?" Ian mumbled to himself as he sauntered into the kitchen.

"So why should I be moral, mom?" he asked, matter of factly.

Why be moral?

Socrates says we should be moral because it will lead to the "good life." The religious motivation is a prosperous afterlife.

In dialogue with Plato, Glaucon imagines a magic ring—The Ring of Gyges—with the power to make the wearer (and all she touches) invisible. Glaucon believes that anyone wearing the ring will act only to seek out her own interests, regardless of her nature prior to the ring. He concludes that the only reason people act morally is because they fear being punished or being judged by their peers.

"Philosophy is like trying to open a safe with a combination lock: each little adjustment of the dial seems to achieve nothing, only when everything is in place does the door open."
–Wittgenstein

"Because you should?" she responded, hesitantly, almost asking instead of answering.

Ian shook his head, responding rhetorically, "I *ought* to be moral because I *ought to*?"

She answered with a sheepish nod, shrugging her shoulders. His father kept his head down, focusing on whatever work he seemed to be doing at the kitchen table. His mother looked at Ian, "You know Alexis is outside." She paused to let Ian smile. "She's on her way to that concert but I'm sure she could talk this through with you. Okay? We can chat in a bit."

He shrugged his shoulders as if caught off guard by his parents' unusual preoccupation with their work, though partly to disguise his obvious excitement at seeing Alexis.

He walked out the door and saw Alexis sitting in the chair on the front porch, as if expecting him. She sat with her feet out towards him, crossed, and she had her hands in her lap, frolicking with a tennis ball the way a cat playfully bats a cloth mouse with its paws.

Ian stood there with his hands to his side. "Hi."

She smiled at him and tossed the ball, surprising him. He managed to catch it, though somewhat clumsily.

"Wha'cha doin'?" she asked.

He bounced the ball and caught it. "I wanted to talk to my parents about some stuff. They said you'd be out here. So I'm out here now."

"What did you want to talk to them about? Can we talk about it too?" She smiled at him. It was obvious that Ian did want to talk to her.

"Really?" he asked, awaiting her encouragement.

"Yeah, of course. I love talking to you about *stuff*."

Slowly but surely, Ian retold his dream. He told it in segments—first disproving moral relativism, then explaining the issues with religious ethics, and finally his two attempts at determining a universal moral guide himself.

She sat, smiling the whole time, though very focused on him. He continued fidgeting with the ball while he talked.

"You know what I think?" she suggested, after he had finished.

He nodded, encouragingly.

"Too many rules," she said with a straight face. "Too many guidelines or whatever you call them."

"Too many rules?" he responded, with a wince.

"Yes. You probably can't even comprehend that, can you? Like a game. Like a game is impossible to play without rules or something."

His eyes got big as he recalled making that analogy himself.

"Think about all the problems with rules to begin with, Ian. Even the rules of the games and sports you play. No single set of rules can cover *every* conceivable action—there's an infinite number of possible wrongful actions so no rule book can include them all. It's a good

Another Perspective on Ethics

Feminist ethics holds that too much emphasis is placed on rules and rights while ignoring relationships and emotions. Ethical theorists Eve Cole and Susan Coultrap-McQuin write that traditional moral theory has, "reflected interests derived predominantly from men's experience. In other words, because men's experience has often involved market transactions, their moral theories concentrate on promise-keeping, property rights, contracts, and fairness."

Are rules all we have?

J.S. Russell examines limitations of rules in his paper, "Are Rules All an Umpire Has to Work With?" (he answers, no): "Philosophers of law have generally accepted that rules . . . can fail to be definitive guides [for conduct]. . . . [B]ecause language is an imprecise instrument, the core of agreed meaning may break down." He explains ambiguities of a basic rule such as, Dogs must be kept on a leash in public space: "What is a 'leash' or a 'public space'? Is a 100-foot long bungee cord attached to a dog a leash? Is a shopping mall a public place? Does the rule mean that dogs may run free if they are simply attached to a leash that is not held by the owner?"

starting point, but there must be something more than just rules. Plus, it seems like there are times that certain rules may not be quite right for a particular situation—like your 'don't tell lies' rule, for example. Words and rules are just so un-exact." She paused for a moment, almost as though she felt bad for pulling the rug out from under him and his rule-governed sports that he liked.

She changed her tone a bit, asking, "Do you think a mother follows rules when she decides what she *ought* to do for her young child? Do you think that every human situation and relationship can be solved by some formula?" She smiled shyly, almost like she had surprised herself. "It just seems like you're basing your morality totally on equality, on fairness."

"What else is there?" Ian responded.

She shook her head, "Caring for each other. *Caring,*" she repeated, to make sure he understood the word in the context.

"Things *aren't* equal and fair, Ian. But we have all been cared for at some point. That's important. These are *people* involved in these situations. That's all."

"I kind of see your point. But I guess I don't think that caring is enough to solve major ethical and political issues. Not the big issues, anyway. And I don't really think that the mother-child relationship is a good one to be a model for all of society."

She smiled. She enjoyed this. "Maybe it could be a combination of your rules and my idea. After all, your rules didn't seem to give us all the answers. How about that 'Don't steal' rule you came up with at the drug store?"

"What would *you* have done then?" Ian responded quickly.

"Talked to the pharmacist, talked to the man with the money, borrowed the money from that man at least. What if you got caught? What if that man had important plans for that money? When you talk about everyone's rights to things—to life, to their money, property, liberty—it gets very, um," she paused, "sterile, non-human. What about the stories of the relationships? These

Alison Jaggar argues that typical Western ethics emphasizes, "male-associated values of independence, autonomy, intellect, will, wariness, hierarchy . . . over the supposedly feminine or female-associated values of interdependence, community, connection, sharing, emotion, body, trust, absence of hierarchy, nature, immanence, process, joy, peace and life."

Annette Baier writes that because a majority of well-known moral theorists were men, they focused, "so single-mindedly on cool, distanced relations between more or less free and equal adult strangers."

universal rules and duties can get so impersonal. Everyone should act more out of a humanistic care instead."

Ian smiled. "You just made a universal law yourself. You said that *everyone* should do something, like it's a duty."

"You're always so good at catching my logical flaws—always playing by the *rules* of logic," she said in a somewhat sarcastic though charming tone.

"I am just curious," she asked, "If you finally do come up with a set of moral rules and of rights, who will they apply to? Will you give rights to everyone? To every living being? Every living thing? Aliens from outer space? Super advanced robots? Fetuses of one day? Of nine months? Humans with no brain function? How will you decide?" She shrugged her shoulders to try to hide the seriousness of her question.

Then she held out her hands, opening her fingers towards him asking for the ball. He threw it to her and she caught it. "I should get going," she said as she walked up to him and hugged him. He stood with his hands still by his side.

In 1992, Harvard psychologist Carol Gilligan wrote one of the first works in feminist ethics, In a Different Voice. She noted that females often appear as morally underdeveloped, yet that this results from the male-centric framework (i.e., Kholberg's moral stages) versus females' lack of moral character. In interviews with an 11-year old boy and girl regarding the Heinz Dilemma she explains, "these two children see two very different moral problems— Jake a conflict between life and property that can be resolved by logical deduction, Amy a fracture of human relationship that must be mended with its own thread."

Who Has Rights?

Peter Singer argues that it is not rationality that determines moral rights, nor communication, nor self-awareness: some animals exhibit these qualities more than some humans. Nor can it be the mere fact that we are human—to hold this position would be what he calls speciesism: *"a prejudice or attitude of bias toward the interests of members of one's own species." He likens this with racism and sexism: each ascribes moral status based on irrelevant factors (species, skin color, and sex, respectively). Instead, what ought to determine who deserves moral consideration is* sentience—*the ability to feel pain.*

Carl Cohen suggests that rights are strictly a human idea; having rights requires having obligations. He imagines a lioness that rips open the throat of a baby zebra, eats part of it, and leaves the carcass. We do not deem this lion immoral like we would a human who acted similarly towards another human: "Lions and rats are totally amoral; there is no morality for them; they do no wrong, ever. In their world there are no rights."

Who Has Rights? (Continued)

Mary Anne Warren suggests five traits most common to determining if a being ought to have moral status: consciousness, reasoning, self-motivated activity, capacity to communicate, self-awareness. She suggests we might want to consider "intelligent inhabitants of other worlds" and "self-aware robots" as moral beings.

The Respect Human Life Act amendment, introduced in the 98th Congress in 1983, held that U.S. government policy is, "to protect innocent life, both before and after birth"—holding human life sacred regardless of the being's developmental stage. This position is in line with many Western religions as well.

As she walked backwards down the path from his house she asked, "You don't even know his name, do you? The Old Man. Say 'hi' to him for me next time you see him." They waved to each other as she walked down the sidewalk.

"I *should* have hugged her back," Ian mumbled as he walked back through the door.

His parents looked up at him, smiling refreshingly as he entered the kitchen. "Did your chat with Alexis help?"

He shrugged his shoulders and mumbled some sort of affirmation.

"Son, I'm not sure what you explored in your dream," his father said. "I'm guessing that you tried making lots of rules about what you should and shouldn't do. I have another possible solution."

Ian seemed almost fearful that his father might propose the same thing as Alexis. "Caring?" Ian suggested, hesitantly.

"Caring?" his father asked, making sure he had heard correctly.

Ian pursed his lips and shook his head as if to erase the comment.

His father nodded, "Virtue."

"Virtue? What do you mean? How will that help figure out what we ought to do?"

"That's just part of the issue, Ian—framing the question. Maybe instead of focusing on specific actions and moral codes, we could instead ask, *What kind of person do I want to be?* The answer to this will help to guide your actions. It might also help with your other question, *Why be moral?*"

Ian nodded slowly, awaiting his father's explanation.

"Let's start with something simple. What would it mean for a hammer to be *excellent*? Think about it."

Ian smiled almost an embarrassing smile at this question. His father nodded to show that he asked the question for a reason.

Ian answered, "Well, I guess that it would be able to hammer nails into wood really well."

"Sure," his father answered. "Why do you say that?"

"That's the purpose of a hammer, I guess," Ian responded. "So it should be sturdy, with a kind of heavy head and flat striking surface, along with an easy-to-hold handle." He sat calmly awaiting the connection with virtue.

"Exactly. An excellent hammer serves its purpose most effectively. An excellent eye sees well. An excellent pencil writes well." And he raised his eyebrows in anticipation. "And an excellent human lives well.

"So asking the question, *Why be moral?* is just like asking *Why should I live well?* It becomes silly to ask, just like it would be silly to ask *Why should I be healthy?* or *Why should I flourish?*"

"Okay, so how do we figure out how to live well, how to flourish?" Ian asked.

"I might ask you that same question. Tell me, what makes us different from all other objects in the universe, from all other beings? Just like the hammer hammers and the eye sees, what do we do?"

"Reason?"

"Yes. So part of this flourishing requires that we utilize our capacity to *reason*, to contemplate. This allows us to be *excellent* human beings. We can use this reason, then, to determine virtue."

Ian nodded as he followed his father's line of reasoning. His dad continued, "Tell me, do you think being a coward is virtuous—that any time anything scary or potentially dangerous arises, you run and hide?"

Ian shook his head.

"What about being foolhardy—jumping in front of trains to save a cat, for example?"

Ian shook his head again, responding, "No, neither is virtuous. In the first instance you would never defend what you believed, but in the other you would probably die pretty quickly—not much chance for *flourishing* there."

Pursuit of Excellence & Happiness

The concept of arête *(Greek for "excellence") played a key role in Plato's view of virtue.* Arête *is achieved when one: a) is properly educated, b) has a proper mentor, and c) practices that in which he hopes to achieve excellence. A carpenter, for example, achieves excellence by creating fine furniture. A human, then, achieves excellence by flourishing through a balanced use of reason, natural desires, and the will.*

*Aristotle wrote that the goal of every human is happiness. We achieve this by fulfilling our primary function (*telos*): what we can do best. For example, the* telos *of an eye is to see. The telos of a human, writes Aristotle, is to reason. Through reasoning we experience what the Greeks called* eudaimonia—*living well.*

"We are what we repeatedly do."

According to Aristotle, virtue is not an inherent trait but is instead something we acquire through practice. Just as a painter becomes good by painting well, a person becomes good by acting well: "Excellence, therefore, is not an act, but a habit."

He proposed a method for determining virtue called the "Doctrine of the Mean." He wrote, "Virtue is a kind of moderation inasmuch as it aims at the mean or moderate amount." For example, he posited the virtue of gentleness as the mean of two vices: wrath (an excess of anger) and timidity (a total lack of anger); and the virtue of wittiness (between the extremes of tediousness and buffoonery).

"It is better to rise from life as from a banquet—neither thirsty nor drunken."
—Aristotle

"Very good, son. So courage is a virtue. It's what lies between two extremes, two vices: cowardice and foolhardiness. It's the same with a lot of things. Think about temperance—you know, 'all things in moderation.' If you over-indulge in pleasurable things—if you play video games all day long and only eat dessert—it could be very bad for you. Yet by completely refraining from all of this and never engaging in *anything* pleasurable, you miss out on an important part of life as well. There's a happy median."

"So like with honesty," Ian started in, pausing to think. "It wouldn't be virtuous to be completely honest all the time, going around telling everyone how you feel about them all the time—like when someone asks if you like their new hair cut that you hate, or if lying could prevent someone from being harmed. But it also wouldn't be virtuous to be dishonest all the time either."

"Exactly. So virtue is something that you develop over time. It can be taught. In flourishing, you learn more and more how to approach that mean, that middle ground."

Writing a century before Aristotle, Confucius also explored virtue and the doctrine of the mean. He wrote, "Without a sense of proportion, courtesy becomes oppressive; calmness becomes bashfulness; valor becomes disorderliness; and candor becomes rudeness."

"Wow, dad. I actually like this. Because even with all the rules there are for acting ethically, no one would even bother to follow them if they weren't virtuous to begin with. Like when we determine duties—if the person isn't virtuous in the first place, they're not going to be concerned with doing their duty.

"And this really takes the *person* into account—the person becomes responsible for making themselves virtuous and not just a rule-follower. It's a little more real-life, more humanistic."

Virtue Supersedes Duty

Superogatory actions—*acts which are morally praiseworthy though not morally required (i.e., holding the door open for someone) as opposed to obligatory acts such as those required by duty.*

Justine Oakley recounts consoling a friend saddened by his failed marriage. She comforts him much longer than required by any duty and cancels a business appointment to do so. Oakley writes, "What makes it right to console the friend here is that this is the sort of thing which someone with an appropriate conception of friendship will be disposed to do, rather than because this brings about the best overall consequences, or because this is our duty as a friend."

"I agree, son. But even more important than that, this view actually helps give a positive guide for living. Instead of telling you what you should *not* do, it helps determine what you *should* do. That just seems to make more sense."

Ian nodded. "So even if there isn't a rule that you *should* do something, this still gives you a reason for doing it. Like greeting someone when they enter a room, or giving someone directions when they're lost, or letting someone cross the street when you're driving. There's no rule that says you *should* greet people, or that you have a duty to do so, but that doesn't mean you shouldn't. Doing these kinds of actions is *virtuous*. None of the rule-based theories talk about that." Ian was smiling, as though he'd solved a major issue.

One of the merits of virtue ethics is that it allows our moral lives to be viewed as a whole, not just as sequential dilemmas and situations.

"The moral life is not . . . best regarded as a set of episodic encounters with moral dilemmas or moral uncertainty . . . it is rather a life-long pursuit of excellence of the person."

–David Solomon

His mom leaned in with her hands on Ian's father's shoulders as if to comfort him. "Can we really help how we feel though?" she seemed to be asking the both of them. "If I am inclined to steal something because I really want it—if my character is such that I want to steal—should I really be faulted if I refrain from stealing *only* because I have a duty not to? Is that so bad? And maybe I don't want to give my money to charity, but I do it out of duty.

"Plus, it does seem like different people and different cultures have different values and, thus, hold different qualities virtuous, doesn't it?"

She paused to take a short breath and continued, "Just because the ability to reason is unique to humans, is that enough to say that we

Immoral in thought only?

In a 1976 interview, 39th President Jimmy Carter admitted he had committed adultery despite the fact that he never acted in an adulterous way. Instead, he explained, "I've looked on a lot of women with lust. I've committed adultery in my heart many times." This raises the question as to whether one can be immoral in thought only.

"Christ condemns even adultery of mere desire."
–Catholic Church Catechism

should do it? It seems like we are assigning value to something factual. Why is reason *good* to begin with? If the purpose of a nuclear weapon is to kill lots of people, does that mean it is good when it does so? Just because something has a unique quality, does that mean it's good?"

"But mom, I don't think you really would *feel good* about stealing something. I certainly don't think that *most* people feel good about it. Shouldn't that count for something?"

His dad nodded his head slowly, deliberately, and boldly stated, *"The human conscience."* He let that float amongst them for a moment and then continued, "It's something I've considered mentioning all along. I actually think we can almost approach morality scientifically just by looking at this notion of moral *feelings.*"

"A science of morals?" Ian's mom said suggestively. "I'd love to hear it," she said looking at Ian who smiled back at her.

"Basically," his dad began, "I don't think reason can help us make value judgments—judgments that involve beauty or, in this case, morality. Reason provides facts—what *is*. Yet morality is a value—what *ought to be*. Think back to our discussion of the passions and how they often guide us in correct action. Morals could very much be a product of tastes and emotion—things universal to human beings."

Ian's mom raised her eyebrows in agreeable anticipation.

The Nature of Ethics and Humans

David Hume argued that ethics could be "naturalized"—studied scientifically— since ethics are based on human nature and not on logical reasoning. He wrote, "To have a sense of virtue is nothing, but to feel *a satisfaction of a particular kind from the contemplation of a character. The very* feeling *constitutes our praise or admiration." He added, "We do not infer a character trait to be virtuous . . . but in feeling that it pleases . . . we in effect feel that it is virtuous."*

Elsewhere he writes, "Reason being cool and disengaged, is no motive to action, and directs only the impulse received from appetite and inclination. . . . Taste, as it gives pleasure or pain, and thereby constitutes happiness or misery, becomes a motive to action, and is the first spring or impulse to desire and volition.

He continued, "So determining moral principles can be accomplished by first assuming that all humans have good feelings that result from good acts. We also have to account for our ability to sympathize with others—to recognize their feelings—and our ability to view situations impartially, without taking into account one's personal interests. From this basis, character traits and actions can be considered moral and virtuous."

With that same agreeable anticipation Ian's mom asked, "So how exactly would we deem a trait as virtuous under this scheme?"

"A character trait is considered virtuous if it first produces that positive feeling within oneself and within others."

"A positive feeling?" she asked, rhetorically.

"Yes, you know, like when someone does something honorable, for example: you always say you get the chills when we go to the movies and a character acts out of honor. That's a positive, agreeable feeling."

She nodded agreeably. "Okay, and secondly?"

"And secondly, the trait must be *useful* to oneself and to others."

Ian smiled at his dad and suggested, "Like honor."

"Yes, son, like honor."

Ian added, "And not stealing. Not selfishness."

"Yes," his dad said, smiling, as if he felt the agreeable positive feelings attached with caring for one's son.

Ian's mom smiled and his father added, "I just view morality as actually *provided by human nature* and not some sterile creation *of* humans."

"But dear," his mom interjected, "what if two people have dissimilar feelings upon examining one particular trait or action?"

Is Moral Sentiment Universal?

Hume answers yes to the above question. He writes that there is, "some internal sense or feeling, which nature has made universal in the whole species."

He goes on to write, "The notion of morals implies some sentiment common to all mankind."

Is it in our nature to be moral?

Hume argues that the human mind must naturally distinguish between moral and immoral characteristics. Otherwise, he writes, how else would we ever distinguish honor from shame, noble from despicable, or lovely from odious? Social virtues must then, "be allowed to have a natural beauty."

Contemporary theorist Michael Shermer argues that humans have evolved a moral sense, at both individual and group levels. He writes, "Asking, 'Why should we be moral?' is like asking 'Why should we be hungry?' . . . The answer is that it is as much a part of human nature to be moral as it is to be hungry."

"Then I would argue that either they didn't both know all there is to know about the situation *or* that one person is maybe overtly self-interested and thus his conscience is tainted."

Ian's smile faded a bit as he realized the problem of varying tastes amongst different people.

Then what was left of his smile turned to a disenchanted blank stare. He sat for a moment and his eyes widened, "Is it possible that there is no such thing as right and wrong? I mean, that humans really just made it up? Maybe like numbers. One plus one only equals two because humans made it up. So maybe stealing is only wrong because humans made it up."

His parents looked at each other, as if realizing the consequences of a morality-free society.

Ian continued, "If I say, *The Earth is spherical*, that's either true or false—the Earth is just the shape it is. But if I say, *It is wrong to kill innocent people*, the truth of that statement is different from the one about the Earth. It seems like it is only true because we say it is. Just like, *One plus one equals two*."

Ethical Egoism—*people ought to do that which is in their best interests.*

What would you choose in the following scenarios:

- *Either you will be killed or one other person in the world chosen at random will be. What about ten others? A hundred others?*
- *Either you will lose a thousand dollars or ten other people will lose a thousand dollars. What about ten other people losing a hundred dollars?*

"Ian, are you suggesting that there's no such thing as morality all together? Do you remember that first part of the dream that you recalled—all those instances? None of those were wrong?"

He immediately shook his head. "I know. I'm just frustrated that I can't come up with a good way to determine morality.

"And it seems like people would only be moral if it benefited themselves. I can't imagine a poor person who is starving and has the chance to steal a loaf of bread just not doing it because it's immoral."

His father nodded a conceding nod towards Ian's mother. He leaned in towards Ian and said, "You are way ahead of where I was at your age, son. Just thinking about these issues and how to determine their ethical status is a step in the right direction. Developing a moral framework takes time and a lot of mental energy. Don't forget to follow your heart, son. You've got a good one. There's something to be said for that conscience we all have." Ian's mom put her hand on his and he looked up and smiled at his father.

"I think I'm going to get a slice of the sky," Ian suggested, now somewhat solemn. "I have kind of a bad feeling—or really, a *sad* feeling—that this was my last night with the Old Man."

His parents looked at each other and nodded as if they agreed with him. They looked at Ian and gave him one of those canned smiles—the smile from parents who want their son to think *everything is okay* when they know it's not.

Can You (Not) Believe It?

As I left the house, Jeff was waiting outside on his bike as if he knew I would be there. We had planned to explore the town fair. Seeing as it was a small town, it was a small fair. But it created some excitement, nonetheless.

As I got on my bike we chatted about the usual stuff, racing through the middle of the street, weaving in and out of the little plastic things that divide the street. The fair was pretty close so we didn't get much practice on our bikes. If you do something for fun and in doing that activity you improve, are you practicing it? When I talk, am I talking or am I practicing my talking? When I play baseball, am I practicing baseball or really playing baseball? What about breathing? What distinguishes my *really doing* something from my just *practicing* it? I wonder what Alexis would say if instead of just kissing her, I asked her if we could *practice* kissing. It would make me a lot less nervous. It would just be practice.

We parked our bikes and I saw the usual little rides, a couple of ponies, and about 20 booths for games. They were the typical games too—the kind that you think you should easily win, but obviously don't win easily, and so the fair makes money:

- The basketball hoop that's as skinny as the basketball.
- The ring-a-bottle game where it looks like there's no way to miss ringing a bottle because there are so many, but the ring is small and there's a lot of space between the bottles and you're really just aiming for *one* bottle anyway.
- The Plinko game where you drop the big chip and it falls through all the pegs and you watch it and plan your next drop, only to have absolutely no effect on where it lands because the pegs are designed to have the chip land in the "Sorry, try again" slot at the bottom.

I guess these are just like gambling is for grown-ups. You believe you should win, you believe you have some effect on the odds, and the times you do win keep you coming back. But in the end you lose. Funny too, because you know that the games are designed so that you lose more than you win.

Regardless, I was back. We played the balloon-popping-dart game, and despite the dull darts and under-inflated balloons, I won once out of three tries. That earned me a candy diamond ring. Even though I could have bought this for 25 cents, I figured that the dollar I spent on it and the fun I had earning it made it all the better. Another life lesson, maybe.

Jeff pointed curiously at another booth. "Look at all these people, here to check their beliefs with an ethicist," he said, as if he knew what that was.

"An ethicist?"

"Yeah, an expert in ethics. People come here to share their beliefs with the ethicist and she tells them if their specific belief is ethical or not."

"How could a *belief* be right or wrong? I mean, a person should be able to believe whatever they want."

"Yeah, you'd think so. That's what I thought at first. Let's get closer and listen in on some of the beliefs people are sharing. We won't get to hear her response because she always writes it out. She believes it will mean more to them that way."

A man nervously walked up to the window—it was like the window of a bank teller. Above it was a sign that read, "Belief Ethicist—On Duty." "Hello," he said. The woman nodded politely. "My psychic correctly predicted that I would experience some disappointment at some point last year. She was right—I didn't get the job promotion that I was hoping for. She recently predicted that because of my date of birth and the alignment of the stars, money would result in great suffering for our family and that I should give half of it to her to balance out my psychic aura. I believe that giving her half of our life savings will help me to avoid this evil."

"How could he really believe that?" I said, turning to Jeff.

Jeff shrugged his shoulders, "People believe pretty weird things. But the question here is, do you see anything *wrong* with that?"

I crinkled my eyebrows at him, still not seeing how *any belief* could somehow be *wrong*.

The woman handed him a small envelope and the man left the window.

The next person approached the window. It was a kid, and he looked younger than me. "I believe that if I am good all year, Santa Claus will bring me presents on Christmas." The woman smiled and slid an envelope towards him.

Following him was what I guessed was his father. "I believe that giving a person any sort of medical attention is like playing God and so we shouldn't intervene in any way. I believe that God will take care of us without the need of any medical attention."

"Do you act on these beliefs?"

"Well sure," he responded. "How can you have a belief and not act on it? What's the point? I don't allow my son to go to the doctor, or the dentist, or anyone like that."

Jeff looked at me. "What do you think of that one?" I nodded. I was starting to see how beliefs—if they lead to action—could be considered right or wrong. The woman gave the father his envelope.

Next a woman approached the window. "I am a doctor and I believe that giving sugar pills to patients as a placebo is better than giving them actual drugs. I present it to them like it's a *real* pill—I lie to them. If *they* believe it then it often works." And she received her envelope.

Next was an older woman. She was with a friend but they went one at a time. "I believe that the moment a fetus is conceived, it is a person and should have the same rights as all other people."

"Why do you believe that?" the Belief Ethicist responded.

"It's just what I believe," the woman responded, nicely. And she received her envelope.

Her friend then approached the window. "I believe that a woman should have the right to choose what she does with her body and with anything in her body. And I believe that the fetus does not have any rights until it is able to live on its own."

"Why do you believe that?" the Belief Ethicist responded.

"It's just what I believe," the woman responded, nicely. It was like the exact same conversation that happened a minute ago, and both people equally committed to their beliefs, yet both beliefs were totally opposite. She received her envelope.

A middle-age man sauntered up to the counter. "I believe that humans were created when a giant egg, floating on a globe of only water, cracked and the pieces of egg shell formed the continents and the yolk created people." Before she could respond he added, "I teach this to the students in my sixth grade science class when we talk about the 'Origin of Humans.'" The ethicist mouthed *ah ha* and handed him his envelope.

Another woman came to the window, "I believe that certain people that currently have rights should not have them. Like people with a specific amount of pigment in their skin, or people with lower IQ's. These *things* are actually not people—they are something else."

I squeezed Jeff's arm tightly. This was to help keep me from yelling something out. "Yeah," he turned to me, "I told you. Lots of people just don't know how to organize their thoughts. They can't tell that their beliefs are based on really poor reasoning—or no reasoning at all. It's really bad when it affects other people."

The ethicist asked, "Do you act on this belief?"

"Yes," she responded. "It affects who I hire and basically how I treat people." The ethicist slid an envelope to the woman and she walked away.

Jeff went on, "People always say, 'Ignorance is bliss.' I guess it's true in a way. But it's kind of selfish. It's like saying, 'I'm blissful, I'm happy, so who cares about what's really going on?' It's short-sighted—*myopic*, as I've heard my dad say."

I nodded. I started to look at all the things I believed and why I believed them. Some, I supposed, were out of habit. I'd never even thought to look at why I believed them. Some were because I was taught that way, probably having a lot to do with my upbringing. Yet other things I believed because I wanted to believe them. Like my wanting to believe them helped me to believe them.

"I believe that you are going to give me your new science set," I said to Jeff, smiling. "I don't think it's wrong to believe that, do you?"

Jeff smiled back. "You could ask the expert. I suppose there's nothing *wrong* with believing that, though this might be a time when belief is a lot different than knowledge. Anyway, I have a feeling that you don't really *believe* that."

"I've got to get going now, anyway," I said to him, somewhat secretively.

"Good luck, Ian," he responded.

Good luck? I smiled at him and we rode off in separate directions.

It was a perfectly cloudy day for that slice of sky—not too many clouds, but enough that they would make for a nice contrast with the blue. I wondered how much meaning this slice would have. More than my first? More than the one that Alexis and I got together?

Chapter 14

The Final Excursion

The soul makes assertions in sleep.

–Aristotle, On Dreams

While we are asleep in this world, we are awake in another one; in this way, every man is two men.

–Jorge Luis Borges

Ian came back through that door still clutching his latest slice of the sky. His parents were sitting at the kitchen table as if they hadn't moved since Ian left.

"How is Jeff?" his mom asked. "What did you two talk about?"

Ian stared at her for a moment, "How did you know I saw Jeff?"

"Don't you always see him *out there*?" she asked, pointing to the door.

Ian seemed to sense something strange about his parents. He placed his slice of the sky on the counter and sat down with them at the table.

"Mom," Ian spoke cautiously.

"Yes, dear," she replied equally cautiously, anticipating the following question. Ian held the diamond of her wedding ring and asked, "Is this real?"

"Yes, it is."

"A real cubic zirconia?" he asked, smiling.

"No, no it's not."

Then he went to the bowl of plastic fruit and grabbed the apple. "Is this real?"

"No, it's not. You know that."

"It's not real? It's not really in my hand? Am I imagining it?" He and his mom had a surprisingly good time going through this whole routine.

"Well, I suppose that's an actual fake apple. It's a real fake apple. Or a fake real apple."

Ian laughed playfully. He knew that she would eventually become somewhat exasperated with this game so when she played along Ian got a real kick out of it.

"What about unicorns? Do they exist?"

"No, Ian, they don't."

"They don't? Well, how can we talk about them then? They must exist in some way for us to talk about them. Otherwise, what are we talking about? And anyway, do they have white horns or black ones?"

She sat, exhaling slowly, smiling slightly, shrugging her shoulders.

"Is this real?" he asked as he pointed off to the living room.

"Is what real?" she responded.

"This house. What about this?" pointing towards the stairway.

"The stairs? Yes."

"No, not that. *This*. This molecule. This electron."

"Well, I don't see anything, but scientists tell us that electrons are real. So I suppose so. Why don't you go back outside and play?"

"Because I have one more question." Ian loved actually answering rhetorical questions.

"Is this real?"

He was pointing to himself. This caught her off guard. She nodded assuredly, though Ian could sense her hesitation. "Could I possibly *not* be real?" he said, with a hint of sincerity. "And what would that mean?"

As he left the kitchen and went up the stairs and out the door, he turned around and came back to ask one more *Is this real?* question. As he walked in the kitchen, he saw his mom and dad at the table. Sitting with them was me, the "Old Man." Ian shook his head as he'd seen cartoon characters do when they do a double take. He was startled after the second take.

"Mom! Dad! That's him. This is him! *The Old Man*. This is him. The man from my dreams." Pointing. "This is him." They smiled. Ian was shocked that they weren't shocked.

I cautiously addressed him, "Ian, it is time that we talk now about *you*. We have come to the time for your last lesson. It's a big one, probably the toughest for you to grasp. It's something that Jeff tried to explain to you just this morning."

Ian sat still, frozen.

"It turns out that you are different than human beings. You may ask yourself, *'How is Ian different from other people?'* And I will tell you.

"You have just completed your training as a Dream Weaver—someone who creates dreams for people. You aren't a person in the way that Jack and his readers are."

"Jack? His readers?"

"Yes. Jack is a person in the way that you understand them. He lives in the world that, for beings like Jack, is his reality. Though it's different from yours. As I will explain to you in a moment, he was given access to everything you've been doing—all your thoughts and all the experiences we've had, as well as my documenting your actual *sleep time* when you, *in your dreams*, met with your parents. Your parents are figments of your dreams. You created them as an inner dialogue to help you sort through everything. Kind of an id-ego battle of sorts, I suppose."

Ian was shaking his head frantically. "No. That doesn't make sense at all. This is just a dream anyway. After all, *you're here*. This is just a dream."

"That's just it, Ian. Let me explain to you *'Ian's levels of reality.'*

"What you've understood as dreams have actually been your reality. And your reality, your dreams. When you come downstairs to talk with your parents, you are actually going down into your subconscious and are dreaming. When you meet with me, you are actually in your reality—it's just that your reality is very different from non-Weavers' reality. And when you walk out that front door, it's your work. *That* is where you make everything happen."

I paused for a moment to catch my breath. Explaining this was difficult and I wanted to ease into it so as not to upset Ian.

I continued, "When you and I went on our nightly adventures, you weren't dreaming. That was real. Your meetings with me comprised your training as a Dream Weaver."

I paused again, being careful to let this all have time to sink in.

"Then following each of our meetings, you rested and dealt with everything you had just learned. You dealt with it by dreaming about it. All your confused thoughts and unanswered questions you brought to your subconscious. It was there that you sorted a lot of it out. It was there that you asked questions you were afraid to ask in reality. Because it was just a dream. You created your mom and dad. They were your way of sorting out all of the information and experiences you had with me."

By now I had my arm resting on Ian's shoulders. We had walked outside and sat together on the front porch.

"And that's just it. Dreams. For human beings you are *the reason that dreams happen.* They happen because thousands of people like you and like your friend Jeff make them happen. This project has been one that has been in the works now for hundreds of years.

"Everything that people think every day—their fleeting thoughts, their daydreams, even all the things they think that they aren't even aware of—it's all recorded in their brain. Then Dream Weavers like myself and *like you* take these bits of information and we help them assign meaning to it. Having experienced all of our meetings—your training—you now have a great understanding of human reality. With this insight, you can help them to better comprehend reality and their lot in life. It's actually a very fulfilling existence."

"But dreams aren't real," Ian muttered. "So that's it, then? That's all for me? I'm stuck in this realm, or world, or whatever, and all I do for my whole life is *weave* dreams for real people? That doesn't sound fulfilling at all. It sounds boring. It sounds *un*fulfilling."

"Well, Ian, I have some answers for you.

"First of all, there's a pragmatic answer. You'll be helping people sleep."

"Helping them?" he asked, genuinely intrigued.

"Yes. Let me give you a very brief version of people's sleeping patterns. Basically, there are five stages of sleep. There is one, which has come to be known as REM sleep—short for Rapid Eye Movement—in which a person's heart rate, oxygen consumption, breathing, and eye movement are the same as when they are awake. This stage occurs up to five times a night. *This* is when we go to work. When a person's eyes start twitching, they're on the verge of waking up. But," and I said this *but* with great emphasis, "this is when we provide a dream for them, a reason to stay asleep. As they dream, they relax and go back to the deep sleep of the middle stages. And that's the funny thing. In all of the books on dreams in Jack's world, they say that dreams cause REM sleep. We know that's obviously not right. It's the other way around—*REM sleep causes dreams.*"

Ian sat still, somewhat excited, somewhat overwhelmed.

I could see that I had piqued his interest so I continued. "Okay, so that's the first-of-all. Second of all, you'll be doing something very important for people. You'll be helping them come to terms with their own problems, inner struggles, uncertainties. As many famous psychologists have realized, dreams are one place where the unconscious actually has a conscious voice. It's very powerful.

"Third, you'll make sleeping more fun for people. You know, every night we get thousands of calls from parents—*Sweet Dreams* they whisper into their children's ears. We're in very high demand. So in that sense, many would consider this a very noble and fulfilling existence."

I smiled a bit, watching Ian's reactions.

"And fourth, this should be fun for you as well. You don't know it, but you've already begun your work. You've already woven the dreams of 14 different people. These were all the experiences you had by yourself or with Jeff when I wasn't around. You were weaving dreams. You walked out of your kitchen, up the stairs, and into someone else's subconscious. That whole outside world is a playground of subconsciouses for you."

Ian crinkled his brow. He looked up at me, almost glaring at me, though not in an angry way—more like he really wanted to understand what I was saying, like he wanted to believe it, but just couldn't quite comprehend it.

I nodded as confidently as I could. "You have done it. And you've done a very good job of it. Each of your adventures without me were dreams that a person had. *You created these dreams for people.* For example, when you and Jeff listened in on those mice, you created a dream for a man named John. John had been dealing with his feelings for his wife and struggled with the head-and-heart issue. He wanted to rationalize his love for his wife and couldn't do it. After that dream that you gave him, he woke up, analyzed it with a friend over lunch that day, and came home more in love with his wife than ever. I must say, that was a very crafty little dream you wove for him."

Ian was now nodding proudly, with a smile slowly emerging.

I continued, "With that dream about the porcupine, you gave someone named Anastasia the confidence to continue the pursuit of her art—you even inspired her to try a new medium that she'd been afraid to try. In another, you helped Frederick find a way to deal with his clients—he's got clients worth millions and you wove him the dream of a simple paperboy. Brilliant. You took on so much—Julia's fleeting reflection of existence, a science teacher's discussion with a colleague, a postman's simple thoughts of identifying letters in an address, a young girl's subconscious discomfort of seeing ads in a magazine—and you turned them all into unique, poignant dreams for them. Even your little snippet with the whole *nothingness* when you walked into Byron's head—he woke up at two in the morning and wrote a short story about that and it was just published. And that thing you and Jeff did with the binoculars: amazing. You should see what you did for a lawyer and a case he was working on. He was able to see the case in a completely novel way and to use the insights from the dream in his actual closing arguments. You are *very* good at what you do, and because of that, you greatly enrich the lives of human beings everywhere."

Ian grinned. Now he was nodding approvingly. He was obviously proud of the dreams he had created for people, though unknowingly at the time.

"And, lastly, this—our team effort—*Ian's final dream infiltration* while under my observation. You and I are completing a dream for a soon-to-be writer. Everything you have done has been cataloged and sent—in a dream—to this person named Jack. Jack will be inspired by the dream we've been creating and will hopefully follow through with a book. He may even include this very conversation in it. Once that gets published, then our mission is complete. We will have a true guide to dreams and reality, all in one."

Ian now seemed astounded, as I had expected. "Wow. This is unbelievable," he exclaimed. "Now that you mention it, there were so many things to do and explore in my neighborhood. I saw so many things that I used to ignore. But recently I've felt more drawn to these things. There's just so much."

"Yes, Ian. You're learning to take nothing for granted. You've come to terms with how things are, and what we can know, and you've earned the privilege to weave dreams for people. I'm glad you've realized both how fun and how rewarding this can be."

His enthusiasm dampened just a bit as I could see him thinking through this. "But I won't be real. This is why my mom hesitated when I pointed to myself just now," he said, looking down at his body as if viewing it for the first time. "Will I be real?"

"It depends on what you mean by *real*. You'll be real in the way that a cubic zirconia is real. Or the way that a diamond is real."

"But a diamond *is* real."

"Either that or it's a fake cubic zirconia."

"But everything downstairs *and* upstairs just seemed so normal. It seemed like reality, or whatever. Like it is in Jack's reality. Like I was on that level."

"Well Ian, do you think tigers that are born and raised in a zoo think there's such a thing as lush jungles?" Ian shook his head, and I continued, "They don't long for the jungle. They don't think of the zoo as *just some sort of reality*. The zoo is all they know. But the visitors at the zoo know that there's life outside of the zoo. And I know—and you will learn—that there's life outside of what you call *Jack's World* as well."

"But what about the *I doubt therefore I am* thing that I came up with? I'm doubting right now—more than ever, actually."

"Yes, you certainly exist. But *as what* you do not know—until now. You *seemed* to know all along what it is that you exist as, but your little catchphrase only concluded what followed *therefore* and nothing more."

"But how could I be a *real* dream character?" Ian asked.

"We're just as real as anyone."

"So that's what all this was about—all these nights of visiting with you—I was getting to know the *actual* world in which the worldly people live?"

"Yes. That's how you weave their dreams. Reality's tricky. If we get to know it, then we can affect people more effectively in their dream state."

"But it seems like there are still so many questions left unanswered. Like maybe I haven't grasped their reality like I'm supposed to," Ian noted, concerned.

"Yes, Ian. You have gained something so much more important than knowledge of *facts*. You have learned *how to think*. You have learned to take nothing for granted. You have learned that there is so much depth to reality. And just as importantly, you have learned what you don't know." I stopped talking for a moment. I stood, almost as if I were looking through Ian.

"Ian," his mother called from behind him.

He turned toward the call. His mother and father walked up the entryway stairs toward him on the front porch. "Ian, you will be amazing. You have really opened yourself up and challenged all that you know. You have confronted conclusions that scared you at first and have worked through them. Your world and the world of all those you affect will be so much brighter because of that. We will always be with you."

As Ian and his parents came together in an embrace, a bright light came from them. Ian turned his head away and felt a soft, warm glow come over his whole body. He turned to where they were and there was nothing. "I feel strangely whole. Happy," he said as he turned to me.

I smiled at him. "Those parents are your inner self. You created them—to deal with your fears and to seek answers to the questions you've had. No one in our world has parents—we're created in a different way. You should be aware that it was *you* who reasoned through all of those things. You're hardly conscious of ninety percent of what you know. You've picked up so much from all those books you have read. You just get overwhelmed by it and suppress it, and much of it only comes out in your dreams.

"As you'll see, Ian, because present-day Dream Weavers have been so successful, dreams really do become difficult to decipher from reality. I have been Weaving for a long time. It's time for me to retire. And now we have this manual finished. Once you start mentoring, your job will be exponentially easier having this. You really will be amazing.

"Come to think of it, I wonder how it is that *I* dream. Who weaves *my* dreams?" I paused, realizing my genuine confusion regarding this matter. "Regardless, you have been remarkable. You will be great. You will have such a strong effect on those whom you touch.

"Now it's time for a little nap. Or, is it time to wake up . . . ? Good luck, Ian. Good luck."

* * *

The Old Man lay down under the big oak tree in the shade and fell asleep. At least he *seemed* to be asleep. He lay there, strangely still in contrast to the subtle rustling of the leaves. He looked almost unnaturally peaceful, *very* restful. I wanted to run to him but my body wouldn't do it. As I stared at him, I became distracted by the feelings I had for the Old Man, and then distracted more so by all of this new information.

I felt a strange feeling of confidence. I was almost surprised at my lack of apprehension given all of this. I'd say that I was even a bit excited about what I'd just learned. *A world of subconsciouses.* And a book! A book about this great, amazing adventure I'd been on. Great, yes. *And* amazing. I suppose something can be amazing and not great and vice versa. This had definitely been both. I wonder what the author will call this book. I wonder if I have any say in it. If I create this dream, then I should get to create the title. Something simple, catchy. "The

Dream Weaver's Handbook." That'd be pretty good. I would read a book with that title. Or maybe "Jack and Ian's Guide to Reality." *My* name really should be in the title. I guess he could keep it simple—"The Dream Weaver," maybe—but they'd probably make him come up with some sort of subtitle for that.

I walked to the oak tree and picked an apple—an apple on an oak tree? Of course. The apple was purple. It seemed purple.

As I reached to pick the apple, I heard what sounded like Alexis' voice. "Are you sure you want one of those?" she asked, in her kind of silly tone. "They look a little rotten."

I turned and saw her standing with a red apple in her hand. She was smiling—a smile that was definitely a happy smile, but also one with a lot behind it. I was so happy to see her. Could *she* be a Dream Weaver?

"Ian, I am so happy to see you. I've just had the most amazing adventure. And I was worried that maybe you weren't," she paused, "I guess, just that maybe you *weren't*. I've been spending time with, well, with the Old Woman—at least that's what I call her. I have a feeling that explains the old man I've seen you with recently."

She paused, standing slightly pigeon-toed, ducking her head and almost wincing a little bit for fear that I had no clue what she was talking about.

"A red apple, eh?" I asked, to tease her a little bit. I was so happy to hear this, to see her. I was so overwhelmed with feelings that I felt like I was almost going to cry.

She smiled a big smile and shook her head happily, her pigtails bouncing back and forth.

"Wanna go make some dreams for a few people?" I asked. "I've got a lot of good ideas."

"I'd love to," she responded enthusiastically, as though her view of her lot in life had just become infinitely better. Mine had. "I have some pretty good ideas myself."

We hugged. We smiled. We took our two apples and walked down the middle of the street together. The sun shone on us and it seemed brighter than ever. It was as if I had been chained down in a dark room and the chains had just been released. I thought of that cave story the Old Man used to always tell me. I looked to the sky to soak in the sun. I looked at Alexis. She was looking at the sun too, and smiling. *This* could be a lot of fun.

Chapter 15

The Words After All Previous Words: Souls (Revisited) and Brains (Visited) . . . and Humans

Evidence shows that we do much less thinking than we believe we do—except, of course, when we think about it.

—Nassim Taleb

Two-thirds of what we see is behind our eyes.

—Chinese Proverb

What I felt now, staring at Alexis, caused me to smile almost against my will. Since our indoctrination as Dream Weavers, we had spent two years together weaving dreams for people, exploring our interests, and then sharing them with others as they slept. I suppose you could say we had been "working," though I finally started to understand the adage, "If you love what you do, you never work a day in your life."

But now, this moment sitting with her hand resting just beside mine so I could feel her little pinky, I felt like we were ready for something more. A next step. I sensed from her gaze that she reciprocated this. I could only compare my feelings to the awkward nervousness I felt around her three years ago from my lifelong secret crush on her.

"I'm ready to mentor, Ian," she said, in response to my telling smile, I suppose. "We'll never know *everything*—we can't wait around until that time or we'll never work with anyone. Our mentors didn't claim to know everything. Think about it—they were the perfect teachers: so knowledgeable about so many things, and so thoughtful in their questions for us and their challenging us, but also free to admit their lacking, to say, 'I don't know.' Can't we do that?" Her smile had turned serious, and I immediately felt like we could do that, like we could do anything, really.

> *"Good teaching is more a giving of right questions than a giving of right answers."*
>
> –Josef Albers

"How?" I asked sincerely, really wanting to know.

She tilted her head, nudging my attention toward a cozy-looking two-story home, surrounded by billowy oak trees. Against it rested a wooden ladder with a sign dangling from it that I couldn't make out from the distance. Alexis continued her nudging as though she were now leading this expedition. She reached back for my hand and smiled at me—I would pretty much have followed her anywhere at that point.

The lettering on the sign hanging from the ladder looked vaguely familiar, handwritten in felt pen, crisp lettering, all caps, just perfectly askew. It read: IAN AND ALEXIS with an arrow pointing up the ladder. It was signed, –TOM.

"Tom?" I asked her, as though she really had assumed the role of tour guide.

"Look closer," she whispered. It was an acronym, but I still didn't know anyone named or referred to as Tom.

"The," she paused, "Old . . . Man." My eyes teared uncontrollably the moment she said that—also the moment that I realized she was right. Emotion swelled in my chest—nothing like sadness. The sound of it conjured up so much on so many levels that it overwhelmed me. She wiped my eyes and kissed my cheek, and *I* now confidently led the way up the ladder. My heart beat both in reaction to the essence of The Old Man and in anticipation of the unknown that lay immediately ahead.

The smooth wooden rungs seemed familiar as I felt the impression of them melting into my hands and supporting my every step. I gripped the final wooden rung, perched against what appeared to be a window, though the other side seemed more like the back of a poster than a window shade.

Of course.

I climbed through the makeshift hole, reaching back to grasp Alexis' hand. I stood in a child's bedroom—splashed with colors and a ceiling of sky-blue and clouds painted above. A boy peered at me from under a comforter in his bed, quizzically yet unafraid, almost as though he were expecting us. Alexis made her way through the surreal entrance, and I watched the poster of a sky-blue-and-cloud-filled eye flap back into place, as if there were nothing extraordinary behind it. The boy's glare became friendly once Alexis came into view. Above his bed dangled a framed photo of what looked to be a graduation ceremony with the text, "Congratulations Connor. Spangler Middle School Graduation."

"So," I began without thinking, my voice cracking, "how do we know what's really there, Connor?" I surprised myself, though it felt somehow familiar as I recalled my first meeting with The Old Man years ago.

"Why does it matter?" Connor answered defiantly, remaining under the covers.

I frowned a bit, thoughtfully, and nodded turning to Alexis as if to suggest, "Great question. Why *does* it matter?", ready to return to our playground we call the Dream World.

"You're done?" she asked, raising her eyebrows at me. "Perspective, Ian. Perspective." She climbed onto the desk adjacent to the near wall and stood up. The wall behind her held a parody of an award, framed: "Certificate of Accomplishment For All Those Who Want To Show Others They Have Accomplished Something." Edgy.

I followed her lead, climbing onto the low dresser along the wall opposite his desk. "Try standing on your bed for a sec," I suggested. With us standing on the furniture, our heads near the sky-laden ceiling, maybe we seemed more intimidating, more legitimate. Connor slid out of his bed and stood up, showing off an unremarkable pair of terrycloth shorts and a cream-colored T-shirt emblazoned in green with, "No Something. Know Nothing." The shirt hung on his frame as though it were a size too big, though a size smaller would have been too small. He looked scrawny, yet oddly healthy. His straw-like light-brown hair fell down to his thick eyebrows, and he looked curiously mature for what I assumed was a fourteen-year-old.

"How does everything look up there?" I asked him.

"Different, I guess," he mumbled, still somewhat defiant.

"Do you like it?"

"It's fine. Just different."

I let the silence settle, resisting the temptation to look to Alexis for help (and for comfort).

"Well," he said with a tone of happy sheepishness, "I can see where the rubber ball went that I thought I had lost. So, I like that."

I nodded in response. Nothing more. To my surprise, he looked upward instead of downward, which was my inclination.

"I always thought there were actually different shades of blue in this painting," he shared. "But it's the same blue and the artist just made some of the clouds wispy instead of solid." He seemed happy with this insight as well. So at least he gained something, and I felt comfortable and ready to move on.

But he continued, "The braces on my bookshelf are actually quite amazing—I'd never noticed how they really held all that weight." I nodded and he continued, pointing at the globe near his bed, "And I never really noticed how close North America is to Russia. I always think of it as really far away 'cause that's how it is on maps or when I look at the globe from where I usually stand.

"And these springs in my bed now feel like actual springs. When I lie on my bed it just feels like one big spring. But with my foot I can feel the individual springs," he said, now standing on one foot. "The result of decreased surface area, I suppose."

> "The art of teaching is the art of assisting discovery."
> —Mark Van Doren

> "Philosophy could actually change your experience of the world . . . . Coming to see something in a wholly different way was like discovering a new thing."
> —Larissa MacFarquhar (*The New Yorker*) in interview with philosopher Patricia Churchland

I looked to Alexis to show off my ability to *teach without teaching*. I hopped off the dresser and asked him how he felt now, looking down at me.

"Different, again," he said, now more quick to respond. "Almost like I have some weird power over you. Like I could push you over if I wanted. And it's funny to look down at someone like this and see the top of their head instead of always looking up at the bottom of their chin. You look different to me, that's all." And with that, he sat down on his bed, and Alexis sat down on the table.

"So to answer your question," I said, confidently, "*that* is one reason 'it matters'— perspective. At the very least, you gain a new perspective. From that new perspective you may gain nothing more than just a new way of seeing things. Though you may learn something: where your ball is, where Russia is relative to other continents, the color of your ceiling, or how your bookshelf and your bed are constructed. You may get in touch with new feelings. And you may be better able to *empathize*—to see things from another's perspective, even if it is just from the perspective of someone a foot taller than you, as in this case."

"Okay. A new perspective. But we don't really care *that much* about perspective *out there*," he responded, pointing out his window. "I mean, we've pretty much got it all figured out. Perspective is like something you get from going to an art museum," he said, matter of factly, "or standing on your bed."

"Well, let's just go outside and see what we can see," I suggested, confident that I knew what we would see, that I could create what we would see.

It felt strange going down the ladder as a leader now instead of a follower. Connor followed much more eagerly than I would have expected—even though I remember being eager when in his shoes, I also remember a distinct feeling of trepidation that I didn't sense from Connor as he scurried down the ladder, shaking it as I neared the bottom.

Connor jumped to the ground, skipping the ladder's bottom three rungs. I greeted him with the first unsolved question I could think of, "So, when does a human being truly become a human being?"

"*This* is the question to show that we do *not* have it all figured out?" Connor asked, looking to Alexis as if showing off for her.

"What he means," she responded supportively, "is, 'When does a human entity get the same rights that all human beings have?' It's

---

Policy and Humanity

Roe v. Wade *(1973): Permitted an abortion up until the time of the fetus' "viability"—ability to live outside the womb—typically at 24–28 weeks. The Supreme Court ruled, "We need not resolve the difficult question of when life begins. When those trained in the respective disciplines of medicine, philosophy, and theology are unable to arrive at any consensus, the judiciary, at this point in the development of man's knowledge, is not in a position to speculate as to the answer."*

* * *

In 2007, President George Bush vetoed a bill that would have allowed for research on stem cells derived from five-day-old human embryos. He noted, "Each of these human embryos is a unique human life with inherent dignity and matchless value."

In 1987, a five-months-pregnant woman driving alone in the carpool lane in California was ticketed for not having more than one person in the car. The court overturned this based on her pregnancy, allowing that there were two people. In 2005 an eight-months-pregnant woman in Arizona was in the same situation, yet the court denied her claim based on a "common sense" definition of "person."

wrong to kill an innocent human walking down the street. So, *when* does it become wrong to kill that person?"

I thought back to my visit with Jeff to "We the People" and how tricky this situation really was. Alexis continued, "Currently, much policy assumes that at the moment of human conception, a soul appears or is injected and that entity then has rights. This affects conclusions relating to stem cell research, abortion, and cloning. It's actually very relevant *out here*," she said, waving her finger around to reference Connor's earlier mention of the "outer world."

"Doesn't that make sense?" Connor asked, as though she had just framed his own views. "Why can't the, um, the thing . . ."

"The zygote—"Alexis interjected, "the initial fertilized egg immediately following the meeting of the sperm with the egg during conception."

Connor smiled at her, "Yeah, the zygote. Why can't that get a soul the second it's made? Conceived."

"It *could*," I responded, "but conception isn't really an event—it's more like a process. So why don't you ask it?" I suggested, pointing to some very small creatures on a leaf that had fallen onto a bush from the adjacent tree, officially employing my powers as a Dream Weaver.

Connor looked at what appeared to be animated cartoon figures of sorts, nicely shaped, colorful, symmetrical—nothing at all like they were in *real life* but nicely formed caricatures (if I do say so myself).

Aristotle held that semen contained the soul-power which was then manifested in the full-grown human.

"Hi Connor," said the creature standing to the far left of the leaf, balanced on a one-and-only foot, with an oversized head. "I'm a human sperm. You can't see my soul, but it's tucked nicely in the middle of my enlarged head."

"Hi," Connor responded, strangely confidently, though also a bit uncertain of how to properly greet a talking spermatozoa.

"Hi Connor," the next in line said, this one more of a perfect sphere, "I'm a human egg. Though no one has really suggested that I have a soul, I do. It's in the exact middle of me, equidistant from all of my

A (Very) Brief Timeline of the Fertilization and Conception Process

1. *(0 hrs.) Before contact with sperm, the egg begins division into two cells ("meiosis").*
2. *(18 hrs.) The sperm fuses with the egg, forming a "zygote."*
3. *(30 hrs.) The zygote completes the first division of the fused cells ("mitosis").*
4. *(4 days) The cells continue dividing to form a spherically shaped "morula."*
5. *(5 days) A "blastocyst" forms, containing an inner cell mass of 50–200 cells. These cells are the* embryonic stem cells, *and all maintain the potential to become any of the 200 human cell types.*

edges. That's what keeps it so protected. No one can see souls, so no one knows it's really inside me!"

I turned to Alexis and whispered, "No one has suggested that human eggs contain the soul because all of the soul-theorists have been men, huh?"

She smiled at me, happy to see that I had actually learned something from our last excursion as trainees.

Next in line stood a slightly larger sphere, with a slightly deeper voice. "I'm a human egg that's actually gone through my second meiotic division, unlike this one next to me," it said, in an arrogant tone, addressing the sphere immediately to its right. "You've only had the first division so you can't fuse with a sperm. I have. And can. So I now have a soul."

"Not so fast," said the less-than-perfect globule to the right. "You are still capable of twinning." It shimmied a bit, as though proud of its age-related maturity.

"So?" responded the sphere.

"So you can't have a soul yet because you don't know if you'll end up being one, two, or even three eventual humans. If you have a soul now and then become twins, there would be a human walking around without a soul. Or two humans with half a soul. You at least need to make it to my developmental position to have a soul."

"Well," said the next object, now looking a bit like a tadpole though strangely more human. "I have bad news for all of you. You don't get your badge of humanity—your soul—until you reach my stage: the stage at which it is more likely than not that you will come to fruition."

The other four responded with a collective, "Huh?"

"First of all, most eggs do not become human beings to begin with. They're not even fertilized. No souls there. Either that, or every day there are like a gazillion deaths!

Timeline continued . . .
Twins and Survival

Identical twins occur when some of the cells resulting from the egg's first mitotic division are implanted. This often occurs after fertilization and as late as 5 days after.

* * *

Of every 100 eggs fertilized, 51 do not implant in the uterus and thus do not continue on to pregnancy.

Of the 49 that do implant, 16 naturally abort because of natural conditions.

Thus 33 of the 100 fertilized eggs continue naturally to full-term pregnancy.

You have no idea my son,
Your journey's just begun,
If you look with eyes
* wide open*
You realize the world
* wonders*
And you are not alone
        —Matt Bowen,
        "Beautiful Colors"

"And for those of you eggs lucky enough to meet a sperm, less than half of you will even get to go to the uterus where the real growth happens. Again, seems unlikely that all of these 'deaths' occur and no one does anything about it.

"And even then, if you do advance to the uterus, practically a third just don't make it. So out of every hundred sperm-and-egg meetings, only about 33 get to come out nine months later and do whatever it is you humans do *out there*. Or, should I say, whatever *we* humans do."

Connor stared at these five creatures, then looked at us as though almost through us. "So how do we know if we even have souls?" he asked, somewhat intrepidly. "And when we got them? And how clones get them? And if stem cells have them?

"And why do we make all of these mistakes in our understanding to begin with?"

I couldn't help feeling a little jealous of Connor at this point. It was like meeting someone who hadn't read an amazing book that I had read and who had the chance to read it for the first time. He was about to embark on a life-changing journey—one that I had been on—though I realized that I too was beginning a journey of sorts, all stemming from where I had already been.

I thought of how much I had learned from the Old Man that helped me to frame this very issue and the questions Connor asked. Not just the learning of facts, but of thinking—of *how* to think:

Knowledge—how we acquire knowledge and the shortcomings involved, especially regarding things like souls;

Science—how science works and frames much of what we know, providing a backdrop for topics like personhood and humanity;

Personal Identity—what it means for me to be *identical* not just with my "self" from yesterday, but with my "self" from *day one* . . . I always thought,

Souls: Afterlife, Sneezing, and eBay

The idea of a soul dates over 30,000 years as evidenced by Cro-Magnons bury-ing their dead with objects thought to be used in the afterlife.

Today, an "sPhone" is available in Taiwan: for $122, one can purchase a paper cell phone look-alike to be burned at one's funeral for use in the afterlife. Paper goods—including real paper money—are thought to be carried into the afterlife.

* * *

Sneezing was once thought of as an attempt for the soul to escape the body, or for the devil to enter. Pope Gregory I (c. 540 AD) introduced the term "God Bless You" as a way of preventing one from catching the bubonic plague. This would also help keep the soul in and the devil out. Scientists now argue that sneezing helps to alleviate irritation in the nose and to aid in expelling any germs.

* * *

In 2006, a man sold his soul on eBay for $504. For every $10, he agreed to spend one hour at a place of worship chosen by the winner. Following a bid-ding war between atheists and religious, an evangelical Christian organization won. Instead of spending the complete 50.4 hours in church, the "now soulless man" spent half in church and half writing about it on their website. He recently published a book titled I Sold My Soul on eBay.

You can't become something that you are.

If I truly *was* that zygote—that ball of cells from 18 years ago—then it did not *become* Ian, but it *was* Ian;

God—what different gods and religions and spiritual paradigms say about the soul, the spirit, and life and death, and what role that should play in our framework of ideas;

Heaps—how something as initially mundane as determining when a heap of sand became a heap now sheds light on determining the exact-ness of moral personhood in the *process* of conception;

Faith—what role non-logical methods of reasoning (faith, intuition, biases) play in the framing of reality;

Language—how important our language is in denoting reality, yet how very imperfect it is (and how tricky that is for us!);

Freewill—which forces determine our actions and thoughts and how these things are affected by society—advertisers, politicians, etc.—and our own biological foundation;

Ethics and Morality—once we take all this into account, how ought we to act on it?

I finally realized the true irony in the statement, "The more you know, the more you don't know." It was humbling, in a way, even if fully engaging and exciting in another. Before meeting Connor, I had again become somewhat complacent, as though I'd learned it all, graduating from my time with The Old Man. But I realized that, truly, my journey was just beginning. Again.

"To teach is to learn twice."

–Joseph Joubert

In teaching the very ideas that I had been taught, I began the process of relearning, of more concisely formulating my ideas. Of having to see once again the other side of issues and experience others' viewpoints. And it made me want to know even more.

I looked at Alexis, and I wanted to know more about her. I realized that this new part of my journey would involve an emotional journey as well, that I could apply all that I had learned not just to the "world" around me, but to the people around me, especially the one person that I care the most about.

I grabbed Alexis' hand and turned to Connor, "Thank you, Connor."

"Thank you?" he responded. "Thank *you*." He paused, thoughtfully. "But I don't feel like we're finished."

"We're not," I said, smiling at him. "You should rest now. Or go back to your room and just be," I said, not wanting to share too much with him. "When you," I paused to choose my words carefully, "When you *wake up*, share this with your parents. My guess is they will have more to share with you than I could."

"Don't you kind of need to stick around?" Alexis asked me knowingly. "Aren't you—more like, aren't *we*—trying to get this part of the journey into that new edition of 'Mr. Jack's' book? If so, someone's got to transcribe it all. And we're the only ones who know about it."

"Yeah, I suppose you're right. Let's see if we can get a view from the kitchen window." We both squeezed together between the trunk of a tree and the pinewood panelled wall of the home, allowing us to peer in through the slightly ajar kitchen window, letting the subtle breeze flow in.

I could see the back of an older man's head, sitting in the kitchen nook, sipping tea and reading a book. He wore an old flannel shirt and had short, grey, thinning hair. He looked up as he heard Connor's footsteps traipsing down the stairs.

"Morning Grandpa. I think we need to talk," Connor said, grabbing a bottle of water from the antique-style refrigerator.

"I agree," he responded in jest.

Connor looked somewhat surprised but continued, "Why haven't we ever talked about what a soul is. How we know if we have it. All that stuff. People just say *soul* over and over, but we never even talk about it."

"I'm more interested in talking about your other question first," his grandfather replied.

"Other question? What *other* question?"

"Why do we make all of these mistakes in our understanding to begin with?" he said, obviously quoting someone.

> *"Our minds are like inmates, captive to our biology; unless we manage a cunning escape."*
> –Nassim Taleb

"Oh yeah. But, um, how'd you know about that question?"

"Did you not ask it? Are you not interested?"

"No, I am. I mean, yes, I did ask it. But . . ."

"Never mind how I know about it. This question of yours is much more relevant and easier to answer. And it will shed light on many of the other questions you have."

Connor nodded, visibly perturbed but also interested in exploring the issue.

"Take that bottle of water there," his grandfather said, waving his finger at it as though it were something not to be touched. "Why do you drink that instead of the tap water from our sink?"

"Well, obviously it's cleaner. And it tastes better. But everyone knows that," Connor replied, taking a swig from the bottle and letting out an exaggerated "ahh" as he swallowed.

"Now, take a sip of my tap water here," his grandfather commanded. "How do you compare the two?"

"The bottled water is just crisper. Tastes pure, not gritty," Connor said, pointing to the photo of the snow-covered mountaintop on the label. "Like I'm drinking straight out of this fresh natural spring," he said as though he were mimicking an advertisement.

"It certainly appears that way, doesn't it?" his grandfather said, nodding. "But I filled

All in Your Head

In the 2003 series of Penn and Teller's television show, they visit an upscale restaurant that serves what patrons believe to be different brands of upscale bottled water from various places throughout the world. In fact, the water is all the same—filled from the hose behind the restaurant. The footage depicts diners reveling in the "different" tastes of each water, praising the water quality for exceeding that of tap water, and accepting the price of $4.99–$9.99.

Is It More "Pure"... ?

- *25–40% of bottled water (BW) is tap water (TW) from a municipal source;*
- *TW is more stringently regulated: 43 states have only one person regulating BW versus hundreds of federal staff assigned to TW regulation;*
- *1 in 3 bottled waters tested either violated state limits for arsenic or other cancer-causing chemicals, or had excessive amounts of bacteria such as E. coli (evidence of fecal matter).*

that bottle with tap water last night. That's why the cap wasn't sealed. The water in that bottle is exactly the *same* as the water in my glass here. Your brain just prompted you to insert that flavor into each water sample—to impart something to reality that wasn't even there.

"Your *wanting* the bottled water to taste better caused the water to taste better.

"So, there's one answer to your question: We believe we see things that we expect—and wish—were really there."

Connor ducked his head a bit as though he were embarrassed.

"What's worse, we act on this. People spend a considerable amount of money on bottled water that they could save and spend on something that actually made sense. Or they could donate it, or do whatever they wanted with it.

"And it turns out that bottled water is *no cleaner* than tap water. In fact, in many cases, tap water is more stringently regulated and cleaner than the water in the bottle. Either that, or the bottled water is literally taken from a municipal water supply—basically a large tap—which has already been paid for by the citizens through their taxes!

"Blue Gold"

In 2005 Americans consumed nearly eight billion gallons of bottled water, and global BW consumption exceeded 41 billion gallons, resulting in—creating— a $50 billion industry.

This required 2.7 million tons of plastic and resulted in considerable carbon dioxide emissions in the transport of the heavy substance.

"And on top of that, shipping all that very heavy water and then dealing with the millions of discarded plastic bottles takes an immense toll on the already fragile environment.

"All this because people *think* it's cleaner and tastes better. But it would be cheaper, more enjoyable, and even more convenient to just have one drinking container that you could simply reuse."

Connor tilted his head, "So . . ."

"So . . . ?" his grandfather encouraged.

"So our brain frames the world according to our wants?"

His grandfather nodded.

Connor continued, "And if we're not aware of this it can affect us in a negative way—

"We are the product."

Jean Kilbourne examines the dangers of advertising, noting that some companies spend more than $200 billion per year on it. In doing so, they often attempt to sell an image instead of a product. She discusses a slogan for the soft drink, Sprite ("Thirst Is Everything"): "The campaign is about nothing but image. Of course, what other way is there to sell sweetened, flavored carbonated water? If thirst is really everything, our best bet is water, and not high-priced bottled water either, such as Evian, which costs more than some champagne (no wonder that Evian backward spells 'naive')."

Another pitfall of advertising is summarized nicely by the title of Jon Spoelstra's 1997 book: Ice to the Eskimos: How to Market a Product Nobody Wants.

---

wasting our money, doing things that are bad for us, doing things that are bad for the environment."

"Exactly. This whole industry is frighteningly like that seemingly silly—though here very apt—analogy of *selling ice to Eskimos*. Perfectly marketed. Or *im*perfectly marketed, I'd say. Anyone can put a sticker of a glacier on a bottle—doesn't mean it has anything to do with the product."

Connor smiled that seeing-beyond-the-curtain sort of smile. "So there are other things like this, though?" he asked. "I mean, you said this would help with the soul question, right?"

"It will help in that it will illuminate the means by which you—and all people—go about framing reality. Just remember, though: *Thinking something doesn't make it so*. If you think the earth is one shape, and someone else believes it to be another, that doesn't affect the actual shape of the earth.

"Having a great imagination will steed you well and allow you to more creatively and playfully interact with the world. But don't forget to turn your imagination off sometimes so you don't miss out on the real stuff. You need that imagination to enjoy a good film, but I wouldn't want you to continue your suspension of disbelief when you left the theater, thinking that you could actually fly."

> *"It is by logic we prove, it is by intuition that we discover."*
> –Henri Poincaré, French mathematician, physicist, and philosopher of science

Connor nodded a satisfied nod. "So what else, then? What else?"

"My favorite—or should I say my *least* favorite—are the psychic tricksters who take money from people and then direct their actions based on no sound reasoning, no evidence whatsoever. All based on the fragility—and the gullibility—of humans."

"I see a billion dollars in our future."

The dial-a-psychic industry brings in more than $1 billon per year. The more popular psychics and "speakers to the dead" demand $1,000 for a 30-minute consultation. Since 1964, paranormal researcher James Randi has offered $1 million to anyone who can prove any sort of paranormal powers. To date, none have passed.

Biologist Richard Dawkins writes of astrology that it is, "an insult to the science of psychology and the richness of human personality." Elsewhere he notes, "It's been suggested that if the supernaturalists really had the powers they claim, they'd win the lottery every week. I prefer to point out that they could also win a Nobel Prize for discovering fundamental physical forces hitherto unknown to science. Either way, why are they wasting their talents doing party turns on television?"

"But if people want to believe that, why shouldn't they? I mean if it makes them feel better, why is it so bad?" Connor asked.

Scientific American columnist and Skeptic magazine editor Michael Shermer explains that psychics are, "Unethical and dangerous [because] they are not helping anyone in what they are doing. They are simply preying on the emotions of grieving people. As all loss, death, and grief counselors know, the best way to deal with death is to face it head on. Death is a part of life, and pretending that the dead are gathering in a television studio in New York to talk twaddle with a former ballroom-dance instructor is an insult to the intelligence and humanity of the living."

"Your question is well-framed in one sense, son. But I think most people would agree there is some harm done. In the same way as the bottled water fiasco, but in a deeper sense, much much worse."

"Worse?"

"Yes. First of all, the amount of money spent per user is much greater. But in this case, people's lives are being directed, they are being told what life choices to make, they are given fraudulent solutions to real problems, and they are given false hopes.

"There is no evidence whatsoever that the alignment of the stars has anything to do with a person's love life, their job, or anything of that nature.

"Likewise, there is no correlation between the lines on your palms and any other facet of your life.

"Nor do we have any confirmation that psychics can speak to dead spirits in any way. Actually, all of the evidence points to the contrary.

"But, as you remember, people hear what they *want* to hear. Believe what they *want* to believe. Imagine how badly you wanted to like bottled water more than tap water."

"Not *that* badly."

"Exactly. And it *still* worked. Now imagine that you lose someone close to you, someone you deeply loved. And in your grieving you give someone $500, and they tell you they can see your dearly departed standing behind you and they can speak to them. Wouldn't you want that?"

Connor nodded solemnly, as if thinking about someone he had lost, or would lose.

"But these people are just using simple statistics and knowledge of basic psychology. They speak to a room of 20 grieving people, for example, and ask who has lost someone recently with an initial J, or M, let's say. Two very popular initials, by the way.

"Five people raise their hands.

"He will tell those five that he sees these dead spirits. That it looks like one of them was an older gentleman who had some interest in sports.

"The odds that one of the five is a man is high and the odds that he had some interest in sports—played it, watched it, had children who played, etc.—is even higher.

"What people in this emotional state don't realize, though, is three things: The psychic is speaking in very general terms, the psychic is wrong more often than they're right but that goes unnoticed because of the bias we have already mentioned, and the psychic is *asking questions*. They always ask questions. But they are supposed to be *telling* me the future or what my dead relatives are saying, not *asking* me.

Shermer notes, *"Anyone can talk to the dead. It's getting them to talk back that's the hard part."*

He explains that psychics appear to succeed only because they employ three "reading" techniques:

1. *Cold—Ask general questions and allow subjects to provide the answers. For example, ask a group at a reading, "I'm getting a P-name, who is this? They are holding something red, what is this?" and one may answer, "My father Paul died. He had a red handkerchief."*

2. *Warm—Make general guesses based on the subject's cues and body language, such as jewelry or their reaction to guesses. The subjects tend to ignore wrong guesses and focus on correct ones.*

3. *Hot—Obtain information about subjects by planting people in the audience, through surveys, etc.*

A newspaper writer alleviated his boredom by writing the horoscope: "All the sorrows of yesteryear are as nothing compared with what will befall you today." Following the newspaper office's jammed phone lines with concerned callers, he was subsequently fired.

In 1999, "Magnet Therapy" grossed over a billion dollars worldwide. Yet, as physician Bruce Flamm explains, nothing in the human body is affected by magnetic fields. If it were then, "people might explode or be flung across the room when exposed to the extraordinarily powerful magnetic field of a MRI scan." An intensive study concluded it to be "useless."

As "Penn & Teller" illustrate, some subjects respond favorably to demagnetized magnets, substantiating the notion that the effects are merely mental.

"Anyway, when do you ever see a horoscope that tells someone something negative? Can you imagine getting the newspaper and seeing that all Scorpios will have a miserable month, that they have no romance in their lives, and they will get fired from their jobs?

"Or imagine seeing the headline, Psychic wrongly predicts a hurricane in Florida? Psychics predict hurricanes every day—what would be amazing is if they were never right, not that they are right sometimes."

Connor took a deep breath as though it were sinking in.

"I believe that all of this is what leads to the pseudo-success of so-called 'alternative medicine.' There's a reason they call it 'alternative,' you know? It's an alternative to what works."

"But if it works then it works, right?" Connor asked.

"I'm curious as to what you mean by 'works,' Connor. People waiving magnets over their body when there is nothing a magnet could do to one's body 'works' in one sense: it makes them feel better. But it does nothing to the body. Bathing in magic water makes you feel better and I'm sure one in a million people will have their cancer disappear, but that same cure-rate exists for people who do nothing at all. Sometimes cancer goes away.

"If you take lots of alternative herbs to cure your cold then your cold goes away after a few days. But colds last an average of five days to begin with. Colds go away."

Connor smiled and his grandfather summarized, "It works because you think it will work. You don't have to spend thousands of dollars on it in the first place. You don't have to waste your time and your energy chasing a chimera. You can do it yourself. Here's what I think should be on the market. Actually, you and I should look into this because it would be cheap—the only ingredients in these would be sugar and maybe some food dye to make it all look magical:

Outside of the Natural World

–*In 2006, a 36-year-old woman paid a New York psychic $75 for meditative candles, then bought her a $20,000 watch to "reset time" and gave her, in total, $220,000 to help remove curses.*

–*Following £15,000 ($30,000) of work on a building property in St. Fillans, Perthshire, in 2005, builders were ordered by the community council to cease working because they would disrupt fairies that lived under a nearby rock.*

–*September of 2007: A Nepal Airlines jet experienced technical difficulties before takeoff, and so two goats were brought in and sacrificed in its presence.*

–*Powdered rhinoceros horn is still used as an aphrodisiac for the mere reason that it appears slightly phallic.*

–*Health and Corporeal Well-being Pill*. Very potent. Take one in the morning and consume *at least* eight 12-ounce glasses of water and six servings of fresh vegetables to aid digestion. Allow a full eight hours of rest daily.

–*All-Natural Muscle Enhancer*. Take *two* of the "Health and Corporal Well-being Pill" daily. Follow the same instructions. *Warning*: Involve yourself in at least one hour every other day of an intensive weight-training program in order to help pills absorb into muscle tissue, otherwise the affects are negligible.

–*Psychical Happiness and Cosmic Welfare Serum*. Consume twice daily. Within one hour of consumption, complete at least one "random act of kindness." Each week spend three hours at a charity of your choice. This aids serum dispersion optimally throughout the brain and body.

–*Enhanced Personal Growth Body Rub*. Does not work in patient's native country; requires that you travel, see other countries, meet people from different cultures. It reacts negatively with television signals, and thus you will be required to stay 20 yards away from any functioning television.

–*Deep Interpersonal Connection Magic Grain*. Pinch the magic grain tightly between the index finger and thumb of the off-hand while simultaneously looking a loved one in the eye and saying, "I love you," or, "I care about you."

Connor smiled, laughing to himself, and nodded in approval.

> "*The danger to society is not merely that it should believe wrong things, though that is great enough; but that it should . . . lose the habit of testing things and inquiring into them, for then it must sink back into savagery.*"
>
> –William Clifford
> *The Ethics of Belief*

Nassim Taleb explains in his book, Black Swans, *that our over-reliance on generalizations causes us to be unnecessarily surprised by anomalous events. (His reference of black swans can be explored in chapter 3 of this book.) He concludes his book:*

"a. *I can't do anything to stop the sun from nonrising tomorrow (no matter how hard I try)*

b. *I can't do anything about whether or not there is an afterlife*

c. *I can't do anything about Martians or demons taking hold of my brain.*

But I have plenty of ways to avoid being a sucker.*"

His grandfather took much more of a shotgun-approach than I remembered my parents— or, should I say the *embodiment of my parents*—taking, though his points were all quite powerful and serious. I imagined that Jack would have fun plugging in all of those side boxes for all of these.

"People are just neurologically wired for confirmation, Connor. Two people can hear the same set of facts and make them fit wholly different worldviews.

"In addition, we all have this natural inclination to simplify the world around us. To force the universe into categories. To simplify the chaos and frame it in bite-sized chunks so we can more easily deal with it.

"These sorts of biases can be really helpful, almost necessary. But that doesn't mean that they frame the world as it really is. They're just another tool to help us navigate our way around.

"You don't want to confuse your little onboard navigational system . . ." he said, pausing.

"My brain?" Connor suggested.

His grandfather nodded and continued, ". . . with the terrain in which that system is navigating.

"This is where that distinction you mentioned was important—the *out there* that you were waving your finger about."

Distaste for Chaos and Randomness

One of the major pitfalls—and at times, skills—of human reasoning is our inclination to categorize in order to decrease natural randomness. Sir Francis Bacon writes, "The human understanding supposes a greater degree of order...in things than it really finds."

* * *

Taleb writes, "Categorizing is necessary for humans, but it becomes pathological when the category is seen as definitive, preventing people from considering the fuzziness of boundaries, let alone revising their categories."

He continues, "The same condition that makes us simplify pushes us to think that the world is less random than it actually is."

Connor smiled as though he had made a good distinction, though unbeknown to him.

"And all of these biases are not just manifested by your *nature*. There's a lot of societal *nurturing* going on as well. Though I'm not sure *nurturing* is the right word here."

"It's kind of overwhelming, grandpa. Doesn't paint a very nice picture of us."

"Well, there's something to be gained from all of this, you know. Something quite positive."

Connor raised his eyebrows in anticipation.

"I personally find it kind of exciting. This knowing that the world around us is so complex, so fascinating. And that understanding all of this can increase awareness. Your awareness that you, Connor, are biased toward confirmation. That you come pre-programmed with biological tendencies. That your own society biases you. That you are biased against some people and toward others. And that you can do something about it."

"Biased toward people?"

"Yes. Biased toward yourself, for one. And toward whatever the current societal standards demand of you. It's hard to escape. The only real escape being that you recognize it and then try to do something about it. It's the *knowing* and the *doing* that are important here.

"Ignorance is the root and stem of all evil."

–Plato (whose real name was Aristocles; named Plato, meaning "broad," likely for his broad shoulders.)

How Biased Are We?

Studies show biases on many levels:

1. *Attractive children are more likely to be seat-buckled in a car.*
2. *When black applicants are interviewed by a Caucasian (in comparison with Caucasian applicants), interviews ended 25% earlier, the interviewer sat further away and made 50% more speaking errors.*
3. *When a subject believes that the woman on the phone is more attractive, the subject assesses the woman as speaking more warmly than if she were deemed unattractive.*
4. *When scientific hiring proposals are viewed "blindly" (with no names), men and women are equally hired versus when gender-specific names are included on the same proposals, in which case men are disproportionately hired.*
5. *When asked who will go to heaven, 62% checked Michael Jordan, 78% Mother Theresa, and 82% "Person filling out this form."*

Cognitive Behavioral Therapy (CBT)

A recent form of psychotherapy, CBT has been empirically shown to reduce mild depression, anxiety, and other mood disorders. It is based on the notion that many disorders result from irrationally held beliefs, negatively-biased thinking or improper methods of framing one's world-view. In CBT, the therapist helps the patient to reframe their illogical or negative beliefs in a logically consistent manner that helps them view their situation in a more positive, consistent light, thus alleviating any dissonance or negativity that may cause depression or anxiety.

Never-Ending Pursuit of Happiness

Economist Richard Easterlin illustrates what is called the hedonic treadmill. *A study asked people to note items on a list that they owned and then to designate items they wanted. They conducted the study 16 years later with the same group of people. At both times people owned 2.5 items fewer than they wanted—as they accumulated more, they wanted more.*

"The alternative—complete ignorance—is saddening. Selfish, even. *Not* knowing about all of this. You'd be like a puppet. A slave of sorts. A detriment to yourself and all those harmed as a result.

"And I hate to admit it for some reason, but all of this gives credence to one of those little life-slogans I typically don't care for. But here, it's really true. *The glass is half-full.* You really do have control over how you frame your own worldview and your place in it. Confirmation bias comes into play here as well—you'll hear someone say that they're having a bad day and then all the traffic lights were red and more people than usual cut them off. But very often, they're just clued in to the negative: They're counting the hits—red lights—and ignoring the misses—green lights—in order to show to themselves that the world has somehow conspired against them on that day.

"In a sense, you can choose how you interact with the world. It's not what you have but how you look at it that matters. This is not to say that you can *change* the world just by looking at it, and it does take a lot of work. But, perspective matters."

He rustled Connor's already messy hair and got up, the conversation having gone full circle. Connor stared out the window right at us, but with no reaction at all. As if we weren't even there. Or as if he weren't even awake . . .

The "First" Excursion—The Author Authors

Alexis turned to me and smiled. "Pretty insightful," she said, to fill the void of our silence. I didn't know what to expect from it, though I certainly agreed with her caricature.

"Much more psychological than I remember my training being," I responded. "But all pretty relevant. I mean, that really does play a major part in how we view reality. And then most of us go on assuming that what we take to be reality actually *is* reality."

She smiled back, asking playfully, "So now what?"

"Well, the standard has already been set. Aren't we supposed to go create a dream for someone and catalog it so Jack can finish the chapter? Isn't that how all the other chapters are done?"

Her playful smile now appeared more mischievous. "But now that we know we're in control, why don't we take control? Do something different. Put him on the spot, maybe."

"Put Jack on the spot?"

"Let the last part of this chapter be from him. Let's see what he has to say. He's been looking in on us all this time. Plus, I bet he'd like it. A chance to finally write in his own voice."

Ian grinned at Alexis, and they gazed off into the distance, as if looking at something—or someone. He put his arm around her and walked off, looking over his shoulder and smiling.

* * *

I welcome this opportunity given to me by Ian and Alexis. "Welcome" is perhaps too weak—I embrace it. (Though I feel a bit slighted as I thus forfeit the chance to see what they would have created themselves!)

While on my book tour for the original edition of this book, I focused on the topic of the soul and its relation to four areas: morality, personhood, science, and the self. This part of the experience—having the opportunity to discuss these topics with strangers, people of all ages, on radio and television shows, and with my students, my athletes, my friends—turned out to be the real gift of being an author. I only wish I had been encouraged to do so earlier in life, as such discussions didn't occur in my religious upbringing nor very often while studying human biology at Stanford. Only within the mind-nurturing discipline of philosophy did it really flourish.

Not surprisingly, the most common responses from readers were split between, "I can't believe I never really considered this all," and, simply, "Wow, this is actually cool!" This sentiment accurately frames my own for the most part (minus the "actually" because I knew it was "cool" already).

But it is here that I diverge somewhat from the great poet Keats who wrote, "Philosophy will clip an Angel's wings, Conquer all mysteries . . . Unweave a rainbow." While I agree that philosophy likely eliminates angels from the realm of reality (thus clipping any supposed appendages to begin with), this in no way devalues our own existence nor even removes the meaning of the metaphorical adjective, *angelic*. Ironically, it makes it all the more powerful. To continue in an allegorical vein, I very much celebrate Eve's apple of knowledge as coaxed by the talking serpent of the human mind in all of its curiosity and quest for wonder. And to further wax poetic, I welcome the mysteries hidden within Pandora's Box. I recognize that they may be fearful and unknown, though also believe that this is something we can handle— that we shouldn't sell ourselves short.

Were I alive at the time of the paradigm-shifting Copernican Revolution, I would like to think that I could have celebrated the shift and not condemned it. While it may have been an affront to my ego—and to the hubris of humanity—I imagine I would have preferred it to the falsities of the geocentric story being sold. And I appreciate the advance of knowledge in showing that my neighbor's sneeze is not an attempt to thwart invading demons nor to expel the ghostly soul dwelling within, but is simply the body's way of helping in our quest for health. (I will still "bless" them and even those around them—anything that provides an opportunity to connect on *that* level.) And if I had grown up believing one could communicate with the dead, I would like to think that I would embrace a thinker (a.k.a. "skeptic") who had the wherewithal to expose their fraudulence: That while I missed out on speaking to my deceased grandparents, I gained much more. (This, in contrast to some who have cursed the skeptic who proves psychic tricksters to be nothing more than well-studied magicians who might as well be sawing people in half.)

And this is where I am today: with a sense of a celebration of the mundane. Not the mundane of small talk about weather patterns or the reality show *du jour*, but the *seemingly* mundane—the leaf that falls and is registered as green by my limited sensory receptors, captured by a language we recognize as merely a tool we use to map the terrain we have come to inhabit as a gift from our ancestors and of those who begot them. Within this contextual framework, it is a celebration of the complexities—the real magic of being human.

The imagination that good thinking requires reveals the boundless possibilities of things that *could* be; but the rigor that good thinking requires reveals the uniquely singular reality—that I am doing this one thing, right now, right here.

This process of worldly investigation can result in something daunting: not just that souls might not exist or that we're not the center of creation, but something more personally substantial—that I don't know everything. Worse (or better?), that I *cannot* know everything. It instills a sense of humility that I did not discern from any other venture and demands a sense of open-mindedness that I lacked before engaging in such inquiry. It provides a platform from which the depth of the landscape is simply marvelous, for lack of any better word.

That the feelings of love coincide with a certain rush of chemicals in the brain does not diminish the power of love in any way. It only illuminates it, if anything. That the soul is not needed in order to move my arm or to feel happy does not dampen the simple (yet amazingly complex) act of motion, or feelings of euphoria. That I am often compelled by forces outside of my immediate control—be they nature- or nurture-driven—only makes the forks in the road all that much more profound and enticing. That there is an innate sense of moral virtue in humans which is not inscribed on any tablet or list of rules only provides hope, not despair.

So, as I sit around the table with my family and other loved ones, I am humbled by what I do not know: if there is an afterlife, exactly how we got here, if the planet will be spinning tomorrow. But I can consciously recognize the trillions of things that occurred to allow us to be there at that moment, looking each other in the eye and sharing the here and the now. Heaped upon that are the reverberations in the air that we call music stirring newfangled thoughts and emotion, the taste of the food, the color of a flower, and the shade created by a tree blocking the way of the fiery sun hung perfectly in the sky—it really does cause me to catch my breath and is far more than I could ever want from existence.

It is with this overwhelming sense of awe that I move forward in pursuit of more. And just as Ian develops the desire to turn that lens inward, so do I. It is another equally enticing and frightful venture: a quest for knowledge in the face of realizations that may be less than ideal. To borrow a line from my previous book, "Learning about what you think teaches you something about who you are, for in many ways we are what we think."

This entire process gives me the confidence that, when I close my eyes and honestly "look" at what I believe, I know that those beliefs rest on a foundation that is earned. And I can remain humble, while celebrating the fruits of my own dreams that have been woven—and unwoven—and provide a foundation for authentic being.

JACK BOWEN
Menlo Park, California, February 2008

Reading Group Discussion Questions

Prologue and Note from the Old Man

1. Do you agree with the phrase, "Ignorance is bliss"? What would be an example of something that you could know that you'd rather not? What would be an example of something that you should know that you don't?

   Would you want to know:
   - Your exact date of death? (If you answered "no" then how would you answer: "If you had a terminal disease?")
   - If you were actually liked by others for reasons unknown to you (i.e., your social status, job connections, physical appearance, etc.)
   - If God exists?
   - How humans and the universe were created/came to exist?
   - If you lived in a false reality that was actually much more grim than it appears? (i.e., the movies *The Matrix* or *The Truman Show*.)

2. The Old Man uses the words "domesticated" and "indoctrinated" when referring to Ian's education. Is there a negative connotation to that? What are the negative aspects of education as we know it today?

3. What value do you see, if any, in asking a question yet not coming up with a satisfactory answer?

4. If C. S. Lewis is right when he writes, "Friendship is unnecessary, like philosophy . . . it has no survival value; rather it is one of those things that give value to survival," what *are* the necessary components of life? What else "gives value to survival"?

5. How would your view of life change if you . . . :
   a. were sentenced (wrongly, of course) to 5 years in prison, 25 years, or life?
   b. were told that you have one year to live? Were paralyzed?
   c. won a million dollars? Lost all your money?

    d. found out that the end of the world was going to occur in the next 5 years?

6. What if you were told each of the things separately, and then told a week later that this was not the case (e.g., there was a mistake in the records, you were miraculously healed, etc.)?

Chapter 1: Knowledge

1. Can you distinguish between your dream state and waking state? If so, how? Have you ever confused the two (i.e., not being sure if something happened in a dream or while awake)?

2. Is there anything that you are completely certain about? How important is complete certainty (i.e., the inability to doubt) in your claiming to know something?

3. Is one level of magnification in the table-example closer to the *real* table than another? Could it be true that the table is *both* solid *and* primarily empty space? How so? Is the function of the table or usefulness of the term "table" important in determining the real table? Explain.

4. If we cannot know whether our point of view is the same as another's (i.e., our green could be another's red), what relevance does that have? Is it counterintuitive to think that an object's color is "in" you versus in the object? What about the sound of something being "in" you, or the sweetness?

5. What is the moral of "What Really *Really* Happened"? Did Ian finally "get it right"—does he see the event from a purely objective point of view? What is the significance of Jeff's disagreement? How might the lessons from this story apply to something like a court case in which witness testimony is often used as evidence?

Chapter 2: Self, Mind, Soul

1. Do you seem to have more than one "self"? Are you different in an interview or a classroom than you are around your friends? Is this a problem for your identity? Does this mean that sometimes you're not "real" or "true to yourself"? What is essential to your *self*? What factors might interfere with you *knowing* your real self?

2. How does plastic surgery play into the personal identity discussion? In what ways could it alter one's identity?

3. If we do have a mind, what function does it serve? How would it be different from the brain? From the soul? If the mind were just a concept—like the center of gravity—used to help us explain things, would that lessen its importance for you? Why or why not?

4. If humans do have souls, at what point in their conception do they acquire them (for example, Aristotle believed it to be 40–90 days after a fetus is conceived)? And when, evolutionarily, did humans acquire them?

5. How would your existence be different if you couldn't remember your past experiences? If you couldn't plan for the future? Researchers believe that in the near future, they will be able to erase memories and create new ones. Would you want this? If so, to what extent? Would this change your identity?

6. If we define "mental states" as purely behavioral, then could computers *have* mental states? For example, if *pain* is just a response to something that is harmful or damaging for the organism, then could a computer feel pain?

7. Could something like *love* really be reduced to the physical brain, chemicals, evolution, etc.? If so, would that change your view of love in any way?

8. If we don't have a soul, would an afterlife still be possible?

9. What other organisms have souls? Chimpanzees? Dogs? Ants? Cells?

10. What would necessitate a computer being conscious? Could a computer be sarcastic? Would it be possible for a computer to turn against humans? What ethical concerns might there be regarding artificial intelligence, such as robots in wartime, or hackers using computers wrongly?

11. If we develop the ability to download your entire consciousness into a computer and save a copy of it, would that interest you? Would you consider that as extending your life?

12. What are your criteria for personhood? Is the being who is transferred from tube to tube the *same* person as before the transfer? Which of the following beings in "What's in a Name?" are persons (or which should have moral rights?):

    a. talking chimpanzee

    b. human clones

    c. man with mechanical/electrical brain

  d. human-like robot

  e. man constructed from the parts of 317 people

  f. human-like alien

  g. a mouse/human chimera (mix of both)

13. In "What's In a Name?" the doctor mentions "Playing God." What does this constitute? *Any* scientific advancement? Birth control? Cloning? Cryogenics? In what sense is "Playing God" a negative thing?

14. You have a concept of how people see you. But others inevitably see you differently than you imagine. This is the case with how you view others as well. Does this realization change your interaction with another person?

15. What happens to your "self" when:
 • you sleep and dream?
 • you're under hypnosis? Under anesthetic?
 • someone has Multiple Personality Disorder?

What is it to be the same "self" at age 5, 25, and 80? What about being the same self as you were as a 9-month-old fetus? A 3-month-old fetus? A zygote? Were "you" ever a zygote?

Chapter 3: Science

1. How does your paradigm affect who you are and what you see? Think of what you consider fashionable, art, your relationships, truth, etc. How about paradigms of medicine, such as Eastern versus Western?

2. If scientific theories are useful in explaining the universe, would it matter if they were not true?

3. Do you agree that we would see the world differently if we spoke a completely different language? How so? On the other hand, do you think language captures the world as it really is? Can you describe everything in words? How about: Feelings of anger? Being in love? What a beautiful landscape looks like?

4. If you don't have a word to describe something, can you experience that thing? Dogs don't have our language—can they experience jealousy?

5. How much testing would be "enough" testing to determine that there is no life anywhere other than on Earth? Could we ever know this?

6. Does knowledge of how science works enhance or detract from your view of science?

7. Should science progress as far as possible? Are there any ethical ramifications (e.g., cloning; atom bomb; etc.)?

8. A "miracle" is often defined as a phenomenon that goes against scientific theory. (Can you come up with a more precise definition?) Given that definition, can a scientist consistently believe in miracles? Why/why not?

Chapter 4: The Liar, Motion, and a "Surprise"

1. In what way is it meaningless to say, "I know what I'm thinking" as Wittgenstein suggests? How does it differ from saying, "I know what you are thinking"? Elsewhere, Wittgenstein argues that one cannot correctly identify the same sensation (such as a pain) repeatedly due to this problem of self-reference. Given that, what problems might you encounter when you try to know yourself?

2. If logic and math lead to paradoxes like the "Liar" and show that motion is impossible, what does that tell us about these two modes of thought?

3. Does it seem that, theoretically at least, you could still divide a Planck Length (the smallest length known)? If so, what implications would that have? If no, why not?

4. How do you respond to the issues presented in "Silent Lonesome Tree" that argue for and against a falling tree making a noise when no one is there?

5. Is silence possible? If so, does that support or oppose the notion that the "lonesome tree" makes a noise? If silence is not possible, what does this mean? When someone blows a dog whistle and no humans (or dogs) hear it, does it make a noise?

6. How do you define "sound"? The deaf person in the story claims that he "heard" the airplane—is this a good definition of "hearing"? How much does your definition of "sound" affect your answer to the "Lonesome Tree" question?

Chapter 5: God

1. What is the relevance of the comic quoted before the chapter: "I'll have to believe it to see it"?

2. Can God *hope* that we act or believe a certain way? How can an all-knowing entity have faith or hopes, given that one must be uncertain in order to have faith or hope?

3. Do you agree that religion is an "opiate" (sedative) for the masses, as Marx stated? If so, in what way? If it were, in what ways would it be a good or a bad thing?

4. Is the analogy of the watch in relation to the creation of the universe a good one? Why or why not?

5. The response to Dorothy in the epigram from the "Wizard of Oz" is, "You're wasting my time." Is it reasonable to try to rationalize about something that is infinitely powerful such as God? If it isn't, then why would God create humans to be such rational creatures?

6. Regarding Anselm's proof:
   - Can you conceive of a perfect being?
   - Have you ever experienced anything perfect? If not, do you think it is possible to experience perfection? Can we even conceive of perfection? If not, how can we know it? If we can, when/how?
   - Do you think that everything that exists is somehow flawed? If so, then how would this relate to God's existence?
   - Does being perfect require existing? Can something be perfect yet not exist? What would that mean?

7. Did the man in the woods with the watch use it incorrectly? What relation does *purpose* have to *meaning*? Can a thing have one without the other? Does this distinction help you address the broad question of the meaning of life? How would the meaning of life be different if you never died?

8. Imagine both scenarios:
   a. God exists, or, God doesn't exist.
   b. God created the universe, or, God did not create it.

   How would each affect your view of the meaning and purpose of life?

Chapter 6: Evil

1. What is the significance of Einstein's quote, "God doesn't play dice?"

2. Reread Dostoevsky's quote at the beginning of the chapter—how can we establish a sense of morality (right and wrong) if it doesn't come from God? If there were no humans would there be evil? Would there be morality?

3. Given that God does exist, must He be good? Could a being like God create the universe yet not be good? And how would we know?

4. Looking back on any "bad" event in your life, are you ever thankful in a way for its positive long-term effects? What "evils" do you think are unnecessary? Long classes? Work? Pain? Death?

5. Would it be "hell" if *everything* went perfectly all the time? After trillions of years of nothing but A+'s on exams, never losing any game, dating whomever you want, etc., would you get bored? Does a "perfect" place like the popular conception of heaven (no sadness, challenges, losing, rejection, etc.) sound good? If so, why? If not, what would you change?

6. Camus writes that Sisyphus should be happy. Would you be happy given his fate?

7. Think of something you value, for example, the music performed by a world-class violinist. Do you value this solely intrinsically (i.e., just because it sounds nice) or is there something more (i.e., respect for the violinist's dedication, uniqueness, etc)? Would you hold the violinist and his music in the same regard if *everyone* could play at that level without ever practicing? Would you assign greater value to the ability to walk upright if only one percent of humans could do it?

8. If you had never experienced any smell that you currently think is "bad," then would the current "good" smells still be good? Would the "least good" smells become bad? What about the reverse: if you'd never experienced anything you currently think smells good, would your current bad smells become good? How would your answer to this compare to the previous one about the "goodness" of a violinist?

9. Some believers say that God is unknowable. If this is so, then what would they believe in?

10. How could someone argue that 200,000 dead from a tsunami is consistent with an all-loving god? What about a person (or even a deer as the dad suggests) burning to death unknown to anyone else?

Chapter 7: Going East

1. Is it realistic to eliminate all desires? The desire for money? For food? For life? Is this humanly possible? What could be the downside of eliminating all desire?

2. Take a moment and think of one specific desire that you have—maybe a desire for something tangible (like a car) or maybe for a relationship, an education, or even a craving you have (chocolate, a cigarette, etc.). How might your *pursuit* of that desire result in something negative? How might your *obtaining* that desire result in something negative? Is it possible for the cycle of desires to end—that once you get something, you stop wanting more?

3. Now think about where that desire (from question 2) stems from—is this something that *you* want, or is this desire caused externally, maybe by advertisements, your parents, your friends, society? Is it possible to determine this?

4. Before we had certain words (e.g., soul, love, infinity) would it be possible to still experience their concepts? Can you currently feel something that does not match any known word? How would your thinking be different if you were born and grew up on a deserted island?

5. Try to clear your mind so that you think nothing—it will likely take a quiet place where you feel safe and may take some practice. When you try this, do you succeed? If not, what prevents you?

6. In the second half of the chapter, the father presents the stoic approach—relying purely on logic and reason and eschewing passion and intuition. What pitfalls/downsides do you find in this approach? What benefits do you find? How important is intuition/passion to knowing your self and the world around you?

7. Can you imagine what it would be like with no universe? Can you imagine "nothing"? Can there be nothing without something? Is nothingness even possible?

8. What is your reaction to the proposed solutions given in "The Problem With Solutions"?

Chapter 8: Faith and Reason

1. In Ian's situation, would you choose just the black box or would you choose both? Why?

2. If the "Predictor" *knows* what you will choose, then what point is there in deliberating? If a being predicts the future, does it *make* it happen or does it just *know* it will happen? How does your answer to this question affect what you choose in Ian's situation?

3. Have you ever wished that you believed differently than you do? Have you ever held beliefs that you realized were irrational yet you still maintained them? What did you do to try to change these beliefs, if anything?

4. Does your understanding of something help you believe in it? Or does your belief in something help you to understand it?

5. Is Pascal's justification for believing in God a good one? If so, could you force yourself to believe simply because it could be beneficial? Why/why not? Do you agree with the values placed in the outcomes of Pascal's Wager?

6. Many religions claim that their god is the *only* God to be worshipped. Is it a problem that Pascal doesn't address *which* god you should believe in, and that the same faith is needed to believe in all forms of supreme beings?

7. What is the difference between faith, belief, and knowledge? Can you *believe* you are reading this? Can you *know* that God exists? Nearly everyone claims that you need faith to believe God exists—is it true that you need faith to believe that God does *not* exist? Why/Why not?

8. In the box on "The Ethics of Belief," Clifford argues that it is wrong to believe anything based on insufficient evidence while James writes that it is necessary to formulate beliefs when sufficient evidence is not available. Which do you agree with? How could it be "wrong" to believe something? How important is your acting on beliefs?

9. In what other areas in your life might you make a leap of faith? Relationships? Work? A sporting team?

10. If you *feel* that you are one way, can you actually *be* another? In what sense is Aristotle right when he writes, "We are what we do"? How does that differ from Vonnegut's, "We are who we pretend to be"?

11. Have you ever experienced a self-fulfilling prophecy: a time in which your knowing that something would happen actually aided it in happening? Looking back on that, can you see how you might have affected the turnout, even unconsciously?

12. Numerous hoaxes have occurred recently such as the appearance of a Virgin Mary statue crying or Jesus on the crucifix bleeding. Before being exposed as a hoax, these "miracles" drew multitudes of believers (and also their money). If this provides hope and joy for them, should it matter if these "miracles" were staged? Could this be an example of "ignorance is bliss"?

13. This chapter contrasts with the second half of the previous chapter by showing the use and even need for faith and intuition. After reading both, how do you approach this juxtaposition? Is one better than the other? If we need both, how do you know when to employ one over the other?

Chapter 9: Free Will

1. If an infant/child has a first free act, what is it? When is it? How could a first free act result from repeated un-free acts?

2. If human beings are free, are other animals free as well? Which ones?

3. Regarding Darrow's defense (his client's "decision" to murder was pre-determined by his biology and thus not his fault) how does that relate to the insanity plea? If a person is biologically predisposed to commit a crime, should that factor into her punishment (for example: kleptomania—the impulse to steal)?

4. What does it mean for a desire to be wholly *authentic*? Wholly *free*? Can you think of an example of a completely random, *uncaused* action?

5. People often say that they "had to" do something—that they "had no choice" (i.e., I had to go to class, I had to pick my brother up, etc.). Look at the box about the girl who professed her belief in God in the face of death at Columbine—if you were in her situation, would you have done that? Would you have understood if she instead denounced God, later claiming that she "had no choice"? What does it mean to "have to" do something? What is something that you are so commited to that you would retain your conviction in the face of death?

6. Given the argument that we, to a great extent, are programmed (either by our society—education, parents, peers—or our biology) how are we any different than a computer that is programmed?

7. If you play against a computer in a game (e.g., poker) and the computer plays with an illegal card (e.g., a fifth king), did the computer

cheat? If not, why? If so, do you think the computer has the ability to act intentionally? Is acting intentionally necessary for cheating?

8. What effect do advertisements have on you? Could there be a strong unconscious effect as well? Is this a good or a bad thing? What could you do to control that influence (that is, if it is something you think to be unfavorable)?

9. Accounting for the "authoring your own character" analogy, when was the last time you made a character-enhancing decision?

10. Do you find it ironic that, with the "authoring your character" analogy, the more character-enhancing decisions you make, the more (not *less*) determined your "character sketch" becomes? Is this a problem for the analogy?

11. Some argue that your subconscious causes you to act in a way that you don't recognize and, thus, these actions are not free. Isn't your subconscious part of you? If so, if your subconscious chooses freely (even if you don't consciously recognize it) then don't *you* choose freely?

12. Does doing the opposite of what you wanted to do or "would have done" in a certain situation prove your free will?

13. What significance does the topic of free will/determinism have in your life and in society around you? If we are determined (i.e., no free will) does that give us an excuse to act on any impulse and do whatever we want?

14. If we do not have free will, would you want to know or would this be an example of "ignorance is bliss"?

Chapter 10: Selfishness (and Science Revisited)

1. How would you classify a self*less* act? How important is the motive of the actor? Are humans naturally selfish? Would it be possible for someone to freely give an anonymous gift to charity yet not be happy about it?

2. Is an act selfless if you act towards another purely out of duty (for example, giving a friend a ride to the airport only because you feel it is your duty or giving money to your church because you feel a duty to do so)? Why/why not?

3. How would you classify "natural"? Is it anything not influenced by humans? Is an apple on the shelf at the store natural?

4. If it's wrong to say, "What's right is whatever *I* think is right," then how can we determine what is right?

5. Would it be possible for you to use a language that no one else knew (for example, one that you invented)? If so, how? If not, why not?

6. Many people find great value in Freud's theory of psychoanalysis (e.g., it provides healing power, diagnostic capacity, etc.). If Popper's critique of Freud's theory is correct (that it is unscientific) how important is this? If an approach (i.e., Freud, astrology, etc.) were useful to you, would it matter if it wasn't scientific? Is science somehow better than pseudo-science?

7. Would there be any difference if *everything* in the universe were shifted three feet to the right? If so, what would it be? If not, are you surprised at your conclusion?

8. In what ways do you experience "confirmation bias" (seeking evidence that supports your position/preferences instead of what might refute it)? Your political views? Religion? Ethics? Relationships?

9. Baseball umpire Doug Harvey is quoted: "When I'm right no one remembers. When I'm wrong no one forgets." Oftentimes fans, players, and parents talk about all of the bad "calls" an umpire or referee made during the game; have you ever heard anyone talk about all of the good calls? Isn't it likely that a majority of the calls are good? How would confirmation bias explain this? As a sports fan what could you learn from this?

10. Ian's father (and earlier, a book that Ian reads) argues that art doesn't improve upon itself—do you agree?

Chapter 11: Heaps and Eggs

1. In determining when someone ceases to be a "child," is it defined by age, physical development, mental development (and do you think this is the same for every person)? How or why do you choose that cut-off point?

2. Where do you draw the line for when a fetus should have the same moral status as other people? Why do you choose that criterion?

3. Develop a list of criteria that define a "game." Are all of your criteria *necessary* for games (i.e., if "fun" is a criterion you suggest, yet someone does not have fun playing checkers, does it cease to be a game?)? Are any of your criteria *sufficient* (i.e., if something is "fun" is that enough to determine it is a game?)? How would you answer whether the following are games: Frisbee; boxing; Olympic ballroom dancing; Russian roulette; bull fighting; war?

4. What do you mean when you say you are *certain* of something? Does it make sense to say that you're *"fairly* certain" of something?

5. Which came first, the chicken or the egg? Why? In naming the egg that contained the first chicken, do you refer to that egg based on the non-chicken that laid it or based on it having an actual chicken in it? Does surrogate motherhood pertain to this example (i.e., whose baby is it, the donor's or the host's?)?

6. How can you know if your meaning for a word matches another's meaning for that same word (think of specific words, for example, *love, angry, impossible, success*)? If you can't, how might this be important in conversation? Have you ever had a discussion or argument with someone in which you realize that you used different definitions for the same terms?

7. In the Hanging Town, *did* Jeff walk around the squirrel? What if the tree wasn't there, and instead the squirrel still walked around in a circle, facing Jeff as he walked his same path? If you disagree with someone on this, where does the disagreement lie?

Chapter 12: Society, Politics, and Money

1. Many people equate anarchy with chaos. Would this necessarily be the case? Do you think that some sort of government might eventually result from an anarchist state? Do you think that people who lived with no system of government would live lives that were "nasty, brutish, and short," or that they would be more like "noble savages"?

2. How do the two concepts of fairness relate to taxation? Is it fair to more heavily tax wealthy people and give it to people with less? Would it matter how the wealthy acquired their wealth?

3. Look at the criteria in the box that suggest when going to war is justified. Are the criteria sufficient? What problems might arise from them? Do you think going to war is ever justified? Does it make sense to have rules within war? Would you trust your enemy to follow them in a life-and-death wartime situation? Could a country be said to fight fairly even if the war was not justified?

4. The courts hold that affirmative action is needed in order to promote diversity throughout schools and in the workplace. Others hold that affirmative action should be implemented to make up for past injustices. Which approach, if any, do you find most plausible? Does affirmative action solve the problem or might it imbed the racial stigma? How does reverse discrimination factor into the issue?

5. Which economic system mentioned (Socialism or Capitalism) seems more efficient to you? Are there questions of fairness here? What reasons would make you choose one over the other?

6. Regarding the National Endowment for the Arts:
   a. Do you think the government should support art through something like the National Endowment for the Arts? How would you deal with the arguments against your position stated in the chapter?
   b. Can art be defined? How about defining "good" art? If so, how would you define it? If not, how might you justify the government's funding of art?
   c. Has art somehow "evolved" or progressed over time?
   d. How would you answer the question posed in the chapter: Can art be good without people thinking it is? And what would that mean?

7. Should people have a right to anything other than life? If so, how would you go about defending people's having such rights?

8. What other kinds of beings would you grant rights to? Imagine you found out that, all along, your best friend was an alien (i.e., didn't have human DNA); or imagine that he or she was a robot. Would he or she be worthy of all the rights that you have? How might this relate to animal rights? Rights of a human fetus?

9. Do you think the "Shouting Fire" example is analogous to rescinding rights related to pornography? Why/why not?

10. Given Ian's predicament in jail, which action would you take? Why?

Chapter 13: Ethics and Morality

1. Is morality something that can be defined objectively—i.e., are moral statements (such as, "It's wrong to lie") true or false, or are they just a matter of personal taste? If they are objective, how do we determine it? If a matter of taste, then how can we morally prohibit occurrences like slavery and genocide?

2. If you do believe there are moral truths, do you adhere to them? Why? If you were desperate (i.e., homeless and starving) how important would morality be?

3. Imagine someone had a ring similar to Plato's "Ring of Gyges" that made them and all they touched invisible. Do you think they would act morally? Would you? What does your answer say about human nature?

4. Aristotle writes that humans are happy when they pursue their goal (*telos*) of reason. Do you think that humans have a "purpose" and, if so, what is it? What does it mean for you to be happy? What does it mean to live up to your potential?

5. If morality is driven by religion, how do we reconcile the differing views amongst religions?

6. Is Euthyphero's Dilemma (mentioned in a box) a problem as Plato thinks it is? Which formulation do you think is correct for Divine Command Theory—i.e., why is an act considered "good"?

7. Do you hold someone in higher regard for acting morally strictly out of duty *or* because that is "just the way they are"? Why?

8. In the previous chapter, a comparison is made to sports—that simply by playing in a game, you agree to play by the rules. Do you agree?
   - What does it mean to cheat in a game?
   - Is it always okay to intentionally foul someone (i.e., to purposely break the rules) if you accept the consequences (i.e., the corresponding penalty)? Is it *ever* okay?
   - Is it ethical to deceive the referee (i.e., to make it look like you were tripped in soccer when you were not)?

9. Are the following actions moral or immoral? Why?
   a. Speeding on a freeway
   b. Looking at a classmate's test during an exam
   c. Reporting false numbers on your taxes
   d. While in a committed monogamous relationship, having a sexual encounter with a person other than your partner
   e. Incest between two consenting adults
   f. Pornography
   g. Homosexuality
   h. Physician-assisted suicide (euthanasia)
   i. Abortion
   j. Death penalty

10. Holland prohibits resuscitating any baby born before 25 weeks (just past the sixth month of pregnancy). Do you agree with this ruling? Is it moral? Does this value/devalue human life?

11. Look at Singer's quote about the "Global Village." How do we determine just what is of "comparable moral worth" when we discuss our moral obligations to those seriously in need? Do you feel a stronger moral obligation to those who are very close to you in

proximity versus those who are not? Why? What about those who are close in time (i.e., alive now, versus in the future)?

12. Alexis asks Ian *who* should get rights. How do you determine the answer to this? How does this relate to the discussion of persons in chapter 2?

13. Can a price be put on human life? Imagine that two people get in a near-fatal car accident. Do we do *everything* to save them (i.e., fly in specialists, run tests, administer all possible medications, utilize every machine we know of)? What if one is a cancer researcher and the other is a seventy-year-old man?

14. How do you answer the question in the boxes in the text:
    • Kill 1 or let 20 die?
    • 2 trolley car scenarios
    • Ethical Egoism

    What does this tell you about morality?

Chapter 14: The Final Excursion

1. Having gone on this adventure with Ian, how has your view of philosophy changed, if at all? Does your response to the phrase "Ignorance is bliss" change from how you felt at the beginning of the book?

2. How do we use the terms "real" and "reality" differently? What does it mean for a phenomenon or an object to be *real*?

3. Are you happy for Ian or sad for him, given what you learn at the end?

4. Can newborn infants dream? A fetus in the womb with a functioning brain? If so, what do you think they dream about?

5. Do you believe that dreams contain hidden truths about yourself? Do you analyze your dreams?

6. Was it wrong of the Old Man to deceive Ian? If you were in Ian's position, would you rather continue living with the comfort of believing your parents were real or would you prefer to know the truth, as Ian learns in the end?

7. Some people are amazed by certain phenomena (like rainbows, sunsets, human emotion, etc.) when they deeply examine and deconstruct them, thus learning all there is to know about them, while others feel that this examination removes any mystery and thus diminishes their amazement. Which type of person are you and why?

Chapter 15: The Words After All Previous Words: Souls (Revisited) and Brains (Visited) . . . and Humans

1. How do you answer the question, "When does a human acquire a soul?" (If you don't believe in souls, "When does a human acquire full moral rights?") How does your view of souls and personhood inform your stance on stem cell research? On abortion? What is your view on using stem cells for research?

2. Should a woman who is pregnant be legally permitted to drive in a carpool lane by herself? How does your answer to this question inform your stance on abortion?

3. In what ways does philosophy provide a new perspective for you? What value do you see in "doing" philosophy?

4. Does the discussion of bottled water in this chapter change your use of the product? Why/why not?

5. Given the deception and dishonesty that psychics and alternative "doctors" employ, do you see any harm in allowing them to continue doing what they do? Do you see any value in it?

6. In what way do you notice the "hedonic treadmill" (p. 370) playing a role in your life?

7. How would you summarize the author's final note ("The Author Authors")? Do you agree with him? Disagree with him? Why?

KQED's *Forum* with Michael Krasny

Interview with Jack Bowen
Monday, April 3, 2006

Krasny: I know you work with young people, college-aged, and have coached high school, and so forth—how do you make philosophy relevant to them? You know you're dealing with some pretty heavy-duty philosophers here—ideas from Wittgenstein, Pascal, and the like. Bringing them down, really, to the level of everyday is kind of where it's at, isn't it?

Bowen: Yes, I think so. You know, in my talks that I've been giving—I've talked to a few middle schools, and I've spoken to and teach high school and college—these ideas, they are so relevant, and so we talk about ideas like love. We even talk about Chris Rock's joke—when you go out on a first date, you're going out with someone's representative, not the person themselves. And we talk about what it means to be an authentic person, and all of these personas, and this notion—this philosophical notion—of the self. And right there we bring up Chris Rock or we bring up Owen Wilson from the *Wedding Crashers* and talk about how love is one soul's counterpart in another.

Krasny: You can't talk philosophy with kids without bringing in popular culture.

Bowen: There you go.

Krasny: But you talk about free will here, the chicken and the egg, God, evil, the big questions; questions that certainly a lot of young people, if they have an intellect and if they have an interest and curiosity, really love to grapple with. But making those ideas relevant to their lives again—that's difficult sometimes, isn't it?

Bowen: It seems like it would be difficult, but after spending five years writing a book—so I guess the short answer is yes, it was difficult. But with this approach, what I noticed students are really drawn to, and when I go back to what I was really drawn to and excited about initially, was that philosophy is very different from all the other courses. It's sort of the how-to-think rather than the what-to-think. And when I see students realizing that their ideas are not only as important but maybe even *more* important than René Descartes' ideas, or my ideas . . . I mean, my philosophy course is not about teaching students what I think, and this book is actually not about that. As you mention, I do solve the chicken and the egg question and the meaning of life, but 99 percent of this book is a chance for the reader—or in my class the student—to author their own ideas, and I think when the students realize that it really becomes fun because it's now about their own personal journeys and not just another form of education.

Krasny: Talk about a way of brilliantly promoting your own book: "I do solve the chicken and the egg and the meaning of life, but I can't tell you." That will most certainly pique some curiosity. Let's talk about, for example, you have been involved in water polo—on the Olympic level, as a competitor, and you have been a coach. Where does philosophy play its role in coaching young people?

Bowen: Boy, that's a big question.

Krasny: You've used it, haven't you?

Bowen: We use it a lot. First of all, for me one thing it's done is it's really given me a healthy perspective on athletics and sports, not only in my life but societally. I think we get one perspective from the newspapers and the media about how important sports and athletics are on one level, but I think when I take into account Eastern ideas—there's this conversation in the book about the Dalai Lama and a Western philosopher watching a volleyball game. The Dalai Lama weeps when the ball hits the ground and the Westerner is sitting there thinking, why are you weeping, we just annihilated the other team, or we destroyed them, or all these terms that we use in sports. But isn't it partly a cooperative adventure and this thing that we're all doing together, and isn't there a sort of beauty in keeping the ball in the air as opposed to slamming it down? So when we take these ideas—and I push this on my kids that I coach—I say what do you guys think? When we're doing our leg work, which is the conditioning part of our training, we'll talk about these issues to help them get their mind off of it. But to really put it in perspective and realize that what we're doing together is we're sort of taking risks together, we're going out on a limb, we're trying to do our best, pursuing this goal together.

Krasny: Do you still tell them to annihilate their opponents? Get their testosterone going?

Bowen: No. By all means, I think a blending of the East and West provides a real healthy approach to that.

Krasny: Well, your first chapter ends with an umpire's call. An umpire's call gives us this whole sense of the bifurcated nature of reality: you see it one way, and somebody sees it another way—where is the reality?

Bowen: Well, there's your underlying question, certainly with the first chapter. And my theory . . . I actually was able to go back and give a presentation where I got my graduate degree, and one of the professors was reading the book, one of my favorite professors of all time, he said, "Jack, I was concerned after the first chapter that your book was promoting this undercurrent of relativism and postmodernism." And I sat on the edge of my seat, and I said, "Oh no, Professor Spangler thinks I'm a postmodernist," but then he read on and he said he was so happy by Chapter Two—

Krasny: Your professor's name is Spangler?

Bowen: Yes, Al Spangler. But to your question, yes, that's the subtitle of the book, the journey through the landscape of reality. But realizing that we are these subjective viewers, whether we're viewing "reality" or ourselves, at the least, sheds light on what it is we're viewing and how we're establishing this sort of epistemological framework.

Krasny: You called it the dreamscape of reality too to some degree—

Bowen: Well, we wanted something a little bit harder; we already had the word "dream" in there—

Krasny: Yes, you wanted it to be on terra firma, I understand. In fact, I could understand where Professor Spangler would say that because there's a sense . . . I thought, after reading the first chapter, I said to myself, well the beginning of wisdom is doubt, questioning and not knowing is a form of finding out what you know, and what you don't know is a way of finding out what you know, and kids can get a whole sense of this uncertainty that can really put them on shaky ground and can make them not know what is terra firma again.

Bowen: Yes, I think the aim of Chapter One is to show all the possibilities for doubt, but in the end we do bring in Descartes' solution and Plato's solution. It is not my hope to thoroughly confuse a reader, and as Professor Spangler mentioned, this goes away after the first chapter. And it is my hope to sort of show the landscape and to at least give the reader a sense of what skepticism is and was. And this is Ian's mentor's position, is this whole skeptical position, but then Ian comes back and realizes that of course knowledge is possible; there are certain lackings in our senses and reason and logic and science that they're not perfect, which I think is very enlightening, but it also doesn't lead us down the path of pure relativism and skepticism.

Krasny: We're talking to Jack Bowen, who teaches philosophy at De Anza College in Cupertino and has written a book called *The Dream Weaver.* I see this book as not only an educational book, which obviously it is, but also it's really about the consolations of philosophy. Normally, people don't necessarily think that philosophy—and particularly philosophy tied to skepticism—and not knowing, and all that, can lead us in directions of illumination. But of course that's your basic premise.

Bowen: Certainly. And like I said, this is stemming from the personal excitement that I had in studying these ideas and in coming to take authorship of my own ideas. My undergraduate degree was in human biology—and never once did I step back or was I asked to step back and not look at just what I know through science, but how do we know it. What is science? What is the scientific method? What is induction? What is pseudoscience? Why isn't astrology considered a science? So not only the "*how* is science functioning," but, then what? If evolution is true, then what? Or if it's not true, then what? There are so many, I guess, metaquestions—is the almost annoying term—there are so many underlying themes throughout all of these major subjects that I was so excited to see were going on there; there's just so much going on that I never had the chance to explore.

Krasny: You know John Barth, I think it was in *The End of the Road*—in one of his earlier novels, could have been *The Floating Opera*, but anyway—you talked about how you started out questioning, and you say, for example, people say what do you do? Well I teach philosophy. Why do you teach philosophy? Because I want to enlighten young people and get them thinking and get them curious and expand their consciousness. And you can say why? Well because I think it's valuable for them. And you can just keep going on with the "why" and you can do that with simply every kind of assertion.

Bowen: Yes, and we do talk about that in my class, this incessant asking of why, and that is part of what philosophers do. And that's why it's often said that children are the best philosophers. You know, "We're going to the store. Why? We need to eat. Why? We need to stay alive. Why? Well, let's see here." But there's a little more rigor to that in the sense that we're trying to look at things logically and to see what will play out given certain truths about the world. I think in what you just said, there is fun. We have fun in our classroom—we talk about the chicken and the egg question—

Krasny: Philosophy can be fun, but also, some people find it overwhelming, as I'm sure you realize.

Bowen: Yes.

Krasny: It can be paralytic, in fact.

Bowen: Right, there's certainly the agnostic approach to everything where you end up just sitting on the fence—

Krasny: That's Barth again. *Cosmastris*, I think he calls it at one point. The cosmic sense of the futility of everything, so it's just paralytic.

Bowen: Yes, and that's one of the challenges I work with the students, and, actually, I'm now giving seminars in a few schools where we talk about how you can balance being really convicted to your conclusions and beliefs yet also be open—how can you be really convicted and open-minded simultaneously?

Krasny: I'm responding because of your use of the word "convicted," because earlier on in the book you talk about things like a crime scene. Here's a strange man in Ian—the fourteen-year-old's—bedroom, which is a little bit odd, but here he is, and he's questioning things like, you try to reconstruct a crime scene, and you try to go by the evidence and that's what philosophy does for you, metaphorically in some ways.

Bowen: I think so. Ian's mentor in that situation is trying to give us motivation or almost make it OK for us to ask a question and not get an answer. Very often the criticism is, "Well, you ask this question, but there's no right answer." But in asking the question, at the least it illuminates these issues, and we don't critique crime scene investigators, as you mention, for asking a question that doesn't have an answer; it very often leads to another question that *is* the right question that leads to an answer.

Krasny: So who is the Old Man that you have in this as Ian's mentor?

Bowen: You're really delving. These are answers that I don't share with friends. I suppose as an author there's a little bit of me in every character. Certainly I identify with Ian because he's just so free and he's getting a chance to ask questions that sometimes I wish I were asking more blatantly. The Old Man is really the skeptic. Ian's almost this naïve romantic—he believes we know things, we have souls, God exists, science is perfect, we have free will, there's right and wrong, and everything's great. But Ian's smarter than that, and I think the Old Man brings some of those concerns out overtly, in a sort of caricature of skepticism.

Krasny: But also like a philosopher.

Bowen: Yes.

Krasny: In many ways the consummate philosopher in terms of what he's offering this young boy. It's important, I guess, that he's a teenager, that Ian is a teenager; he's fourteen years old, and like you said, he's open to experience, even though he's got some answers, or thinks he does.

Bowen: Right, I chose that age just because the kids I've worked with at that age are so . . . I actually work with a group of middle schoolers in water polo and we have discussions like these all the time. I remember sitting with the sister of a girl—her older sister was playing in a water polo game and we were keeping score—and she was very excited about how her sister was playing. Her name was Chelsea. And I said to Chelsea, "Why don't we add a point on the scoreboard, no one will notice." And we had about a fifteen-minute discussion about why that would be wrong, and we have a duty to others, and there's this notion of fairness and competition, and without competition the game breaks down. She was in seventh grade at the time, and it was a fascinating discussion to listen to her talk freely and unabatedly about those issues.

Krasny: Well you're right about ethics in this book, and kids really want an ethical code—a lot of kids do—don't they?

Bowen: I think so. I think they want some sort of framework, because when we start to talk about theses issues, it's very much—and this is where relativism, almost nihilism, comes into play—it's like, saying "something is wrong" is like saying "steak is better than shrimp," which is really just a personal taste. And we go through and say, well then the Holocaust was right for some people. Oh no, no. If someone murders your family it isn't morally permissible; no, not that. So we need to establish a foundation. OK, yes, how do we do that? And then we get into what it means to have this sort of metaethical thinking, and then, obviously, the more pertinent aspect of applying that to issues. Students really grasp onto it; that's why I left that chapter for the end—because I think a lot of it builds up to that.

Krasny: Well it also builds up to the idea that there's value in the application of knowledge. That's an underlying girder in your work and also a kind of faith in the possibility of human choice.

Bowen: Certainly. It's important to me—as we touched on, Chapter One does seem overtly skeptical and relativistic—that as the book builds, you see that what I'm giving up in the skepticism is that I'm protecting the reader from feeling like I'm trying to convince them of my views. At the end of the semester-long course, students say, "Now we want to know what *you* think. We have no idea what you think." And to me that's a success. I know what I think: I've written papers, gone to conferences—

Krasny: You're like the ideal of an NPR journalist. You've been mediating between these issues, hearing from both sides. That would be called commercial radio, though sometimes it slips in anyway. But you know, you've got a whole list of philosophers that you cover here, and some of them in fact might not necessarily even be in peoples' minds as philosophers, people like Mencken, and Lewis Carroll, and Carol Gilligan, who's a psychologist, or Noam Chomsky, who's a linguist and a political analyst, so the word *philosopher* takes on a very broad, capacious mantle.

Bowen: Yeah, you chose a pretty good group of three right there. We go back and look at Aristotle or even Newton and Einstein, and they're all considered natural philosophers, and very often something like science spills into philosophy by definition because you're exploring these unknown entities, and there is a crossover there, in my mind. We talk about Gilligan or Chomsky, and, boy, the ideas, the issues with language—to look at Chomsky and how important a role language plays in a lot of these philosophical issues and how some of those dissolve when you look at it from maybe an Eastern approach, where language isn't this paradigm of pure knowledge—it actually gets in the way of knowledge. Or you look at Gilligan and these feminist ideas in ethics and what that does. Granted, she's looking at it from more of a psychological standpoint, but I think someone like William James is considered by many to be a psychologist as well, but—

Krasny: Because he's a pragmatist.

Bowen: Certainly. But all of these ideas . . . and I suppose that's one of the other things that really excited me about philosophy, is that I remember thinking of my professors, and how do they know so much about so much, because it all is pertinent and we need to know about psychology, sociology, science, etc., in order to look at the philosophical importance of certain issues.

Krasny: It's all interdisciplinary.

Bowen: Certainly.

Krasny: The more you learn about philosophy the more you realize you don't know—isn't that true?

Bowen: There's a little Gödel in the whole process, yes.

Krasny: Most philosophers I know—we were just talking about Stanford philosophers—we had Richard Rorty on recently, and this is a man of extraordinary knowledge in terms of philosophy, an iconic figure and so forth, but he'll be the first to tell you, there are certain things that . . . there are epistemological walls: you can't get past them unless you make a leap of faith or decide to invent something that's on the other side of the wall.

Bowen: Certainly, for me that's part of the excitement, is realizing that wall, and realizing not just what we can't or don't know, but why we can't or don't know it, and then like you said—you brought up this phrase "leap of faith," and we think of Kierkegaard, which we talk about in Chapter Eight here, and what the role of faith and intuition is in philosophy, because if I am really trying to give you a view of the landscape of reality, I can't just give it to you from a purely logical standpoint. If we ignore intuition and faith then we're ignoring a huge part of what it means to be human.

Krasny: Is that what you mean by seeing more of the beautiful colors— you're seeing faith, or seeing things that perhaps aren't necessarily there within our visual sight?

Bowen: Yes, and I suppose when you say, "Is that what *you* mean," that is technically—

Krasny: I'm asking you the question that your students ask you—"is that what you mean."

Bowen: Well, because my brother wrote that song. Yes, so absolutely, and maybe the best thing for me as a writer that came through this experience of five years was realizing my close-mindedness, to be quite frank about it. I was born and raised on this small tropical island off the coast of San Diego, and it was a military town, and everyone's Republican, and everyone goes to the same church, and I left thinking that this is how everybody thinks. I had a great upbringing and a great education, but this must be how everyone thinks. Everyone here is smart and we've got it all solved. And in looking at these issues and taking ideas from feminism; if you asked me about feminism in high school I probably would have mocked you. I would have said that there's no way a male can be a feminist. So I wasn't even open to these ideas. You're talking about Eastern philosophy, which is a huge portion of the landscape of reality—I would have said there's no value in that. But these things solve a lot of the issues. So I suppose this idea, from the theme song of the beautiful colors, is realizing that as much as I personally want to put the world in black and white, that's not how the world functions.

Krasny: It's in Technicolor.

Bowen: Exactly.

Beautiful Colors

The world is quite peaceful,
  With my head down in the sand.
  It's cool and it's quiet here,
  no need to understand
  Life's great mysteries,
  seeing only shadows of reality.
  So I lift my head to the world,
  and I'm blinded by the light.

If you see the world in black and white,
  you're missing out on all the beautiful colors.

Dark and light, wrong and right,
  May or might, and all the rest.
  If you keep on traveling to the east,
  You'll end up west.
  Your paradigms are affected,
  When you see it's all connected.
  You embrace both heart and mind
  in seeking what you find.

You have no idea my son.
  Your journey's just begun.
  If you look with eyes wide open,
  you realize the world wonders,
  and you are not alone.

The world is quite full of wonder,
  with my head out of the sand.

Questions for Discussion

1. People often say "ignorance is bliss." In what ways might this be true? What are the negative consequences of this ideal? How do you evaluate the opening and closing stanzas of the song, which seem to be totally opposing views?

2. What virtue might there be in seeing the world in "black and white"? What would this mean? If right-and-wrong (morality) is not a black-and-white issue, then how could we come to any answers regarding morality? If morality is a matter of black and white, why can't we all agree on moral issues?

3. What produces greater insights for you—your heart (intuition, faith, passion) or mind (logic, math, reason)? Is one "better" than the other?

4. What kind of things affect your paradigm (worldview)— Science? Advertising? Religion? "Society"? With all of these influences, how can you make truly authentic choices?

5. Do you find greater beauty/wonder in something the more or less you know about it? How does your answer affect the way you approach knowing yourself, others, and the world around you?

* THIS SONG CAN BE HEARD AT THE BOOK'S WEBSITE HOME PAGE: www.dreamweaverphilosophy.com

Index